VISUAL QUICKSTART GUIDE

PYTHON

Chris Fehily

Peachpit Press

Visual QuickStart Guide
Python
Chris Fehily

Peachpit Press
1249 Eighth Street
Berkeley, CA 94710
510/524-2178
800/283-9444
510/524-2221 (fax)
Find us on the World Wide Web at: http://www.peachpit.com
To report errors, send a note to errata@peachpit.com.
Peachpit Press is a division of Addison Wesley Longman

Copyright © 2002 by Chris Fehily

Editor: Clifford Colby
Production Coordinator: Connie Jeung-Mills
Copyeditor: Kathy Simpson
Technical Editor: Cliff Vick
Compositors: Lisa Brazieal, Maureen Forys, Myrna Vladic
Indexer: Joy Dean Lee
Cover Design: The Visual Group

ISBN 0-201-74884-3

9 8 7 6 5 4 3 2

Printed and bound in the United States of America

Dedication

To my mother

Special Thanks to:

Cliff Colby for never panicking (outwardly).

Marjorie Baer for being compellingly listenable.

Kathy Simpson for spotting the fused genitives and comma-less nonrestrictive appositives.

Connie Jeung-Mills for those eyes, those eyes.

Lisa Brazieal for the asterisks.

Cliff Vick for retyping.

Nancy Aldrich-Ruenzel for the green light.

Judy for encouraging, Lynn for listening, Phil and Melanie for tipping, Darren for updating, Deb and Kate for distracting, Deanne for suggesting, and Irene for not calling.

Some people who inspired me but are unaware of it: Stephen Schonberg (my former English teacher), Art Owen (my former Statistics professor), Sherrie (Librarian), Jane (Dry Cleaner), and Cyndi (Pharmacist).

TABLE OF CONTENTS

INTRODUCTION

Welcome to Python, a popular open-source programming language. You can use Python to do everything from writing simple scripts to developing Web sites to creating complex applications. To keep this book to a manageable size, I've limited its scope to Python's core language and libraries. After finishing this book, you'll know how to use Python for routine and advanced programming tasks. At the end, I'll point you toward other topics and information sources. OK? Then turn the page.

About Python

Python is a programming language that is:

- Free and freely available

- Reliable and well supported

- Portable

- Compatible

- Easy(ish)

- Interpreted

- Object-oriented

- Versatile

- Named after British comedians

Free and freely available. Python is open-source software available free from the official Python Web site, www.python.org (**Figure i.1**). Python's license lets you copy, modify, distribute, extend, embed, and resell it without paying fees or signing license agreements. (Some restrictions apply. You must leave the copyrights in, for example.) You can learn more about the Open Source Initiative at www.opensource.org (**Figure i.2**).

Reliable and well supported. Python has been around for more than 10 years. It's a mature product whose source code has been created, poked, prodded, tested, and debugged by many people. Python's attentive development team, led by Python's principal author, Guido van Rossum, regularly releases updates and upgrades. The Python development community will (usually) answer your questions.

Python also comes with a complete set of documentation, including a tutorial, language reference, and library reference. As a last resort, you can read the empyreal documentation: the C source code.

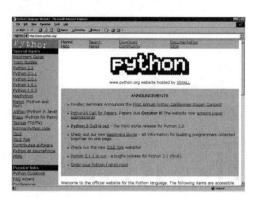

Figure i.1 The official Python Web site, www.python.org, is the best starting point for all things Pythonic. You can download Python, read the latest Python news, read the FAQ, and find out about other Python Web sites and resources.

Figure i.2 The Open Source Initiative board voted to certify the Python license as open-source. You can read more about Open Source (in plain English) at www.opensource.org.

✔ Tip

- For information about where to get support, see the Appendix.

Portable. Python is written in portable ANSI C, so it compiles and runs on all viable operating systems, including Unix, Windows, Mac OS, and Palm OS. (For a complete list, see www.python.org/download/.) Python's core language and libraries run the same way on all platforms, so you can program in mixed environments. You can write and test your programs in Windows and upload them to a production Linux server, for example. Note that a few Python extensions are operating-system-specific. You can't call the Windows COM module in Unix, for example.

Compatible. Python is a "glue language" that can connect to existing libraries written in C, C++, Fortran, Java, Visual Basic (using the COM package), and other languages. You can write the computationally intensive parts of your weather prediction program in C and the rest in Python, and then compile them into a single, stand-alone, "frozen" executable file by using the `freeze` utility.

Python/C integration is beyond this book's scope, but it's covered in the *Python/C API Reference Manual* and *Extending and Embedding the Python Interpreter* books, which come with Python. Also see the Appendix for information about Jython, which allows Python and Java programs to communicate.

Easy(ish). Python generally is simpler to install, learn, and use than other programming languages. It's also easier to read thanks to many clever features, such as:

♦ A line structure that forces consistent indentation,

♦ Syntax and semantics that make it suitable for simple scripts or large programs,

♦ Flexible data structures and dynamic typing that allow you to get a lot done in a few lines.

Python vs. Other Languages

You can safely ignore the comparisons I make to Perl, C, and other languages throughout this book. But if you'd like to know more, start with Guido van Rossum's *Comparing Python to Other Languages* at www.python.org/doc/essays/comparisons.html and then visit www.python.org/doc/Comparisons.html for links to other articles. Most of the articles are even-handed and discuss Python's strengths and weaknesses.

ABOUT PYTHON

Interpreted. The Python interpreter runs your program as soon as you type or load it. When the interpreter encounters an error, it raises an exception and prints an error message. You can test and debug your code quickly, because you have no compilation or link step. An interpreter can run programs written for earlier interpreter versions. Python also supports *byte compilation,* in which the interpreter translates Python programs into portable code that can be run on any computer with a Python interpreter.

Object-oriented. You can use Python as a procedural language, but it was conceived as an object-oriented language. Python implements all the concepts usually associated with object-oriented programming (OOP). I'll just list them here and explain them in Chapters 11 and 12:

- Exceptions
- Classes
- Instances
- Methods
- Automatic memory management (garbage collection)
- Inheritance
- Overloading

Objects

In most object-oriented programming literature, *object* refers only to what in Python is called a class instance (see Chapter 12). But in Python, an instance of *any* data type is an object: lists, strings, numbers, functions, modules, and so on. In this book, I follow formal Python documentation conventions and refer to instances of any type (not just class instances) as *objects*.

Versatile. Python is sometimes called a "scripting language." But even though it's a great choice for writing utility programs and simple CGI scripts, it's also suitable for large projects. If you're a Web programmer, for example, you can create complex server programs using Python's modules for Internet protocols, data handling, markup languages, multimedia, and cryptography. The Grail Web browser (`http://grail.sourceforge.net/`) and Zope (`www.zope.com`), a free Web application server for creating and maintaining large Web sites, are written mostly in Python.

Named after British comedians. Guido van Rossum named the language after the British comedy troupe Monty Python. No knowledge of Monty Python is required, but Python documentation is littered with references to the group's television series and movies. You might notice that the generic identifiers `foo` and `bar` have become `spam` and `eggs` or that the phrase "And now for something completely different" is overused.

ABOUT PYTHON

About This Book

This book is appropriate for you if you are learning Python with an instructor or have already done some programming in another language (not a lot, but you should know about variables, loops, and conditions). This book is *not* appropriate if you're learning your first programming language on your own or if you want to learn Python programming techniques for system administration, Web programming, or other specialized areas. (Keep all these assumptions in mind when you post a book review on Amazon.com.)

This book isn't an exhaustive guide to Python. I have limited the scope to Python's core language and most popular library modules. For information about Python's other modules, see the *Python Library Reference,* which comes with the Python distribution. I survey Python's other popular uses and modules in the Appendix.

Conventions

I use the following typographic conventions:

Italic type introduces new terms or represents replaceable parameter names in text.

`Monospace type` denotes Python code in programs and in regular text. It also shows output screen text in Python's interactive interpreter or a command-prompt window (shell).

`Bold monospace type` denotes statements and commands that you type in Python's interactive interpreter or a command-prompt window (shell).

`Italic monospace type` denotes a replaceable parameter name whose actual value depends on the context. You'd replace *`filename`* with an actual file name, for example.

Companion Web Site

At `www.peachpit.com/vqs/python`, you'll find the full table of contents, corrections, updates, all source code (with bugs fixed), and other stuff. You also can write to me directly at `fehily@pacbell.net` with questions, suggestions, corrections, and gripes related to this book.

ABOUT THIS BOOK

I use the following icons to indicate topics of special interest:

LANG This icon indicates a comparison with another programming language.

NEW This book covers Python version 2.1. This icon indicates a feature that differs or is unavailable in earlier versions. As this book goes to press (September 2001), the release of Python 2.2 is approaching. I'll mention some of its new features, but I won't describe them in detail.

OS This icon denotes Python code that may work differently on different platforms, such as a file operation under Windows and Linux.

Other things to keep in mind:

◆ All quote marks in Python code are straight quotes (such as ' and "), not curly, or smart, quotes such as ' and ". Curly quotes prevent code from working.

◆ Python is case-sensitive, which means that myName, MyName, and MYNAME are considered to be separate and unrelated identifiers.

◆ Brackets used in syntax lines indicate optional items. (Don't type the brackets.) The function round(x [,n]), for example, can be called as round(3.56) or round(3.56,2). In the syntax [param = value], value denotes the default value of param. (In actual code examples, brackets indicate a Python list.)

◆ When a column is too narrow to hold a single line of code, I break it into two or more segments. The gray arrow → indicates a continued line. Python also has several built-in ways of splitting long lines; see "Splitting Statements Across Lines" in Chapter 7.

◆ If you type my examples in your Python interpreter and your answers differ from mine, exit and restart the interpreter and try again, as you may have some leftover variables improperly initialized from previous examples.

◆ **OS** Python runs on a variety of operating systems. You can write programs on one OS and run them on another. Many people write programs in Windows and then upload and run them on a Unix server, for example.

◆ I use a consistent style to improve code readability and maintenance. To save space in this book, my indentation level is two spaces (in practice, it's usually four spaces). I use CapitalWords to name classes and exceptions and lowercase or lower_case for everything else. For style advice, see the *Python Style Guide* at www.python.org/doc/essays/styleguide.html.

ABOUT THIS BOOK

A Preview

Script i.1 shows a Python program. The sidebar explains what it does, but right now, *you don't have to understand it in its entirety.* I'm just going to use it to introduce you to some individual concepts:

- ```
  #Simulate coin-flipping experiments and
  #print a histogram showing the number of
  #heads that occurred in each experiment.
  ```
  These lines are comments, introduced by a pound sign (#). Comments are for human edification; the interpreter ignores them. Comments are also allowed at the end of a line of code, as shown in the following statement.

- ```
  import random  #For random flips
  ```
  This statement finds and loads the `random` module, making the `random()` function available for later use. Although Python's built-in functions are always available, you must load others explicitly—including ones you create—with an `import` statement, which loads external library files that define functions and other objects.

- ```
  experiments, flips = 500, 16
  ```
  This assignment statement creates and assigns two variables: `experiments` gets the integer value 500, and `flips` simultaneously gets the integer value 16. No type declaration is needed; any Python variable can hold any type of object.

Script i.1 This Python program simulates repeated coin flips and prints a histogram showing the number of heads that occurred for each set of flips. It illustrates some basic Python concepts and constructs.

```
script
#Simulate coin-flipping experiments and
#print a histogram showing the number of
#heads that occurred in each experiment.

import random  #For random flips

#Define the number of experiments, the
#number of coin flips per experiment,
#and initialize a list to hold results.
experiments, flips = 500, 16
heads = [0] * (flips + 1)

#Perform each experiment.
for i in range(experiments):
    count = 0
    #Accumulate the number of heads.
    for j in range(len(heads)):
        if random.random() < 0.5: count += 1
    heads[count] += 1

#Print the numeric results.
print "heads:\n", heads, "\n"

#Print the histogram.
for j in range(flips + 1):
    print "%2d " % j,
    i = 0
    #Print a "*" for each 10 occurrences.
    while i < heads[j]:
        print "*",
        i += 10
    print
```
```

◆ `heads = [0] * (flips + 1)`

This statement initializes and sizes a list and assigns it to the variable `heads`. A list is an ordered collection of arbitrary objects, each accessed with a sequential index number starting at 0. `[0]` defines a list with a single item (the number 0), and the repetition operator `*` resizes the list to `flips` + 1 = 17 items (all zeros), indexed 0 through 16.

◆ `for i in range(experiments):`

This `for` statement iterates 500 times over the items in the list created by the `range()` function:

`[0, 1, 2, ..., 499]`

(`range()` creates zero-based sequences by default.)

◆ `count = 0`

`flips`

```
for j in range(len(heads)):
    if random.random() <
    → 0.5: count += 1
heads[count] += 1
```

These statements are indented below the `for` statement and thus form the `for` loop's body; they are executed as a single unit with each repetition of the loop. Python uses indentation to group statements into blocks. Notice that the `if` statement is indented farther right than the other statements, which means that it's the body of the nested `for` loop (`for j in...`). The first unindented statement marks the end of a block. Most languages use `{` and `}` braces (such as C and Perl) or begin/end keywords (such as Pascal) to delimit code blocks. Also note that the end of the line marks the end of a statement. You don't need explicit line terminators, like the semicolon in C and Perl. Next, I look at each block statement separately.

continues on next page

What Script i.1 Does

If you repeatedly flip a fair coin, you expect half the flips to turn up heads—but it's possible to get anywhere from no heads to all heads. Script i.1 runs `experiments` experiments in which each experiment simulates flipping a coin `flips` times. The outcome of each experiment will be "i heads", where $0 \le i \le$ `flips`. The list `heads` keeps track of the outcomes (I use the standard trick of indexing on a computed value). The program prints a histogram, which I expect to be bell-shaped and centered at `flips`/2. **Figure i.3** shows the output of a sample run.

◆ `count = 0`

Variables spring into existence when they're assigned a value and are destroyed automatically when they are no longer needed.

◆ `for j in range(len(heads)):`

Passing `range()` the length of the list heads via `len()` produces a list of the indexes (0...16) for heads's 17 items.

◆ `if random.random() < 0.5: count += 1`

This `if` statement evaluates the condition:

`random.random() < 0.5`

If the condition is true, Python executes this statement:

`count += 1`

The dot operator accesses the `random()` function in the `random` module (loaded earlier with `import`). `random()` returns a random number between 0 and 1, and the comparison operator, `<`, determines whether that number is less than 0.5. If the number is less than 0.5 (which happens about half the time), `count` is incremented by 1 with the augmented assignment operator, `+=`.

By the way, these statements could have been written on two lines, as follows:

```
if random.random() < 0.5:
    count += 1
```

◆ `heads[count] += 1`

This line adds 1 to the count-*th* item of the list heads. (Remember, the item count is zero-based.)

```
heads:
[0, 0, 1, 3, 17, 33, 58, 84, 96,
→ 90, 56, 41, 17, 2, 2, 0, 0]

 0
 1
 2  *
 3  *
 4  * *
 5  * * * *
 6  * * * * * *
 7  * * * * * * * *
 8  * * * * * * * * * *
 9  * * * * * * * * *
10  * * * * * *
11  * * * * *
12  * *
13  *
14  *
15
16
```

Figure i.3 Output from Script i.1. As expected, flipping a coin 16 times usually yielded about eight heads. Each time you run the program, the histogram will change (because of the random() function), but it will still be bell-shaped and centered at or near 8.

◆ The rest of the program contains several print statements. print evaluates expressions and writes them to your screen (or a file).

```
print "heads:\n", heads, "\n"
```

This statement prints three expressions. (The commas separate the expressions; they're not printed.) The first and last expressions are strings. The \n escape sequence, called a *newline*, forces a new line. The middle expression, heads, is converted automatically from a list to a string and printed.

```
print "%2d " % j,
```

This statement prints a formatted string, the way that the C or Perl printf() function does. print writes a newline (\n) at the end automatically. Here, however, the trailing comma suppresses the newline.

```
print "*",
```

This statement prints an asterisk (*), again suppressing the newline.

```
print
```

This statement writes a blank line.

◆ while i < heads[j]:

The while statement executes a block of statements as long as a condition is true. Again, indentation determines the loop body. This nested while loop executes as long as i is less than the j-*th* item of heads:

```
print "*",
```
```
i += 10
```

The value of i changes within the body of the while loop itself. j is the index of the outer for loop.

Built-In Types

Each Python object has a type that determines its allowable values and the operations it supports. An integer object, for example, can represent any whole number that is between −2147483648 and 2147483647 and supports the usual arithmetic operations: addition, subtraction, multiplication, and division (among others). But an integer can't represent a nonnumeric value such as "schadenfreude" and doesn't support string operations such as capitalization.

Python's built-in types are the building blocks used to construct programs. Script i.1 introduced integers, strings, and lists. Python's *standard type hierarchy* lists all the built-in types, grouped by similarity and purpose.

Numbers

Numbers represent numerical values (**Figure i.4**). Plain integers are whole numbers written without a decimal point: −38, 0, 62262. Long integers are arbitrary-precision integers that can grow as large as needed. These numbers are written like integers, followed by a lowercase or capital L: −100L, 0L, 99l. Floating-point numbers have a fractional component and are written with a decimal point or expressed in scientific notation: −55.0, −2.5e−5, 0.0, 1.010010001, 1E2. Complex numbers comprise a real part and an imaginary part. These numbers are written as the sum of two floating-point numbers followed by a lowercase or capital J: −5.5+4j, 0+0J, 2−3.5E3j.

For information about numbers, see Chapter 3.

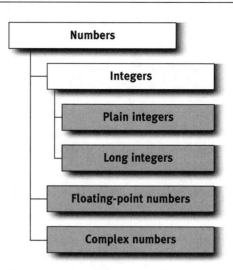

Figure i.4 Python supports the usual integer and floating-point numeric types. It also supports integers of unlimited size and complex numbers (if you don't know what complex numbers are, you won't need them).

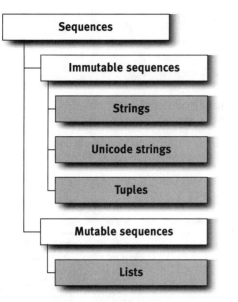

Figure i.5 Strings and Unicode strings are quoted literals (or constants) that can hold an unlimited number of characters. Lists and tuples are arrays of arbitrary objects. Lists can be modified; tuples can't.

Table i.1

Mutable and Immutable Objects		
Type	Category	Mutable?
Number	Number	No
String	Sequence	No
Unicode	Sequence	No
Tuple	Sequence	No
List	Sequence	Yes
Dictionary	Mapping	Yes

Sequences

Sequences are ordered sets of items, with each item identified by a sequential index number (**Figure i.5**). When an immutable sequence is created, its items or size can't change; the items or size of a mutable sequence can change. **Table i.1** summarizes immutable and mutable object types.

Strings are sequences of characters enclosed in single or double quotes: 'crepuscular', "38", " ". *Unicode strings* are like standard strings but hold Unicode characters instead of ASCII characters, and have a small u in front of the first quote: u"ß 本 ä". For information about strings, see Chapter 4.

Tuples are immutable collections of comma-separated objects between parentheses: (1, 'two', 3.0). *Lists* are mutable collections of comma-separated objects between brackets: [1.0, u"two", 3.0L]. For information about lists and tuples, see Chapter 5.

BUILT-IN TYPES

Mappings

Mappings are unordered sets of items, with each item identified by an arbitrary key that you define (**Figure i.6**). The only built-in mapping is a *dictionary,* which is a collection of key-value pairs. The key, which can be an immutable object (number, string, or tuple), is used to access the value, which can be any type of object. Dictionaries are written as comma-separated items between braces. Each item contains a key, with its associated value separated by a colon: {'name': 'Rich', 'occupation': 'sycophant', 'age': 28}.

Mappings, along with sequences, are called *collections* because they contain references to other objects.

For information about dictionaries, see Chapter 6.

Callable types

Callable types include reusable objects that perform well-defined tasks (**Figure i.7**). Simple scripts aside, well-designed programs are not monolithic sequences of statements that execute successively from beginning to end. Instead, programs are broken into modular subroutines that are invoked, or *called,* from elsewhere in the program (or by other programs).

Functions and *methods* perform similar tasks but have different syntax. Python has both an `rstrip` function and an `rstrip` method to remove trailing white-space characters from a string, for example. The function is called with the string object as its argument: `rstrip("stripme ")`. The method is invoked on the string object with the dot operator: `"stripme ".rstrip()`. Functions and methods are either *built-in,* which come free with Python (the interpreter implicitly understands them), or *user-defined,* which you define and write yourself. For information about functions, see Chapter 8.

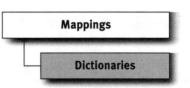

Figure i.6 Dictionaries, called hashes or associative arrays in other languages, hold pairs of objects. The first object in each pair is called the key, which uniquely identifies the second object, called the value.

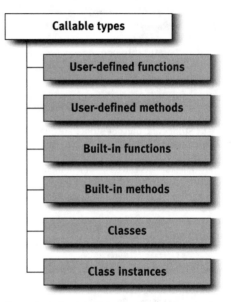

Figure i.7 Python's built-in functions and methods are described in the *Python Library Reference*. You also can write your own functions, methods, and classes and then use them in any program.

A *class* is a broad category that defines a set of attributes and methods for more specific items, called *class instances,* that exist within it. An instance of the Planet class could be uranus, for example. For information about classes and methods, see Chapter 12.

Modules are text files containing Python statements that define related variables, functions, and classes. Module files end with the *.py* extension and are loaded with the import statement. For information about modules, see Chapter 9.

Files are text or binary files. Python has many built-in functions and methods to open, read, write, and otherwise process files. For information about files, see Chapter 10.

The *None* type defines a single empty None object, sometimes called the *null object,* which is used in a few contexts. None is returned by functions that lack a return statement, for example. It's also commonly used as a placeholder for an unknown or not-yet-calculated value. There's only one instance of None; all references to None point to the same object. None has no methods.

The *Ellipsis* type defines a single Ellipsis object, represented by the . . . syntax. The ellipsis (. . .) appears in recursive objects—that is, lists or dictionaries that contain references to themselves. It's also used in extended-slice syntax in Numerical Python (which is not covered in this book). There's only one instance of Ellipsis; all references to Ellipsis point to the same object.

BUILT-IN TYPES

Internal types

Internal types define objects that you can access even though they're used internally by the interpreter (**Figure i.8**).

Code objects are modules compiled into *byte-codes,* which are portable, low-level (not human-readable) instructions that can run on any machine with a Python interpreter. Python quietly creates compiled bytecode files when you first import or reload a module. These *.pyc* files appear in your module directories after running programs. For information about code objects, see Chapter 9.

Frame objects contain debugging information and define the namespaces that keep track of how objects are identified. For information about namespaces, see Chapter 9.

Traceback objects provide debugging information such as the error type, offending code, file name, and line number. When an error occurs in your program, the interpreter prints a *stack trace* and halts (**Figure i.9**). In Python, an error condition is called an *exception.* You can use exceptions to write code to handle errors gracefully. You can also generate, or *raise,* your own exceptions. For information about exceptions, see Chapter 11.

Slice objects represent extended slices, which are used in Numerical Python (NumPy). Extended slices don't work with standard sequences (lists, strings, and tuples) and are beyond the scope of this book.

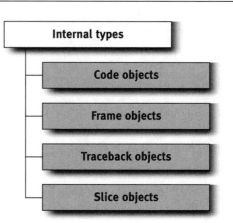

Figure i.8 The Python interpreter automatically builds code objects to speed subsequent load (but not execution) times. Frames help you resolve object-naming problems. Tracebacks appear whenever Python encounters a run-time or syntax error. Slice objects are handy for handling multidimensional arrays in Numerical Python (see the Appendix).

```
>>> 5 + 'five'
Traceback (most recent call last):
  File "<stdin>", line 1, in ?
TypeError: unsupported operand types for +
```

Figure i.9 Here, I tried to add a number and a string illegally. The Python interpreter responded with a stack trace complaining that the operation's types are incompatible. This particular error raised a TypeError exception.

GETTING STARTED

To run Python programs, you need the (free) Python interpreter, which is available from the Python Web site (www.python.org). In this chapter, I explain how to get the Python distribution, offer installation and setup tips, and show you how to run programs interactively or as scripts.

To get Python up and running, you'll need to tinker with some of your operating system's settings. I explain how to add the Python directory to your path so that you can start the interpreter from any directory, and how to use command-line options to change the interpreter's default behavior or pass arguments to a Python program.

Getting Python

The Python distribution includes the Python interpreter, standard modules, and other files you need to run Python programs. Python runs on most operating systems, and each system's installation procedure differs. (In some cases, you must compile Python's C source code.) I describe how to get the distribution for different OSes, but I don't rehash the installation procedures, which are given on the download pages. Python may already be installed on some Linux systems; see the first tip in this section to determine whether it is.

To get the Python distribution:

1. Visit the Download Python Software page at www.python.org/download/.

2. In the Download Standard Python Software section, click the link for the latest release (**Figure 1.1**) to go to the final-release page.

3. In the Download section (**Figure 1.2**), read the download instructions for your operating system, and click the appropriate link.

   You're taken to another link on the same page or to another page.

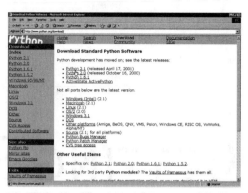

Figure 1.1 The Python download page is the starting point for getting the Python distribution for your operating system. The latest release is at top of the list. The Python folks release new versions once or twice a year.

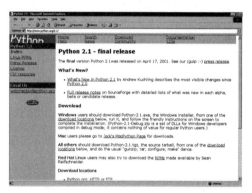

Figure 1.2 The Download section of the final-release page gives download instructions for various operating systems.

Figure 1.3 You can go to the HTTP or FTP download location. (FTP is faster, but your firewall may prevent FTP downloads.)

GETTING PYTHON

Index of /ftp/python/2.1

Name	Last modified	Size	Description
Parent Directory	24-Jan-2001 11:04	-	
Python-2.1-Debug.zip	16-Apr-2001 23:06	1.3M	
Python-2.1.exe	16-Apr-2001 23:03	6.0M	
Python-2.1.tgz	16-Apr-2001 17:01	4.1M	
Python-2.1a1.exe	23-Jan-2001 23:33	5.7M	
Python-2.1a1.tgz	24-Jan-2001 14:02	3.9M	
Python-2.1a2.exe	02-Feb-2001 17:53	5.8M	
Python-2.1a2.tgz	02-Feb-2001 17:11	3.9M	
Python-2.1b1.exe	02-Mar-2001 16:23	5.9M	
Python-2.1b1.tgz	02-Mar-2001 16:36	4.0M	
Python-2.1b2-Debug.zip	23-Mar-2001 17:11	1.3M	
Python-2.1b2.exe	23-Mar-2001 17:11	5.9M	
Python-2.1b2a.tgz	24-Mar-2001 08:26	4.1M	

Figure 1.4 This page shows a list of Python distribution files. To get the Windows version of Python, you need to download only one file.

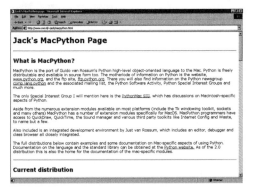

Figure 1.5 The Windows distribution comes with the standard Windows installer.

Jack's MacPython Page

What is MacPython?

MacPython is the port of Guido van Rossum's Python high-level object-oriented language to the Mac. Python is freely distributable and available in source form too. The motherlode of information on Python is the website, www.python.org, and the ftp site, ftp.python.org. There you will also find information on the Python newsgroup comp.lang.python and the associated mailing list, the Python Software Activity, Python Special Interest Groups and much more.

The only Special Interest Group I will mention here is the PythonMac SIG, which has discussions on Macintosh-specific aspects of Python.

Aside from the numerous extension modules available on most platforms (include the Tk windowing toolkit, sockets and many others) MacPython has a number of extension modules specifically for MacOS. MacPython programmers have access to QuickDraw, QuickTime, the Sound manager and various third party toolkits like Internet Config and Waste, to name but a few.

Also included is an integrated development environment by Just van Rossum, which includes an editor, debugger and class browser all closely integrated.

The full distributions below contain examples and some documentation on Mac-specific aspects of using Python. Documentation on the language and the standard library can be obtained at the Python website. As of the 2.0 distribution this is also the home for the documentation of the mac-specific modules.

Current distribution

Figure 1.6 Mac OS distributions are maintained on a separate Web site.

4. Depending on your OS, do one of the following:

For Windows, click either HTTP or FTP in the Download Locations section (**Figure 1.3**). You're presented with a list of files (**Figure 1.4**). Click the file indicated by the on-screen instructions in step 3. When the download completes, double-click the file to launch the standard Windows installer (**Figure 1.5**), and follow the directions on the screen.

For Macintosh, you're directed to the Mac-Python Page (**Figure 1.6**), which contains download and installation instructions. Note that Mac OS X, unlike its predecessors, is a Unix OS.

continues on next page

GETTING PYTHON

For Red Hat Linux, you're directed to the Linux RPMs page (**Figure 1.7**), where you can get RPM (Red Hat Package Manager) files. Use GnoRPM or the `rpm` command to install the package.

For other Unix systems, click either HTTP or FTP in the Download Locations section. You're presented with a list of files. Click the file indicated by the on-screen instructions in step 3. The file is a source tarball (.tgz file); ask a system administrator to install it if you've never compiled source code.

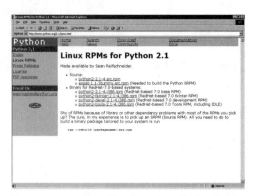

Figure 1.7 You can install Red Hat Linux distributions by using Red Hat's RPM (Red Hat Package Manager) tools.

✔ Tips

- In Unix, type `which python` at a command prompt and press Enter to determine whether Python is already installed. If so, type `python -V` (or `python -v`) and press Enter to determine the version.

- Python also runs on Palm OS; click the Pippy link at www.python.org to get to the download site (**Figure 1.8**). To reduce memory requirements, Pippy is missing a few core Python features, such as floating-point numbers.

Figure 1.8 You can install Python on your Palm, Visor, or any other handheld that runs the Palm OS.

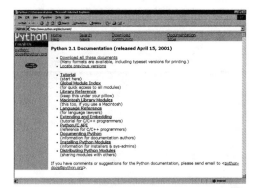

Figure 1.9 The index page for downloaded documentation.

Figure 1.10 The index page for online documentation.

Reading Python Documentation

Python includes a standard set of manuals. As a new user, you'll be most interested in the following:

◆ *Python Tutorial*—an introduction to Python programming written by Python's creator. It includes many examples and explains the rationale for many of the language's features.

◆ *Python Library Reference*—describes the standard library that comes with the Python distribution, including built-in data types, functions, and methods. Reading this manual is necessary to understand Python's scope and power.

◆ *Python Language Reference*—describes the exact syntax and semantics of the Python language. Some parts may be difficult for beginning programmers.

The Windows distribution contains the standard Python manuals in HTML format that you can read in a browser. For other platforms, you can read the documentation online or download it for quicker access.

To display the documentation in Windows:

◆ Choose Start > Programs > Python > Python Manuals.

The Python documentation index page appears (**Figure 1.9**).

To browse the documentation online:

◆ In your browser, go to www.python.org/doc/current/ (**Figure 1.10**).

To download the documentation:

1. In your browser, go to the documentation download page at www.python.org/doc/current/download.html (**Figure 1.11**).

2. Click the link for the desired content and format to download the documentation.

3. Follow the Unpacking directions on the download page to install the documentation.

✔ Tips

- The Python installation script embeds the Python version number in the names of some installation directories, so locations and commands may differ slightly by version.

- The documentation page, www.python.org/doc/, provides links to Python documentation, essays, how-to guides, and other Python-related publications (**Figure 1.12**).

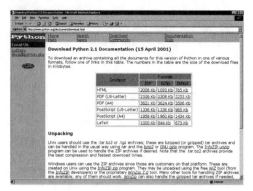

Figure 1.11 Windows and Mac users should download Zip files. Unix users should download GZip or BZip2 files. You can read HTML documents in a browser. PDF documents are suitable for printing; to read or print them, you need Adobe Acrobat Reader, available for free at www.adobe.com.

Figure 1.12 The Python documentation page is the starting point for finding Python-related publications.

Figure 1.13 A Unix command shell. This one is the bash shell running in Linux.

Figure 1.14 The Windows 2000 command-prompt window.

Opening a Command-Prompt Window

Configuring and running Python means typing commands at a command prompt. Several Unix command shells and configurations exist, so I won't review them here (**Figure 1.13**). Instead, I'll refer you to your local computerphile and product documentation. Or you can consult *UNIX: Visual QuickStart Guide,* by Deborah S. Ray and Eric J. Ray, from Peachpit Press.

To open a command-prompt window in Windows:

◆ In Windows 95/98/NT, choose Start > Programs > Command Prompt (or MS-DOS Prompt).

or

In Windows 2000/Me, choose Start > Programs > Accessories > Command Prompt (or MS-DOS Prompt).

The command-prompt window opens (**Figure 1.14**).

To exit a command-prompt window:

◆ Type exit at the command prompt and press Enter.

This method works in Windows and Unix.

✔ Tip

■ Shells have convenient features such as command-line editing (to correct typos) and command history (to repeat a command typed earlier). To learn more about the Windows command prompt, search Windows Help for "command prompt" (Windows 2000 and later) or "MS-DOS prompt" (other Windows versions). To learn more about your Unix shell, type man *shell,* where *shell* is the name of your shell (typically, csh, bash, ksh, or sh); then press Enter.

Setting Your Path

Programs and other executable files can live in many directories, so operating systems provide a search *path* that lists the directories that the OS searches (in the order listed) for executables. This setup relieves you of the burden of having to remember (and type) the path name of each command.

The path is stored in an *environment variable,* which is a named string maintained by the operating system. These variables contain information available to the command shell and other programs. The path variable is named PATH in Unix or Path in Windows (Unix is case-sensitive; Windows is not). In Mac OS, the installer handles the path details. To invoke the Python interpreter from any particular directory, you must add the Python directory to your path.

In Windows, Python usually is located in C:\Python*xx*, where *xx* is the Python version number. In the examples in this book, I don't indicate a version number, but you must type the Python directory name exactly as it appears on your system. In Unix, Python usually is in /usr/local/bin/python or /usr/bin/python. If you can't find it, ask your system administrator.

To view the path:

◆ In Windows, type path at a command prompt and press Enter.

or

In Unix, type echo $PATH at a command prompt and press Enter. The $ character tells the shell to print the contents of the variable, not the string "PATH".

You can add the Python directory to the path for the duration of the command session or have it added automatically whenever you log on. The procedure for changing the path differs by operating system.

Figure 1.15 Using the command prompt to add the Python directory to the Windows path for a particular session.

```
SET windir=C:\WINDOWS

SET winbootdir=C:\WINDOWS

SET PATH=C:\WINDOWS;
→ C:\WINDOWS\COMMAND;C:\Python

SET PROMPT=$p$g

SET TEMP=C:\temp
```

Figure 1.16 Adding the Python directory to the path in the autoexec.bat file.

To add the Python directory to the path for a particular session in Windows:

◆ At a command prompt, type path %path%; *C:\Python* and press Enter.

C:\Python is the path of the Python directory (**Figure 1.15**).

In Unix, the command varies by command shell.

To add the Python directory to the path for a particular session in Unix:

◆ In the csh shell, type setenv PATH "$PATH:*/usr/local/bin/python*" and press Enter.

or

In the bash shell (Linux), type export PATH="$PATH:*/usr/local/bin/python*" and press Enter.

or

In the sh or ksh shell, type PATH="$PATH:*/usr/local/bin/python*" and press Enter.

/usr/local/bin/python is the Python directory.

To add the Python directory to the Windows 95/98/Me path at login automatically:

1. Start a text editor (Notepad will do).

2. Choose File > Open, and open *C:\autoexec.bat*

   C is the letter of the Windows drive.

3. At the end of the SET PATH statement, type ;*C:\Python*

   C:\Python is the Python directory (**Figure 1.16**).

   Don't forget the initial semicolon.

4. Choose File > Save.

5. Choose File > Exit.

   The changes take effect when you restart your computer.

To add the Python directory to the Windows NT/2000 path at login automatically:

1. Make sure that you are logged on as an administrator.

   Administrator privileges permit you to change system variables; otherwise, you can change only user variables.

2. Choose Start > Settings > Control Panel.

3. Double-click the System icon.

4. In Windows NT, click the Environment tab.

   or

   In Windows 2000, in the Advanced tab, click Environment Variables.

5. In the System Variables list, click the Path variable. In Windows 2000, click Edit.

6. In the Value text box, at the end of the string type ; *C:\Python*

   C:\Python is the Python directory (**Figure 1.17**).

   Don't forget the initial semicolon.

7. In Windows NT, click Set; then click OK.

   or

   In Windows 2000, click OK; then click OK again.

   The changes take effect the next time you log on or restart your computer.

To add the Python directory to the Unix path at login automatically:

◆ In a text editor, add the Python directory to the end of the PATH statement in your login initialization file.

   This file is located in your home directory and, depending on your version of Unix, usually is named .login, .profile, or .bash_profile.

Figure 1.17 Adding the Python directory to the Windows 2000 path.

✔ Tips

■ Windows searches the current directory before it searches directories in the path. Unix searches only directories in the path; it does not search the current directory unless it's included in the path. To add the current directory to the Unix path, add the ./ (dot-slash) directory to the path.

■ Note that the Windows path separator is a backslash (\) and that the Unix path separator is a forward slash (/).

SETTING YOUR PATH

Using Python Environment Variables

Python also recognizes the environment variables listed in **Table 1.1**. You can view your environment variables with the set command.

To display your current environment variables:

◆ Type set at a command prompt and press Enter.

✔ Tips

■ Type python -h at a command prompt and press Enter to print a brief description of the Python environment variables.

■ You also can use the set command at a command prompt to create an environment variable for a particular session.

■ To add an environment variable at login automatically, add a set command to your autoexec.bat (Windows 95/98/Me) or login file (Unix). In Windows 2000/NT, you can use the Control Panel's System utility that I described in the preceding section.

Table 1.1

Python Environment Variables	
VARIABLE	**DESCRIPTION**
PYTHONPATH	Has a role similar to PATH. This variable tells the Python interpreter where to locate the module files you import into a program. PYTHONPATH should include the Python source library directory and the directories containing your Python source code. PYTHONPATH is sometimes preset by the Python installer. See "Specifying the Module Search Path" in Chapter 9.
PYTHONSTARTUP	Contains the path of an initialization file containing Python source code that is executed every time you start the interpreter (similar to the Unix .profile or .login file). This file, often named .pythonrc.py in Unix, usually contains commands that load utilities or modify PYTHONPATH.
PYTHONCASEOK	Used in Windows to instruct Python to find the first case-insensitive match in an import statement. Set this variable to any value to activate it.
PYTHONHOME	An alternative module search path. It's usually embedded in the PYTHONSTARTUP or PYTHONPATH directories to make switching module libraries easy.

Running Programs in Interactive Mode

Interactive mode is the easiest way to run Python programs: Just type statements at the interpreter's command line. Python evaluates each statement line by line and, if appropriate, prints the result (or an error message).

To start the interpreter in interactive mode:

◆ In Windows, choose Start > Programs > Python > Python (command line).

   or

   In Unix, make sure that Python is on your path, type python at a command prompt, and press Enter.

   or

   In the Mac OS, double-click the Python Interpreter icon in the Python folder.

   The Python interpreter starts (**Figures 1.18** and **1.19**).

The three greater-than signs (>>>), called the *primary prompt,* indicate that the interpreter is waiting for the next statement. The *secondary prompt* (. . .) indicates that you're typing a multiple-line statement.

To run interactive programs:

1. Start the interpreter in interactive mode.

2. At the >>> prompt, type a Python statement.

3. Press Enter.

   The interpreter prints the results of the statement and displays the >>> prompt again (**Figure 1.20**).

   Alternatively, the interpreter displays the >>> prompt again without printing anything because the statement doesn't display a result (**Figure 1.21**).

Figure 1.18 The Windows Python interpreter in interactive mode.

Figure 1.19 The Python interpreter in Unix.

```
>>> print "area =", 7 * 5
area = 35
>>> 1 + 1
2
>>>
```

Figure 1.20 The interpreter prints the results of arithmetic operations, making it a handy desktop calculator.

```
>>> a = 38
>>>
```

Figure 1.21 The interpreter doesn't print the results of some statements, such as this assignment.

```
>>> for x in range(1,6):
...     print x, x*x
...
1 1
2 4
3 9
4 16
5 25
>>>
```

Figure 1.22 The interpreter displays the . . . prompt for multiple-line (or compound) statements. Enter a blank line to tell Python you're finished typing.

```
>>> a === 7
  File "<stdin>", line 1
    a === 7
        ^
SyntaxError: invalid syntax
>>> x = 7.5
>>> y = 0
>>> x/y
Traceback (most recent call last):
  File "<stdin>", line 1, in ?
ZeroDivisionError: float division
```

Figure 1.23 I've made some errors here. In the first statement, Python points to where it encountered a syntax error. In the last statement, Python chokes when I try to divide by zero.

```
>>> rate = 7.125 / 100
>>> principal = 50.3
>>> rate * principal
3.5838749999999995
>>> _ + principal
53.883874999999996
>>> round(_, 2)
53.880000000000003
```

Figure 1.24 The underscore character (_), which stores the preceding result, is useful for chaining calculations.

Or the interpreter may display the . . . prompt, indicating that it requires continuation lines. After typing the final line, press Enter *twice;* the blank line signals the end of the statement (**Figure 1.22**).

If an error occurs, the interpreter prints an error message and a stack trace. Retype the corrected statement and press Enter (**Figure 1.23**).

To quit the interpreter:

◆ Press Ctrl-C (Windows), Ctrl-D (Unix), or Command-Q (Mac OS).

✔ Tips

■ In this book, I use interactive mode to demonstrate new concepts and give short examples.

■ In interactive mode, the built-in underscore (_) variable holds the result of the last printed expression (**Figure 1.24**).

RUNNING PROGRAMS IN INTERACTIVE MODE

Running Programs in Script Mode

Interactive mode is useful for quick tasks and tests, but you lose everything you type when you exit the interpreter. In *script* (or *noninteractive*) *mode,* you run a Python script that you have already saved in a text file. Python source-code files end with the *.py* suffix and are called *modules,* which I cover in more detail in Chapter 9. **Script 1.1** shows the squares.py script, which I use in the following examples.

To run a program in script mode:

1. At a command prompt, make sure that Python is on your path and that you are in the same directory as the script.

2. Type python *script.py* and press Enter. *script.py* is the name of a script file.

   Python runs the script and displays another command prompt (**Figures 1.25** and **1.26**).

In Unix, you can turn a Python script into an executable program by adding a *shebang line* and changing the file permission. The shebang line has the following characteristics:

◆ Starts with #! (*sharp* + *bang*),

◆ Specifies the path of the Python interpreter,

◆ Is always the first line in the script file.

To find the Python interpreter in Unix:

◆ Type which python at a command prompt, and press Enter.
   The Python path is displayed.

To make a script an executable program in Unix:

1. Open the script in a text editor.

2. Type the following line at the top of the file:
   #! */usr/local/bin/python*

Script 1.1 The script squares.py prints the integers from 1 to 5 and their squares. The range() function returns a list of integers that goes up to, but doesn't include, its second argument.

```
for x in range(1,6):

    print x, x*x
```

Figure 1.25
The script squares.py run in Windows.

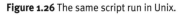

Figure 1.26 The same script run in Unix.

Script 1.2 This script, squares2.py, is the same as Script 1.1 except for a shebang line indicating the location of the Python interpreter.

```
                   script
#! /usr/local/bin/python


for x in range(1,6):

    print x, x*x
```

```
pythonfortheweb - SecureCRT
File  Edit  View  Options  Transfer  Script  Window  Help

[chris@ada chris]$ chmod +x squares2.py
[chris@ada chris]$ ./squares2.py
1 1
2 4
3 9
4 16
5 25
[chris@ada chris]$
```

Figure 1.27 The chmod (change mode) command changes a file's permission to execute. Type ./ and the file name to run the script.

/usr/local/bin/python is the path to the Python interpreter you found in step 1. #! must be the first two characters of the file; otherwise, Python will interpret the line as a comment.

3. Save the file (**Script 1.2**), and exit the editor.

4. At a command prompt, use the cd command to change to the directory containing the script.

5. Type chmod +x *script.py* and press Enter. *script.py* is the name of a script file.
   The file permission changes to execute.

6. Type ./*script.py* and press Enter to run the script (**Figure 1.27**).
   ./ tells Unix to search in the current directory.

✔ Tips

- If you place an executable script in a directory on your path (such as your bin directory), you can execute it from any directory.

- The shebang line may include command-line options; see "Specifying Command-Line Options" later in this chapter.

- I recommend that you write scripts in a dedicated text editor, such as Notepad, vi, BBEdit, or one of the many excellent shareware editors. (Search for "text editors" at www.download.com.) You *can* use a word processor such as Microsoft Word and save as text only, but that practice usually leads to maintenance problems (and professionals consider it to be bad form).

- **OS** The shebang line is ignored in Windows and Mac OS.

- **OS** To learn how to use the Python interpreter in Mac OS, double-click the Documentation icon in the Python folder.

RUNNING PROGRAMS IN SCRIPT MODE

Using IDLE

IDLE (Integrated DeveLopment Environment) is an application that wraps the Python interpreter in a graphical user interface (GUI) and adds considerable functionality to the basic command-shell interpreter. Its features include menus, automatic indentation, colorized code, command completion, pop-up syntax tips, a debugger, and file editing tools. IDLE is available for Windows and Unix. (The Mac OS has a similar tool called Python IDE.) The complete IDLE documentation is available at www.python.org/idle/doc/idle2.html (**Figure 1.28**), so I'll review just the basics. IDLE usually is bundled with the Python distribution, but you can download it at www.python.org/idle/.

To start IDLE:

◆ In Windows, choose Start > Programs > Python > IDLE (Python GUI).

   or

   In Unix, type idle at a command prompt and press Enter.

   IDLE starts and displays the Python Shell window (**Figure 1.29**).

To run interactive programs:

◆ Type Python statements at the >>> prompt just as you would in basic interactive mode; see "Running Programs in Interactive Mode" earlier in this chapter.

To run programs in script mode:

1. In the Python Shell, choose File > Open.

2. Select a Python script file, and click OK.
   A script window appears (**Figure 1.30**).

3. In the Python script window, choose Edit > Run script.
   The Python Shell window is activated, and the script runs (**Figure 1.31**).

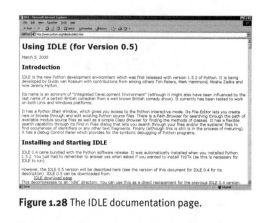

Figure 1.28 The IDLE documentation page.

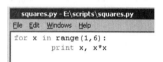

Figure 1.29 IDLE in Windows.

Figure 1.30 An IDLE script window.

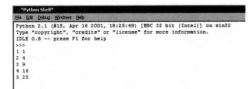

Figure 1.31 Results from a script run in IDLE.

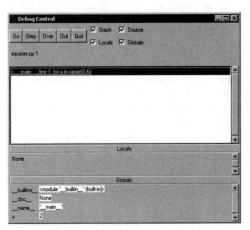

Figure 1.32 The IDLE Debug Control window during a debugging session.

4. If the prompt doesn't appear after the script runs, press Ctrl-C to get it back.

To debug programs:

1. In the Python Shell, choose Debug > Debugger.

The Debug Control window appears.

2. Select the appropriate checkboxes to display the stack, source code, and local and global variables.

3. Activate or open a Python script window.

4. Choose Edit > Run script.

The Debug Control window opens.

5. Use the control buttons to step through the code line by line.

Click Step to step into calls to nested functions, or click Over to execute nested functions without stepping into them.

The Debug Control window displays the stack and variable values (**Figure 1.32**). IDLE for Windows does not support breakpoints.

To quit IDLE:

◆ Choose File > Exit.

✔ Tips

■ If IDLE doesn't start, you may have to install Tcl/Tk or add it to your path. (This tool is installed by default but may have been deselected during installation.) Tcl/Tk is a cross-platform GUI toolkit necessary for IDLE to run. Instructions are on the IDLE documentation Web page at www.python.org/idle/doc/idle2.html.

■ Run IDLE on your local machine and not over a telnet connection (unless you're running a remote X-Windows session).

■ IDLE is an excellent free tool, but more powerful commercial and shareware Python IDEs are available. For more information, see the Appendix.

Specifying Command-Line Options

When you invoke the Python interpreter at a command prompt, you can specify *command-line options* (also called *switches*) to change the interpreter's default behavior or display extra information. I show a few of the common options here and discuss others where they're relevant.

To display a complete list of command-line options:

◆ Type python -h and press Enter (**Figure 1.33**).

To display the Python version:

◆ Type python -V and press Enter.

To execute Python statements from the command prompt:

◆ Type python -c "*cmd*" and press Enter.

cmd is a string containing one or more Python statements separated by semicolons (**Figure 1.34**).

To remain in the interpreter after running a script:

◆ Type python -i *script.py* and press Enter.

script.py is the name of a script file.

This command keeps the interpreter from quitting as soon as the script finishes.

To detect inconsistent use of tabs and spaces in indentation:

◆ Type python -t *script.py* and press Enter.

script.py is the name of a script file. See Figure 7.9 in Chapter 7 for an example.

Figure 1.33 The Python interpreter help message displays syntax, command-line options, arguments, and environment variables.

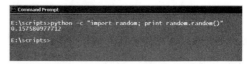

Figure 1.34 With the -c option, you can execute Python statements directly from the command line. This command prints a random number.

Script 1.3 The script `printargs.py` prints a list of its command-line arguments.

```
                    script
import sys

print sys.argv
```

```
Command Prompt
E:\scripts>python printargs.py -w 1.5 abc "a string"
['printargs.py', '-w', '1.5', 'abc', 'a string']

E:\scripts>
```

Figure 1.35 Every word after *python* is placed in the list *argv*, including the name of the script file. All arguments are converted to strings.

Passing Arguments to a Script

You can pass arguments from the command line to a Python program. Python automatically stores command-line arguments as a list of strings in the *argv* variable of the sys module. **Script 1.3**, named `printargs.py`, prints the *argv* list. **Figure 1.35** shows a test run.

To pass command-line arguments to a script:

1. Create a script that contains the statement `import sys`.

   `import` statements usually are placed near the beginning of a script.

2. Use list indexing and slicing to retrieve the arguments from the end of the list `sys.argv`.

   For information about indexing and slicing lists, see "Indexing a List or Tuple (Extracting an Item)" and "Slicing a List or Tuple (Extracting a Segment)" in Chapter 5.

3. Assign the arguments to variables or pass them to functions, converting them from strings to other data types if necessary.

4. At a command prompt, type the following line and press Enter:

   python *script.py arg1 arg2...*

   script.py is the name of the script file, and *arg1 arg2...* represents an arbitrary number of arguments separated by spaces.

continues on next page

The following example shows how to pass command-line arguments to a script. I modified the squares.py script (refer to Script 1.1) to take two command-line arguments. The new script, squares3.py (**Script 1.4**), takes minimum and maximum values from the command line and passes them to the range() function. To run the script, type the following line at a command prompt and press Enter:

```
python squares3.py min max
```

min and *max* are integers, and *max* should exceed *min*. **Figure 1.36** shows a test run. For this run, sys.argv is:

```
['squares3.py', '6', '11']
```

The following statements use negative index values to count from the end of sys.argv:

```
min = int(sys.argv[-2])

max = int(sys.argv[-1])
```

The next-to-last and last items in argv are converted from strings to integers and assigned to the variables min and max, respectively. The range() function in the for loop uses min and max as bounding values.

✔ Tip

- You can use the getopt module for advanced parsing of command-line options and arguments. The functionality of this module is similar to the Unix getopt function. For information about getopt, see the *Python Library Reference*.

Script 1.4 The script squares3.py prints the integers from min to max - 1 and their squares.

```
import sys

min = int(sys.argv[-2])

max = int(sys.argv[-1])

for x in range(min, max):

    print x, x*x
```

Figure 1.36 The minimum (6) and maximum (11) values specified in the command line are passed to the range() function.

EXPRESSIONS AND STATEMENTS

Tokens are the basic indivisible particles of programming languages; they cannot be reduced grammatically by the interpreter. Examples of tokens are variable names, keywords, operators, literals, and delimiters. Tokens are assembled into *expressions,* which create objects, and *statements,* which are executable lines of source code that manipulate objects and carry out commands. An *object* is an instance of any Python data type and has a value, identity, and type. This chapter describes the basic properties of objects and how to construct valid Python tokens, expressions, and statements.

By the way, a file that contains a sequence of one or more statements is a *module*, and a collection of one or more modules is a *program*. Modules are covered in Chapter 9.

Documenting Programs

A *comment* is text that you embed in your program source code to explain it. Comments usually describe what a program does and how, but they can also explain why code was changed and give copyright and author information.

The interpreter ignores comments; they are for future programmers who must understand your script to change it. **Script 2.1** shows some examples.

To add a comment on its own line:

1. At the beginning of the line, type # to begin the comment.

2. Type *comment*, replacing *comment* with explanatory text.

You can also add *inline comments* at the end of a line of code.

To add an inline comment:

1. At the end of a statement, type a space and then # to begin the comment.

2. Type *comment*, replacing *comment* with explanatory text.

Script 2.1 Indent comments at the same level as the code they describe. Use inline comments sparingly.

```
# Print the names of files and
# directories in the current
# working directory.
import os
dir = os.getcwd()  # Current directory
for file in os.listdir(dir):
    # Build a fully-qualified path.
    f = os.path.join(dir, file)
    # Append a separator to
    # indicate directories.
    s = " "
    if os.path.isdir(f): s = os.sep
    print f + s
```

✔ Tips

- Comments continue until the end of the line (the return).

- In interactive mode, you may type a comment at the >>> or . . . prompt. A comment typed at the >>> prompt is followed by the . . . prompt.

- You don't have to indent comments at the same level as the code, but doing so is a good idea.

- For testing, you can *comment out* (disable) lines of code by converting them to comments temporarily.

- Python doesn't support multiple-line comments. Each comment line must have its own pound sign (#).

- Exercise restraint when writing comments. A program with too many comments sometimes is as hard to read as a program with none. Don't include explanations of the obvious such as "Open the file" or "Increment counter."

Blank Lines

Like all modern programming languages, Python permits blank lines, which you should use judiciously; a little white space will make your scripts easier to read. Space permitting, the scripts in this book follow the *Python Style Guide* guidelines at www.python.org/doc/essays/styleguide.html.

As it does comments, the interpreter ignores blank lines in script mode. But Python's sensitivity to indentation yields a twist in interactive mode: you must enter a blank line to terminate a multiple-line statement (that is, just press Enter at the . . . prompt).

DOCUMENTING PROGRAMS

Naming Variables

A *variable* is a named storage location for data. Every variable has a name, called the *variable name, identifier,* or just *name*. Python's rules for naming variables are

◆ Names are unlimited in length,

◆ Names start with a letter or underscore character followed by any number of letters, digits, or underscores. x, _render, and The_Bronx are valid variable names; 100bottles, %hash, and huh? are not,

◆ Names are case-sensitive. filename is not the same as FILENAME,

◆ Names cannot be *keywords,* which are words reserved by Python because they have special meaning in the language (**Table 2.1**).

✔ Tips

■ Python names conventionally have lower-case letters, with multiple words separated by underscores (number_of_links).

■ The more meaningful your variable names are, the less you have to comment your code.

■ Names that begin with an underscore character (_myvar) have a special meaning when you are importing modules; see Chapter 9. Names that begin and end with two underscores (__init__) are system-defined names. To prevent confusion, don't begin names with underscores without a specific reason.

■ To print a list of Python keywords, type the following statements:

```
import keyword
print keyword.kwlist
```

Table 2.1

Python Keywords		
and	exec	lambda
assert	finally	not
break	for	or
class	from	pass
continue	global	print
def	if	raise
del	import	return
elif	in	try
else	is	while
except		

NAMING VARIABLES

Creating Expressions

An *expression* is a legal combination of symbols (variables, literals, objects, functions, parentheses, operators, and so on) that returns an object when evaluated by the Python interpreter. Functions and operators may be built in or user-defined.

Expressions are classified by the type of object they return or action they perform. **Table 2.2** lists some common Python expression types and examples. I'll discuss each type of expression in more detail when it arises.

Table 2.2

Types of Expressions

Type	Description and Examples
Arithmetic	Yields a number using unary, binary, shifting, or bitwise arithmetic operators: x+2, -y, x*y
Atom	A literal, identifier, display, or string conversion: 3.14159, x, [1,2], `x`
Attribute reference	An object's attribute: obj.attr
Boolean	A Boolean operation that yields true or false: a and b, x or y, not c
Call	Invokes a function or method: len(x), x.append(a)
Comparison	A comparison operation that yields 1 (true) or 0 (false): a!=0, x<y<z, m is n, s not in t
Display	A tuple, list, or dictionary: (1,2),(3,), [1,2], [], {"a":1, "b":2}
Lambda	A lambda form: lambda x:x*x
Literal	A string or numeric literal: "mimetic", 3.14159
Slicing	A range of items in a sequence (string, tuple, or list): x[2:4], x[-3:], x[:5]
Subscription	An item in a sequence (string, tuple, or list) or dictionary: x[0], x[-1], dict[key]
String conversion	A string representation of an object: str(x), repr(x), `x`

Creating Expression Statements

One or more comma-separated expressions is called an *expression list*. When an expression list is used as an entire statement itself rather than as part of a larger statement, it's called an *expression statement*.

In interactive mode, expression statements evaluate and print expressions (**Figure 2.1**). If the expression list contains multiple expressions, they are printed as a tuple (that is, surrounded by parentheses). An interactive expression statement is like a shorthand `print` statement; see "Printing Objects" later in this chapter.

In script mode, expression statements don't print anything (you need an explicit `print` statement for that purpose), but they call functions and methods that produce useful *side effects*. A side effect is a change in a variable as a by-product of the evaluation of an expression. The `sort()` method, for example, saves memory by modifying an existing list in place; it returns the `None` (null) object, not a new sorted list object. So although `sort()` doesn't return a useful value, it does have the desirable side effect of sorting a list. See also "Using Functional Programming Tools" in Chapter 8.

```
>>> x = 5
>>> s = "mailbox"
>>> lst = [1, 2, 3]
>>> s, lst
('mailbox', [1, 2, 3])
>>> (x * 2) - 7
3
>>> "echo"
'echo'
>>> x
5
```

Figure 2.1 Typing an expression at an interactive prompt evaluates it and prints its value. Multiple expressions on one line are printed as tuples.

```
>>> lst1 = [9, 3, 7]
>>> lst1 = lst1.sort()
>>> print lst1
None
>>> lst2 = [8, 2, 6]
>>> lst2.sort()
>>> print lst2
[2, 6, 8]
```

Figure 2.2 Oops. Here, lst1 is assigned the result of a method that returns the null object None, thus losing the list. Because sort() sorts a list as a side effect, the correct thing to do is call sort() in an expression statement, as done with lst2.

✔ Tips

■ A common programming error is assigning a None result to a variable, thus losing the original reference (**Figure 2.2**).

■ The result of an expression statement that returns None is not printed in interactive mode.

■ You can use expressions as statements, but you can't do the reverse. Python (unlike C) doesn't support *inline assignments,* which are assignment statements used as expressions. The prohibition of inline assignments obviates the common programming error of using = (and erroneously changing a variable's value) when you really want to use == to compare two values. So typing this:

```
if a = 0:
```

instead of this:

```
if a == 0:
```

is a syntax error.

■ For a full treatment of expressions, see Chapter 5 of the *Python Reference Manual.*

Creating Variables

A variable springs into existence the first time it's assigned a value with an *assignment statement,* which binds the variable name to an object. Python doesn't assign default values to names, so if you try to use a name that hasn't been defined, Python raises a NameError exception (**Figure 2.3**).

Python variables aren't restricted to a particular data type, so any variable can represent any object: number, string, list, and so on. Python keeps track of the data type internally; see "Determining an Object's Type" later in this chapter.

Variables actually store *object references,* which are pointers to objects residing in memory (**Figure 2.4**). Python permits single or multiple assignments in a single statement. By convention, a variable being assigned a value is called a *target.*

To assign a value:

◆ Type *target = expr*

target is the variable being assigned a value, and *expr* is an expression (**Figure 2.5**).

```
>>> x
Traceback (most recent call last):
  File "<stdin>", line 1, in ?
NameError: name 'x' is not defined
>>> x = 5
>>> x
5
```

Figure 2.3 Python raises an exception if you try to use a variable that hasn't been defined.

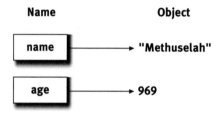

Figure 2.4 Variables hold references that point to objects stored in memory.

```
>>> s = "mephitic"
>>> lst = [1, 2, 3]
>>> num = 10.5
>>> x = 10 * num
>>> tup = ("one", "two", 3)
>>> dict = { 1:"one", 2:"two" }
```

Figure 2.5 A simple assignment binds a single variable name to an object.

```
>>> s, lst = "mephitic", [1, 2, 3]
>>> s
'mephitic'
>>> lst
[1, 2, 3]
>>> num, x = 10.5, 10 * num
Traceback (most recent call last):
  File "<stdin>", line 1, in ?
NameError: name 'num' is not defined
>>> s, t, r = 1, 2, 3, 4
Traceback (most recent call last):
  File "<stdin>", line 1, in ?
ValueError: unpack tuple of wrong size
```

Figure 2.6 These are some multiple assignments using expressions. The first statement is a normal assignment. The second assignment shows that you can't define a name and then use it later in the same multiple assignment. (Two separate assignments are needed here.) The third assignment shows that you must have the same number of expressions as variables.

```
>>> s, t, r = [1, "two", 3.0]
>>> s,t,r
(1, 'two', 3.0)
>>> x, y, z = "ABC"
>>> x,y,z
('A', 'B', 'C')
>>> a, b, c, d = range(4)
>>> a,b,c,d
(0, 1, 2, 3)
```

Figure 2.7 These are some multiple assignments using sequences. The first statement is a normal assignment. The second assignment works only if the length of the string equals the number of variables (use the len() function to determine length). The third assignment uses the list returned from the range() function.

To assign multiple values:

◆ Type *target1, target2,... = expr1, expr2,...*

target1, target2,... are one or more comma-separated variables being assigned values, and *expr1, expr2,...* are expressions.

You must have the same number of expressions as targets (**Figure 2.6**).

or

Type *target1, target2,... = seq*

target1, target2,... are one or more comma-separated variables being assigned values, and *seq* is a sequence (string, list, or tuple) with the same number of items as targets (**Figure 2.7**).

Python pairs each target with its corresponding value and assigns target–value pairs from left to right.

Spaces Between Tokens

You should use spaces to separate tokens in expressions and statements. This statement:

```
a = (b + c) or (d != e)
```

is easier to read than this one:

```
a=(b+c)or(d!=e)
```

In Chapter 7, you'll see that Python uses indentation to define code blocks, so don't add spaces (or tabs) before the first token unless you're indenting a line. Styles vary; look at the spacing recommendations in the *Python Style Guide* at www.python.org/doc/essays/styleguide.html.

CREATING VARIABLES

To assign a value to multiple variables:

◆ Type *target1 = target2 = ... = expr*

  target1, target2, and so on are one or more variables being assigned the same value, and *expr* is an expression (**Figure 2.8**).

✔ Tips

■ When you assign multiple values, Python recognizes both the left and right sides of the assignment as tuples of values. So this:

  a, b, c = 1, 2, 3

  really is shorthand for this:

  (a, b, c) = (1, 2, 3)

  This arrangement is called a *tuple packing and unpacking* assignment, because Python first packs the right-side values into an internal temporary tuple and then unpacks that temporary tuple's values as it assigns each item to the corresponding item in the left tuple. You can use this behavior to swap the values of variables easily (**Figure 2.9**).

■ I have more-detailed examples of assignments that create and modify numbers, strings, lists, tuples, and dictionaries in Chapters 3, 4, 5, and 6.

■ To print the names you've defined in an interactive Python session, type print dir() (**Figure 2.10**); see "Accessing Namespaces" in Chapter 9.

■ An *augmented assignment* combines a binary operation and an assignment in a single statement; see "Making Augmented Assignments" in Chapter 3.

■ Names are not created only with an = assignment statement. The class, def, for, from, and import statements (all covered in later chapters) create names implicitly.

```
>>> x = y = z = 0.0
>>> x,y,z
(0.0, 0.0, 0.0)
>>> a = b = c = None
>>> a,b,c
(None, None, None)
```

Figure 2.8 These assignments usually are used to set a batch of variables to default or initial values.

```
>>> x = 1
>>> y = 2
>>> x, y = y, x
>>> x,y
(2, 1)
```

Figure 2.9 A Python show-stopper: swapping the values of two variables without the need for a temporary variable. This also works with more than two variables; you can type a, b, c = b, c, a, for example.

```
>>> dir()
['__builtins__', '__doc__', '__name__']
>>> a, b = 5, "B"
>>> c = a
>>> dir()
['__builtins__', '__doc__', '__name__',
→ 'a', 'b', 'c']
```

Figure 2.10 The dir() function prints a list of currently defined names. (For now, ignore the built-in names that begin and end with __.)

■ **LANG** You don't need to declare variable names as you do in C, Pascal, and other languages. Unlike a Perl variable, a Python variable doesn't have a special prefix ($, @, or %) that indicates its type.

```
>>> x = y = z = "genome"
>>> x,y,z
('genome', 'genome', 'genome')
>>> del x, y
>>> x,y,z
Traceback (most recent call last):
  File "<stdin>", line 1, in ?
NameError: name 'x' is not defined
>>> dir()
['__builtins__', '__doc__', '__name__', 'z']
```

Figure 2.11 The `dir()` function shows that the names x and y were deleted. Python won't delete the "genome" object because z still refers to it.

Deleting Variables

Whereas a new assignment will clear a variable's current value, the del statement deletes a variable. If you try to use a deleted variable, Python raises a NameError exception, just as though the variable had never existed in the first place.

To delete variables:

◆ Type:

del *var*

var is a variable name.

or

To delete multiple variables, type:

del *var1, var2,...*

var1, var2,... are one or more comma-separated variable names (**Figure 2.11**).

✔ Tips

■ Note that del deletes only a variable, not the object to which it points, because another variable may be pointing to the same object. Python keeps track of objects internally and deletes them automatically when they're no longer in use.

■ Deleting a variable doesn't forfeit its name. You can create another variable with the same name later in the same program.

■ You needn't delete variables yourself when you're done with them; Python deletes them automatically (see "Destroying an Instance" in Chapter 12).

■ In later chapters, you'll see that you can also use del to delete list items, dictionary items, and attributes.

Printing Objects

In interactive mode, you simply type expressions to evaluate and print them. That method won't work in script mode; the statement is legal, but nothing will happen. To print values explicitly, use the print statement, which takes an expression list and does the following:

◆ Evaluates each expression as an object,

◆ Internally converts each object to a nicely formatted printable output string by calling the str() function; see "Converting Strings" in Chapter 4,

◆ Writes each output string to *standard output*, separating them with single spaces,

◆ Terminates the output with a newline, which you may suppress if you want to continue printing on the same line with subsequent print statements.

What is standard output? Technically, it's the stdout file object in the standard sys module. By default, this output is where you expect it to be: in the window where you started your Python program, but you can redirect it elsewhere. For more information about standard output, see "Accessing Standard Input and Output Files" in Chapter 10.

To print objects:

◆ Type:

print *expr*

expr is an expression.

or

To print multiple objects, type:

print *expr1, expr2,...*

expr1, expr2,... are one or more comma-separated expressions (**Figure 2.12**).

```
>>> print "x"
x
>>> "x"
'x'
>>> print "x", "y"
x y
>>> "x", "y"
('x', 'y')
>>> a, b = 5, 10
>>> print "a" + "b", a + b
ab 15
>>> print "a * b =", a * b
a * b = 50
>>> print a, "\n\n", b
5


10
```

Figure 2.12 The print statement evaluates and prints expressions, separated by spaces and followed by a newline. You can add a manual newline with \n. Note the differences between using print and typing expressions to print them interactively.

Script 2.2 The first `print` statement prints the same output as the following three `print` statements combined, because a trailing comma suppresses a newline at the end of printed output. Figure 2.13 shows the output of this script.

```
script
x, y, z = "xxx", "yyy", "zzz"

print x, y, z, 5 * 10

print x,

print y, z,

print 5 * 10
```

```
xxx yyy zzz 50
xxx yyy zzz 50
```

Figure 2.13 The output of Script 2.2.

- You can print formatted output by using the % operator; see "Printing Formatted Strings" in Chapter 4.

- You can redirect output to a file by using the >> operator; see "Printing to a File" in Chapter 10.

- `print` *expr* is equivalent to `sys.stdout.write(expr)`

To print objects without a trailing newline:

- Type:
  `print expr,`

  or

  Type:
  `print expr1, expr2,...,`

  The syntax is the same as the `print` statements in "To print objects" above, except for the trailing comma, which suppresses a newline at the end of the printed output. **Figure 2.13** shows the output of **Script 2.2**.

To print a blank line:

- Type:
  `print`

  or

  To print multiple blank lines, type:
  `print m * "\n",`

  m is the number of blank lines to print.

  The \n escape sequence is the newline character, and the trailing comma suppresses the extra blank line at the end.

✔ Tips

- To print objects without intervening spaces, create an output string by concatenating individual strings; see "Concatenating Strings" in Chapter 4. The following example prints xy:

  `print "x" + "y"`

  You may have to use `str()` to convert an object to a string explicitly. This example raises a `TypeError` exception, because a string and a number can't be concatenated:

  `print "x" + 2`

  But this example prints x2:

  `print "x" + str(2)`

PRINTING OBJECTS

Determining an Object's Identity

Every object has a unique *identity*, which is the address of the object in memory, expressed as an integer or long integer. An object's identity doesn't change; it is constant during the object's lifetime. Use the id() function to determine an object's identity.

To determine an object's identity:

◆ Type id(*expr*)

expr is an expression (**Figure 2.14**).

✔ Tips

■ Use the is comparison operator to determine whether two names refer to the same object; see "Using Comparison Operators" later in this chapter.

■ An object's identity doesn't really *have* to correspond to its location in memory—which actually depends on the implementation of the Python interpreter—but accepted parlance is to refer to the identity as a pointer to a memory location.

```
>>> a = "mephitic"
>>> id(a)
8253288
>>> id(7 - 7)
7955708
>>> id(None)
504964216
```

Figure 2.14 The id() function returns an object's unique and unchangeable identifier, expressed as an integer. Built-in objects such as None have identifiers too.

```
>>> a = "mephitic"
>>> b = a
>>> print a, b
mephitic mephitic
>>> print id(a), id(b)
8253288 8253288
```

Figure 2.15 An assignment such as b = a doesn't duplicate the object to which a points, but it causes b to point to the same object.

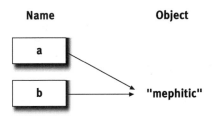

Figure 2.16 An illustration of what's going on in Figure 2.15.

```
>>> a = "diapason"
>>> print a, b
diapason mephitic
>>> print id(a), id(b)
8124672 8253288
```

Figure 2.17 Continuing from Figure 2.15: The value of a isn't changed in place (and can't be, because strings are immutable), so Python creates a new string object and binds a to it, leaving b unchanged.

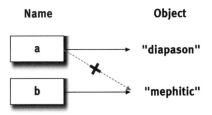

Figure 2.18 An illustration of what's going on in Figure 2.17.

Creating References to the Same Object

When you assign a variable the value of an existing object, Python doesn't make a copy of the object; instead, it duplicates the object reference. You can use the id() function to verify this reference. **Figure 2.15** shows that the assignment b = a assigns the object reference of a to b, so a and b point to the same object in memory (**Figure 2.16**). Multiple variables that refer to the same object are called *aliases*, and the object itself is said to be *aliased*.

Suppose that the value of a changes. Because a and b point to the same memory location, you might expect the value of b to change also. In fact, as **Figure 2.17** shows, Python constructs a new object in a new memory location for a, and b retains its original value and memory location. As illustrated in **Figure 2.18**, the binding of a to the original value is lost.

continues on next page

You can make changes in one alias that are visible to other aliases only when the aliased object is modified *in place*. An in-place operation changes the value an existing object without creating a new one. You may recall from the introduction, however, that mutable objects can change after they're created, whereas immutable objects cannot, so only mutable objects can be changed in place. Lists and dictionaries are mutable; numbers, strings, and tuples are immutable. Python created a new string object in Figure 2.17 because it couldn't modify the existing one. Repeating the process using a mutable list, **Figure 2.19** shows that the aliases x and y still refer to the same object when the object is changed in place.

✔ Tips

- When you assign a new value with an immutable type to a variable, Python may or may not assign the object reference of an existing object with the same type and value. This situation doesn't happen with mutable types. Python won't reuse an object reference; it always creates a new object (**Figure 2.20**).

- To make a copy of a list, see "Copying a List or Tuple" in Chapter 5.

```
>>> x = [1, 2, 3]
>>> y = x
>>> print x, y
[1, 2, 3] [1, 2, 3]
>>> x[1] = "two"
>>> print x, y
[1, 'two', 3] [1, 'two', 3]
>>> x = [4, 5, 6]
>>> print x, y
[4, 5, 6] [1, 'two', 3]
```

Figure 2.19 Here, x and y are assigned to the same list. If the (mutable) list is changed in place, the changes are visible to both variables. If a new list object is created and assigned x, y is left unchanged.

```
>>> a = 0
>>> b = 0
>>> print id(a), id(b)
7955708 7955708
>>> x = [1, 2, 3]
>>> y = [1, 2, 3]
>>> print id(x), id(y)
8241532 8237044
```

Figure 2.20 Python often reuses immutable objects but never mutable ones. Here, a and b both refer to the same integer object with value zero, even though they were assigned separately. But Python creates different lists for x and y even though the lists have the same value.

```
>>> x = 123
>>> type(x)
<type 'int'>
>>> x = "goetic"
>>> type(x)
<type 'string'>
>>> x = [1, "two", 3.0]
>>> type(x)
<type 'list'>
>>> x = 3.0
>>> type(x)
<type 'float'>
```

Figure 2.21 A variable can take any type of object.

Determining an Object's Type

An object's *type* establishes how Python represents it internally. The type determines the range of values an object can take and the operations it supports. Integer objects, for example, can represent only whole numbers between given minimum and maximum values and support arithmetic operations but not string operations such as concatenation. An object's type, like its identity, cannot change during its lifetime.

Python is a *dynamically typed* language, which means you can bind names to objects of different types while the program is running. Use the type() function to determine an object's type or determine whether two objects are of the same type.

To determine an object's type:

◆ Type type(*expr*)

expr is an expression (**Figure 2.21**).

To determine whether two objects are the same type:

◆ Type type(*expr1*) == type(*expr2*)

   expr1 and *expr2* are expressions.

   This expression returns 1 (true) if the objects are of the same type, or 0 (false) otherwise (**Figure 2.22**).

Each value returned by type() has a corresponding name defined in the types module. The type() value <type 'int'>, for example, corresponds to the name IntType in types.

To list the standard object types:

1. Type import types to load the types module.

   You need to load the module only once before its first use.

2. Type dir(types) to print a list of Python's standard object types.

   You can ignore the names that begin with underscores (**Figure 2.23**).

```
>>> a = "diapason"
>>> b = "mephitic"
>>> lst = [1, "two", 3.0]
>>> type(a) == type(b)
1
>>> type(a) == type(lst)
0
>>> type(a) == type(lst[1])
1
>>> type(a) != type(1)
1
>>> type(1) == type(1.0)
0
>>> type(1) == type("1")
0
>>> type(a) == type(b) != type(lst)
1
```

Figure 2.22 Comparing the types (but not values) of objects.

```
>>> import types
>>> dir(types)
['BufferType', 'BuiltinFunctionType', 'BuiltinMethodType', 'ClassType', 'CodeType',
→ 'ComplexType', 'DictType', 'DictionaryType', 'EllipsisType', 'FileType', 'FloatType',
→ 'FrameType', 'FunctionType', 'InstanceType', 'IntType', 'LambdaType', 'ListType', 'LongType',
→ 'MethodType', 'ModuleType', 'NoneType', 'SliceType', 'StringType', 'TracebackType',
→ 'TupleType', 'TypeType', 'UnboundMethodType', 'UnicodeType', 'XRangeType', '__builtins__',
→ '__doc__', '__file__', '__name__']
```

Figure 2.23 The types module defines names for all built-in types.

Table 2.3

Standard Type Names	
TYPE NAME	**DESCRIPTION**
BufferType	Buffer object returned by buffer()
BuiltinFunctionType	Built-in function such as range() or math.sqrt()
BuiltinMethodType	Same as BuiltinFunctionType
ClassType	User-defined class
CodeType	Byte-compiled code returned by compile()
ComplexType	Complex number
DictionaryType	Same as DictType
DictType	Dictionary
EllipsisType	An Ellipses object used in an extended slice
FileType	Open file object such as sys.stdout
FloatType	Floating-point number
FrameType	Execution frame object
FunctionType	User-defined and lambda functions
InstanceType	Instance of a user-defined class
IntType	Integer
LambdaType	Same as FunctionType
ListType	List
LongType	Long integer
MethodType	Method of a user-defined class instance
ModuleType	Module
NoneType	The null object None
SliceType	Extended slice returned by slice()
StringType	Character string
TracebackType	Stack traceback of an exception, such as sys.last_traceback
TupleType	Tuple
TypeType	Type object returned by type()
UnboundMethodType	Same as MethodType
UnicodeType	Unicode character string
XRangeType	Returned by xrange()

Table 2.3 lists the built-in types and their corresponding types names. Use these names in your programs for *type checking,* which tests whether an object is of a specific type. I'll discuss each type in detail when it arises.

To check an object's type:

1. Type from types import * to import the type names from types.

   You need to import a type name only once before its first use. The from statement is covered in "Loading Specific Module Names with *from*" in Chapter 9.

2. Type type(*expr*) == *typename*

   expr is an expression, and *typename* is the name (defined in types) of a standard object type.

   This expression returns 1 (true) if the object is of type *typename,* or 0 (false) otherwise (**Figure 2.24**).

   continues on next page

DETERMINING AN OBJECT'S TYPE

✔ Tip

■ For information about determining the type of user-defined classes of objects, see "Determining Class Membership" in Chapter 12.

```
>>> from types import *
>>> x = 1
>>> type(x) == IntType
1
>>> type(1.0) == FloatType
1
>>> type(None) == NoneType
1
>>> type([]) != ListType
0
>>> type(id) == BuiltinFunctionType
1
>>> type(type) == BuiltinFunctionType
1
>>> a = type(" ")
>>> type(a) == TypeType
1
```

Figure 2.24 Type-checking objects. Note that even the object returned by type() has a type (TypeType).

Using Boolean Operators

A *Boolean expression* (also called a *logical* or *conditional expression*) evaluates to one of two states: true or false, called *Boolean* or *truth values*. Truth values are complementary: "true" means "not false." In Python, a false expression evaluates to one of the values listed in **Table 2.4**. Consequently, a true expression evaluates to any value *not* listed in Table 2.4: a nonzero number or nonempty string, tuple, list, or dictionary.

Table 2.5 shows Python's three *Boolean operators* (or *logical operators*); the operands *x* and *y* represent expressions. If you've used other languages, you'll find that these operators perform standard Boolean algebra, except that *and* and *or* return one of their operands rather than a Boolean value or an integer.

The not operator takes a single operand and negates, or inverts, its Boolean value. This operator returns 1 (true) if its operand is false or 0 (false) otherwise. **Table 2.6** lists possible outcomes. See **Figure 2.25** for examples.

The *and* operator takes two operands and performs a left-to-right evaluation to determine whether *both* operands are true. Python won't evaluate the right operand if the expression's truth value is determined by the left operand. If *x* is false, for example, *x and y* evaluates and returns *x* and ignores *y*, no matter what its value is. Refer to Table 2.6, which lists the possible outcomes. See **Figure 2.26** for some examples.

The or operator takes two operands and performs a left-to-right evaluation to determine whether *either* operand is true. Like *and*, Python won't evaluate the right operand if the expression's truth value is determined by the left operand. If *x* is true, for example, *x or y* evaluates and returns *x* and ignores *y*, no matter what its value is. See **Figure 2.27** for some examples.

continues on next page

Table 2.4

False Values	
VALUE	DESCRIPTION
0, 0.0, 0L, 0+0J	The number zero
" "	Empty string
()	Empty tuple
[]	Empty list
{}	Empty dictionary
None	The null object

Table 2.5

Boolean Operators	
OPERATOR	DESCRIPTION
not x	Returns 1 if x is true, 0 (zero) otherwise.
x and y	Returns x if x is false, y otherwise.
x or y	Returns y if x is false, x otherwise.

Table 2.6

Boolean Operation Results				
x	y	x and y	x or y	not x
F	F	x	y	1
T	F	y	x	0
F	T	x	y	
T	T	y	x	

F = FALSE, T = TRUE

```
>>> not -4
0
>>> not "mephitic"
0
>>> not "", not 0, not None
(1, 1, 1)
>>> not [" "], not ({},), not [None]
(0, 0, 0)
```

Figure 2.25 The not operator negates its argument and returns 1 (true) or 0 (false).

✔ Tips

- You can assign the result of a Boolean expression to a variable. This method is commonly used to replace an empty object with a default value. The following statement assigns country the value "US" if s is " " (or any other false value):

  country = s or "US"

- print a or b or c or... prints the first nonempty (true) object.

- If the second operand of an and or or expression is a function or method, it won't be invoked if evaluation stops at the first operand. You'll have a bug in your program if its logic depends on the function's side effects. In this example, the list lst won't be sorted if a is false:

  a and lst.sort()

  In this example, lst won't be sorted if b is true:

  b or lst.sort()

- A list, tuple, or dictionary that contains a false value still evaluates to true. The list [" "], for example, is true because it contains one item.

- The truth value of some objects isn't useful. Code and file objects (which are always true) have no sensible meaning as Boolean operands. Class instances default to true, but you can make them false by defining a special method; see "Setting the Truth Value of an Instance" in Chapter 12.

- For jargon fans: NOT is *logical negation,* AND is *logical conjunction,* and OR is *logical inclusion.*

- **LANG** Python doesn't have an exclusive-OR (XOR) Boolean operator or a built-in Boolean type.

```
>>> "a" and "b"
'b'
>>> "a" and ""
''
>>> 0 and "b"
0
>>> "a" and "b" and [1, 2, 3]
[1, 2, 3]
>>> "a" and "b" and [] and "c"
[]
```

Figure 2.26 The *and* operator returns the last evaluated argument.

```
>>> "a" or "b"
'a'
>>> "a" or ""
'a'
>>> 0 or "b"
'b'
>>> "a" or "b" or []
'a'
>>> 0 or "" or () or []
[]
>>> 1 and "a" or "b"
'a'
>>> "a" and "" or "b"
'b'
```

Figure 2.27 The or operator (like *and*) returns the last evaluated argument.

- You can combine multiple Boolean operators in a single expression. From highest to lowest priority, the operators are not, and, and or. The expression x and not y or z, for example, is equivalent to (x and (not y)) or z. For more information about the order of evaluation, see "Determining the Order of Evaluation" later in this chapter.

Table 2.7

Comparison Operators	
OPERATOR	DESCRIPTION
<	Less than
<=	Less than or equal to
>	Greater than
>=	Greater than or equal to
==	Equal to
!=	Not equal to
is	Same object identity
is not	Different object identity
in	Member of
not in	Not a member of

```
>>> a = 1
>>> b = 10
>>> a == b
0
>>> a < 5, 5 < b
(1, 1)
>>> a < 5 < b
1
>>> a > 5, 5 > b, b == 10
(0, 0, 1)
>>> a > 5 > b
0
>>> a < 10 == b
1
>>> (a == 1) and (b >= 5)
1
>>> (a != 1) or (b >= 5)
1
```

Figure 2.28 The comparison operators can be mixed with the Boolean operators.

Using Comparison Operators

Python's *comparison operators* (or *relational operators*) compare two objects and return the integer 1 for true or 0 for false (**Table 2.7**).

The <, <=, >, >=, ==, and != operators compare the values of two objects. The way that the objects are compared depends on their type. Numbers are compared arithmetically, for example, and strings are compared by characters' numerical equivalents. Objects of different types always compare unequal, but numbers (integers, long integers, floats, and complex numbers) are converted to a common type for comparisons. I cover the criteria used to compare numbers, strings, lists, tuples, and dictionaries in the "Comparing..." sections of Chapters 3, 4, 5, and 6 (**Figure 2.28**).

continues on next page

The is and not is operators determine whether two objects have the same identity; see "Determining an Object's Identity" in this chapter. *x* is *y* returns 1 (true) only if *x* and *y* refer to the same object, or 0 (false) otherwise. *x* is not *y* returns the inverse truth values of *x* is *y* (**Figure 2.29**).

```
>>> a = b = "mephitic"
>>> a is b
1
>>> lst1 = [1, 2, 3]
>>> lst2 = [1, 2, 3]
>>> lst1 is lst2
0
>>> lst3 = [lst1, 4, 5]
>>> lst4 = [-1, 0, lst1]
>>> lst3[0] is lst4[-1]
1
>>> x = None
>>> y = None
>>> x is y is None
1
```

Figure 2.29 The is and is not operators test for identical objects. Some built-in objects, such as None, have a single instance.

```
>>> lst = [1, "two", 3.0, ""]
>>> str1 = ""
>>> str2 = "two"
>>> str3 = "ABC"
>>> str4 = "ABC\n"
>>> 5 in lst, 3 in lst, str2 in lst
(0, 1, 1)
>>> "" in lst
1
>>> "" in str2
Traceback (most recent call last):
  File "<stdin>", line 1, in ?
TypeError: 'in <string>' requires character
→ as left operand
>>> "a" not in str3, "A" in str3,
→ "\n" in str4
(1, 1, 1)
>>> 3.00 in (1, 2, 3, 4)
1
```

Figure 2.30 The in and not in operators test for membership in strings, lists, and tuples. Comparisons are case-sensitive. You can search for single characters only in strings.

The in and not in operators determine whether an object is a member of a sequence. A sequence is a string, list, or tuple. *x* in *seq* returns 1 (true) only if *seq* contains the item *x*, or 0 (false) otherwise. *x* not in *seq* returns the inverse truth values of *x* in *seq*. If *seq* is a string, *x* must be a single character. (An escape sequence such as \n is considered to be a single character.) If *seq* is a tuple or list, *x* can be any object (**Figure 2.30**).

✔ Tips

- An is comparison matters only for mutable objects such as lists and dictionaries; see "Creating References to the Same Object" in this chapter.

- a is b is equivalent to id(a) == id(b); see "Determining an Object's Identity" earlier in this chapter.

- The find() method is more flexible than in for finding string characters; see "Searching For Substrings" in Chapter 4.

- The <> operator is equivalent to != but is obsolete.

- **LANG** In Java, the == operator (object identity) is equivalent to Python's is operator, and the equals method (value equality) is equivalent to Python's == operator.

USING COMPARISON OPERATORS

Chaining Comparisons

You can chain comparisons to create expressions such as this:

```
x <= y < z
```

That expression is equivalent to the following one, except that y is evaluated only once:

```
(x <= y) and (y < z)
```

✔ Tips

- Only adjacent operands are compared, so in a < b > c (which is legal but stylistically best avoided), a is not compared with c.

- Chained comparisons can be arbitrarily long, but the implied and means evaluation halts as soon as the truth value of the entire expression is determined. In the following example, f and g will not be evaluated if d < e is false:

  ```
  d < e < f < g
  ```

Table 2.8

Order of Evaluation (Highest to Lowest)	
OPERATOR	**DESCRIPTION**
(), [], {}, `	Tuple, list, dictionary, string conversion
x.attr, *x[i]*, *x[i:j]*, *f()*	Attribute, index, slice, function call
+*x*, -*x*, ~*x*	Unary identity, unary negation, unary bitwise invert
**	Exponentiation (right-to-left associativity)
*, /, %	Multiplication, division, modulo
+, -	Addition, subtraction
<<, >>	Bitwise shifts
&	Bitwise AND
^	Bitwise XOR
|	Bitwise OR
<, <=, >, >=, ==, !=, is, is not, in, not in	Comparison operators
not	Boolean NOT
and	Boolean AND
or	Boolean OR
lambda	Lambda expression

Determining the Order of Evaluation

Precedence determines the priority of various operators when more than one is used in an expression. Operations with higher precedence are performed first. This expression:

```
x > y and a == 1
```

is equivalent to this:

```
(x > y) and (a == 1)
```

and not this:

```
x > (y and a) == 1
```

Comparison operators have higher precedence than Boolean operators do. Operators with lower precedence are said to be less *binding* than those with higher precedence. **Table 2.8** lists operator precedences from most to least binding and includes operators that I have not yet covered. Operators in the same row have equal precedence.

Associativity determines the order of evaluation in an expression when adjacent operators have equal precedence. Python uses left-to-right associativity for all operators except ** (exponentiation), which groups from right to left.

You don't need to memorize all this information. You can use parentheses to override precedence and associativity rules. It's a good idea to add parentheses (even when they're unnecessary) to complex expressions to ensure your intended evaluation order and to improve readability.

Summarizing Objects

This section provides a quick summary of the important characteristics of objects covered in this chapter. This definition will expand as I introduce more object types, including user-defined ones.

A Python object has the following characteristics:

- Stores data in a Python program

- Is an instance of any Python data type

- Is created by an expression

- Can be referenced by one or more names

- Has a changeable value that represents a quantity assigned to it

- Is uniquely identified by an unchangeable identity, returned by the id() function

- Has an unchangeable type, returned by the type() function, that determines what values it can take and what operations it supports

- Is mutable or immutable, depending on its type

- Can be converted to a string representation with the str() function

- Can be printed with the print statement

- Is deleted by the Python interpreter automatically when it's no longer needed

WORKING WITH NUMBERS

This chapter introduces you to Python's numeric capabilities. Many of the mathematical operators and functions will be familiar to you if you've taken (and passed) high-school mathematics. I also review Python's numeric types and how to convert among them.

You have several ways to create a number in Python, most commonly by:

◆ Typing a numeric literal (6.22)

◆ Using a numeric attribute (math.pi)

◆ Making a comparison (x<y, a in b, m is n)

◆ Using the not operator (not x)

◆ Calling a function or method that returns a number (abs(x))

Understanding the Types of Numbers

Python has four numeric types (**Table 3.1**):

Plain integers, often called just *integers* or *ints,* are positive or negative whole numbers with no decimal point.

Long integers, or *longs,* are integers of unlimited size, written like integers and followed by an uppercase or lowercase *L.*

Floating-point numbers, or *floats,* represent real numbers and are written with a decimal point dividing the integer and fractional parts. Floats may also be in scientific notation, with *E* or *e* indicating the power of 10 ($2.5e2 = 2.5 \times 10^2 = 250$).

Complex numbers are of the form *a* + *b*J, where *a* and *b* are floats and J (or j) represents the square root of −1 (which is an imaginary number). *a* is the real part of the number, and *b* is the imaginary part. Complex numbers are not used much in Python programming.

Table 3.1

Numeric Types	
TYPE	EXAMPLES
Integer	-10000, 0, 38
Long (integer)	-1L, 0L, 99999999999L
Float	-2.5E4, -1., 0.001, 10e2
Complex number	-6+3j, 2.0J, 4.2-5.0J

```
>>> type(1), type(1.0)
(<type 'int'>, <type 'float'>)
>>> type(1L), type(1J)
(<type 'long int'>, <type 'complex'>)
```

Figure 3.1 The types of numbers.

Roundoff Error

Sometimes, floats appear differently than you expect, as in these examples:

```
>>> 0.1
0.10000000000000001
>>> 0.2
0.20000000000000001
>>> 0.3
0.29999999999999999
```

The difference occurs because Python (like Perl, Java, C, and other languages) uses internal binary (base 2) representations of decimal (base 10) numbers. Unfortunately, most decimal fractions can't be represented exactly in binary, so small differences occur. This difference, called *representation error* or *roundoff error,* is discussed in "Floating Point Arithmetic: Issues and Limitations" on the online *Python Tutorial* at python.sourceforge.net/devel-docs/tut/node14.html.

This situation is a design issue (speed versus accuracy) and generally not considered to be a bug. Python rounds floats to 17 significant digits, which is enough precision for most applications. If you need more precision, try the FixedPoint class at ftp://ftp.python.org/pub/python/contrib09-Dec-1999/DataStructures/FixedPoint.py.

✔ Tips

- Python supports *octal* (base 8) and *hexadecimal* (base 16) integers. Octal values start with a leading 0 (zero) followed by octal digits (0...7). Hexadecimal, or *hex,* values start with a leading 0x or 0X followed by hex digits (0...9, A...F, or a...f). You can't start a normal (base 10) integer with a zero; Python will interpret it as an octal value.

- To determine the largest representable positive integer, type the following statements:

  ```
  import sys
  print sys.maxint
  ```

  The largest representable negative integer is -maxint-1.

- Use the type() function to determine a number's type; see "Determining an Object's Type" in Chapter 2 (**Figure 3.1**).

- Calculations involving only integers are much faster than those involving floats. Always use integers for operations such as counting, numbering, and indexing.

- To extract the real part of a complex number z, type z.real. Type z.imag to extract the imaginary part.

- Use an uppercase *L* in a long integer; a lowercase letter *l* is easily confused with the digit 1.

- **LANG** A plain integer is the same as a C long, and a float is the same as a C double.

UNDERSTANDING THE TYPES OF NUMBERS

Understanding Promotion

When you mix numeric types in an arithmetic expression, Python converts, or *coerces*, all the numbers to the type of the expression's most complex operand and returns the result in this type. Here are the rules of this process, called *promotion,* from the *Python Reference Guide*:

◆ If either operand is a complex number, the other is converted to a complex number,

◆ Otherwise, if either operand is a floating-point number, the other is converted to a floating-point number,

◆ Otherwise, if either operand is a long integer, the other is converted to a long integer,

◆ Otherwise, both operands must be plain integers, and no conversion is necessary.

If you add a plain integer and a float, for example, Python converts the plain integer to a float, adds the numbers, and returns the sum as a float. You can also convert numbers to other types explicitly by using Python's conversion functions; see "Converting Among Number Types" later in this chapter.

✔ Tip

■ You can use the coerce() function to see how Python promotes numbers. Type coerce(*x*, *y*), where *x* and *y* are numeric expressions that represent different types of numbers. Python returns a two-item tuple containing the arguments converted to a common type using promotion rules. coerce(1,2.5), for example, is (1.0,2.5).

Table 3.2

Unary Arithmetic Operators	
OPERATOR	WHAT IT DOES
-x	Reverses the sign of x
+x	Leaves x unchanged

Table 3.3

Binary Arithmetic Operators	
OPERATOR	WHAT IT DOES
x + y	Sums x and y
x - y	Subtracts y from x
x * y	Multiplies x and y
x / y	Divides x by y
x ** y	Raises x to the power y
x % y	Remainder of x / y

```
>>> 5 + -3
2
>>> principal = 1000
>>> rate = 0.07125
>>> interest = principal * rate
>>> principal + interest
1071.25
>>> 3 * 10.0
30.0
>>> 3 * 5L
15L
>>> 3 * 5L * 10.0
150.0
>>> 1 / 0
Traceback (most recent call last):
  File "<stdin>", line 1, in ?
ZeroDivisionError: integer division or
→ modulo by zero
```

Figure 3.2 Python as desktop calculator. Note that mixed numeric types are converted automatically to a common type.

Performing Basic Arithmetic

The *unary arithmetic operators* (**Table 3.2**) perform mathematical operations on a single operand to produce a result. The – (negation) operator changes the sign of its operand. The not very useful + (identity) operator leaves its operand unchanged.

To change the sign of a number:

◆ Type -x

x is a numeric expression.

Python's *binary arithmetic operators* (**Table 3.3**) perform mathematical operations on two operands to produce a result. These operators include the usual ones: + (addition), – (subtraction), * (multiplication), and / (division).

To add, subtract, multiply or divide:

◆ Type x + y to add, x - y to subtract, x * y to multiply, or x / y to divide.

x and y are numeric expressions (**Figure 3.2**).

See "Getting the Quotient of a Division" later in this chapter for information about dividing integers.

continues on next page

✔ Tips

- When you use multiple operators in a single expression, you may need to use parentheses to control the calculation order; see "Controlling Calculation Order" later in this chapter.

- An operation on (only) plain integers will not produce a long integer if the result is too large for a plain integer to store. You must designate one of the operands a long integer; otherwise, Python raises an OverflowError exception (**Figure 3.3**).

- The *shifting operators* and *bitwise operators* (**Table 3.4**) perform logical and shift operations on the bits of integers. These operators are not used much in Python, but someday you may need them to deal with image files or external C libraries. See Sections 5.5, "Unary arithmetic operations," 5.7, "Shifting operations," and 5.8, "Binary bit-wise operations," of the *Python Reference Manual*.

- **LANG** Perl automatically converts strings to numbers in arithmetic operations: 5 + "5" is 10 in Perl but raises a TypeError exception in Python.

```
>>> 123456 * 123456
Traceback (most recent call last):
  File "<stdin>", line 1, in ?
OverflowError: integer multiplication
>>> 123456 * 123456L
15241383936L
>>> import sys
>>> sys.maxint
2147483647
```

Figure 3.3 A plain integer is too small to hold the result of this calculation. You must change one of the operands manually to a long integer. The sys.maxint attribute holds the largest representable plain integer.

Table 3.4

Shifting and Bitwise Operators

Operator	What It Does
~x	Inverts the bits of x
$x << n$	Shifts x left by n bits
$x >> n$	Shifts x right by n bits
$x \& y$	Bitwise AND of x and y
$x \wedge y$	Bitwise exclusive-OR (XOR) of x and y
$x \mid y$	Bitwise OR of x and y

```
>>> 3 ** 2
9
>>> 2 ** 3
8
>>> 1 / (2.0 ** 3)
0.125
>>> 2.0 ** -3
0.125
>>> (2.0 ** 3) ** -1
0.125
>>> 25 ** 0.5  # Square root
5.0
```

Figure 3.4 Exponentiation raises a number to a power.

Raising a Number to a Power

The ** (exponentiation) operator and the pow() function raise a number to a power. The expression $x**y$ (or, mathematically, x^y) shows how many times the *base, x,* is multiplied by the *exponent, y.* A positive exponent indicates multiplication ($2^4 = 2 \times 2 \times 2 \times 2$), a negative exponent indicates division ($2^{-4} = 1/2^4$), and a fractional exponent indicates the root of the base ($16^{1/2} = 4 =$ the square root of 16).

To raise a number to a power:

◆ Type x ** y

 or

 Type pow(x, y)

 x and y are numeric expressions (**Figure 3.4**).

✔ Tip

■ You can't raise an integer to a negative integer power by using **. In the expression $x**y$, either x or y must be a float if y is negative. Type 2.0**-4, for example, not 2**-4. The function call pow(2, -4) works, however.

Getting the Remainder of a Division

The % (modulo) operator yields the remainder of a division. 20 % 6 is 2 because 20 equals 3 * 6 + 2. You usually perform *modular division* to check whether one number is evenly divisible by another. If x % 2 is 0, for example, x is even. You can also use modular division to scale numbers to a desired range. If x is a random integer, (x % 6) + 1 will always be between 1 and 6, inclusive (the roll of a die, perhaps). Here's another trick: x % (10 ** n) returns the n rightmost digits of x. Modular division usually is performed on integers, but Python supports floats too. 2.4 % 0.7 is 0.3, for example, because 2.4 equals 3 * 0.7 + 0.3.

To get the remainder of a division:

◆ Type x % y

x and y are numeric expressions.

y must be nonzero. The result will have the same sign as y (or zero) and be less than y (**Figure 3.5**).

✔ Tips

■ If x and y are integers, x % y is equivalent to the following expression:

$x - y * (x / y)$

/ represents integer division; see "Getting the Quotient of a Division" later in this chapter.

■ **LANG** Perl truncates the decimal part of a number before calculating the modulus; Python performs modular division on floats.

```
>>> 10 % 3, 10 % 4, 10 % 5, 10 % 6
(1, 2, 0, 4)
>>> 15 % 4, -15 % 4, 15 % -4, -15 % -4
(3, 1, -1, -3)
>>> 15L % 4
3L
>>> 1234567890 % (10 ** 5)
67890
>>> 1.7 % 0.5
0.19999999999999996
>>> 2 % 0.4
0.39999999999999991
>>> 0 % 10
0
>>> 10 % 0
Traceback (most recent call last):
  File "<stdin>", line 1, in ?
ZeroDivisionError: integer division or
→ modulo by zero
```

Figure 3.5 Modular division returns the remainder of a division.

```
>>> 20 / 6
3
>>> -20 / -6
3
>>> 1 / 2
0
>>> -1 / 2
-1
>>> 13L / 3
4L
>>> 1 / float(2)
0.5
>>> q, r = divmod(20,6)
>>> q,r
(3, 2)
```

Figure 3.6 Integer division returns the quotient of a division. `divmod()` returns both the quotient and remainder.

Getting the Quotient of a Division

Integer division complements modular division: it yields the quotient of a division and drops the remainder. The result of a (plain or long) integer divided by an integer is always an integer, rounded down toward minus infinity.

To get the quotient of a division:

◆ Type x / y

x and y are integer expressions (**Figure 3.6**).

Note that integer division uses the ordinary division operator. To divide two integers and get the true floating-point answer, convert one of the operands to a float by using the `float()` function. (Python converts the other operand automatically.)

To divide integers and get a floating-point result:

◆ Type `float(`x`)` / y or x / `float(`y`)`

x and y are integer expressions.

✔ Tips

■ The `divmod(`x`,`y`)` function returns the quotient and remainder of x and y in the tuple $(x / y, x \% y)$.

■ **NEW** In Python 2.2, you optionally may use the / operator for true division and the // operator for integer division; see "Enabling Language Features" in Chapter 9.

Controlling Calculation Order

The calculation order of arithmetic expressions is determined by precedence and associativity, which are described in "Determining the Order of Evaluation" in Chapter 2. **Table 3.5** (a subset of Table 2.8) lists arithmetic operator precedences. Operators in the same row have equal precedence. The expression 2 + 3 * 4 is 14 rather than 20 because multiplication has higher precedence than addition. Python first computes 3 * 4 and then adds 2.

Python uses left-to-right associativity for all arithmetic operators except ** (exponentiation), which is right to left. * and / have the same precedence, so 6 / 2 * 3 is 9 (not 1) because 6 / 2 is evaluated first, and 2 ** 3 ** 2 is 512 (not 64) because 3 ** 2 is evaluated first.

You can use parentheses to override precedence and associativity rules. Expressions inside parentheses are evaluated before expressions outside them. Adding parentheses to the preceding examples, you get (2 + 3) * 4 is 20, 6 / (2 * 3) is 1, and (2 ** 3) ** 2 is 64.

✔ Tips

- It's good programming style to add parentheses to long expressions to increase readability. 5 ** 2 * 4 / 2 is equivalent to ((5 ** 2) * 4) / 2, but the latter is clearer.

- Arithmetic operators (+, -, *, ...) have higher precedence than comparison operators (<, ==, >, ...), which have higher precedence than Boolean operators (not, and, or), so this expression:

  a or b * c >= d

  is equivalent to this one:

  a or ((b * c) >= d)

Table 3.5

Arithmetic Operator Precedence*	
OPERATOR	**DESCRIPTION**
+X, -X	Unary identity, unary negation
**	Exponentiation (right-to-left associativity)
*, /, %	Multiplication, division, modulo
+, -	Addition, subtraction

*FROM HIGHEST TO LOWEST PRECEDENCE

Table 3.6

Augmented Assignment Operators	
OPERATOR	ASSIGNS THIS VALUE TO x
$x += y$	x incremented by y
$x -= y$	x decremented by y
$x *= y$	x multiplied by y
$x /= y$	x divided by y
$x **= y$	x raised to the power y
$x \%= y$	Remainder of x / y

```
>>> a = b = c = d = e = f = 5
>>> x = 2
>>> a += x + 1
>>> b -= x + 1
>>> c *= x + 1
>>> d /= x + 1
>>> e **= x + 1
>>> f %= x + 1
>>> a,b,c,d,e,f
(8, 2, 15, 1, 125, 2)
```

Figure 3.7 Some augmented assignments.

- Python also has augmented assignments for bitwise operators: &=, |=, ^=, >>=, and <<=; see "Performing Basic Arithmetic" earlier in this chapter.

- **NEW** Python 2.0 introduced augmented assignment operators.

- **LANG** Python doesn't have the C and Perl ++ (increment) or - - (decrement) operators. Python interprets - - 4 as -(-4) = 4.

Making Augmented Assignments

Assignment expressions such as x = x + 1 are so common that Python provides short-cuts called *augmented assignments*. Python provides one *augmented assignment operator* (**Table 3.6**) for each binary arithmetic operator; see "Performing Basic Arithmetic" earlier in this chapter. x += 1 is equivalent to the preceding expression.

To make an augmented assignment:

◆ Type $x += y$ to increment x by y.
  Type $x -= y$ to decrement x by y.
  Type $x *= y$ to multiply x by y.
  Type $x /= y$ to divide x by y.
  Type $x **= y$ to raise x to the y power.
  Type $x \%= y$ to assign $x \% y$ to x.

  x is a numeric variable and y is a numeric expression (**Figure 3.7**).

✔ Tips

- An augmented assignment such as x = x + 1 isn't *exactly* the same as x += 1. The former computes x twice: once when it evaluates the right x and again when assigns the result to the left x. The latter computes x only once or *in place*, meaning that Python saves time and memory by modifying only the original x object.

- x *op* y is evaluated as x *op* (y), where *op* is any augmented assignment operator. The statement:

  x *= y + 1

  is equivalent to:

  x = x * (y + 1)

  and not:

  x = (x * y) + 1

Converting Among Number Types

Python converts numbers internally in an expression containing mixed types to a common type for evaluation. But sometimes, you'll need to coerce a number explicitly from one type to another to satisfy the requirements of an operator or function parameter. The int(), long(), float(), and complex() functions perform numeric conversions.

To convert a number to a specific type:

◆ Type int(*x*) to convert *x* to a plain integer.

Type long(*x*) to convert *x* to a long integer.

Type float(*x*) to convert *x* to a floating-point number.

Type complex(*x*) to convert *x* to a complex number with real part *x* and imaginary part zero.

Type complex(*x*, *y*) to convert *x* and *y* to a complex number with real part *x* and imaginary part *y*.

x and *y* are numeric expressions (**Figure 3.8**).

✔ Tips

■ When you convert a float to a (plain or long) integer, Python discards the float's fractional part, losing information. See also the round() and floor() functions in "Using Advanced Mathematical Functions" later in this chapter.

■ You may lose precision when you convert a very large long integer to a float.

■ These functions can also convert a string to a number, provided that the string is a valid numeric literal of corresponding type. float("1.0") returns 1.0, for example, but int("1.0") is an error.

■ Use the str() function to convert a number to a string; see "Converting Strings" in Chapter 4.

```
>>> x = 0
>>> int(x), long(x), float(x),
→ complex(x)
(0, 0L, 0.0, 0j)
>>> x = 1
>>> int(x), long(x), float(x), complex(x)
(1, 1L, 1.0, (1+0j))
>>> x = 1.5
>>> int(x), long(x), float(x), complex(x)
(1, 1L, 1.5, (1.5+0j))
>>> x = "1"   # An "int" string
>>> int(x), long(x), float(x), complex(x)
(1, 1L, 1.0, (1+0j))
>>> x = "1.5"   # A "float" string
>>> float(x), complex(x)
(1.5, (1.5+0j))
>>> y = 111222333444555666777888L
>>> float(y)   # Loses precision
1.1122233344455567e+023
>>> oct(256), hex(256)
('0400', '0x100')
>>> str(1), str(1.5), str(1/3.3)
('1', '1.5', '0.30303030303')
```

Figure 3.8 Some numeric conversions.

■ The oct() and hex() functions convert integers to octal and hexadecimal strings.

```
>>> 3 < 1, 3 > 3, 3 == 2.9999999
(0, 0, 0)
>>> (1 == 1.0) + (0 < -1) + (1 >= 1)
2
>>> x = 3
>>> x and (x > 4)
0
>>> x or (x > 4)
3
```

Figure 3.9 Comparing numbers.

Comparing Numbers

You can compare numbers using the comparison operators introduced in "Using Comparison Operators" in Chapter 2. Comparisons have the expected mathematical interpretation and return 1 (true) or 0 (false).

To compare numbers:

◆ Type *x op y*

x and *y* are numeric expressions, and *op* is the <, <=, >, >=, ==, or != operator (**Figure 3.9**).

✔ Tips

■ Python converts numbers to a common type internally for comparisons.

■ Numeric comparisons can be chained. x < y != z, for example, is legal; see "Chaining Comparisons" in Chapter 2.

■ Numbers and non-numbers always compare unequal, that is, x == obj is always false if x is a number and obj is not. Python won't convert obj to a number internally.

■ Comparing complex numbers with == and != tests both the real parts and imaginary parts for equality. It's not mathematically meaningful to compare complex numbers by using <, <=, >, or >=; Python raises a TypeError exception if you do.

■ **NEW** Python 2.1 introduced complex number comparisons.

■ **LANG** Perl and C use the same operators for comparing numbers.

Using Mathematical Functions

Python includes functions that perform mathematical calculations. **Table 3.7** lists the popular ones; others are described in Section 2.3, "Built-in Functions," of the *Python Library Reference*. **Figure 3.10** shows some examples.

To get the absolute value of a number:

◆ Type abs(*x*)

   x is a numeric expression.

To get the sign of the difference of two numbers:

◆ Type cmp(*x*, *y*)

   x and *y* are numeric expressions.

To find the largest or smallest of several numbers:

◆ Type max(*x1*, *x2*, . . .) to find the largest number.

   or

   Type min(*x1*, *x2*, . . .) to find the smallest number.

   x1, x2,... are one or more comma-separated numeric expressions. These functions also work with sequences (strings, lists, and tuples).

To round a number:

◆ Type round(*x*) or round(*x*,0) to round *x* to the nearest integer.

   or

   Type round(*x*, *n*) to round *x* to *n* digits to the right of the decimal point.

   or

   Type round(*x*, -*n*) to round *x* to closest multiple of 10**n. (This expression rounds to the left of the decimal point.)

   x and *n* are numeric expressions. If *n* is not an integer, its fractional part is truncated.

Table 3.7

Mathematical Functions	
FUNCTION	**RETURNS**
abs(*x*)	The absolute value of *x*: the (positive) distance between *x* and zero.
cmp(*x*, *y*)	-1 if *x* < *y*, 0 if *x* == *y*, or 1 if *x* > *y*
max(*x₁*, *x₂*,...)	The largest of its arguments: the value closest to positive infinity
min(*x₁*, *x₂*,...)	The smallest of its arguments: the value closest to negative infinity
round(*x* [,*n*])	*x* rounded to *n* digits from the decimal point. Python rounds away from zero as a tie-breaker: round(0.5) is 1.0 and round(-0.5) is -1.0.

```
>>> abs(-4), abs(0.0), abs(99L)
(4, 0.0, 99L)
>>> cmp(-4, -5), cmp(0, 0.0), cmp(5*2, 5/0.1)
(1, 0, -1)
>>> max(-4, -5, 0)
0
>>> min(-4, -5, 0)
-5
>>> lst1 = [1, 2, 3]
>>> lst2 = [4, 5, 6]
>>> max(lst1), max(lst2), max(lst1, lst2)
(3, 6, [4, 5, 6])
>>> min(lst1), min(lst2), min(lst1, lst2)
(1, 4, [1, 2, 3])
>>> str1 = "abcABC"
>>> str2 = "xyzXYZ"
>>> max(str1), max(str2), max(str1, str2)
('c', 'z', 'xyzXYZ')
>>> min(str1), min(str2), min(str1, str2)
('A', 'X', 'abcABC')
>>> x = 123456.567
>>> round(x), round(x, 2), round(x, -3)
(123457.0, 123456.57000000001, 123000.0)
>>> x = -123456.456
>>> round(x), round(x, 2), round(x, -3)
(-123456.0, -123456.46000000001, -123000.0)
```

Figure 3.10 Mathematical functions.

Using Advanced Mathematical Functions

Advanced perhaps is too strong a word; these functions are just mathematical functions that Python's designers decided to place in the math module rather than build in. **Table 3.8** lists some commonly used math module functions; others are described in Section 5.3, "math—Mathematical functions," of the *Python Library Reference*. All functions take float and integer arguments and return float values.

To call a `math` module function:

1. Type `import math` to load the math module. You need to do this only once before the first function call.

2. Type `math.`*function*`()` to call the function. *function()* is any math function, including arguments (**Figure 3.11**).

Table 3.8

`math` Module Functions	
FUNCTION	**RETURNS**
ceil(x)	The ceiling of x: the smallest integer not less than x
exp(x)	The exponential of x: e^x
floor(x)	The floor of x: the largest integer not greater than x
log(x)	The natural logarithm of x, for $x > 0$
modf(x)	The fractional and integer parts of x in a two-item tuple. Both parts have the same sign as x. The integer part is returned as a float.
sqrt(x)	The square root of x, for $x \geq 0$

```
>>> import math
>>> math.ceil(-5.5), math.ceil(1.99)
(-5.0, 2.0)
>>> math.floor(-5.5), math.floor(1.99)
(-6.0, 1.0)
>>> x = 1
>>> math.exp(x), math.log(x)
(2.7182818284590451, 0.0)
>>> math.exp(1) == math.e
1
>>> x = 12.34
>>> math.log(math.exp(x))
12.34
>>> math.cos(math.pi)
-1.0
>>> math.modf(4.5)
(0.5, 4.0)
>>> math.sqrt(1), math.sqrt(2)
(1.0, 1.4142135623730951)
>>> math.sqrt(-1)
Traceback (most recent call last):
  File "<stdin>", line 1, in ?
ValueError: math domain error
>>> import cmath
>>> cmath.sqrt(-1)
1j
```

Figure 3.11 math module functions.

✔ Tips

- Python raises a ValueError exception if an argument is outside the function's domain, as in math.sqrt(-1). A OverflowError exception occurs if the result is too large to store in a plain integer or float, as in math.exp(1000).

- The math module defines useful float values: math.pi is the value pi = 3.14159..., and math.e is the value e = 2.71828....

- The math module also defines the usual trigonometric functions: acos(x), asin(x), atan(x), atan2(y, x), cos(x), cosh(x), sin(x), sinh(x), tan(x), and tanh(x). x and y are angles expressed in radians. To convert degrees to radians, multiply degrees by math.pi/180.

- You can't use math module functions with complex numbers. Instead, use the cmath module functions described in Section 5.4, "cmath Mathematical functions for complex numbers," of the *Python Library Reference*. cmath.sqrt(-1), for example, is 1J.

- For advanced numerical methods, array operations, and scientific computing, use Numeric Python, or NumPy; see the Appendix.

- **LANG** Most math module functions have counterparts in the math.h C standard library.

USING ADVANCED MATHEMATICAL FUNCTIONS

Generating Random Numbers

Random numbers are used for games, simulations, testing, security, and privacy applications. **Table 3.9** shows some commonly used functions in the random module.

To call a random module function:

1. Type import random to load the random module.

   You need to do this only once before the first function call.

2. Type random.*function*() to call the function.

   function() is any random function, including arguments (**Figure 3.12**).

Table 3.9

random Module Functions	
FUNCTION	RETURNS
seed([*x*])	Sets the integer starting value used in generating random numbers. Call this function before calling any other random module function. Returns None.
randrange ([*start*,] *stop* [,*step*])	A randomly selected element from range(start, stop, step), see "Looping over a Range of Integers" in Chapter 7.
choice(*seq*)	A random item from a list, tuple, or string.
shuffle(*lst*)	Randomizes the items of a list in place. Returns None.
random( )	A random float r, such that $0 \leq r < 1$.
uniform(*x, y*)	A random float r, such that $x \leq r < y$.

```
>>> import random
>>> random.seed()
>>> random.random()
0.34745484082159694
>>> random.random()
0.7074581488922288
>>> lst = range(5)
>>> lst
[0, 1, 2, 3, 4]
>>> random.shuffle(lst)
>>> lst
[4, 3, 0, 2, 1]
>>> random.choice(lst)
3
>>> random.choice("AbCdE\n")
'd'
>>> random.choice("AbCdE\n")
'\n'
>>> random.randrange(6,10)
9
>>> random.randrange(-10,-6)
-10
>>> random.uniform(0,1)
0.86333698132139158
>>> random.uniform(-5,-4)
-4.7267319892312729
```

Figure 3.12 *random* module functions.

✔ Tips

■ Identical seeds yield identical sequences of random numbers (handy for testing). If you don't call seed(), Python sets the seed based on the system time and generates different sequences every time.

■ Computer-generated random numbers aren't truly random; they're *pseudorandom.* Pseudorandom numbers are knowable because they come from a mathematical function, but they have many of the properties of truly random numbers, which usually are generated by observing natural phenomena (such as cosmic rays).

■ The theoretical properties of Python's pseudorandom numbers make them unsuitable for cryptography; see Chapter 15, "Cryptographic Services," of the *Python Library Reference.*

WORKING WITH STRINGS

Here's a string: `'mimetic polyalloy'`. Here's another: `""`. A *string* is a sequence of zero or more characters surrounded by quotes. The quotes tell Python to treat the characters as a single item, so you can't embed comments, extra white space, or anything else that you don't want to be part of the string.

You've seen strings in many examples. Anything a Python program prints is a string representation of an object. These statements assign `s` a string object reference and print the value of `s`:

```
s = "valorize"
```

```
print s
```

Printing a string representation of a string object is not always straightforward. There are escape sequences, Unicode strings, and triple-quoted strings—all covered in this chapter, along with string-related methods, functions, and operators.

Creating a String

First, a little terminology: I use *string* to refer to both string objects and string literals, unless the distinction is important. A *string object*, like any Python object, has a value, identity, and type. A string object's value is a *string literal*, which is zero or more characters enclosed by single quotes ('), double quotes ("), or three single or double quotes (''' or """), called a *triple-quoted string*.

To create a string:

♦ Type '*chars*'.

Or type "*chars*".

Or type '''*chars*'''.

Or type """*chars*""".

chars is zero or more characters (**Figure 4.1**).

The same type of quote that starts a string literal must end it. Some string differences depend on the quoting style:

♦ You can embed double quotes in a single-quoted string, and vice versa. You can embed both single and double quotes in a triple-quoted string (**Figure 4.2**). Alternatively, you can use escape sequences to insert quote characters and other characters with special meaning; see "Inserting Special Characters in a String" later in this chapter.

♦ Single- and double-quoted strings must be specified on one line. Triple-quoted strings may span multiple lines.

♦ Triple-quoted strings that span multiple lines retain their formatting. Python concatenates the lines to a single string with a newline (\n) character terminating each line (**Figure 4.3**).

```
>>> "covey"
'covey'
>>> str1 = 'A'
>>> str2 = "covey"
>>> str3 = '''of'''
>>> str4 = """strings"""
>>> str2
'covey'
>>> str1,str2,str3,str4
('A', 'covey', 'of', 'strings')
>>> print str1, str2, str3, str4
A covey of strings
```

Figure 4.1 Quotes define a string but are not part of it.

```
>>> s1 = "It's too much."
>>> s2 = '"Quite old," he said.'
>>> s3 = '''Oh, it's an "antique".'''
>>> print s1, "\n", s2, "\n", s3
It's too much.
"Quite old," he said.
Oh, it's an "antique".
>>> s1
"It's too much."
>>> s2
'"Quite old," he said.'
>>> s3
'Oh, it\'s an "antique".'
```

Figure 4.2 Python's different quoting mechanisms provide an easy way to define strings containing quote characters themselves.

```
>>> s = """  So she prodded
...     and I replied
... at once"""
>>> print s
  So she prodded
    and I replied
at once
>>> s
'  So she prodded\n    and I replied\nat once'
```

Figure 4.3 Python retains line breaks in triple-quoted strings.

✔ Tips

- You also can create strings by using string attributes (`string.letters`) or by calling a function or method that returns a string (`chr(x)` or `str(a)`).

- A string with no characters (`""`) is called an *empty string* or *null string*.

- **LANG** Unlike C, Python has no separate character type. (A string with one item represents a character.) Python tracks string length internally, so you don't need to terminate a string with a null character (`\0`). In fact, a null *won't* terminate a Python string. Perl and C strings are mutable; Python's are not. In both Perl and Python, strings can be single- or double-quoted. There's no difference between the two in Python, but in Perl, double-quoted strings are interpolated and single-quoted strings are not. Perl's q and qq functions, like triple-quoted strings, permit strings with embedded quotes.

Inserting Special Characters into a String

Within a string literal, you can include *escape sequences* for characters that either don't appear on the keyboard or would cause Python to misinterpret the string literal.

An escape sequence begins with a backslash (\), meaning that you must use an escape sequence to insert the backslash character itself. You've already seen the newline (or *linefeed*) escape sequence (\n). which inserts a line break into a string. **Table 4.1** lists the complete set of escape sequences. **Figure 4.4** shows some examples.

Table 4.1

Escape Sequences	
CHARACTER	DESCRIPTION
\	Statement continues on next line (ignored)
\\	Backslash (one \)
\'	Single quote (one ')
\"	Double quote (one ")
\a	Bell (beep!)
\b	Backspace
\f	Formfeed
\n	Newline (or linefeed)
\r	Carriage return (different from \n)
\t	Horizontal tab
\v	Vertical tab
\0 *or* \000	Null value
\ooo	Octal value, where *ooo* is one to three octal digits (0...7)
\xhh	Hexadecimal value, where *hh* is one or two hex digits (0...9, a...f, A...F)
\uxxxx	Unicode character value, recognized only in Unicode strings; see "Creating a Unicode String" later in this chapter

```
>>> a = "A\n\tB"
>>> a
'A\n\tB'
>>> print a
A
        B
>>> print "\"antique\""
"antique"
>>> print "\\A\\B\\"
\A\B\
>>> s = "Oh, it's an \"antique\"."
>>> print s
Oh, it's an "antique".
>>> s
'Oh, it\'s an "antique".'
```

Figure 4.4 Escape sequences represent hard-to-type or invisible characters. Note that in the last example, Python uses an escape sequence to display a single quote within a single-quoted string.

✔ Tips

- If Python doesn't recognize an escape sequence, it leaves the string unchanged. `print "\w"`, for example, prints "\w" (without the quotes).

- \e is recognized as the escape character on some platforms.

- `print "\a"` makes the terminal beep.

- An escape sequence looks like more than one character but represents only one. `len("\n")`, for example, is 1; see "Finding the Length of a String" later in this chapter.

- \u*xxxx* can be used in Unicode strings only; see "Creating a Unicode String" later in this chapter.

- Python also supports *raw strings,* which turns off processing of escape sequences. Raw strings have an r or R immediately before the first quote. The raw string `r"A\nB"` has four characters (not three) because the \n is interpreted as a backslash and the letter *n* (not the newline escape sequence). Raw strings often are used for writing regular expressions, which contain lots of backslashes.

- **LANG** As in C, \ooo permits only three octal digits in Python, and \x*hh* permits only two hex digits. Unlike C, Python doesn't allow the null character (\0) to terminate a string.

INSERTING SPECIAL CHARACTERS INTO A STRING

Creating a Unicode String

Unicode strings hold Unicode characters (see the sidebar in this section), which are used in software internationalization (that is, making software portable to other locales). Unicode strings integrate well with standard strings and can be used in the same operations: indexing, slicing, concatenation, comparison, conversion, search-and-replace, built-in function arguments, dictionary-key lookup, and so on.

Learning Unicode requires a substantial effort. A complete treatment of Python's Unicode capabilities involves a discussion of notation, hexadecimal values, codecs (for *coder/decoders*), input-output operations, error handling, comparisons, and so on. These topics are beyond the scope of this book, so this section is meant to be used as a reference. You can find broader Unicode discussions in the Python documentation and on the Python Web site. You may skip this section safely if you're not interested in Unicode.

Unicode

Computers store characters (letters, digits, punctuation, control characters, and other symbols) internally by assigning them numeric values. The mapping of characters to numeric values is determined by an *encoding*. Many different native encodings are used for different languages and operating systems. Standard Python strings use *ASCII* encoding, which assigns values to as many as 256 (2^8) different characters—not much, and not even enough to hold all the Latin characters used in modern European languages, much less all the Chinese ideographs.

Unicode is a single character set developed to represent the characters of almost all the world's written languages. Unicode can encode 65,536 (2^{16}) characters. The Unicode Standard is developed and maintained by the Unicode Consortium (www.unicode.org). The actual Unicode mappings are available in the latest online or printed edition of *The Unicode Standard*, available at the Unicode Web site.

```
>>> u""
u''
>>> u1 = u"mimetic polyalloy"
>>> u1
u'mimetic polyalloy'
>>> u2 = u"mimetic\u0020polyalloy"
>>> u2
u'mimetic polyalloy'
>>> print u"\u0041\u0020\u0042"
A B
>>> print u"\u41"
UnicodeError: Unicode-Escape decoding
→ error: truncated \uXXXX escape
>>> print u"\u0041"
A
```

Figure 4.5 Unicode literals convert ASCII strings to Unicode strings. The escape sequence \u0020 represents the ordinal hexadecimal value 0x0020 (decimal 32), which is the Unicode space character. (\u0041 is *A*, and \u0042 is *B*.)

Creating Unicode strings is similar to creating standard strings, except that Unicode strings are preceded by u or U.

To create a Unicode string:

◆ Type u'*chars*'.

Or type u"*chars*".

Or type u'''*chars*'''.

Or type u"""*chars*""".

chars is zero or more characters. *chars* may include \u*xxxx* escape sequences, called *Unicode-Escape* encoding, where *xxxx* specifies a (16-bit) Unicode character value as a four-digit hexadecimal number (**Figure 4.5**).

The unicode() function is a more flexible way of creating a Unicode string. It converts a standard string to a Unicode string by using a specified encoding.

To convert a standard string to a Unicode string:

◆ Type unicode(*string* [,*encoding* [,*errors*]])

    string is the standard string to convert, *encoding* is the codec for encoding, and *errors* specifies how encoding errors are handled. The codec specifies how (8-bit) standard string characters are mapped to (16-bit) Unicode values, and vice versa. *encoding* takes one of the values listed in **Table 4.2.** If this argument is omitted, the default encoding for your system is used; see "To get the default encoding for your system" later in this section. *errors* takes one of the values listed in **Table 4.3.** If this argument is omitted, 'strict' is used (**Figure 4.6**).

```
>>> unicode("mimetic", "ascii")
u'mimetic'
>>> unicode("mimetic", "latin-1")
u'mimetic'
>>> unicode("groß", "ascii")
Traceback (most recent call last):
  File "<stdin>", line 1, in ?
UnicodeError: ASCII decoding error:
→ ordinal not in range(128)
>>> unicode("groß", "latin-1")
u'gro\xe1'
>>> unicode("groß", "ascii", "ignore")
u'gro'
>>> unicode("groß", "ascii", "replace")
u'gro\ufffd'
>>> str(u"mimetic")
'mimetic'
>>> str(u"groß")
Traceback (most recent call last):
  File "<stdin>", line 1, in ?
UnicodeError: ASCII encoding error:
→ ordinal not in range(128)
```

Figure 4.6 The characters of "mimetic" are common to ASCII and Latin-1 encodings, but the character ß (0xe1 or decimal 225) is outside ASCII. The str() function (see "Converting a String" later in this chapter) uses the default (usually, ASCII) encoding to convert Unicode to standard strings.

Table 4.2

Supported Encodings	
VALUE	**DESCRIPTION**
'ascii'	ASCII
'iso-8859-1'	ISO 8859-1 Latin-1 (used in many Western countries, same as the lower 256 Unicode characters)
'latin-1'	Same as 'iso-8859-1'
'utf-8'	8-bit variable-length encoding
'utf-16'	16-bit variable-length encoding (big- or little-endian)
'utf-16-be'	UTF-16 with big-endian encoding
'utf-16-le'	UTF-16 with little-endian encoding
'unicode-escape'	Same as Unicode literal u"chars"
'raw-unicode-escape'	Same as raw Unicode literal ur"chars"

Table 4.3

Unicode Error Handling	
VALUE	**DESCRIPTION**
'strict'	Raises a UnicodeError exception if Python encounters a character it can't convert (the default)
'ignore'	Ignores an invalid character and continues to the next
'replace'	Replaces an invalid character with a replacement character: ? in standard strings or 0xfffd in Unicode.

```
>>> s = "gro\341"
>>> s
'gro\xe1'
>>> print s
groß
>>> u = unicode(s, "latin-1")
>>> u
u'gro\xe1'
>>> u.encode("latin-1")
'gro\xe1'
>>> print u.encode("latin-1")
groß
>>> u.encode("utf-8")
'gro\xc3\xa1'
>>> u.encode("ascii")
Traceback (most recent call last):
  File "<stdin>", line 1, in ?
UnicodeError: ASCII encoding error:
→ ordinal not in range(128)
```

Figure 4.7 The character ß is hexadecimal e1 (\xe1) or octal 341 (\341); you can use either escape sequence to specify characters you can't type on your keyboard. The 1-byte Latin-1 encoding of ß ends up as a 2-byte UTF-8 encoding.

The encode() method converts a standard string to a Unicode string by using a specified encoding.

To convert a Unicode or standard string by using a specified encoding:

◆ Type *s*.encode(*encoding* [,*errors*])

s is the Unicode or standard string to convert, *encoding* is the codec for encoding, and *errors* specifies how encoding errors are handled. *encoding* takes one of the values listed in Table 4.2 earlier in this section. If this argument is omitted, the default encoding for your system is used; see "To get the default encoding for your system" later in this section. *errors* takes one of the values listed in Table 4.3 earlier in this section. If this argument is omitted, 'strict' is used (**Figure 4.7**).

CREATING A UNICODE STRING

The sys module contains a method to retrieve the default encoding for your system.

To get the default encoding for your system:

◆ Type:

```
import sys
print sys.getdefaultencoding()
```

The method returns the name of the default encoding as a string (**Figure 4.8**).

The unichr() function converts a Unicode code to a Unicode character.

To convert a Unicode code to a Unicode character:

◆ Type unichr(*i*)

i is an integer or long integer between 0 and 65535 (inclusive) that represents the code of a Unicode character (**Figure 4.9**).

```
>>> import sys
>>> sys.getdefaultencoding()
'ascii'
```

Figure 4.8 This system uses ASCII as the default encoding for conversions.

```
>>> print unichr(65), unichr(66),
→ unichr(67)
A B C
>>> unichr(10)
u'\n'
>>> print unichr(65), unichr(10),
→ unichr(67)
A

 C
>>> unichr(120), unichr(121),
→ unichr(122)
(u'x', u'y', u'z')
>>> unichr(0)
u'\x00'
>>> unichr(622)
u'\u026e'
>>> print unichr(622)
Traceback (most recent call last):
  File "<stdin>", line 1, in ?
UnicodeError: ASCII encoding error:
→ ordinal not in range(128)
>>> unichr(65535)
u'\uffff'
>>> unichr(65536)
Traceback (most recent call last):
  File "<stdin>", line 1, in ?
ValueError: unichr() arg not in range(65536)
```

Figure 4.9 The unichr() function returns the Unicode character that maps to the numeric (integer) value defined by the Unicode Standard.

```
>>> ord(u'A'),ord(u'Z'),ord(u'a'),
↪ ord(u'z')

(65, 90, 97, 122)

>>> print ord(u' '), ord(u'\n'),
↪ ord(u'\t')

32 10 9

>>> print ord(u'0'), ord(u'1'),
↪ ord(u'9')

48 49 57

>>> u = unichr(92)

>>> u

u'\\'

>>> print u

\

>>> ord(unichr(65))

65
```

Figure 4.10 ord() is unichr()'s inverse: ord(unichr(*i*))
is *i*.

The ord() (for *ord*inal) function does the
opposite of unichr(): it converts a Unicode
character to a Unicode code.

To convert a Unicode character to a Unicode code:

◆ Type ord(*c*)

 c is a Unicode character (**Figure 4.10**).

✔ Tips

■ The chr() function is the analogue of
 unichr() for standard strings. ord()
 works for both types of strings; see
 "Comparing Strings" later in this chapter.

■ When you mix Unicode and standard strings
 in operations, Python promotes standard
 strings to Unicode (using unicode())
 before carrying out the operation. In this
 example:

 a = "mimetic"

 b = u"polyalloy"

 c = a + b

 the last statement is equivalent to:

 c = unicode(a) + b

■ The codecs module provides access to the
 standard Python encoders and decoders
 that manage the lookup process; it also
 contains base classes that let you write
 your own codecs. The unicodedata module provides access to the Unicode character database, which contains Unicode
 character properties. See Chapter 4,
 "String Services," of the *Python Library
 Reference*.

■ **NEW** Python 2.0 introduced Unicode
 support, unichr(), and unicode().

Finding the Length of a String

The len() function counts the number of characters in a string. len() counts everything in the string: letters, digits, punctuation, white space, symbols, escape sequences, and so on.

To find the length of a string:

◆ Type len(*s*)

s is a string expression (**Figure 4.11**).

✔ Tips

■ An escape sequence represents one character. len("\n"), for example, is 1.

■ len() also counts items in lists, tuples, and dictionaries.

■ **LANG** Perl's length function returns string length.

```
>>> len("")
0
>>> print len(" ")
1
>>> len("\n")
1
>>> len("\"antique\"")
9
>>> s1 = "A\n\tB"
>>> len(s1)
4
>>> s2 = "mimetic polyalloy"
>>> len(s2)
17
>>> len(s2) + len(s1)
21
>>> len(s1 + s2)  # Concatenate strings
21
>>> len("012345")
6
>>> len(123)
Traceback (most recent call last):
  File "<stdin>", line 1, in ?
TypeError: len() of unsized object
```

Figure 4.11 An escape sequence is considered to be a single character.

```
>>> "sequoia"[0]
's'
>>> 'one\ntwo'[3]
'\n'
>>> s = 'sequoia'
>>> print s[0], s[7/3], s[-3], s[-1]
s q o a
>>> s[len(s)]
Traceback (most recent call last):
  File "<stdin>", line 1, in ?
IndexError: string index out of range
>>> s[len(s) - 1]
'a'
>>> s[-len(s)]
's'
>>> s[-len(s) + 1]
'e'
>>> n = -3
>>> s[n] == s[len(s) + n]
1
>>> s[1.5]
Traceback (most recent call last):
  File "<stdin>", line 1, in ?
TypeError: sequence index must be integer
```

Figure 4.12 Python uses zero-based integer indexes.

Indexing a String (Extracting a Character)

Strings are ordered sequences of characters. An individual character is identified by its position, or *index*, in a string. Python uses zero-based indexes: The first character is at index 0, the second is at index 1, and so on. The index of the last character is the length of the string minus 1—that is, len(s) - 1.

You also can use a *negative index* to retrieve characters from the end of a string. The index of the last character is –1, the next-to-last is at index –2, and on down to -len(s).

To index a string:

◆ Type *s*[*i*]

   s is a string expression, and *i* is an integer expression representing the index (**Figure 4.12**).

✔ Tips

■ If the index is out of range, Python raises an IndexError exception. If the index is not an integer (or long integer), Python raises a TypeError exception.

■ Python adds a negative index to the length of the string. If *n* is negative, s[*n*] is equivalent to s[len(s) + *n*].

■ Python has no "negative zero" index: s[-0] is equivalent to s[0].

■ Indexing also works with lists and tuples; see "Indexing a List or Tuple (Extracting an Item)" in Chapter 5.

Slicing a String (Extracting a Substring)

A *slice* is a substring of a string specified by two indexes that demarcate a sequence of contiguous characters. In the preceding section, you saw that indexing involves a single index that points *at* a character. In slicing, the indexes point *between* characters (**Figure 4.13**).

If both indexes are positive, slicing returns the substring starting with the first index and up but not including the second index. A negative index starts counting from the end of the string.

Slicing and indexing take practice, but they're fundamental, frequently used Python techniques.

To slice a string:

◆ Type *s*[*i*:*j*]

s is a string expression, and *i* and *j* are integer expressions representing the indexes. If *i* is omitted, it defaults to 0; if *j* is omitted, it defaults to the length of *s* (**Figure 4.14**).

Strings are immutable, so you can use simple assignment to make a copy; see "Creating References to the Same Object" in Chapter 2.

To copy a string:

◆ Type *t* = *s*

s is the string you want to copy, and *t* is the variable assigned the copy.

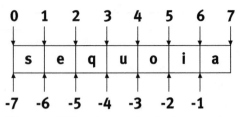

Figure 4.13 Slicing returns a substring that comprises the characters between two indexes.

```
>>> s = 'sequoia'
>>> s[0:2]
'se'
>>> s[1:3]
'eq'
>>> s[-3:-1]
'oi'
>>> s[1:-1]
'equoi'
>>> s[3:-3]
'u'
>>> print s[2:], s[:2], s[-2:], s[:-2]
quoia se ia sequo
>>> s[:]
'sequoia'
>>> s[:2] + s[2:]
'sequoia'
>>> s[:-3] + s[-3:]
'sequoia'
```

Figure 4.14 Slicing strings.

```
>>> s = 'sequoia'
>>> print s[-100:100]
'sequoia'
>>> s[1:100]
'equoia'
>>> s[100:]
''
>>> s[:100]
'sequoia'
>>> s[-100:]
'sequoia'
>>> s[:-100]
''
>>> s[-100:2]
'se'
>>> s[6:2]
''
```

Figure 4.15 Python implicitly constrains indexes that are too small or too large to sensible values. Reversed indexes return empty strings.

```
>>> s = 'sequoia'
>>> id(s)
8127464
>>> s = s[1:-1]
>>> print s
'equoi'
>>> id(s)
8279720
>>> s[2:4] = "XX"   # Oops, strings are
→ immutable
Traceback (most recent call last):
  File "<stdin>", line 1, in ?
TypeError: object doesn't support slice assignment
```

Figure 4.16 Strings can't be changed. The statement s = s[1:-1] doesn't modify the value of s, it instead creates a new string object with a different identity. If you try to change a string in place with a slice assignment, Python raises an exception.

✔ Tips

- An index that is too small is replaced by zero, and one that is too large is replaced by the string length. If the second index indicates a position before the first index, an empty string is returned (**Figure 4.15**).

- Strings are immutable. The following statement doesn't modify the existing string object but creates a new one:

  s = s[i:j]

  You can't modify a string in place with an assignment such as this:

  s[i:j] = "*chars*" # Error

  In this example, *chars* represents replacement characters (**Figure 4.16**).

- For any integer *n*, s equals s[:*n*] + s[*n*:].

- Slicing also works with lists and tuples; see "Slicing a List or Tuple (Extracting a Segment)" in Chapter 5.

- **LANG** Perl's substr function extracts substrings.

Concatenating Strings

Use the + (concatenation) operator to combine, or *concatenate*, strings. Concatenation joins two strings into a single string.

To concatenate strings:

◆ Type *s1 + s2*

s1 and *s2* are string expressions (**Figure 4.17**).

You can concatenate string literals just by placing them next to each other.

To concatenate string literals:

◆ Type *'s1' 's2'*

's1' and *'s2'* are string literals (**Figure 4.18**).

You also can use the += augmented assignment operator to concatenate strings (see "Making Augmented Assignments" in Chapter 3).

```
>>> 'formal' + 'dehyde'
'formaldehyde'
>>> "" + ""
''
>>> r = "A" + "\n" + "\t" + "B"
>>> r
'A\n\tB'
>>> print r
A
        B
>>> s = 'sequoia'
>>> t = s[0:4] + 'el'
>>> print t
'sequel'
>>> a = "He loves her"
>>> b = "obeys"
>>> a[:3] + b + a[3 + len(b):]
'He obeys her'
```

Figure 4.17 Concatenating strings.

```
>>> "a""b"
'ab'
>>> s = 'formal' 'de' 'hyde'
>>> print s
formaldehyde
>>> t = 'Plan ' str(9)
  File "<stdin>", line 1
    t = 'Plan ' str(9)
                   ^
SyntaxError: invalid syntax
```

Figure 4.18 This method works only with string literals, not with string expressions.

```
>>> s = 'formal'
>>> s += 'de'
>>> s += 'hyde'
>>> print s
formaldehyde
```

Figure 4.19 Concatenating strings by using augmented assignment.

To concatenate strings by using augmented assignment:

◆ Type *s1* += *s2*

s1 is a string variable, and *s2* is a string expression (**Figure 4.19**).

✔ Tips

■ Concatenation doesn't add a space between the strings.

■ If you try to concatenate a string and a nonstring a TypeError exception is raised. Before concatenation, use str() to convert the nonstring to a string; see "Converting a String" later in this chapter.

■ Concatenation also works with lists and tuples; see "Concatenating Lists or Tuples" in Chapter 5.

■ **LANG** Perl's dot operator concatenates strings.

Operator Overloading

Recall that the + operator also is used to add two numbers. Using + for both addition and string concatenation is your first example of *operator overloading*, which is the assignment of more than one function to a particular operator. The operation performed depends on the data types of the operands involved. Here, + behaves differently with numbers than it does with strings. Later in this book, you'll see that Python also overloads the *, %, augmented assignment, and other operators. You can even overload operators for user-defined objects; see "Using Special Methods to Overload Standard Behavior" in Chapter 12.

CONCATENATING STRINGS

Repeating a String

Use the * (repetition) operator to repeat a string a given number of times.

To repeat a string:

◆ Type s * n (or n * s)

s is a string expression, and n is the integer number of times to repeat s. An empty string is returned if n is less than or equal to zero (**Figure 4.20**).

```
>>> t = "toyboat "
>>> t * 3
'toyboat toyboat toyboat '
>>> t * 0
''
>>> t * -2
''
>>> t * 3.5
Traceback (most recent call last):
  File "<stdin>", line 1, in ?
TypeError: unsupported operand type(s) for *
>>> '' * 1000
''
>>> s = 'sequoia'
>>> s[0:4] + 'el ' * 3
'sequel el el '
>>> (s[0:4] + 'el ') * 3
'sequel sequel sequel '
>>> print "<" + s * 3 + ">"
<sequoiasequoiasequoia>
```

Figure 4.20 Repeating strings.

```
>>> s1 = '1'
>>> s2 = '22'
>>> s1 *= len(s1)
>>> s2 *= len(s2)
>>> print s1, s2
1 2222
>>> s3 = 'abc '
>>> s3 *= len(s3) + 1
>>> print s3
abc abc abc abc abc
>>> s3 *= 0
>>> s3
''
```

Figure 4.21 Repeating strings by using augmented assignment.

You also can use the *= augmented assignment operator to repeat strings (see "Making Augmented Assignments" in Chapter 3).

To repeat a string by using augmented assignment:

◆ Type *s *= n*

   s is a string variable, and *n* is the integer number of times to repeat *s* (**Figure 4.21**).

✔ Tips

■ Repetition doesn't add a space between the strings.

■ Trying to repeat a string by using a non-integer raises a TypeError exception.

■ Repetition is more efficient than multiple concatenations.

■ Repetition also works with lists and tuples; see "Repeating a List or Tuple" in Chapter 5.

■ **LANG** Perl's x operator repeats strings.

REPEATING A STRING

Using String Methods and Functions

NEW Python 2.0 introduced built-in string methods to replace most of the like-named functions in the standard `string` module. If you're using an earlier version, use the `string` module functions.

You can invoke built-in string methods at will, but to use string functions, you first must import the `string` module. The examples in this book favor built-in methods over the equivalent `string` functions (unless a function has no counterpart method). The syntax of equivalent method and function calls differs. The method call:

```
s.find(sub, start, end)
```

is equivalent to the function call:

```
string.find(s, sub, start, end)
```

String methods are described in this chapter and in Section 2.1, "Built-in Types," of the *Python Library Reference*. `string` module functions are described in Section 4.1, "`string`—Common string operations," of the *Python Library Reference*.

✔ Tips

- When you use `string` module functions, you need to import the module only once before the first function call.

- Most string methods, functions, and operators (including indexing and slicing) also work with Unicode strings; see "Creating a Unicode String" earlier in this chapter. I'll indicate which operations don't support Unicode strings.

- When you import the `string` module, it replaces parts of itself with the redundant parts of the built-in string methods, so you incur no extra cost by using `string`.

```
>>> s = "The Man from UNCLE"
>>> s.upper()
'THE MAN FROM UNCLE'
>>> s.lower()
'the man from uncle'
>>> s.swapcase()
'tHE mAN FROM uncle'
>>> s.capitalize()
'The man from uncle'
>>> s.title()
'The Man From Uncle'
>>> import string
>>> string.capwords(s)
'The Man From Uncle'
>>> t = "   The 5th element:\t boron"
>>> print t
   The 5th element:        boron
>>> print string.capwords(t)
The 5th Element: Boron
>>> r = 'dot.com dot_com dot@com'
>>> r.title()
'Dot.Com Dot_Com Dot@Com'
```

Figure 4.22 Changing the case of strings.

Changing String Case

Python includes several methods that change the case of strings. A *cased* character is a letter, which can be lowercase (*a*) or uppercase (*A*). Case changes affect only letters; digits, punctuation, white space, and escape sequences are left unchanged (except by capwords(), which deletes white space). These methods usually are used to format printed output, although lower() is useful for making case-insensitive comparisons. **Figure 4.22** shows some examples.

To convert a string to uppercase:

◆ Type *s*.upper()
    s is a string expression.

To convert a string to lowercase:

◆ Type *s*.lower()
    s is a string expression.

To invert the case of a string:

◆ Type *s*.swapcase()
    s is a string expression.

To convert a string to sentence case:

◆ Type *s*.capitalize()
    s is a string expression. This method capitalizes the first character of *s* and converts the other letters to lowercase.

To convert a string to title case:

◆ Type *s*.title()
    s is a string expression. This method capitalizes the first character of each word in *s* and converts all the other letters to lowercase.

To convert a string to title case and strip white space:

◆ Type:

```
import string
string.capwords(s)
```

s is a string expression. This capitalizes each word of *s*, converts the other letters to lowercase, trims leading and trailing white space, and replaces runs of white space with a single space. (White space includes spaces, tabs, and newlines.)

✔ Tips

■ Python has no built-in method that is equivalent to capwords().

■ To capitalize the first character of a string, s, without changing the case of any other letters, type s[0].upper() + s[1:].

■ **LANG** Perl's uc, ucfirst, lc, and lcfirst functions change case. C's case functions are in the ctype.h standard library.

```
>>> alpha = "abc"
>>> num = "123"
>>> space = " \n\t"
>>> print alpha.isalpha(),
⤷ num.isdigit()
1 1
>>> (alpha + num).isdigit()
0
>>> (alpha + num).isalnum()
1
>>> (alpha + num + space).isalnum()
0
>>> space.isspace()
1
>>> "".isalpha()
0
```

Figure 4.23 The methods test whether *all* the string's characters (not just any character) match the criteria.

Testing a String

The is methods test whether strings contain certain characters and return 1 (true) or 0 (false). These methods often are used to test the validity of user-entered or database values.

To test for letters, digits, or white space:

◆ Type *s*.isalpha() to test whether all the characters in *s* are letters.

Or type *s*.isdigit() to test whether all the characters in *s* are digits.

Or type *s*.isalnum() to test whether all the characters in *s* are letters or digits (alphanumeric).

Or type *s*.isspace() to test whether all the characters in *s* are white space. White space includes the characters space, tab, newline, carriage return, formfeed, and vertical tab.

s is a string expression (**Figure 4.23**).

To test the case of letters:

◆ Type *s*.isupper() to test whether all the letters in *s* are uppercase (and the string contains at least one letter).

Or type *s*.islower() to test whether all the letters in *s* are lowercase (and the string contains at least one letter).

Or type *s*.istitle() to test whether all the words in *s* are title-cased. In title case, uppercase letters follow nonletters, and lowercase letters follow only letters (of any case).

s is a string expression (**Figure 4.24**).

The string module defines data attributes that are useful for determining how the is methods work. isspace(), for example, determines whether all the characters in a string are contained in string.whitespace.

Some string attributes are combined to form others. letters is lowercase and uppercase combined; and printable is digits, letters, punctuation, and whitespace combined.

You can use these constants to create your own is functions. You could define an ispunc() function that determines whether all the characters in a string are punctuation characters.

To use string-related constants:

◆ Type:

import string

string.*attribute*

attribute is one of the following values: digits, hexdigits, letters, lowercase, octdigits, punctuation, printable, uppercase, or whitespace (**Figure 4.25**).

✔ Tips

■ The is methods return 0 (false) for empty strings.

■ **LANG** Most of these methods have counterparts in the ctype.h C standard library.

```
>>> upper = "ABC"
>>> lower = "xzy"
>>> title = "Title"
>>> num = "123"
>>> print upper.isupper(), lower.islower()
1 1
>>> (upper + num).isupper()
1
>>> title.isupper()
0
>>> title[1:].islower()
1
>>> title.istitle()
1
>>> (title + num).istitle()
1
>>> (num + title).istitle()
1
>>> ("\n" + title).istitle()
1
>>> (num + title).istitle()
1
>>> (upper + title).istitle()
0
```

Figure 4.24 These methods test whether only the string's *letters* match the criteria and ignore nonletters.

■ Don't change the values of the string module attributes, because some methods depend on their definitions. upper() and swapcase() depend on string.lowercase, and strip() and split() depend on string.whitespace.

```
>>> import string
>>> string.digits
'0123456789'
>>> string.hexdigits
'0123456789abcdefABCDEF'
>>> string.letters
'abcdefghijklmnopqrstuvwxyzABCDEFGHIJKLMNOPQRSTUVWXYZ'
>>> string.lowercase
'abcdefghijklmnopqrstuvwxyz'
>>> string.octdigits
'01234567'
>>> string.punctuation
'!"#$%&\'()*+,-./:;<=>?@[\\]^_`{|}~'
>>> string.printable
'0123456789abcdefghijklmnopqrstuvwxyzABCDEFGHIJKLMNOPQRSTUVWXYZ!"#$%&\'()*+,./:;<=>?@[\\]^_`{|}
→ ~ \t\n\r\x0b\x0c'
>>> string.uppercase
'ABCDEFGHIJKLMNOPQRSTUVWXYZ'
>>> string.whitespace
'\t\n\x0b\x0c\r '
>>> "\n" in string.whitespace
1
>>> "\f" in string.whitespace
1
>>> " " in string.printable
1
>>> (string.whitespace).isspace()
1
```

Figure 4.25 Constants defined in the string module.

Trimming and Justifying a String

Trimming strips extraneous white space from the beginning or end of a string. *Justifying* pads a string with extra spaces at the beginning or end. Trimming often is used to clean up user-entered values. Justification adjusts spacing to form tidy columns on a page or to ensure that lines end evenly at a margin.

To trim a string:

◆ Type s.lstrip() to remove leading white space.

Or type s.rstrip() to remove trailing white space.

Or type s.strip() to remove leading and trailing white space.

s is a string expression (**Figure 4.26**).

To justify a string:

◆ Type s.ljust(*width*) to left-justify a string of length *width*.

Or type s.rjust(*width*) to right-justify a string of length *width*.

Or type s.center(*width*) to center a string of length *width*.

s is a string expression, and *width* is an integer expression. If *width* is not an integer, its fractional part is truncated (**Figure 4.27**).

```
>>> s = "   John Q. Public    "
>>> s.lstrip()
'John Q. Public    '
>>> s.rstrip()
'   John Q. Public'
>>> s.strip()
'John Q. Public'
>>> t = "\t \t Middle \n Part \n \n "
>>> t.lstrip()
'Middle \n Part \n \n '
>>> t.rstrip()
'\t \t Middle \n Part'
>>> t.strip()
'Middle \n Part'
```

Figure 4.26 Trimming strips *all* white space, not just spaces.

```
>>> s = "Mimetic Polyalloy"
>>> len(s)
17
>>> s.ljust(20)
'Mimetic Polyalloy   '
>>> s.rjust(20)
'   Mimetic Polyalloy'
>>> s.center(len(s) + 4)
'  Mimetic Polyalloy  '
>>> s.rjust(0)
'Mimetic Polyalloy'
>>> s.ljust(-2)
'Mimetic Polyalloy'
>>> s.center(10)
'Mimetic Polyalloy'
>>> s.rjust(len(s) + 2.99)
'  Mimetic Polyalloy'
```

Figure 4.27 If the justification width is less than the length of the string, the original string is returned.

```
>>> import string
>>> s = "123.45"
>>> len(s)
6
>>> string.zfill(s,8)
'00123.45'
>>> string.zfill(s,4)
'123.45'
>>> string.zfill(-11,5)
'-0011'
>>> string.zfill(0.01,6)
'000.01'
>>> string.zfill('1' * 3, 5)
'00111'
```

Figure 4.28 zfill() works with both numbers and numeric strings, and handles signs correctly.

The string module contains a function that pads a numeric string or number on the left with zeroes. Note that you can't start a decimal (base 10) number with a leading zero; if you do, Python interprets it as an octal (base 8) number; see "Understanding the Types of Numbers" in Chapter 3.

To pad a numeric string with zeroes:

◆ Type:

```
import string
string.zfill(s, width)
```

s is a number or numeric string expression, and *width* is an integer expression. If *width* is not an integer, Python raises a TypeError exception (**Figure 4.28**).

✔ Tips

■ Trimming does not remove white space from *within* a string.

■ White space includes the characters space, tab, newline, carriage return, formfeed, and vertical tab. To determine the white-space characters for your system, see "Testing a String" earlier in this chapter.

■ As an alternative to zfill(), you can use conversion specifiers to pad numbers; see "Printing Formatted Strings" later in this chapter.

■ **LANG** Perl's format function justifies strings. Trimming is done with chomp, chop, or substitution.

Searching for Substrings

The search methods count and find substrings in strings. You can search forward from the start of a string or backward from the end.

These methods take optional *start* and *end* arguments that restrict the search area, which is useful for finding a substring beyond its initial occurrence. Normally, the entire string *s* is searched, but if *start* and *end* are specified, only *s*[*start:end*] is searched. *start* and *end* are interpreted as in slice notation; see "Slicing a String (Extracting a Substring)" earlier in this chapter. If either *start* or *end* is omitted, its default is used: zero for *start* or the length of the string being searched for *end*.

To count substrings:

◆ Type *s*.count(*sub* [,*start* [,*end*]]) to return the number of times the substring *sub* occurs in the string *s*.

  s and *sub* are string expressions. *start* and *end* are integer expressions that restrict the search area to *s*[*start:end*] (**Figure 4.29**).

```
>>> s = "Peter: pepper eater"
>>> len(s)
19
>>> s.count("ter")
2
>>> s.count("er")
3
>>> s.count("er", 7)
2
>>> s.count("er", 7, 13)
1
>>> s.count("pe")
2
>>> s.lower().count("pe")
3
>>> s.count("X")
0
>>> s.count(" ")
2
>>> s.count("")
20
>>> s.count("", 0, 6)
7
```

Figure 4.29 Counting substrings.

```
>>> s = "Peter: pepper eater"
>>> len(s)
19
>>> s.find("er")
3
>>> s.find("er", 7)
11
>>> s.find("er", 13)
17
>>> s.find("pe")
7
>>> s.lower().find("pe")
0
>>> s.find("\n")
-1
>>> s.find("X")
-1
>>> s.index("X")
Traceback (most recent call last):
  File "<stdin>", line 1, in ?
ValueError: substring not found in string.index
>>> s.find(" ")
6
>>> s.find("")
0
>>> s.find("", 7)
7
```

Figure 4.30 Finding the first substring in a string.

To find a substring:

◆ Type s.find(*sub* [, *start* [, *end*]]) to return the lowest index in the string *s* in which the substring *sub* occurs or –1 if *sub* is not found.

or

Type s.index(*sub* [, *start* [, *end*]]), which behaves like find() but raises a ValueError exception if *sub* is not found.

s and *sub* are string expressions. *start* and *end* are integer expressions that restrict the search area to *s*[*start:end*] (**Figure 4.30**).

To find a substring searching from the end of a string:

◆ Type s.rfind(*sub* [,*start* [,*end*]]) to return the highest index in the string *s* in which the substring *sub* occurs or –1 if *sub* is not found.

or

Type s.rindex(*sub* [,*start* [,*end*]]), which behaves like rfind() but raises a ValueError exception if *sub* is not found.

s and *sub* are string expressions. *start* and *end* are integer expressions that restrict the search area to *s*[*start:end*] (**Figure 4.31**).

```
>>> s = "Peter: pepper eater"
>>> len(s)
19
>>> s.rfind("er")
17
>>> s.rfind("er", 7, 13)
11
>>> s.rfind("er", 0, 7)
3
>>> s.rfind("pe")
10
>>> s.rfind("Pe")
0
>>> s.rfind("\n")
-1
>>> s.rfind("X")
-1
>>> s.rindex("X")
Traceback (most recent call last):
  File "<stdin>", line 1, in ?
ValueError: substring not found in string.rindex
>>> s.rfind(" ")
13
>>> s.rfind("")
19
>>> s.rfind("", 0, 7)
7
```

Figure 4.31 Finding the last substring in a string.

```
>>> s = "Peter: pepper eater"
>>> len(s)
19
>>> s.startswith("Pe")
1
>>> s.startswith("Pe", 7)
0
>>> s.startswith("pe", 7)
1
>>> s.endswith("er")
1
>>> s.endswith("er", 0, 13)
1
>>> s.endswith("er", 0, 5)
1
>>> s.startswith("")
1
>>> s.endswith("")
1
>>> t = "\t" + s + "\n"
>>> t.startswith("Pe")
0
>>> t.startswith("\t")
1
>>> t.endswith("er\n")
1
```

Figure 4.32 Testing the starting and ending text.

To find an initial or terminating substring:

◆ Type *s*.startswith(*prefix* [,*start* [,*end*]])
   to return 1 (true) if the string *s* starts with
   prefix or 0 (false) otherwise.

   or

   Type *s*.endswith(*suffix* [,*start* [,*end*]])
   to return 1 (true) if the string *s* ends with
   suffix or 0 (false) otherwise.

   s, prefix, and *suffix* are string expressions.
   start and *end* are integer expressions that
   restrict the search area to *s*[*start:end*]
   (**Figure 4.32**).

✔ Tips

■ Counts and searches are case-sensitive.

■ Counts and searches find nonoverlapping
   substrings. The string "Ba-booom!" contains only one occurrence of oo, not two.

■ You can use the in and not in operators
   to determine whether a single character
   is in a string; see "Using Comparison
   Operators" in Chapter 2.

■ **LANG** Perl's index and rindex functions
   find substrings.

Replacing Substrings

The replace methods replace one set of characters with another in a string.

To replace substrings:

- Type *s*.replace(*old, new* [,*maxreplace*]) to return a copy of the string *s* with occurrences of the substring *old* replaced by the string *new*. The first *maxreplace* occurrences are replaced. If *maxreplace* is omitted, all occurrences are replaced.

   s, old, and *new* are string expressions; *maxreplace* is an integer expression (**Figure 4.33**).

```
>>> s = "Peter: pepper eater"
>>> s.replace("eat", "purg")
'Peter: pepper purger'
>>> s.replace("Pe", "Dei")
'Deiter: pepper eater'
>>> print s.replace(" ", "\n")
Peter:
pepper
eater
>>> t = "pepper"
>>> s[s.find(t):].replace(t, "lotus")
'lotus eater'
>>> s.replace("X", "Y")
'Peter: pepper eater'
>>> s.replace("er", "")
'Pet: pepp eat'
>>> s.replace("er", "", 1)
'Pet: pepper eater'
>>> s.replace("", "X")
Traceback (most recent call last):
  File "<stdin>", line 1, in ?
ValueError: empty pattern string
>>> s.replace("e", "E").replace("p", "P")
'PEtEr: PEPPEr EatEr'
```

Figure 4.33 Changing matching substrings.

```
>>> s = "A\tB\tC"
>>> t = s.expandtabs()
>>> s,t
('A\tB\tC', 'A       B       C')
>>> print s
A       B       C
>>> print t
A       B       C
>>> print s.expandtabs(0)
ABC
>>> print s.expandtabs(-1)
ABC
>>> print s.expandtabs(1)
A B C
>>> print s.expandtabs(2)
A B C
>>> print s.expandtabs(2.5)
A B C
>>> print s.expandtabs(4)
A   B   C
>>> print s.expandtabs(12)
A           B           C
```

Figure 4.34 Changing tabs to spaces.

To replace tabs with spaces:

◆ Type *s*.expandtabs([*tabsize*]) to return a copy of the string *s* with all tab (\t) characters replaced by *tabsize* spaces. If *tabsize* is omitted, it defaults to 8.

s is a string expression, and *tabsize* is an integer expression. If *tabsize* is not an integer, its fractional part is truncated (**Figure 4.34**).

✔ Tips

■ Replacements are case-sensitive.

■ Nonoverlapping substrings are replaced. Replacing oo in the string "Ba-booom!" replaces only the first and second o, and leaves the third o unchanged.

■ **LANG** Perl's tr function replaces substrings.

Translating a String

If you're making several single-character replacements, it's more efficient to use the translate() method than to invoke replace() multiple times. translate() requires a 256-character string, called a *translation table,* to make replacements. You can build a translation table manually, but it's easier to create one with the string.maketrans() function.

To translate characters in a string:

1. Type import string to load the string module.

2. Type *table* = string.maketrans(*from, to*) to create a translation *table* suitable for translate().

   from and *to* are string expressions containing the same number of characters. During translation, each character in *from* is converted to the character at the same position in *to*. Other characters are not translated.

3. Type *s*.translate(*table* [,*deletechars*]) to return a string that is the translation of the string expression *s* using the translation *table* that you created in step 2.

   If specified, all characters in the string expression *deletechars* are removed in the returned string. Deletion occurs before translation (**Figure 4.35**).

✔ Tips

■ Translations are case-sensitive.

■ You can't translate Unicode strings.

```
>>> s = "sequoia"
>>> import string
>>> table = string.maketrans("aeiou",
→ "AEIOU")
>>> s.translate(table)
'sEqUOIA'
>>> t = "Peter: pepper eater"
>>> t.translate(table, "pt")
'PEEr: EEr EAEr'
>>> t.translate(table, "e")
'Ptr: pppr Atr'
```

Figure 4.35 This translation converts vowels to uppercase.

```
>>> s = "I replied at once."
>>> lst = s.split()
>>> lst
['I', 'replied', 'at', 'once.']
>>> " ".join(lst)
'I replied at once.'
>>> "".join(lst)
'Irepliedatonce.'
>>> print "\n".join(lst)
I
replied
at
once.
>>> print ". ".join(lst).title()
I. Replied. At. Once.
>>> t = "543235,3800 Waldo
→ Ave,Bronx,NY,10463"
>>> t.split(",")
['543235', '3800 Waldo Ave', 'Bronx', 'NY',
→ '10463']
>>> t.split(",", 1)
['543235', '3800 Waldo Ave,Bronx,NY,10463']
>>> t.split(",", 2)
['543235', '3800 Waldo Ave', 'Bronx,NY,10463']
>>> r = "Peter: pepper eater"
>>> r.split("er")
['Pet', ': pepp', ' eat', '']
>>> r.lower().split("pe")
['', 'ter: ', 'p', 'r eater']
>>> "I    replied  \n at \t
→ once.\n".split()
['I', 'replied', 'at', 'once.']
```

Figure 4.36 Splitting strings into substrings, and joining substrings into strings.

Splitting and Joining Strings

Splitting a string divides it into pieces and puts those pieces into a list. *Joining*, the inverse of splitting, joins all the items of a list (or tuple) into a single string. (For information about lists and tuples, see Chapter 5.) One or more *delimiter* characters separate individual items during split and join operations. The fields of a database record could be delimited by commas, for example. Splitting and joining often are used for parsing or preparing data for databases and log files. **Figure 4.36** shows some examples.

To split a string:

◆ Type s.split([*delim* [,*maxsplit*]]) to return a list containing the words in the string *s*, using *delim* as a delimiter.

Delimiter characters are stripped from the returned list. If *delim* is omitted, the default delimiter is white space (spaces, tabs, newlines, and so on). Consecutive white-space characters count as a single delimiter. The string is split *maxsplit* times. If *maxsplit* is omitted, all splits are made.

s and *delim* are string expressions, and *maxsplit* is an integer expression.

To join strings:

◆ Type *delim*.join(*sequence*) to return a string containing the items in the sequence *sequence*, separated by *delim*.

s is a string expression, and *sequence* is a list or tuple containing only string items.

The splitlines() method breaks strings into lines.

To split a string into lines:

◆ Type s.splitlines([*keepends*]) to return a list containing the lines of the string *s*. If *keepends* is true, the line breaks are included in the list. If *keepends* is false or omitted, line breaks are not retained.

 s is a string expression, and *keepends* is a Boolean expression (**Figure 4.37**).

✔ Tips

■ For join(), all the list or tuple items must be string expressions; otherwise, Python raises a TypeError exception.

■ When you are concatenating many strings, it's more efficient to use join() with an empty delimiter ("") than it is to use the + operator, because join() creates fewer temporary string objects.

■ It's common to want to separate the first part of a string (up to the first delimiter) from the rest. If the first field of a database record contains an identifier that isn't useful for your analysis, set *maxsplit* equal to 1 in split() and discard the first item in the returned list. The second item contains the database record without the identifier.

■ Although the join() *sequence* argument usually is a list or tuple, it also can be a string (a sequence of characters). This example:

```
print "\n".join("321")
```

prints this:

3
2
1

■ ![LANG] Perl's split and join functions split and join strings.

```
>>> s = "Line 1\nLine 2\nLine 3"
>>> print s
Line 1
Line 2
Line 3
>>> s.split("\n")
['Line 1', 'Line 2', 'Line 3']
>>> s.splitlines()
['Line 1', 'Line 2', 'Line 3']
>>> s.splitlines(1)
['Line 1\n', 'Line 2\n', 'Line 3']
>>> t = "Line 1\n\nLine 3"
>>> print t
Line 1

Line 3
>>> t.splitlines()
['Line 1', '', 'Line 3']
>>> t.splitlines(1)
['Line 1\n', '\n', 'Line 3']
```

Figure 4.37 splitlines() is like split("\n"), except that you have the option to retain the line breaks.

```
>>> s = "polyalloy"
>>> s = list(s)
>>> print s
['p', 'o', 'l', 'y', 'a', 'l', 'l', 'o', 'y']
>>> s[4:] = []
>>> s.sort()
>>> s.reverse()
>>> s = "".join(s)
>>> s
'ypol'
```

Figure 4.38 Here, you use list operations to truncate and reverse-sort a string.

Performing List Operations on a String

Recall that strings are immutable and can't be changed in place the way that lists can (see "Creating References to the Same Object" in Chapter 2). Sometimes, however, it's useful to treat a string as a sequence of characters and manipulate them as you would items in a list.

To manipulate a string as a list:

1. Type s = list(s) to convert the string expression s to a list.

2. Perform list operation(s) on s, such as s.sort() to alphabetize the characters of s.

   For information about list operations, see Chapter 5.

3. Type s = "".join(s) to convert s back to a string (**Figure 4.38**).

✔ Tips

■ For information about list(), see "Converting a String" later in this chapter. For information about join(), see "Splitting and Joining Strings" earlier in this chapter.

■ You also can convert strings to tuples with tuple(), but tuples, like strings, are immutable and lack the in-place operations supported by lists.

■ String and list type conversions are computationally expensive; use them judiciously.

Converting a String

Python has functions for converting strings to other objects, and vice versa.

The numeric type-conversion functions convert strings to numbers. The string to be converted must be a valid numeric literal for the target conversion type. int("1.5") won't work, for example, because "1.5" represents a float.

To convert a string to a number:

◆ Type int(*s*) to convert *s* to a plain integer.
   or
   Type long(*s*) to convert *s* to a long integer.
   or
   Type float(*s*) to convert *s* to a floating-point number.
   or
   Type complex(*s*) to convert *s* to a complex number.

   s is a string expression representing a valid numeric literal (**Figure 4.39**).

The list() and tuple() functions convert strings (and other sequences) to lists and tuples. For information about lists and tuples, see Chapter 5.

To convert a string to a list or tuple:

◆ Type list(*s*) to convert *s* to a list.
   or
   Type tuple(*s*) to convert *s* to a tuple.
   s is a string expression (**Figure 4.40**).

```
>>> int('39'), long('10L'),
→ float('6.22')
(39, 10L, 6.2199999999999998)
>>> print int('39'), long('10L'),
→ float('6.22')
39 10 6.22
>>> complex('0'), complex('5j'),
→ complex('6+22j')
(0j, 5j, (6+22j))
>>> int('39.0')
Traceback (most recent call last):
  File "<stdin>", line 1, in ?
ValueError: invalid literal for int(): 39.0
>>> float('39')
39.0
>>> long("39")
39L
>>> long("39.0")
Traceback (most recent call last):
  File "<stdin>", line 1, in ?
ValueError: invalid literal for long(): 39.0
```

Figure 4.39 Python raises a ValueError exception if it can't convert a string to a number.

```
>>> list('mimetic')
['m', 'i', 'm', 'e', 't', 'i', 'c']
>>> t = "I'll tell.\n"
>>> print tuple(t)
('I', "'", 'l', 'l', ' ', 't', 'e', 'l', 'l',
→ '.', '\n')
>>> print list(''), tuple('')
[] ()
```

Figure 4.40 Each character in a string becomes an individual item in a list or tuple.

```
>>> s = "mimetic"
>>> s, str(s), repr(s)
('mimetic', 'mimetic', "'mimetic'")
>>> print s, str(s), repr(s)
mimetic mimetic 'mimetic'
>>> t = s + "\n"
>>> t, str(t), repr(t)
('mimetic\n', 'mimetic\n', "'mimetic\\n'")
>>> print t, str(t), repr(t)
mimetic

mimetic

'mimetic\n'
>>> repr(len)
'<built-in function len>'
>>> import math
>>> repr(math)
"<module 'math' (built-in)>"
>>> str(math.pi)
'3.14159265359'
>>> repr(math.pi)
'3.1415926535897931'
>>> lst = ['one' + str(2), len,
→ (math.pi, 1/3.0)]
>>> str(lst)
"['one2', <built-in function len>,
→ (3.1415926535897931, 0.33333333333333331)]"
>>> `lst`
"['one2', <built-in function len>,
→ (3.1415926535897931, 0.33333333333333331)]"
>>> str(SyntaxError)
'exceptions.SyntaxError'
>>> repr(SyntaxError)
'<class exceptions.SyntaxError at 007AB8FC>'
>>> str(None)
'None'
```

Figure 4.41 Even functions, modules, and exceptions have string representations.

The str() and repr() (for *representation*) functions convert almost any type of object to a string. They often return the same value, but when they differ, the str() value is more concise and readable. Surrounding an expression with *backquotes* (or *reverse quotes*) is equivalent to using repr(). The backquote (`) key is above the Tab key on most keyboards.

To convert an object to a string:

◆ Type str(*expr*)

 or

 Type repr(*expr*)

 or

 Type `expr`

 (Note the backquotes; a backquoted expression is equivalent to repr(*expr*).)

 expr is an expression (**Figure 4.41**).

 continues on next page

CONVERTING A STRING

107

✔ Tips

- The numeric-conversion functions also can convert among numeric types; see "Converting Among Number Types" in Chapter 3.

- When you type a variable name in inter- active mode, Python uses `repr()` internally to display the variable's value. Python uses `str()` internally to display objects with the `print` statement, however. You can over- ride this behavior with `print repr(expr)`.

- For most data types, the string returned by `repr()` can be passed to `eval()` to (re)create an object with the same value; see section "Running Code Programmatically" in Chapter 9.

- Use `repr()` rather than `str()` to print debugging data, as `repr()` may contain more information. The formatting precision of floating-point numbers, for example, in `repr()` exceeds that of `str()`. `repr()` uses the `%.17g` conversion specifier and `str()` uses `%.12g`, so `repr()` will show more dec- imal places than `str()` for certain numbers. For information about conversion speci- fiers, see "Printing Formatted Strings" later in this chapter.

- **NEW** The `string` module's numeric conversion functions were dep- recated in Python 2.0. The functions are `atof()` (replaced by `float()`), `atoi()` (replaced by `int()`), and `atol()` (replaced by `long()`). These functions are still useful for working with non-base-10 numbers. See Section 4.1, "`string` Common string operations," of the *Python Library Reference*.

- **LANG** Perl's `pack` and `unpack` functions convert between strings and lists. C's `stdlib.h` standard library contains functions that convert string to numbers.

```
>>> 'Zero' == 'zero'
0
>>> 'zero' == ('zero' + '')
1
>>> "A" < "a"
1
>>> "A" < "AA"
1
>>> "A" < ""
0
>>> 'formal' >= 'formaldehyde'
0
>>> 'able' <= 'baker' != 'c'
1
>>> '\t' < '\n' < '.' < '4' < 'A' < 'z'
1
>>> 'home wrecker' < 'home_wrecker'
→ < 'homewrecker'
1
```

Figure 4.42 Python compares strings by evaluating the lexicographical ordering of their characters.

Comparing Strings

You can compare strings by using the comparison operators, introduced in "Using Comparison Operators" of Chapter 2. Comparisons return 1 (true) or 0 (false).

To compare strings:

◆ Type *s1 op s2*

s1 and *s2* are string expressions, and *op* is the <, <=, >, >=, ==, or != operator (**Figure 4.42**).

Python compares strings by looking at the (integer) ASCII values of their individual characters (or Unicode values for Unicode strings; see "Creating a Unicode String" earlier in this chapter). To determine whether one string is "less" than another, Python first compares their initial characters. If the characters are different (that is, have unequal ASCII values), Python determines the truth of the comparison; otherwise, it compares the second characters, and so on.

continues on next page

You can determine a character's ASCII value with the ord() (for *ord*inal) function. The chr() function, the inverse of ord(), converts an ASCII code to a character (**Figure 4.43**).

```
>>> print ord('\t'), ord('\n'), ord('.')
9 10 46
>>> print ord('A'), ord('Z'),
→ ord('a'), ord('z')
65 90 97 122
>>> ord('')
Traceback (most recent call last):
  File "<stdin>", line 1, in ?
TypeError: ord() expected a character,
→ but string of length 0 found
>>> ord('Zzz')
Traceback (most recent call last):
  File "<stdin>", line 1, in ?
TypeError: ord() expected a character,
→ but string of length 3 found
>>> chr(65), chr(10), chr(9), chr(66)
('A', '\n', '\t', 'B')
>>> print chr(65), chr(10), chr(9),
→ chr(66)
A

   B
>>> chr(6)
'\x06'
>>> chr(256)
Traceback (most recent call last):
  File "<stdin>", line 1, in ?
ValueError: chr() arg not in range(256)
>>> chr(ord('F'))
'F'
>>> ord(chr(65))
65
```

Figure 4.43 Use chr() and ord() to display the values used for lexicographical ordering.

```
>>> for i in range(0, 256):
...   print `i` + " = " + chr(i)
...
0 =
...<snip>...
40 = (
41 = )
...<snip>...
47 = /
48 = 0
49 = 1
...<snip>...
64 = @
65 = A
66 = B
...<snip>...
89 = Y
90 = Z
91 = [
...<snip>...
96 = `
97 = a
98 = b
...<snip>..
```

Figure 4.44 An abridged printout of the 256 ASCII characters for this particular system. Some characters (such as tabs and newlines) are invisible.

To convert a character to an ASCII value:

◆ Type ord(*c*)

   c is a string expression with one character.

To convert an ASCII value to a character:

◆ Type chr(*i*)

   i is an integer expression. *i* must be between 0 and 255 (inclusive); otherwise, Python raises a ValueError exception.

Figure 4.44 shows how to print all ASCII values and their corresponding characters.

continues on next page

The max() and min() functions return the largest or smallest of several strings, or the largest or smallest character in a single string (**Figure 4.45**).

To find the largest or smallest of several strings:

◆ Type max(*s1,s2,...*), to return the largest string.

or

Type min(*s1,s2,...*), to return the smallest string.

s1,s2,... represent one or more comma-separated string expressions.

To find the largest or smallest character in a string:

◆ Type max(*s*), to return the largest character in *s*.

or

Type min(*s*), to return the smallest character in *s*.

s is a string expression.

✔ Tips

■ Comparisons are case-sensitive. *A* is less than *a*.

■ You also can use the cmp() function to compare two strings; see "Defining a Custom List Sort Order" in chapter 5.

■ String comparisons can be chained. The expression 'a' < 'b' != 'c', for example, is legal; see "Chaining Comparisons" in Chapter 2.

■ The == operator tests value equivalence, and the is operator tests object identity. For information about the is operator, see "Using Comparison Operators" in Chapter 2.

■ Strings and nonstrings always compare unequally—that is, s == obj is always false if s is a string and obj is not. Python won't convert obj to a string internally.

```
>>> r = 'vermicelli'
>>> s = 'mimetic'
>>> t = 'polyalloy'
>>> print min(r, s, t), max(r, s, t)
mimetic vermicelli
>>> print min(r), min(s), min(t)
c c a
>>> print max(r), max(s), max(t)
v t y
>>> min('mimetic'.capitalize())
'M'
>>> min('Mimetic', "")
''
>>> max(t, t + "\n")
'polyalloy\n'
>>> min(t + "\n")
'\n'
>>> min(s + " " + t)
' '
>>> min(chr(68), chr(70))
'D'
```

Figure 4.45 You can use max() and min() to determine whether your phone book is sorted correctly.

■ The chr() function doesn't work with Unicode strings. Use unichr() instead; see "Creating a Unicode String" in this chapter. All the other functions and operators in this section work with Unicode strings.

■ **LANG** Unlike Perl, Python uses the same operators for comparing numbers and comparing strings. Perl's string-comparison operators are lt, le, gt, ge, eq, and ne.

```
>>> s = "mimetic"
>>> t = "polyalloy"
>>> x = 2
>>> import math
>>> dict = { "e": math.e, "pi":
→ math.pi }
>>> print "s is %s" % s
s is mimetic
>>> a = "%s %s" % (s, t)
>>> a
'mimetic polyalloy'
>>> print "x = %d, sqrt(x) = %.4f" %
→ (x, x**0.5)
x = 2, sqrt(x) = 1.4142
>>> print "pi = %(pi)f, e = %(e)f"
→ % dict
pi = 3.141593, e = 2.718282
>>> print "-x * pi = %.4g" %
→ (-x * dict["pi"])
-x * pi = -6.283
>>> print "|" "%*.*f" "|" %
→ (7,3,dict["e"])
|  2.718|
>>> p = 0.3
>>> print "%d%% of %d is %.2f" %
→ (p * 100, x, x * p)
30% of 2 is 0.60
```

Figure 4.46 The % operator makes it easy to format data stored in tuples and dictionaries.

Printing Formatted Strings

Python's % operator lets you produce formatted output. % takes two operands: a format string and a tuple or a dictionary containing replacement values. The format string contains ordinary characters (which are not changed) and *conversion specifiers,* each of which is replaced by a new formatted string corresponding to the tuple or dictionary item. You can print the result (with print) or assign it to a variable (with =). For information about tuples, see Chapter 5. For information about dictionaries, see Chapter 6.

To create a formatted string:

◆ Type *s* % *values*

 s is a string expression containing plain text and conversion specifiers that you want to apply to the data in *values*. If *values* is a tuple, it must contain the same number of items as the number of conversion specifiers in *s*. If *values* is a dictionary, each conversion specifier in *s* must be associated with a key value in the dictionary (**Figure 4.46**).

Conversion specifiers begin with % and end with a conversion type character, which tells Python to how to convert a string, integer, or floating-point number. You can add optional modifiers between % and the conversion character to control the format further.

To create a conversion specifier:

◆ Type

`%[(key)][flags][width][.prec]type`

(*key*) is a dictionary key value in parentheses; specify this value only if the *values* operand is a dictionary. If *key* is not in the dictionary, Python raises a KeyError exception.

flags is zero or more characters that specify padding and alignment settings (**Table 4.4**).

width is a positive integer specifying the minimum field width (the minimum number of characters the output should contain). If the converted value has fewer characters than the field width, it's padded on the left or right (with spaces, by default), according to *flags*.

prec is . (dot) followed by a positive integer specifying the precision. This integer is the number of digits that should appear to the right of the decimal point in a floating-point number or the minimum number of digits in an integer. For f, F, e, E, g, and G conversions, *prec* defaults to 6; a precision of 0 suppresses the decimal point. This option doesn't affect strings.

type is a single character specifying the conversion type (**Table 4.5**).

Table 4.4

Flags	
CHARACTER	**DESCRIPTION**
0	Pad numbers with leading zeroes.
-	Left-align the result within the field. The default is right alignment.
<space>	Add a space before a positive number or empty string.
+	Always begin a number with a sign (+ or –). The default is to begin only negative numbers with a sign (overrides <space>).
#	Display numbers in *alternate form*. For e, E, f, F, g, and G conversions, the result will contain a decimal point even if no digits follow it. For g and G conversions, trailing zeroes are not removed. For o conversions, precision is increased (if necessary) to force the first digit to be a zero. For x and X conversions, a leading ox or oX is added to nonzero numbers. This flag has no effect on other conversions.

Table 4.5

Conversion Types	
CHARACTER	**DESCRIPTION**
d, i	Decimal integer or long integer. (*Decimal* means base 10, not decimal point.)
u	Unsigned (can't be negative) decimal integer or long integer.
f, F	Floating-point number in fixed-decimal notation: [-]*m.dddddd*, in which the number of *d*'s is specified by the precision.
e, E	Floating-point number in exponential (scientific) notation: [-]*m.dddddd*e+*xx*, in which the number of *d*'s is specified by the precision (e or E prints a lowercase or uppercase "e").
g, G	Same as e, E or f, F—whatever Python thinks is best. More precisely, if the exponent is greater than –4 or less than the precision, Python uses e or E; otherwise, it uses f or F.
o	Unsigned integer in octal.
x, X	Unsigned integer in hexadecimal (x or X print lowercase or uppercase letters).
c	Single character (accepts an integer ASCII code or single-character string).
r	String generated with repr(); see "Converting a String" earlier in this chapter
s	String generated with str(); see "Converting a String" earlier in this chapter
%	Literal %. The compete specification is %%.

Table 4.6

String-Conversion Examples	
Specifier	**Result**
%s	|mimetic|
%5s	|mimetic|
%.5s	|mimet|
%.10s	|mimetic|
%10s	| mimetic|
%-10s	|mimetic |
%10.5s	| mimet|
%-10.5s	|mimet |

Table 4.7

Integer-Conversion Examples	
Specifier	**Result**
%d	|123456|
% d	| 123456|
%2d	|123456|
%9d	| 123456|
%09d	|000123456|
%-9d	|123456 |
%+d	|+123456|
%+9d	| +123456|
%+-9d	|+123456 |

Table 4.8

Float-Conversion Examples	
Specifier	**Result**
%e	|1.234560e+002|
%f	|123.456000|
%g	|123.456|
% g	| 123.456|
%+g	|+123.456|
%16e	| 1.234560e+002|
%16.3e	| 1.235e+002|
%-16.3e	|1.235e+002 |
%9f	|123.456000|
%9.2f	| 123.46|
%-9.2f	|123.46 |
%+-9.2f	|+123.46 |
%+09.2f	|+00123.46|

Table 4.6 shows some example string conversions for the string `"mimetic"`. **Table 4.7** shows some example integer conversions for the integer 123456. **Table 4.8** shows some sample floating-point conversions for the float 123.456 (note that Python rounds the last displayed fractional digit). The surrounding pipe (|) characters show the extent of each field.

continues on next page

✔ Tips

■ Parentheses around the *values* operand are optional if *values* is a tuple containing only one item.

■ The width or precision may be specified as *, in which case the value is computed by reading the next item in the *values* tuple (which should be an integer). The value to convert comes after the width or precision item. To print at most five characters of the string *s*, for example, type `print "%.*s" % (5, s)`.

■ You can use the dictionary returned by the `vars()` function as the *values* variable in formatted strings (**Figure 4.47**). For information about `vars()`, see section "Accessing Namespaces" in Chapter 9.

■ You can use the `%=` augmented assignment operator (see "Making Augmented Assignments" in Chapter 3) to create formatted strings. These statements set *a* equal to `"mimetic polyalloy"`:

`a = "%s %s"`

`a %= ("mimetic", "polyalloy")`

■ The specifier `%.2f` often is used to print currency amounts (for example, 23.40). The specifier `%02d` is used to print date and time elements with leading zeroes (for example, 06/22/62 or 07:49).

■ **LANG** Perl and C's `sprintf` and `printf` functions have similar formatting capabilities. For compatibility with C's conversion specifiers, Python permits a length modifier (with the value h, l (ell), or ll (ell ell)) between *prec* and *type*. This modifier is ignored because it doesn't apply to Python.

```
>>> quality = "color"
>>> thing = "orange"
>>> print "What %(quality)s is an
→ %(thing)s?" % vars()
What color is an orange?
```

Figure 4.47 The `vars()` dictionary contains all locally defined names.

Working with Lists and Tuples

Lists and tuples, like strings, are ordered sequences of objects. But whereas strings hold only characters, list and tuples hold collections of arbitrary objects. Lists and tuples are like arrays in other languages.

Lists are mutable; can contain any type of object (including other lists); can grow and shrink as needed; and are easy to sort, search, and modify. Lists are enclosed in brackets, as follows:

```
lst = [1, "two", 3.0]
```

Tuples are like lists but can't be modified; they're immutable (like strings) and have a fixed length. Tuples are enclosed in parentheses, as follows:

```
tup = (1, "two", 3.0)
```

Mutability aside, many list and tuple operations are identical—that's why they're both in one chapter. So why do we need tuples if we have lists? Mainly for efficiency: Tuples are faster to access and consume less memory than lists. Python also requires tuples in certain situations, such as string formatting, dictionary keys, and multiple function arguments. Tuples also are handy when you want to be sure that your data can't be modified by an alias (see "Creating References to the Same Object" in Chapter 2).

Creating a List or Tuple

Creating a list is straightforward: Simply enclose zero or more comma-separated expressions in brackets. Creating a tuple involves a syntactic twist that ensures that one-item tuples can be distinguished from parenthesized expressions.

Lists can contain tuples, and vice versa. A list may contain nested lists (you can have lists of lists of lists of...) and a tuple may contain nested tuples. An *empty list* or *empty tuple* contains no items.

To create a list:

◆ Type [*expr1, expr2,* ...]

expr1, expr2,... are zero or more comma-separated expressions (**Figure 5.1**).

To create a tuple:

◆ Type (*expr1, expr2,* ...)

This expression creates a tuple with two or more items.

or

Type (*expr,*)

This expression creates a one-item tuple, called a *singleton*. You must include the comma after the expression; otherwise, Python will think the expression is parenthetical and evaluate it instead of creating a tuple with the result of the expression.

or

Type ()

This expression creates an empty tuple.

expr is an expression, and *expr1, expr2*,... are two or more comma-separated expressions (**Figure 5.2**).

```
>>> x = 1
>>> [x]
[1]
>>> y = "two"
>>> import math
>>> lst1 = [x, y, round(math.pi)]
>>> print lst1
[1, 'two', 3.0]
>>> lst2 = [0, lst1, 4]
>>> print lst2
[0, [1, 'two', 3.0], 4]
>>> lst3 = [lst2, (10/2, str(6))]
>>> print lst3
[[0, [1, 'two', 3.0], 4], (5, '6')]
>>> lst4 = []
>>> print lst4
[]
```

Figure 5.1 Lists can be nested arbitrarily.

```
>>> ()
()
>>> type(())
<type 'tuple'>
>>> x = 1
>>> (x)  #Not a tuple
1
>>> (x,)  # A tuple
(1,)
>>> lst = [2, "three", str(4)]
>>> tup1 = (0, x, lst, (5, '6'))
>>> print tup1
(0, 1, [2, 'three', '4'], (5, '6'))
>>> dict = {}
>>> lst2 = [dict]
>>> tup2 = (lst2,)
>>> print tup2
([{}],)
```

Figure 5.2 Take care when creating one-item tuples.

```
>>> tup1 = 1,
>>> print tup1
(1,)
>>> tup2 = 1, "two", 10/2.5
>>> print tup2
(1, 'two', 4.0)
```

Figure 5.3 Parentheses are optional for simple tuple assignments. For obvious reasons, you can't create an empty tuple this way.

✔ Tips

■ You can omit the parentheses when creating a tuple if the tuple is not part of a larger expression. An assignment like this one:

a = 1, 2, 3

is called *tuple packing,* because Python internally groups or "packs" the values on the right side into a tuple and then performs the assignment (**Figure 5.3**).

■ The reverse of tuple packing is *sequence unpacking:*

x, y, z = a

Here, Python unpacks the items in the sequence a and then assigns each item to the corresponding variable on the left side. (The number of variables must match the number of items in a.) Sequence unpacking works with a string, list, or tuple on the right side. For information about packing and unpacking assignments, see "Creating Variables" in Chapter 2.

■ Nested lists often are used to represent two-dimensional matrices. The list:

[[1, 2] [3, 4]]

represents the matrix:

$$\begin{bmatrix} 1 & 2 \\ 3 & 4 \end{bmatrix}$$

If you need to perform matrix calculations in Python, try Numeric Python, or NumPy (see the Appendix).

■ You can also create lists with list comprehensions; see "Using List Comprehensions to Create Lists" in Chapter 8.

■ You can create a list of sequential integers with the range() function; see "Looping over a Range of Integers" in Chapter 7.

■ **LANG** A list is like a Perl or C array or a Java Vector.

CREATING A LIST OR TUPLE

Finding the Length of a List or Tuple

The len() function counts the number of items in a list or tuple.

To find the length of a list or tuple:

◆ Type len(*s*)

s is a list or tuple expression (**Figure 5.4**).

✔ Tips

■ len() also counts characters in strings and items in dictionaries.

■ **LANG** Perl uses scalar assignment or the *scalar* function to determine array length.

```
>>> print len(()), len([])
0 0
>>> lst1 = [1, 'two', 3.0]
>>> len(lst1)
3
>>> lst2 = [[0, lst1, 4], (5, '6')]
>>> len(lst2)
2
>>> tup1 = (0,)
>>> len(tup1)
1
>>> tup2 = (0, [], (), {}, "", None)
>>> len(tup2)
6
>>> tup3 = (0, [1], 2, (3, (4, 5), 6))
>>> len(tup3)
4
>>> len([[1, 1, [2, [3, 3], 2, 2], 1]])
1
```

Figure 5.4 A nested list, tuple, or dictionary counts as one item.

```
>>> ['zero', 1, 2, 3][2]
2
>>> ('zero', 1, 2)[-2]
1
>>> lst = [0, 'one', [2, 3.0], 4, '5']
>>> len(lst)
5
>>> print lst[1], lst[2], lst[3]
one [2, 3.0] 4
>>> tup = ((0, 1), (2, 3), 4, (5, 6))
>>> len(tup)
4
>>> tup[len(tup)]
Traceback (most recent call last):
  File "<stdin>", line 1, in ?
IndexError: tuple index out of range
>>> tup[len(tup) - 1]
(5, 6)
>>> tup[-len(tup)]
(0, 1)
>>> tup[-len(tup) + 1]
(2, 3)
>>> n = -2
>>> lst[n] == lst[len(lst) + n]
1
>>> tup[1.5]
Traceback (most recent call last):
  File "<stdin>", line 1, in ?
TypeError: sequence index must be integer
```

Figure 5.5 Python uses zero-based integer indexes for lists and tuples.

Indexing a List or Tuple (Extracting an Item)

Lists and tuples are ordered sequences of items. An individual item is identified by its position, or *index*, in the sequence. Python uses zero-based indexes: the first item is at index 0, the second is at index 1, and so on. The index of the last item is the length of the sequence minus 1—that is, len(s) - 1.

You can also use a *negative index* to retrieve an item from the end of a sequence. The index of the last item is –1, the next-to-last is at index –2, and so on down to -len(s).

To index a list or tuple:

◆ Type *s*[*i*]

s is a list or tuple expression, and *i* is an integer expression representing the index (**Figure 5.5**).

Nested sequences (lists, tuples, or strings) may be accessed with multiple indexes.

To index a nested sequence:

◆ Type *s*[*i*][*j*]

s is a list or tuple expression, *i* is the index of a sequence nested in *s*, and *j* is the index of an item in that nested sequence. *i* and *j* are integer expressions.

You can add an index for each nesting level (**Figure 5.6**).

✔ Tips

■ If an index is out of range, Python raises an IndexError exception. If an index is not an integer (or long integer), Python raises a TypeError exception.

■ Python adds a negative index to the length of the sequence. If *n* is negative, for example, s[*n*] is equivalent to s[len(s) + *n*].

■ Python has no "negative zero" index. s[-0] is equivalent to s[0].

■ Lists are mutable, but tuples are immutable. You can modify a list (but not a tuple) in place with an item assignment like this one:
lst[i] = x
For information about item assignment, see "Replacing List Items" later in this chapter.

■ Indexing also works with strings; see "Indexing a String (Extracting a Character)" in Chapter 4.

■ **LANG** Perl and C use the same zero-based indexing scheme, but C doesn't support negative indexes. In Python, you can't use a Pascal-type expression like s[i,j] to index a nested sequence.

```
>>> tup = ((0, 1), [2, 3], (4, 5, 6))
>>> tup[1]
[2, 3]
>>> tup[1][0]
2
>>> tup[-1][2]
6
>>> tup[-1][-3]
4
>>> tup[0][-1]
1
>>> lst = [ 1, ["two", [ 3,
→ "sequoia"], 4 ]]
>>> lst[1]
['two', [3, 'sequoia'], 4]
>>> lst[1][1]
[3, 'sequoia']
>>> lst[1][1][1]
'sequoia'
>>> lst[1][1][1][2]
'q'
>>> lst[-1][-2][-2]
3
```

Figure 5.6 Arbitrarily deep nestings may be indexed with a[i][j][k]····.

Vertical left margin text: INDEXING A LIST OR TUPLE (EXTRACTING AN ITEM)

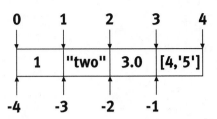

Figure 5.7 Slicing returns a segment that comprises the items between two indexes. A nested sequence counts as one item.

```
>>> i = [1, 2, 3, 4, 5]
>>> i[1:-1]
[2, 3, 4]
>>> print i[0:2], i[1:3], i[-3:-1],
→ i[2:-2]
[1, 2] [2, 3] [3, 4] [3]
>>> print i[2:], i[:2], i[-2:], i[:-2]
[3, 4, 5] [1, 2] [4, 5] [1, 2, 3]
>>> i[:]
[1, 2, 3, 4, 5]
>>> tup = ((0, 1), [2, 3], (4, 5, 6))
>>> tup[1:3]
([2, 3], (4, 5, 6))
>>> tup[1:3][-1][1:]
(5, 6)
>>> lst = ["sequoia", ["mimetic",
→ "polyalloy"]]
>>> lst[tup[0][1]][0][:-3]
'mime'
>>> lst[:1] + lst[1:]
['sequoia', ['mimetic', 'polyalloy']]
>>> tup[:-2] + tup[-2:]
((0, 1), [2, 3], (4, 5, 6))
```

Figure 5.8 Slicing lists and tuples.

Slicing a List or Tuple (Extracting a Segment)

A *slice* is a segment of a list or tuple specified by two indexes that demarcate a sequence of contiguous items. In the preceding section, a single index pointed *at* an item. In slicing, two indexes point *between* items (**Figure 5.7**).

If both indexes are positive, slicing returns the segment starting with the first index and up to but not including the second index. A negative index starts counting from the end of a list or tuple.

To slice a list or tuple:

◆ Type $s[i:j]$

s is a list or tuple expression, and i and j are optional integer expressions representing slice indexes. If i is omitted, it defaults to 0; if j is omitted, it defaults to the length of s (**Figure 5.8**).

continues on next page

✔ Tips

- Python constrains indexes logically. An index that is too small is replaced by zero, and one that is too large is replaced by the list or tuple length. If the second index indicates a position before the first index, an empty list or tuple is returned (**Figure 5.9**).

- For any integer n, s equals s[:n] + s[n:].

- Slicing also works with strings; see "Slicing a String (Extracting a Substring)" in Chapter 4.

- **LANG** Perl uses s[i,j] to extract array segments.

```
>>> i = [1, 2, 3, 4, 5]
>>> i[-100:100]
[1, 2, 3, 4, 5]
>>> i[1:100]
[2, 3, 4, 5]
>>> i[100:]
[]
>>> i[:100]
[1, 2, 3, 4, 5]
>>> i[-100:]
[1, 2, 3, 4, 5]
>>> i[:-100]
[]
>>> i[-100:2]
[1, 2]
>>> i[6:2]
[]
```

Figure 5.9 Python implicitly constrains indexes that are too small or too large to sensible values. Reversed indexes return empty lists or tuples.

```
>>> a = (1, 2, 3)
>>> b = a
>>> print b
(1, 2, 3)
>>> a = (4, 5, 6)
>>> print a
(4, 5, 6)
>>> print b
(1, 2, 3)
```

Figure 5.10 Tuples are immutable, so the assignment b = a effectively makes a copy of a.

```
>>> a = [1, 2, 3]
>>> b = a
>>> print b
[1, 2, 3]
>>> a[1] = -99
>>> print a
[1, -99, 3]
>>> print b
[1, -99, 3]
```

Figure 5.11 Lists are mutable, so b = a doesn't make a copy of a. Changes in a still affect b.

```
>>> a = [1, 2, 3]
>>> b = a[:]
>>> print b
[1, 2, 3]
>>> a[1] = -99
>>> print a
[1, -99, 3]
>>> print b
[1, 2, 3]
```

Figure 5.12 Use slicing to make a true copy of a (and not just duplicate a's object reference).

Copying a List or Tuple

You may recall from "Creating References to the Same Object" in Chapter 2 that the assignment b = a creates a new object reference to a. For an immutable object such as a tuple, this assignment effectively creates a copy of a.

To copy a tuple:

◆ Type b = a

a is the tuple you want to copy, and b is the variable assigned the copy (**Figure 5.10**).

If a is a mutable object such as a list, however, a = b doesn't create a copy of a but instead creates an alias. a and b will refer to the same object, so changes in one are reflected in the other (**Figure 5.11**). To create a completely new object that is a copy of a list, use slice notation.

To copy a list:

◆ Type b = a[:]

a is the list you want to copy, and b is the variable assigned the copy (**Figure 5.12**). This technique works for tuples, too.

Item assignment preview

The examples in this section use item assignment to illustrate how Python's copying mechanisms work. Item assignment changes the value of a list item. This statement, for example, changes the first item of the list s to 39:

```
s[0] = 39
```

Item assignment doesn't work for tuples because they're immutable. For information about item assignment, see "Replacing List Items" later in this chapter.

Shallow and deep copies

The preceding techniques for copying a tuple or list create *shallow copies*. If a list or tuple contains a nested list (or nested dictionary or other nested mutable object), a shallow copy will contain references to—not copies of—the nested items in the original. So even though *a* and *b* are separate objects, a change in a shared reference is still reflected in both (**Figure 5.13**).

To get around this problem, Python provides the deepcopy() method in the copy module. A *deep copy* is one that contains actual copies of *all* the objects in the original, no matter how deeply nested.

To create a deep copy of a list or tuple:

◆ Type:

```
import copy
b = copy.deepcopy(a)
```

a is the list or tuple you want to copy, and *b* is the variable assigned the copy (**Figure 5.14**).

```
>>> a = [1, [2, 3], 4]
>>> b = a[:]
>>> print b
[1, [2, 3], 4]
>>> a[0] = -99
>>> print a
[-99, [2, 3], 4]
>>> print b
[1, [2, 3], 4]
>>> a[1][1] = "sequoia"
>>> print a
[-99, [2, 'sequoia'], 4]
>>> print b
[1, [2, 'sequoia'], 4]
```

Figure 5.13 A shallow copy still holds references to—not copies of—nested objects in the original. Changing a "top-level" item in *a* doesn't affect *b*, but changing a nested item does.

```
>>> import copy
>>> a = [1, [2, 3], 4]
>>> b = copy.deepcopy(a)
>>> print b
[1, [2, 3], 4]
>>> a[1][1] = "sequoia"
>>> print a
[1, [2, 'sequoia'], 4]
>>> print b
[1, [2, 3], 4]
```

Figure 5.14 A deep copy makes true copies of all the items in *a*, including all the nested ones.

```
>>> a = (1, [2, 3], 4)
>>> a[0] = -99  # Nope
Traceback (most recent call last):
  File "<stdin>", line 1, in ?
TypeError: object doesn't support item
→ assignment
>>> a[1] = ['two', 'three']  # Nope
Traceback (most recent call last):
  File "<stdin>", line 1, in ?
TypeError: object doesn't support item
→ assignment
>>> a[1][1] = "sequoia"  # Works!
>>> print a
(1, [2, 'sequoia'], 4)
```

Figure 5.15 A tuple is immutable in the sense that you can't assign new values to its items (or add or delete items), but you *can* change items in a nested mutable container (such as a list).

✔ Tips

- If you've been paying attention, you may have noticed that an immutable tuple may contain a mutable object (such as a list or dictionary), which may be changed in place, so the concept of tuple immutability is subtler than I originally explained (**Figure 5.15**).

- The copy module also contains the copy() method, which makes a shallow copy of an object. b = copy.copy(a) is equivalent to b = a[:].

- You also can make a shallow copy with b = a + [] or b = a * 1 (which are less-efficient alternatives to b = a[:]).

Concatenating Lists or Tuples

The + (concatenation) operator combines, or *concatenates*, lists and tuples. Concatenation joins two lists into a single list or two tuples into a single tuple. You can't join a list to a tuple without first converting one to the other's type; see the tips in this section.

To concatenate lists or tuples:

◆ Type *s1* + *s2*

s1 and *s2* are two list expressions or two tuple expressions (**Figure 5.16**).

You also can use the += augmented assignment operator to concatenate lists or tuples (see "Making Augmented Assignments" in Chapter 3).

To concatenate lists or tuples by using augmented assignment:

◆ Type *s1* += *s2*

s1 is a list variable and *s2* is a list expression, or *s1* is a tuple variable and *s2* is a tuple expression (**Figure 5.17**).

✔ Tips

■ Trying to concatenate a list and a nonlist or a tuple and a nontuple raises a TypeError exception. You can convert an object to a list with list() or tuple with tuple(); see "Converting a List or Tuple" later in this chapter.

■ Augmented assignment behaves differently with (mutable) lists and (immutable) tuples; it modifies a list in place but creates a new tuple object.

■ The extend() method also concatenates lists; see "Adding List Items" later in this chapter.

■ Concatenation also works with strings; see "Concatenating Strings" in Chapter 4.

```
>>> print [] + [], () + ()
[] ()
>>> lst = [1, 2, 3]
>>> [] + lst + []
[1, 2, 3]
>>> lst + [4, 5]
[1, 2, 3, 4, 5]
>>> tup = ('four', 'five')
>>> tup + ()
('four', 'five')
>>> tup + ('six',)
('four', 'five', 'six')
>>> lst + [tup]
[1, 2, 3, ('four', 'five')]
>>> (lst,) + tup
([1, 2, 3], 'four', 'five')
>>> lst + tup
Traceback (most recent call last):
  File "<stdin>", line 1, in ?
TypeError: can only concatenate list
→ (not "tuple") to list
```

Figure 5.16 Concatenating lists and tuples.

```
>>> lst = [1, 2, 3]
>>> lst += [4, 5]
>>> lst += []
>>> lst += [6]
>>> print lst
[1, 2, 3, 4, 5, 6]
>>> tup = ('a',)
>>> tup += (lst[1:3],)
>>> tup += tup
>>> print tup
('a', [2, 3], 'a', [2, 3])
```

Figure 5.17 Concatenating lists and tuples by using augmented assignment.

```
>>> a = [1, 2, 3]
>>> a * 3
[1, 2, 3, 1, 2, 3, 1, 2, 3]
>>> a * 0
[]
>>> a * -2
[]
>>> a * 3.5
Traceback (most recent call last):
  File "<stdin>", line 1, in ?
TypeError: unsupported operand type(s) for *
>>> [] * 1000
[]
>>> [0] * 5
[0, 0, 0, 0, 0]
>>> [a] * 2
[[1, 2, 3], [1, 2, 3]]
>>> a[1:] + [4] * 2
[2, 3, 4, 4]
>>> (a[1:] + [4]) * 2
[2, 3, 4, 2, 3, 4]
>>> ('a', 'b', 'c')[0:2] * 2
('a', 'b', 'a', 'b')
```

Figure 5.18 Repeating lists and tuples.

Repeating a List or Tuple

The * (repetition) operator repeats a list or tuple a given number of times.

To repeat a list or tuple:

◆ Type *s* * *n* (or *n* * *s*)

s is a list or tuple expression, and *n* is the integer number of times to repeat *s*. An empty list or empty tuple is returned if *n* is less than or equal to zero (**Figure 5.18**).

You also can use the *= augmented assignment operator to repeat lists or tuples (see "Making Augmented Assignments" in Chapter 3).

To repeat a list or tuple by using augmented assignment:

◆ Type s *= n

s is a list or tuple variable, and n is the integer number of times to repeat s (**Figure 5.19**).

✔ Tips

■ Trying to repeat a list or tuple by using a noninteger raises a TypeError exception.

■ Repetition is more efficient than performing multiple concatenations.

■ [0] * n is an efficient way to initialize a list with n zeroes (or any other value).

■ Repetition creates shallow copies. The second statement in **Figure 5.20** embeds a shallow copy of a in b. To embed a deep copy of a in b instead, replace this statement:

b = [0, a] * 2

with either these statements:

import copy
b = [0, copy.deepcopy(a)] * 2

or this statement:

b = [0, a[:]] * 2

For information about shallow and deep copies, see "Copying a List or Tuple" earlier in this chapter.

■ Augmented assignment behaves differently with (mutable) lists and (immutable) tuples; it modifies a list in place but creates a new tuple object.

■ Repetition also works with strings; see "Repeating a String" in Chapter 4.

■ **LANG** Perl's x operator repeats array elements.

```
>>> a = [1, 2, 3]
>>> a *= a[2]
>>> print a
[1, 2, 3, 1, 2, 3, 1, 2, 3]
>>> b = ('a', 'b')
>>> b *= 0
>>> print b
()
>>> c = [4, 5]
>>> d = (c, 6)
>>> d *= 2
>>> print d
([4, 5], 6, [4, 5], 6)
```

Figure 5.19 Repeating lists and tuples using augmented assignment.

```
>>> a = [1, 2, 3]
>>> b = [0, a] * 2
>>> print b
(0, [1, 2, 3], 0, [1, 2, 3])
>>> a[1] = -99
>>> print a
[1, -99, 3]
>>> print b
(0, [1, -99, 3], 0, [1, -99, 3])
```

Figure 5.20 The assignment b = [0, a] * 2 creates a shallow copy of a.

```
>>> s = "mimetic"
>>> list(s[0:4])
['m', 'i', 'm', 'e']
>>> list((1, 2, ('a', 'b')))
[1, 2, ('a', 'b')]
>>> tup = ('a', 'b', 'c')
>>> list(tup)
['a', 'b', 'c']
>>> print list(()), list([]), list('')
☐ ☐ ☐
>>> a = [1, 2, 3]
>>> list(a + list(tup))
[1, 2, 3, 'a', 'b', 'c']
>>> list((tup,))
[('a', 'b', 'c')]
```

Figure 5.21 Converting sequences to lists.

```
>>> s = "sequoia"
>>> tuple(s[:4] + "el")
('s', 'e', 'q', 'u', 'e', 'l')
>>> lst = [1, 2, 3]
>>> tuple(lst)
(1, 2, 3)
>>> print tuple(()), tuple([]),
→ tuple("")
() () ()
>>> a = ('a', 'b', 'c')
>>> tuple(a + tuple(lst))
('a', 'b', 'c', 1, 2, 3)
>>> tuple((a,) + (lst,))
(('a', 'b', 'c'), [1, 2, 3])
>>> tuple(list(a))
('a', 'b', 'c')
```

Figure 5.22 Converting sequences to tuples.

Converting a List or Tuple

Python has several functions that convert lists and tuples to other objects, and vice versa.

The list() and tuple() functions convert sequences (strings, lists, or tuples) to lists and tuples. When a string is converted to a list or tuple, each character becomes a separate quoted item.

To convert a sequence to a list:

◆ Type list(*sequence*) to convert a *sequence* to a list.

sequence is a string, list, or tuple expression. If *sequence* is already a list, a deep copy of *sequence* is returned (**Figure 5.21**).

To convert a sequence to a tuple:

◆ Type tuple(*sequence*) to convert *sequence* to tuple.

sequence is a string, list, or tuple expression. If *sequence* is already a tuple, it's returned unchanged (**Figure 5.22**).

CONVERTING A LIST OR TUPLE

The str() and repr() functions convert a list or tuple (actually, any object) to a string. These functions are described in "Converting a String" in Chapter 4 but repeated here.

To convert a list or tuple to a string:

◆ Type str(*s*)

or

Type repr(*s*)

or

Type `` `s` ``

(Note the backquotes; a backquoted expression is equivalent to repr(*s*).)

s is a list or tuple expression (**Figure 5.23**).

✔ Tip

■ **LANG** Perl's pack and unpack functions convert between strings and arrays.

```
>>> lst = [1, 2, 3]
>>> tup = ('a', 'b', 'c')
>>> str(lst)
'[1, 2, 3]'
>>> repr(lst)
'[1, 2, 3]'
>>> `tup`
"('a', 'b', 'c')"
>>> str(`lst` + `tup`)
"[1, 2, 3]('a', 'b', 'c')"
>>> str(lst + list(tup))
"[1, 2, 3, 'a', 'b', 'c']"
>>> str([tup])
"[('a', 'b', 'c')]"
```

Figure 5.23 Converting lists and tuples to strings.

```
>>> a = [1, 2, 3]
>>> a < [1, 2, 4]
1
>>> a > [1, 2]
1
>>> a == [int(1), float(2), long('3')]
1
>>> a < [1, 2, '3']
1
>>> a != tuple(a)
1
>>> ['a', 'B'] < ['a', 'b']
1
>>> ['a', 'B'] == ['a', 'b'.upper()]
1
>>> a > []
1
>>> a == a + []
1
>>> import math
>>> ["A", 1, (2, 3)] == [chr(65),
 ↪ a[0], (int(math.e), 6/2)]
1
>>> ('a', ('b',)) != ('a', 'b') > ('a')
1
```

Figure 5.24 Python compares lists and tuples item by item.

Comparing Lists or Tuples

You can compare lists or compare tuples by using the comparison operators introduced in "Using Comparison Operators" in Chapter 2. Comparisons return 1 (true) or 0 (false).

To compare lists or tuples:

◆ Type *s1 op s2*

s1 and *s2* are two list expressions or two tuple expressions, and *op* is the <, <=, >, >=, ==, or != operator (**Figure 5.24**).

Python compares lists and tuples by comparing their corresponding items. To determine whether a list or tuple is "less" than another, Python first compares their initial items. If the items have different values, Python determines the truth of the comparison; otherwise, it compares the second items, and so on. If the compared items are the same object type, Python uses the comparison rules described in the "Comparing..." sections of Chapters 3, 4, and 6. Numbers are compared arithmetically, for example, and strings are compared lexicographically. Objects of different types always compare unequally. Therefore, if you compare a list with a tuple, the result is always false, even if the list and tuple contain items with the same values.

The max() and min() functions return the largest or smallest of several lists or tuples or the largest or smallest item in a single list or tuple (**Figure 5.25**).

To find the largest or smallest of several lists or tuples:

◆ Type max(*s1, s2, . . .*) to return the largest list or tuple.

or

Type min(*s1, s2, . . .*) to return the smallest list or tuple.

s1, s2,... are one or more comma-separated list expressions or tuple expressions.

To find the largest or smallest item in a list or tuple:

◆ Type max(*s*) to return the largest item in *s*.

or

Type min(*s*) to return the smallest item in *s*.

s is a list or tuple expression.

✔ Tips

■ You also can use the cmp() function to compare two lists or tuples; see "Defining a Custom List Sort Order" later in this chapter.

■ List and tuple comparisons can be chained. The expression s1 < s2 != s3, for example, is legal; see "Chaining Comparisons" in Chapter 2.

■ The == operator tests value equivalence, and the is operator tests object identity (**Figure 5.26**). For information about the is operator, see "Using Comparison Operators" in Chapter 2.

```
>>> a = [1, 2, 3]
>>> b = [0, 2, 3]
>>> c = [0, 1]
>>> print min(a, b, c), max(a, b, c)
[0, 1] [1, 2, 3]
>>> print min(a, b, c, [])
[]
>>> print min(a), max(b + c)
1 3
>>> p = ["mimetic", "polyalloy"]
>>> q = [p]
>>> min(p, q)
[['mimetic', 'polyalloy']]
>>> r = [p[0], p[1].title()]
>>> min(p, r)
['mimetic', 'Polyalloy']
>>> max(r)[0:4]
'mime'
```

Figure 5.25 Finding the smallest or largest list, tuple, or item.

```
>>> a = [1, 2, 3]
>>> b = [1, 2, 3]
>>> a == b
1
>>> a is b
0
```

Figure 5.26 These two lists have the same value but are separate objects.

```
>>> a = [1, 'two', 3.0]
>>> 3 not in a[:-1]
1
>>> print "" in a, None in a, [] in a
0 0 0
>>> print 'two' in a, 'Two' not in a
1 1
>>> print float(1) in a, 6/2 in a
1 1
>>> b = (0, a, (4, 5))
>>> a in b
1
>>> (4, 5) in b
1
>>> 4 in b
0
>>> 4 in b[2]
1
```

Figure 5.27 To detect an item in a nested sequence, refer directly to the nested sequence by its index.

Testing List or Tuple Membership

The in and not in operators (see "Using Comparison Operators" in Chapter 2) determine whether a list or tuple contains a particular value and returns 1 (true) or 0 (false).

To test whether a value is in a list or tuple:

◆ Type *x* in *s*

   or

   Type *x* not in *s*

   x is an expression, and *s* is a list or tuple expression (**Figure 5.27**).

✔ Tips

■ in and not in work for any sequence; you also can use them to determine whether a string contains a given character. "m" in "mimetic", for example, returns 1 (true).

■ You can use the count() and index() methods to count and find occurrences of a value in a list (but not a tuple); see "Counting Matching List Values" and "Searching a List" later in this chapter.

Modifying a List

The remainder of this chapter explains how to modify lists. All the subsequent operations and built-in methods, summarized in **Table 5.1.** work with only lists and not tuples. Tuples, you'll recall, are immutable, so if you attempt to use any of these operations or methods on a tuple, Python will raise a TypeError or AttributeError exception (**Figure 5.28**). (Tuples, in fact, have no methods.)

The count(), index(), and pop() methods return useful values; the other methods do their work as side effects and return None. In actual programs, the result of count(), index(), or pop() usually is assigned to a variable or used as part of a larger expression. A method that returns None is almost always used as an expression statement—that is, as a stand-alone method call without assignment (**Figure 5.29**). For information about expression statements and side effects, see "Creating Expression Statements" in Chapter 2.

Table 5.1

List Operations and Methods	
OPERATION	DESCRIPTION
s[i] = x	Item assignment: replaces item s[i] with x.
s[i:j] = t	Slice assignment: replaces slice s[i:j] with the values in list t.
del s[i]	Item deletion: deletes item s[i] from s.
del s[i:j]	Slice deletion: deletes slice s[i:j] from s.
s.append(x)	Appends item x to the end of s.
s.extend(sequence)	Appends the items in the sequence sequence to the end of s.
s.count(x)	Counts occurrences of x in s.
s.index(x)	Returns the smallest i where s[i] == x.
s.insert(i, x)	Inserts x into s at index i.
s.pop([i])	Returns s[i] and removes it from s. i defaults -1 (the last item of s).
s.remove(x)	Searches for x and removes it from s.
s.reverse()	Reverses the items of s in place.
s.sort([cmpfunc])	Sorts the items of s in place. cmpfunc is an optional comparison function.

```
>>> lst = [1, 2, 3]
>>> lst[1] = "two"
>>> print lst
[1, 'two', 3]
>>> lst.append(4)
>>> lst
[1, 'two', 3, 4]
>>> tup = ('a', 'b', 'c')
>>> tup[1] = "B"
Traceback (most recent call last):
  File "<stdin>", line 1, in ?
TypeError: object doesn't support item
→ assignment
>>> tup.append("d")
Traceback (most recent call last):
  File "<stdin>", line 1, in ?
AttributeError: 'tuple' object has no
→ attribute 'append'
```

Figure 5.28 Lists can be modified in place; tuples can't.

```
>>> a = [1, 2, 3]
>>> a.append(4)
>>> print a
[1, 2, 3, 4]
>>> x = a.pop()
>>> print a
[1, 2, 3]
>>> print x
4
```

Figure 5.29 Some methods (such as pop()) return a useful value; others (such as append()) return None. A common programming error is to type a statement like a = a.append(x), which assigns a the value None and loses the original list.

```
>>> a = [1, 2, 3, 4]
>>> a[1] = "two"
>>> a
[1, 'two', 3, 4]
>>> a[2] = -a[2]
>>> a
[1, 'two', -3, 4]
>>> a[-1] = [4, 5]
>>> a
[1, 'two', -3, [4, 5]]
>>> a[0] = []
>>> a
[[], 'two', -3, [4, 5]]
>>> a[3][-2] = "four"
>>> a
[[], 'two', -3, ['four', 5]]
>>> a[4] = 6
Traceback (most recent call last):
  File "<stdin>", line 1, in ?
IndexError: list assignment index out of range
```

Figure 5.30 You can use item assignment only to change list items, not to add or remove them.

Replacing List Items

You can use *item assignment* to replace a particular list item, or you can use *slice assignment* to replace several (contiguous) items. For information about indexing and slicing, see "Indexing a List or Tuple (Extracting an Item)" and "Slicing a List or Tuple (Extracting a Segment)" earlier in this chapter.

To replace an item in a list (item assignment):

◆ Type *s*[*i*] = *x*

s is a list expression, *i* is the index of the item to be replaced, and *x* is an expression representing the replacement value (**Figure 5.30**).

To replace more than one item in a list (slice assignment):

◆ Type *s*[*i*:*j*] = *t*

s is a list expression, *i* and *j* are the slice indexes of the items to be replaced, and *t* is a list containing replacement expressions (**Figure 5.31**).

✔ Tips

■ For slice assignments, *t* must be a list; otherwise, Python raises a TypeError exception.

■ Slice assignments are versatile. You can add item(s) to the beginning of a list with:

s[:0] = *t*

You can add item(s) to the end of a list with:

s[len(*s*):] = *t*

You can remove item(s) from a list with:

s[*i*:*j*] = []

You can insert an item into a list with:

s[*i*:*i*] = *t*

■ **LANG** Perl also uses index and slice assignments to replace array items. Python does not support non-contiguous item replacement.

```
>>> a = [1, 2, 3, 4, 5]
>>> a[0:2] = ["one", "two"]
>>> a
['one', 'two', 3, 4, 5]
>>> a[-2:] = [-a[-2], "five"]
>>> a
['one', 'two', 3, -4, 'five']
>>> a[3:] = [6, 7, 8, 9]
>>> a
['one', 'two', 3, 6, 7, 8, 9]
>>> a[:4] = [10/2]
>>> a
[5, 7, 8, 9]
>>> a[1:1] = [6]
>>> a
[5, 6, 7, 8, 9]
>>> a[-100:1] = ["five"]
>>> a
['five', 6, 7, 8, 9]
>>> a[-2:] = [[8, 9, 10]]
>>> a
['five', 6, 7, [8, 9, 10]]
>>> a[-1][-2:] = ["nine", "ten"]
>>> a
['five', 6, 7, [8, 'nine', 'ten']]
>>> a[1:] = []
>>> a
['five']
>>> a[:] = []
>>> a
[]
```

Figure 5.31 You can use slice assignment to change, add, and remove list items.

```
>>> a = [1] + (2 * ["two"]) + (3 * [3])
>>> a
[1, 'two', 'two', 3, 3, 3]
>>> x, y, z = a.count(1),
→ a.count("two"), a.count(3)
>>> print x, y, z
1 2 3
>>> a[2:].count("two")
1
>>> print a.count(""),
→ a.count("Two"), a.count([])
0 0 0
>>> a[3:] = [[3, 3, 3]]
>>> a
[1, 'two', 'two', [3, 3, 3]]
>>> a.count([3.0, 6/2, int('3')])
1
>>> a.count(3)
0
>>> a[-1].count(3)
3
>>> a[-1][-2:].count(3)
2
>>> b = ["mimetic", "polyalloy"]
>>> b.count("m")
0
>>> b[0].count("m")
2
```

Figure 5.32 Counting occurrences of specific list items.

Counting Matching List Values

The count() method returns the number of times a particular value occurs in a list.

To count occurrences of a value in a list:

◆ Type *s*.count(*x*) to return the number of times the value of *x* occurs in *s*.

   s is a list expression, and *x* is an expression (**Figure 5.32**).

✔ Tips

■ Counts are case-sensitive.

■ You can save the result of count() in a variable with:

   a = s.count(x)

■ To count values in a nested sequence, refer directly to the nested sequence by its index.

■ Use the in and not in operators to determine whether *x* simply occurs in a list or tuple; see "Testing List or Tuple Membership" earlier in this chapter.

COUNTING MATCHING LIST VALUES

Searching a List

The index() method returns the smallest index at which a particular value occurs in a list.

To find a value in a list:

◆ Type s.index(x) to return the smallest index of the list s where the value of x occurs.

s is a list expression, and x is an expression. Python raises a ValueError exception if x isn't in the list (**Figure 5.33**).

✔ Tips

■ Searches are case-sensitive.

■ You can save the result of index() in a variable with:

a = s.index(x)

■ To search for values in a nested sequence, refer directly to the nested sequence by its index.

■ Use the in and not in operators to determine whether x simply occurs in a list (or tuple); see "Testing List or Tuple Membership" earlier in this chapter.

■ Python raises an exception if index() can't find a value, so you must handle a failed search immediately in your program; see Chapter 11.

```
>>> a = [1, 2, 2, [3, ["mimetic",
→ "polyalloy"], 3], 3]
>>> len(a)
5
>>> print a.index(1), a.index(2),
→ a.index(3)
0 1 4
>>> a.index("two")
Traceback (most recent call last):
  File "<stdin>", line 1, in ?
ValueError: list.index(x): x not in list
>>> x = a.index(2)
>>> print a[x + 1:]
[2, [3, ['mimetic', 'polyalloy'], 3], 3]
>>> a[x + 1:].index(2)
0
>>> a[3].index(3)
0
>>> a[1:].index(3)
3
>>> a[3][1].index("polyalloy")
1
>>> a[3][1].index("poly")
Traceback (most recent call last):
  File "<stdin>", line 1, in ?
ValueError: list.index(x): x not in list
>>> a[3][1][1][4:].index("y")  # "alloy"
4
>>> a.index([])
Traceback (most recent call last):
  File "<stdin>", line 1, in ?
ValueError: list.index(x): x not in list
```

Figure 5.33 index() finds the *first* occurrence; use slicing to search for occurrences beyond the first.

```
>>> a = [1, 2]
>>> a.append(3)
>>> a.append(6/2)
>>> a
[1, 2, 3, 3]
>>> a.append([6, 7])
>>> a.append(a[0:2])
>>> a.append([])
>>> a.append("")
>>> a
[1, 2, 3, 3, [6, 7], [1, 2], [], '']
>>> a[4].append(8)
>>> a
[1, 2, 3, 3, [6, 7, 8], [1, 2], [], '']
```

Figure 5.34 Appending items to the end of a list.

```
>>> a = [1, 2]
>>> a.extend([6/2])
>>> a
[1, 2, 3]
>>> a.extend([])
>>> a.extend("")
>>> a
[1, 2, 3]
>>> a.extend([[5, 6]])
>>> a.extend("abc")
>>> a.extend(('d',))
>>> a
[1, 2, 3, [5, 6], 'a', 'b', 'c', 'd']
>>> a[3].extend([7])
>>> a
[1, 2, 3, [5, 6, 7], 'a', 'b', 'c', 'd']
>>> a.extend(8)
Traceback (most recent call last):
  File "<stdin>", line 1, in ?
TypeError: list.extend() argument must be a
→ sequence
```

Figure 5.35 extend() converts its argument to a list and concatenates it with its object.

Adding List Items

The append() method adds a single item to the end of a list. The extend() method concatenates two lists. The insert() method adds an item at a specified position in a list.

To add an item to the end of a list:

◆ Type *s*.append(*x*) to add the item *x* to the end of the list *s*.

   s is a list expression, and *x* is an expression (**Figure 5.34**).

To add more than one item to the end of a list:

◆ Type *s*.extend(*sequence*) to add the items in the sequence *sequence* (a string, list, or tuple) to the end of the list *s*.

   s is a list expression, and *x* is an expression. Python raises a TypeError exception if *sequence* isn't a sequence (**Figure 5.35**).

To add an item anywhere in a list:

◆ Type s.insert(i,x) to insert the item *x* at index *i* of list *s*.

s is a list expression, *x* is an expression, and *i* is an integer index of *s*. If *i* is not an integer, its fractional part is truncated. The items at index *i* and higher are shifted right during insertion (**Figure 5.36**). For information about indexes, see "Indexing a List or Tuple (Extracting an Item)" earlier in this chapter.

✔ Tips

■ The interpretation of a negative index *i* in insert() is different from what you'd expect. Instead of counting backward from the end of *s*, Python always inserts *x* as the first item of *s* if *i* ≤ 0. If a is [1, 2, 3], for example, a.insert(-1, 4) changes a to [4, 1, 2, 3] (not to [1, 2, 3, 4]).

■ append(), extend(), and insert() are convenience methods, because they can be replicated via slice assignment (see "Replacing List Items" earlier in this chapter) as shown by the following three tips.

■ s.append(*x*) is equivalent to s[len(s):len(s)] = [*x*].

■ s.extend(*sequence*) is equivalent to s[len(s):len(s)] = list(*sequence*).

■ s.insert(*i*,*x*) is equivalent to s[*i*:*i*] = [*x*] if *i* ≥ 0.

■ Use [*x*] * *n* to initialize a list with *n* *x*'s. This procedure is much more efficient than calling append(*x*) *n* times.

■ a.extend(b) is a more efficient way to concatenate lists than a = a + b, because the former statement creates one fewer object.

```
>>> a = [1, 2]
>>> a.insert(0, -2)
>>> a
[-2, 1, 2]
>>> a.insert(-100, a[0] - 1)
>>> a.insert(100, abs(a[0]))
>>> a
[-3, -2, 1, 2, 3]
>>> a.insert(3, -99)
>>> a.insert(len(a), [4, 5])
>>> a.insert(len(a), [])
>>> a
[-3, -2, 1, -99, 2, 3, [4, 5], []]
>>> a.insert(len(a)/2, "mid")
>>> a
[-3, -2, 1, -99, 'mid', 2, 3, [4, 5], []]
>>> a[-2].insert(1, 4.5)
>>> a
[-3, -2, 1, -99, 'mid', 2, 3, [4, 4.5, 5], []]
```

Figure 5.36 Inserting items at various places in a list.

■ If lst1 and lst2 are lists, you can append lst2 to lst1 in place with this statement: lst1[-1:] = lst1[-1:] + lst2.

■ For information about inserting items into a sorted list, see "Inserting Items into a Sorted List" later in this chapter.

■ **LANG** Perl's push and unshift functions insert array elements.

```
>>> a = [1, "sequoia", [3, 4, 5], 6, 7]
>>> del a[3]
>>> a
[1, 'sequoia', [3, 4, 5], 7]
>>> del a[2][-2]
>>> a
[1, 'sequoia', [3, 5], 7]
>>> del a[-1]
>>> a
[1, 'sequoia', [3, 5]]
>>> del a[a[0]]
>>> del a[a[0]]
>>> a
[1]
```

Figure 5.37 Deleting items from a list.

```
>>> a = [1, "sequoia", [3, 4, 5], 6, 7]
>>> del a[2][1:]
>>> a
[1, 'sequoia', [3], 6, 7]
>>> del a[1:-2]
>>> a
[1, 6, 7]
>>> del a[:]
>>> a
[]
```

Figure 5.38 Deleting slices from a list.

Removing List Items

Python lets you remove list items by position or value. The del statement removes one or more contiguous items from a list. The pop() method removes an item and returns its value. The remove() method searches for and removes a given value from a list. del and pop() use indexing and slicing; see "Indexing a List or Tuple (Extracting an Item)" and "Slicing a List or Tuple (Extracting a Segment)" earlier in this chapter.

To remove an item from a list:

◆ Type del $s[i]$ to delete the item at index i of the list s.

   s is a list expression, and i is an integer index of s (**Figure 5.37**).

To remove more than one item from a list:

◆ Type del $s[i:j]$ to delete the items in the slice $s[i:j]$ of the list s.

   s is a list expression, and i and j are integer slice indexes of s (**Figure 5.38**).

To remove an item from a list and save its value:

◆ Type *x* = *s*.pop([*i*]) to delete the item at index *i* of the list *s* and assign it to *x*.

s is a list expression, *i* is an integer index of *s*, and *x* is a variable. If *i* is omitted, it defaults to −1, which is the last item of *s* (**Figure 5.39**).

```
>>> a = [1, 2, 3, 4, 5]
>>> x = a.pop()
>>> print x
5
>>> print a
[1, 2, 3, 4]
>>> y = a.pop(2)
>>> print y
3
>>> print a
[1, 2, 4]
>>> a.pop(-2)
2
>>> a
[1, 4]
>>> a.pop(0)
1
>>> a
[4]
```

Figure 5.39 pop() deletes and returns a list item.

```
>>> a = [1, 2.0, 2, "two", [3, 4, 3]]
>>> a.remove(2)
>>> print a
[1, 2, 'two', [3, 4, 3]]
>>> a.remove(2)
>>> print a
[1, 'two', [3, 4, 3]]
>>> a.remove(3)
Traceback (most recent call last):
  File "<stdin>", line 1, in ?
ValueError: list.remove(x): x not in list
>>> a[2].remove(3)
>>> print a
[1, 'two', [4, 3]]
>>> a.remove(a[-1])
>>> print a
[1, 'two']
>>> a.remove("Two")
Traceback (most recent call last):
  File "<stdin>", line 1, in ?
ValueError: list.remove(x): x not in list
>>> a.remove("Two".lower())
>>> a.remove(float(1.0))
>>> print a
[]
```

Figure 5.40 remove() deletes list items by value, not by index.

To search for a value and remove it from a list:

♦ Type *s*.remove(*x*) to delete the first item with the value of *x* that occurs in the list.

  s is a list expression, and *x* is an expression. Python raises a ValueError exception if *x* isn't in the list (**Figure 5.40**).

✔ Tips

■ remove() is case-sensitive.

■ remove() removes only the *first* occurrence of *x*. Call remove() repeatedly to remove all occurrences. count() returns the number of times *x* appears in a list; see "Counting Matching List Values" earlier in this chapter.

■ Python raises an exception when remove() can't find a value, so you must handle a failed removal immediately in your program; see Chapter 11.

■ *s*.pop(*i*) is equivalent to the following statements:

  ```
  x = s[i]
  del s[i]
  return x
  ```

■ *s*.remove(*x*) is equivalent to del *s*[*s*.index(*x*)].

■ **LANG** Perl's pop and shift functions remove array elements.

REMOVING LIST ITEMS

Sorting a List

The sort() method sorts the items of a list in place in ascending order. Python compares objects by using the comparison rules described in the "Comparing..." sections of chapters 3, 4, and 6. Note that objects with different types always compare unequally.

To sort a list:

◆ Type *s*.sort() to sort *s* in ascending order.

s is a list expression (**Figure 5.41**).

✔ Tips

■ sort() modifies the original list. Sort a copy if you want to maintain the original. This example assigns a sorted copy of *a* to *b* and leaves *a* unchanged:

```
a = [4, 2, 3, 1]
b = a[:]
b.sort()
```

■ To sort a list in descending order, first use sort() and then reverse(); see "Reversing a List" later in this chapter.

■ To sort a list using a custom sort order, see "Defining a Custom List Sort Order" later in this chapter.

■ **LANG** Perl's sort function sorts an array.

```
>>> import math
>>> a = [2.0, -0.11, 4, -2, 0, 2, 1,
→ round(math.pi, 0)]
>>> a.sort()
>>> print a
[-2, -0.11, 0, 1, 2.0, 2, 3.0, 4]
>>> print a.sort()  # Oops
None
>>> b = ["Never", "odd", "or",
→ "even", ""]
>>> b.sort()
>>> print b
['', 'Never', 'even', 'odd', 'or']
>>> c = [[4, 2], [0, 1], [-1, 0],
→ [4, 2, 0], []]
>>> c.sort()
>>> print c
[[], [-1, 0], [0, 1], [4, 2], [4, 2, 0]]
>>> d = [[1], (1,), "1", 1, {"one": 1}]
>>> d.sort()  # Arbitrary sort
>>> print d
[1, {'one': 1}, [1], '1', (1,)]
```

Figure 5.41 It generally makes sense to sort objects only of the same type.

```
>>> a = [4, 1, 3, 4, 0]
>>> a.sort()
>>> print a
[0, 1, 3, 4, 4]
>>> x = bisect.bisect(a, 2)
>>> print x
2
>>> bisect.insort(a, 2)
>>> print a
[0, 1, 2, 3, 4, 4]
>>> b = ["Never", "odd", "or", "even"]
>>> b.sort()
>>> print b
['Never', 'even', 'odd', 'or']
>>> y = bisect.bisect(b, "Mimetic")
>>> print y
0
>>> bisect.insort(b, "Mimetic")
>>> print b
['Mimetic', 'Never', 'even', 'odd', 'or']
>>> bisect.insort(b, "")
>>> print b
['', 'Mimetic', 'Never', 'even', 'odd', 'or']
```

Figure 5.42 insort() inserts an item into an already sorted list and preserves the sort order.

Inserting Items into a Sorted List

The bisect module contains functions for manipulating sorted lists. The insort() function inserts an item into a list, and maintains the sort order. The bisect() function returns the list index where a given item would be inserted into a sorted list. These functions assume that the list is already sorted (**Figure 5.42**).

To insert an item into a sorted list:

◆ Type:

```
import bisect
bisect.insort(s, x)
```

This function inserts the item x into the proper position of the sorted list s. s is a list expression, and x is an expression.

To get the insertion point of an item to be inserted into a sorted list:

◆ Type:

```
import bisect
bisect.bisect(s, x)
```

This function returns the index where the item x would be inserted into the sorted list s. s is a list expression, and x is an expression.

For information about indexes, see "Indexing a List or Tuple (Extracting an Item)" earlier in this chapter.

continues on next page

✔ Tips

- To sort a list, see "Sorting a List" earlier in this chapter.

- The value returned by bisect() can be used to partition a list (**Figure 5.43**).

- You can't type a statement like this one:

  bisect.insort(a.sort(), x) # Wrong

  As you may remember, the sort() method returns None, not a sorted list. This statement raises a TypeError exception.

- The bisect functions don't work properly with custom-sorted lists; see "Defining a Custom List Sort Order" later in this chapter.

- ◆ NEW Python 2.1 introduced some new insertion and bisection functions; see Section 5.7, "bisect—Array bisection algorithm," of the *Python Library Reference*.

```
>>> a = [1, 2, 3, 5, 7, 9, 11]
>>> import bisect
>>> a[:bisect.bisect(a, 5)]
[1, 2, 3, 5]
>>> a[bisect.bisect(a, 5):]
[7, 9, 11]
>>> a[bisect.bisect(a, 6):]
[7, 9, 11]
>>> a[bisect.bisect(a, 13):]
[]
>>> a[bisect.bisect(a, -1):]
[1, 2, 3, 5, 7, 9, 11]
>>> a[bisect.bisect(a, len(a)/2):]
[5, 7, 9, 11]
>>> a[:bisect.bisect(a, len(a)/2)]
[1, 2, 3]
```

Figure 5.43 bisect() can be used to partition sorted lists.

```
a>>> cmp("sequoia", "mimetic")
1
>>> cmp(5.0, 5)
0
>>> cmp([], [0, 1])
-1
>>> cmp(("a", "b"),("a", "B"))
1
>>> cmp("aa", "b")
-1
>>> cmp(len("aa"), len("b"))
1
```

Figure 5.44 The cmp() function returns an integer indicating how its arguments compare.

```
>>> def cmp_ignorecase(x, y):
...     return cmp(x.lower(),
→ y.lower())
...
>>> a = "Travis trips trapshooting
→ Trappist traders".split()
>>> print a
['Travis', 'trips', 'trapshooting',
'Trappist', 'traders']
>>>
>>> a.sort()  # Default sort
>>> print a
['Trappist', 'Travis', 'traders',
→ 'trapshooting', 'trips']
>>>
>>> a.sort(cmp_ignorecase)  # Custom
→ sort
>>> print a
['traders', 'Trappist', 'trapshooting'',
→ 'Travis', 'trips']
```

Figure 5.45 Objects can be sorted as long as they can be compared.

Defining a Custom List Sort Order

This section requires an understanding of functions; see Chapter 8.

As stated in "Sorting a List" earlier in this chapter, the sort() method sorts list items according to Python's default ordering rules. sort() uses the cmp() function internally to compare the values of two objects.

To compare the values of two objects:

◆ Type cmp(x, y)

This function compares objects x and y and returns −1 if $x < y$, 0 if $x == y$, and 1 if $x > y$.

x and y are expressions (**Figure 5.44**).

To define a custom sort order, you must create your own cmp()-like function and pass it as an argument to sort().

To sort a list by using a custom sort order:

1. Define a comparison function that takes two arguments (list items) and returns −1, 0 or 1, depending on whether the first argument is considered to be less than, equal to, or greater than the second argument.

2. Type s.sort(*cmpfunc*) to sort s by using the comparison order defined by *cmpfunc*.

   s is a list expression, and *cmpfunc* is the name of the comparison function that you defined in step 1.

In **Figure 5.45**, the custom comparison function cmp_ignorecase() performs a case-insensitive comparison of strings. The code shows (default) case-sensitive and (custom) case-insensitive sorts.

continues on next page

✔ Tips

- A custom sort is very slow compared with the default sort.

- You *can* define *cmpfunc* to sort a list in descending order, but using sort() and reverse() is much faster; see "Reversing a List" later in this chapter.

- *cmpfunc* doesn't strictly have to return −1, 0, or 1. It can return any negative number, zero, or any positive number.

- The bisect module functions don't work properly with custom-sorted lists; see "Inserting Items into a Sorted List" earlier in this chapter.

- **LANG** Perl's sort function takes a *cmpfunc*-like argument that defines a custom sort order. Perl's <=> and cmp operators are similar to cmp().

```
>>> a = [4, 1, 3, 4, 0]
>>> a.reverse()
>>> print a
[0, 4, 3, 1, 4]
>>> a.sort()
>>> a.reverse()
>>> print a
[4, 4, 3, 1, 0]
>>> b = "Never odd or even"
>>> c = list(b)
>>> c.reverse()
>>> b = "".join(c)
>>> print b
neve ro ddo reveN
```

Figure 5.46 Using reverse() to sort a list in descending order and reverse a string.

Reversing a List

The reverse() method reverses the order of items in a list, putting the last item first, the next-to-last item second, and so on. List reversal often is done to reverse a list after it has been sorted with sort(); see "Sorting a List" and "Defining a Custom List Sort Order" earlier in this chapter.

To reverse the order of items in a list:

◆ Type s.reverse() to reverse s.

s is a list expression (**Figure 5.46**).

✔ Tips

■ reverse() modifies the original list. Reverse a copy if you want to maintain the original. This example assigns a reversed copy of a to b and leaves a unchanged:

```
a = [4, 2, 3, 1]
b = a[:]
b.reverse()
```

■ **LANG** Perl's reverse function reverses an array.

Working with Dictionaries

A *dictionary*, like a list, holds a collection of arbitrary objects. Each object, or *value*, is accessed not by an index number but by a unique identifier that you assign, called a *key*. Each value and its associated key are called a *key-value pair*, and a key-value pair is a single dictionary *item* (or sometimes *entry*).

Dictionaries are mutable, can contain any type of object (including other dictionaries), can grow and shrink as needed, and are easy to modify. Dictionaries are enclosed in braces:

```
d = {"one":"eins", "two":"zwei"}
```

A dictionary is *unordered*. If you print a dictionary, you may notice that the printed order of its items is different from the order in which they were entered. This situation happens because Python stores dictionary items in an order that speeds key lookup. You can't control this order, and it changes when the dictionary changes, so practically, you should view dictionary items as randomly ordered. Operations and methods that require a known sequence, such as indexing and slicing, don't work with dictionaries. This restriction doesn't matter, however, because you retrieve a dictionary item by its key, not by its position.

Using Dictionary Operators and Methods

Table 6.1 summarizes Python's dictionary operators and methods, all of which are explained in this chapter.

All the dictionary methods return useful results except update() and clear(), which do their work as side effects and return None. In actual programs, update() and clear() almost always are used as expression statements—that is, as a stand-alone method calls without assignment; see "Creating Expression Statements" in Chapter 2. The results of the other methods are usually assigned to a variable or used as part of a larger expression. In particular, the methods that return lists (items(), keys(), and values()) often are used in for loops; see "Using For Loops" in Chapter 7.

Table 6.1

Dictionary Operators and Methods	
OPERATION	DESCRIPTION
d[key]	Returns the value associated with key from dictionary d
d[key] = value	Sets the value of d[key] to value
del d[key]	Deletes d[key] from d
len(d)	Returns the number of items in d
d.clear( )	Removes all the items from d
d.copy( )	Returns a (shallow) copy of d
d.get(key [,default_value])	Returns d[key] if key exists, default_value otherwise
d.has_key(key)	Returns true if key appears in d, false otherwise
d.items( )	Returns a list of all the items in d
d.keys( )	Returns a list of all the keys in d
d.popitem( )	Returns and removes a random item from d
d.setdefault(key [,default_value])	Returns d[key] if key exists, otherwise sets and returns default_value
d1.update(d2)	Merges the items of d2 into d1
d.values( )	Returns a list of all the values in d

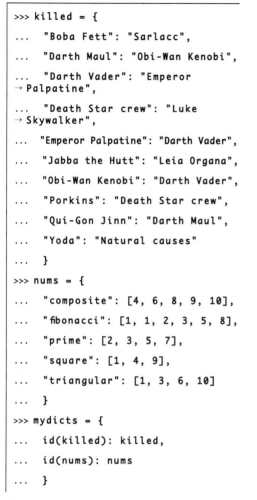

```
>>> killed = {
...    "Boba Fett": "Sarlacc",
...    "Darth Maul": "Obi-Wan Kenobi",
...    "Darth Vader": "Emperor
→ Palpatine",
...    "Death Star crew": "Luke
→ Skywalker",
...    "Emperor Palpatine": "Darth Vader",
...    "Jabba the Hutt": "Leia Organa",
...    "Obi-Wan Kenobi": "Darth Vader",
...    "Porkins": "Death Star crew",
...    "Qui-Gon Jinn": "Darth Maul",
...    "Yoda": "Natural causes"
...    }
>>> nums = {
...    "composite": [4, 6, 8, 9, 10],
...    "fibonacci": [1, 1, 2, 3, 5, 8],
...    "prime": [2, 3, 5, 7],
...    "square": [1, 4, 9],
...    "triangular": [1, 3, 6, 10]
...    }
>>> mydicts = {
...    id(killed): killed,
...    id(nums): nums
...    }
```

Figure 6.1 The killed, nums, and mydicts dictionaries are used in subsequent examples.

Creating a Dictionary

A dictionary (also called a *mapping* or *associative array*) is zero or more comma-separated key-value pairs in braces. A key and its associated value are separated by a colon (:). A key must be an immutable object (a number, string, or tuple), and a value may be any type of object (including a nested dictionary). An *empty dictionary* contains no items: {}.

To create a dictionary:

◆ Type {*key1*: *value1*, *key2*: *value2*,...}
   key1:value1, *key2:value2*,... are zero or more comma-separated key-value pairs. Each *key* is an expression representing an immutable object (number, string, or tuple), and each *value* is an expression (**Figure 6.1**).

I don't have enough room to create a dictionary in every example, so I'll use the dictionaries in Figure 6.1 in subsequent examples without re-entering them.

The killed dictionary contains fictional characters and their killers from an obscure science-fiction film series. The key is the victim, and the value is the perpetrator.

The nums dictionary contains mathematical number types and examples. The key is the name of the number type, and the value is a list of numeric examples between 1 and 10, inclusive. See the tips in this section to learn about each number type.

The mydicts dictionary contains killed and nums as nested dictionaries. The key is a dictionary's identifier (see "Determining an Object's Identity" in Chapter 2), and the value is a reference to the dictionary itself. (The identifiers aren't static throughout this chapter, because I created the examples during various Python sessions.)

Several examples in this chapter use if, for, and while statements; see Chapter 7.

continues on next page

✔ Tips

- Keys are case-sensitive.

- Keys must be unique within a dictionary. If you add an item with a duplicate key, the old value is overwritten.

- A single dictionary's keys may be a mix of numbers, strings, and tuples (**Figure 6.2**).

- A tuple can be a key if it contains only immutable objects (numbers, strings, or tuples). If a tuple directly or indirectly contains a mutable object, such as a list, Python won't allow it as a key and will raise a TypeError exception.

- Tuples can contain *composite keys* that hold several values. A two-item tuple, for example, could hold the latitude and longitude of a location, or the row index and column index of an array.

- In the nums dictionary, a *prime number* has no factors besides 1 and itself. A *composite number* is exactly divisible by at least one number other than 1 and itself—that is, it's not prime. A *square number* is the product of a number multiplied by itself. A *triangular number* is the sum of the first *n* natural numbers (1, 1 + 2, 1 + 2 + 3, and so on). A *Fibonacci number* is in the sequence in which each successive number is equal to the sum of the two preceding numbers (1, 1, 1 + 1, 1 + 2, 2 + 3, and so on).

- In Figure 6.1 (and subsequent figures), I use implicit line joining to format typed input by putting each dictionary item on its own line. Python permits expressions in braces (or parentheses or brackets) to be split across multiple lines; see "Splitting Statements Across Lines" in Chapter 7.

- **LANG** A dictionary is like a Perl hash or Java Hashtable. Perl keys may be only strings. Perl uses (key1 => value1,...) to create a new dictionary.

```
>>> deutsche = {
...    "one": "eins",
...    2.0: "zwei",
...    (3,): "drei",
...    8/2: "vier"
...    }
>>> deutsche
{'one': 'eins', 4: 'vier', (3,):
→ 'drei', 2.0: 'zwei'}
```

Figure 6.2 Keys can be a mix of immutable objects.

```
>>> print killed
```

```
{'Qui-Gon Jinn': 'Darth Maul', 'Darth Vader':
→ 'Emperor Palpatine', 'Yoda': 'Natural
→ causes', 'Obi-Wan Kenobi': 'Darth Vader',
→ 'Death Star crew': 'Luke Skywalker', 'Porkins':
→ 'Death Star crew', 'Boba Fett': 'Sarlacc',
→ 'Emperor Palpatine': 'Darth Vader', 'Jabba
→ the Hutt': 'Leia Organa', 'Darth Maul':
→ 'Obi-Wan Kenobi'}
```

```
>>> print nums
```

```
{'composite': [4, 6, 8, 9, 10], 'fibonacci':
→ [1, 1, 2, 3, 5, 8], 'square': [1, 4, 9],
→ 'triangular': [1, 3, 6, 10], 'prime': [2, 3, 5, 7]}
```

Figure 6.3 Ick.

Script 6.1 The printdict() function prints each dictionary key-value pair on its own line, sorted by key.

```
def printdict(dict):
  """Print sorted key:value pairs"""
  keys = dict.keys()
  keys.sort()
  for key in keys:
    print key, ":", dict[key]
```

```
>>> printdict(killed)
Boba Fett : Sarlacc
Darth Maul : Obi-Wan Kenobi
Darth Vader : Emperor Palpatine
Death Star crew : Luke Skywalker
Emperor Palpatine : Darth Vader
Jabba the Hutt : Leia Organa
Obi-Wan Kenobi : Darth Vader
Porkins : Death Star crew
Qui-Gon Jinn : Darth Maul
Yoda : Natural causes
>>> printdict(nums)
composite : [4, 6, 8, 9, 10]
fibonacci : [1, 1, 2, 3, 5, 8]
prime : [2, 3, 5, 7]
square : [1, 4, 9]
triangular : [1, 3, 6, 10]
```

Figure 6.4 Much better: one item per line.

Printing a Dictionary

You can use the print statement to print a dictionary.

To print a dictionary:

◆ Type print *d*

  d is a dictionary expression.

Figure 6.3 shows some print results. Not very pretty, are they?

The custom printdict() function in **Script 6.1** prints dictionary items sorted by key in a more readable format than print. I haven't yet covered all constructs used in printdict(), but for now, you don't have to understand the function completely. **Figure 6.4** shows printdict() output. I'll use printdict() in subsequent examples.

continues on next page

✔ Tips

■ printdict() is adequate for purposes of illustration in this chapter, but it doesn't do well with nested dictionaries (**Figure 6.5**).

■ If you're curious about printdict(), functions are covered in Chapter 8, the for statement is covered in "Using *for* Loops" of Chapter 7, and the keys() method is explained in "Getting All of a Dictionary's Keys" later in this chapter.

```
>>> printdict(mydicts)
10051340 : {'composite': [4, 6, 8, 9, 10], 'fibonacci': [1, 1, 2, 3, 5, 8], 'square': [1, 4, 9],
→ 'triangular': [1, 3, 6, 10], 'prime': [2, 3, 5, 7]}

10169412 : {'Qui-Gon Jinn': 'Darth Maul', 'Darth Vader': 'Emperor Palpatine', 'Yoda': 'Natural
→ causes', 'Obi-Wan Kenobi': 'Darth Vader', 'Death Star crew': 'Luke Skywalker', 'Porkins':
→ 'Death Star crew', 'Boba Fett': 'Sarlacc', 'Emperor Palpatine': 'Darth Vader', 'Jabba the Hutt':
→ 'Leia Organa', 'Darth Maul': 'Obi-Wan Kenobi'}
```

Figure 6.5 Oh, well, it's not perfect.

```
>>> killed["Yoda"]
'Natural causes'
>>> a = nums["prime"]
>>> print a[0:2]
[2, 3]
>>> b = mydicts[id(nums)]
>>> printdict(b)
composite : [4, 6, 8, 9, 10]
fibonacci : [1, 1, 2, 3, 5, 8]
prime : [2, 3, 5, 7]
square : [1, 4, 9]
triangular : [1, 3, 6, 10]
>>> killed["Boss Hogg"]
Traceback (most recent call last):
  File "<stdin>", line 1, in ?
KeyError: Boss Hogg
```

Figure 6.6 Dictionary values are retrieved by key.

```
>>> a = nums.get("prime")
>>> print a
[2, 3, 5, 7]
>>> b = nums.get("prime", [])
>>> print b
[2, 3, 5, 7]
>>> c = nums.get("even", [2, 4, 6,
→ 8, 10])
>>> print c
[2, 4, 6, 8, 10]
>>> d = nums.get("even")
>>> print d
None
>>> killed.get("Anakin Skywalker", "")
''
>>> killed[killed.get("Anakin
→ Skywalker", "Darth Vader")]
'Emperor Palpatine'
>>> {}.get("mimetic","")
''
```

Figure 6.7 get() returns a default value if the key doesn't exist.

Getting a Value by Using a Key

You can use a value's associated key to retrieve it from a dictionary.

To get a value by using a key:

◆ Type *d*[*key*]

d is a dictionary expression, and *key* is an expression that corresponds to the value's key. If *key* doesn't appear in *d*, Python raises a KeyError exception (**Figure 6.6**).

The get() method returns a specified default value instead of raising an exception if a key doesn't appear in a dictionary.

To get a value by using a key or a default value (if the key doesn't exist):

◆ Type *d*.get(*key* [,*default_value*])

d is a dictionary expression, *key* is an expression that corresponds to the value's key, and *default_value* is an expression. If *key* doesn't appear in *d*, *default_value* is returned. If *key* doesn't appear in *d* and *default_value* is omitted, None is returned (**Figure 6.7**).

The setdefault() method behaves like get(), except that it also adds the default value (with *key*) to the dictionary if the key doesn't exist.

To get a value by using a key, or to get and insert a default value if the key doesn't exist:

◆ Type d.setdefault(*key* [,*default_value*])

   d is a dictionary expression, *key* is an expression that corresponds to the value's key, and *default_value* is an expression. If *key* doesn't appear in *d*, *default_value* is returned and added (with *key*) to *d* as a new item. If *key* doesn't appear in *d* and *default_value* is omitted, None is returned and added (with *key*) to *d* as a new item (**Figure 6.8**).

✔ Tips

■ Keys are case-sensitive.

■ You can get a value by its key, but not vice versa.

■ Getting a value with *d*[*key*] or get() doesn't change the dictionary, whereas setdefault() may add an item to the dictionary.

■ **NEW** Python 2.0 introduced setdefault().

■ **LANG** Perl uses $hash{key} to get hash values.

Figure 6.8 *continued*

```
>>> z = {}
>>> z.setdefault("mimetic","")
''
>>> z
{'mimetic': ''}
```

Figure 6.8 setdefault() returns a default value if the key doesn't exist *and* inserts a new item into the dictionary.

```
>>> a = killed.setdefault
→ ("Radio star", "Video")
>>> b = killed.get("Anakin
→ Skywalker", "Darth Vader")
>>> print a
Radio star
>>> print b
Darth Vader
>>> printdict(killed)
Boba Fett : Sarlacc
Darth Maul : Obi-Wan Kenobi
Darth Vader : Emperor Palpatine
Death Star crew : Luke Skywalker
Emperor Palpatine : Darth Vader
Jabba the Hutt : Leia Organa
Obi-Wan Kenobi : Darth Vader
Porkins : Death Star crew
Qui-Gon Jinn : Darth Maul
Radio star : Video
Yoda : Natural causes
>>> c = nums.setdefault("even",
→ [2, 4, 6, 8, 10])
>>> d = nums.setdefault("imaginary")
>>> e = nums.setdefault("prime", [])
>>> print c
[2, 4, 6, 8, 10]
>>> print d
None
>>> print e
[2, 3, 5, 7]
>>> printdict(nums)
composite : [4, 6, 8, 9, 10]
even : [2, 4, 6, 8, 10]
fibonacci : [1, 1, 2, 3, 5, 8]
imaginary : None
prime : [2, 3, 5, 7]
square : [1, 4, 9]
triangular : [1, 3, 6, 10]
```

(figure continues at left)

```
>>> a = killed.values()

>>> print a

['Darth Maul', 'Emperor Palpatine', 'Natural
→ causes', 'Darth Vader', 'Luke Skywalker',
→ 'Death Star crew', 'Sarlacc', 'Darth Vader',
→ 'Leia Organa', 'Obi-Wan Kenobi']

>>> nums.values()

[[4, 6, 8, 9, 10], [1, 1, 2, 3, 5, 8], [1, 4, 9],
→ [1, 3, 6, 10], [2, 3, 5, 7]]

>>> mydicts.values()

[{'composite': [4, 6, 8, 9, 10], 'fibonacci':
→ [1, 1, 2, 3, 5, 8], 'square': [1, 4, 9],
→ 'triangular': [1, 3, 6, 10], 'prime':
→ [2, 3, 5, 7]}, {'Qui-Gon Jinn': 'Darth Maul',
→ 'Darth Vader': 'Emperor Palpatine', 'Yoda':
→ 'Natural causes', 'Obi-Wan Kenobi': 'Darth
→ Vader', 'Death Star crew': 'Luke Skywalker',
→ 'Porkins': 'Death Star crew', 'Boba Fett':
→ 'Sarlacc', 'Emperor Palpatine': 'Darth
→ Vader', 'Jabba the Hutt': 'Leia Organa',
→ 'Darth Maul': 'Obi-Wan Kenobi'}]

>>> print mydicts[id(nums)].values()

[[4, 6, 8, 9, 10], [1, 1, 2, 3, 5, 8], [1, 4, 9],
→ [1, 3, 6, 10], [2, 3, 5, 7]]

>>> {}.values()

[]
```

Figure 6.9 values() places all of a dictionary's values in a list in random order.

Getting All of a Dictionary's Values

You can use the values() method to create a list containing all of a dictionary's keys.

To get all of a dictionary's values:

◆ Type *d*.values() to place the values in a list.

d is a dictionary expression (**Figure 6.9**).

✔ Tips

■ Values are listed in random order.

■ To sort the values, see "Sorting a Dictionary" later in this chapter.

■ Getting a value doesn't change a dictionary.

■ You can get all of a dictionary's keys with the keys() method; see "Getting All of a Dictionary's Keys" later in this chapter. If you call values() and keys() without any intervening dictionary changes, their list items correspond directly.

■ keys() is used more often than values() in real programs.

■ **LANG** Perl uses values(%hash) to get all of a hash's values. Python can't retrieve a partial list of values, as Perl can with @hash{key1, key2,...}.

Getting All of a Dictionary's Keys

You can use the keys() method to create a list containing all of a dictionary's keys.

To get all of a dictionary's keys:

◆ Type d.keys() to place the keys in a list. *d* is a dictionary expression (**Figure 6.10**).

✔ Tips

■ Keys are listed in random order.

■ To sort the keys, see "Sorting a Dictionary" later in this chapter.

■ Getting a key doesn't change a dictionary.

■ You can get all of a dictionary's values with the values() method; see "Getting All of a Dictionary's Values" earlier in this chapter. If you call values() and keys() without any intervening dictionary changes, their list items correspond directly.

■ **LANG** Perl uses keys(%hash) to get all of a hash's keys.

```
>>> a = killed.keys()
>>> print a
['Qui-Gon Jinn', 'Darth Vader', 'Yoda',
→ 'Obi-Wan Kenobi', 'Death Star crew',
→ 'Porkins', 'Boba Fett', 'Emperor Palpatine',
→ 'Jabba the Hutt', 'Darth Maul']
>>> nums.keys()
['composite', 'fibonacci', 'square',
→ 'triangular', 'prime']
>>> mydicts.keys()
[10117868, 10161660]
>>> print mydicts[id(nums)].keys()
['composite', 'fibonacci', 'square',
→ 'triangular', 'prime']
>>> {}.keys()
[]
```

Figure 6.10 You can iterate through a key list to retrieve all of a dictionary's values.

```
>>> a = killed.items()

>>> print a

[('Qui-Gon Jinn', 'Darth Maul'), ('Darth Vader',
→ 'Emperor Palpatine'), ('Yoda', 'Natural
→ causes'), ('Obi-Wan Kenobi', 'Darth Vader'),
→ ('Death Star crew', 'Luke Skywalker'),
→ ('Porkins', 'Death Star crew'), ('Boba Fett',
→ 'Sarlacc'), ('Emperor Palpatine', 'Darth
→ Vader'), ('Jabba the Hutt', 'Leia Organa'),
→ ('Darth Maul', 'Obi-Wan Kenobi')]

>>> nums.items()

[('composite', [4, 6, 8, 9, 10]), ('fibonacci',
→ [1, 1, 2, 3, 5, 8]), ('square', [1, 4, 9]),
→ ('triangular', [1, 3, 6, 10]), ('prime',
→ [2, 3, 5, 7])]

>>> mydicts.items()

[(10117868, {'composite': [4, 6, 8, 9, 10],
→ 'fibonacci': [1, 1, 2, 3, 5, 8], 'square':
→ [1, 4, 9], 'triangular': [1, 3, 6, 10],
→ 'prime': [2, 3, 5, 7]}), (10161660,
→ {'Qui-Gon Jinn': 'Darth Maul', 'Darth Vader':
→ 'Emperor Palpatine', 'Yoda': 'Natural causes',
→ 'Obi-Wan Kenobi': 'Darth Vader', 'Death
→ Star crew': 'Luke Skywalker', 'Porkins':
→ 'Death Star crew', 'Boba Fett': 'Sarlacc',
→ 'Emperor Palpatine': 'Darth Vader', 'Jabba
→ the Hutt': 'Leia Organa', 'Darth Maul':
→ 'Obi-Wan Kenobi'})]

>>> print mydicts[id(nums)].items()

[('composite', [4, 6, 8, 9, 10]), ('fibonacci',
→ [1, 1, 2, 3, 5, 8]), ('square', [1, 4, 9]),
→ ('triangular', [1, 3, 6, 10]), ('prime',
→ [2, 3, 5, 7])]

>>> {}.items()

[]
```

Figure 6.11 Each key-value pair is a two-item tuple in the list.

Getting All of a Dictionary's Key-Value Pairs

You can use the items() method to create a list containing all of a dictionary's key-value pairs.

To get all of a dictionary's key-value pairs:

◆ Type *d*.items() to place the key-value pairs in a list of two-item tuples, in which the first tuple item is the key and the second is the value.

   d is a dictionary expression (**Figure 6.11**).

✔ Tips

■ Key-value pairs are listed in random order.

■ To sort the key-value pairs, see "Sorting a Dictionary" later in this chapter.

■ Getting a key-value pair doesn't change a dictionary.

■ You can get all of a dictionary's values with the values() method and keys with the keys() method; see "Getting All of a Dictionary's Values" and "Getting All of a Dictionary's Keys" earlier in this chapter.

■ **LANG** You can use Perl's each and foreach functions to get all of a hash's pairs.

Determining Whether a Key Exists

The has_key() method checks to see whether a key exists in a dictionary.

To determine whether a key exists in a dictionary:

◆ Type *d*.has_key(*key*) to return 1 (true) if *key* appears in *d*, or 0 (false) otherwise.

d is a dictionary expression, and *key* is an expression (**Figure 6.12**).

✔ Tips

■ Keys are case-sensitive.

■ To find a key in a nested dictionary, refer directly to the nested dictionary by its key.

■ You can get all of a dictionary's keys with the keys() method; see "Getting All of a Dictionary's Keys" earlier in this chapter.

■ has_key() usually is used as a test condition in an if statement; see "Using If Conditionals" in Chapter 7.

■ **LANG** Perl uses exists %hash{key} to determine whether a hash key exists.

```
>>> nums.has_key("even")
0
>>> nums.has_key("prime")
1
>>> {}.has_key("")
0
>>> killed.has_key("Boss Hogg")
0
>>> def report(victim):
...    if killed.has_key(victim):
...       print killed[victim],
→ "killed", victim
...    else:
...       print victim, "is not dead"
...
>>> report("Han Solo")
Han Solo is not dead
>>> report("Darth Maul")
Obi-Wan Kenobi killed Darth Maul
```

Figure 6.12 has_key() usually is used as an if condition.

```
>>> len({})
0
>>> len(killed)
10
>>> len(nums)
5
>>> len(mydicts)
2
>>> len(mydicts[id(killed)])
10
>>> len(mydicts[id(nums)])
5
```

Figure 6.13 len() counts the number of key-value pairs in a dictionary.

Counting a Dictionary's Key-Value Pairs

The len() function counts the number of key-value pairs in a dictionary.

To count the number of key-value pairs in a dictionary:

◆ Type len(*d*)

d is a dictionary expression (**Figure 6.13**).

✔ Tips

■ len() also counts characters in strings and items in lists in tuples.

■ To count items in a nested dictionary, refer directly to the nested dictionary by its key.

■ **LANG** Perl uses scalar keys %hash to count hash pairs.

Adding or Replacing a Key-Value Pair

You can add a new key-value pair or replace an existing one by assigning a value to a specified dictionary key.

To add or replace a key-value pair:

◆ Type *d*[*key*] = *value* to add a new key-value pair if *key* doesn't appear in *d* or replace an existing pair if it does.

  d is a dictionary expression, *value* is an expression, and *key* is an expression that corresponds to *value*'s key (**Figure 6.14**).

✔ Tips

■ Keys are case-sensitive.

■ Python won't warn you when you're replacing an item rather than adding one. You can use has_key() to determine whether a key exists; see "Determining Whether a Key Exists" earlier in this chapter.

■ **LANG** Perl uses $hash{key} = value to add or replace hash items (or create new hashes).

```
>>> nums["even"] = [2, 4, 6, 8, 10]
>>> nums["prime"] = []
>>> nums["square"].append(16)
>>> printdict(nums)
composite : [4, 6, 8, 9, 10]
even : [2, 4, 6, 8, 10]
fibonacci : [1, 1, 2, 3, 5, 8]
prime : []
square : [1, 4, 9, 16]
triangular : [1, 3, 6, 10]
>>> killed["Greedo"] = "Han Solo"
>>> killed["Boba Fett"] = "Han Solo"
>>> printdict(killed)
Boba Fett : Han Solo
Darth Maul : Obi-Wan Kenobi
Darth Vader : Emperor Palpatine
Death Star crew : Luke Skywalker
Emperor Palpatine : Darth Vader
Greedo : Han Solo
Jabba the Hutt : Leia Organa
Obi-Wan Kenobi : Darth Vader
Porkins : Death Star crew
Qui-Gon Jinn : Darth Maul
Yoda : Natural causes
>>> mydicts[id(killed)] = None
>>> printdict(mydicts)
8148564 : {'composite': [4, 6, 8, 9, 10],
→ 'fibonacci': [1, 1, 2, 3, 5, 8], 'square':
→ [1, 4, 9], 'triangular': [1, 3, 6, 10],
→ 'prime': [2, 3, 5, 7]}
8337852 : None
```

Figure 6.14 Specifying a new key adds a new item. Specifying an existing key overwrites the existing value.

```
>>> del nums["prime"]
>>> printdict(nums)
composite : [4, 6, 8, 9, 10]
fibonacci : [1, 1, 2, 3, 5, 8]
square : [1, 4, 9]
triangular : [1, 3, 6, 10]
>>> del mydicts[id(nums)]["square"]
>>> printdict(mydicts[id(nums)])
composite : [4, 6, 8, 9, 10]
fibonacci : [1, 1, 2, 3, 5, 8]
triangular : [1, 3, 6, 10]
>>> del mydicts[id(nums)],
→ mydicts[id(killed)]
>>> print mydicts
{}
>>> del killed["Boss Hogg"]
Traceback (most recent call last):
  File "<stdin>", line 1, in ?
KeyError: Boss Hogg
>>> del nums["fibonacci"],
→ killed["Yoda"]
>>> printdict(nums)
composite : [4, 6, 8, 9, 10]
triangular : [1, 3, 6, 10]
>>> killed.keys()
['Qui-Gon Jinn', 'Darth Vader', 'Obi-Wan
→ Kenobi', 'Death Star crew', 'Porkins',
→ 'Boba Fett', 'Emperor Palpatine', 'Jabba
→ the Hutt', 'Darth Maul']
```

Figure 6.15 One del statement can delete items in multiple dictionaries.

Removing a Key-Value Pair

You can use the del statement to delete one or more key-value pairs from one or more dictionaries. See **Figure 6.15** for some examples.

To remove a key-value pair:

◆ Type del *d[key]* to remove the key-value pair identified by *key* from *d*.

d is a dictionary expression and *key* is an expression.

To remove multiple key-value pairs:

◆ Type del *d1[key1]*, *d2[key2]*, . . .

d1[key1], *d2[key2]*,.... are one or more comma-separated dictionary items identified by the keys *key1, key2,....* The dictionary expressions *d1, d2,...* may represent different dictionaries.

✔ Tips

■ Keys are case-sensitive.

■ Python raises a KeyError exception if a key doesn't appear in a dictionary.

■ To remove all of the key-value pairs from a dictionary, see "Clearing or Deleting a Dictionary" later in this chapter.

■ **LANG** Perl uses delete $hash{key} to delete hash items.

Removing a Random Key-Value Pair

You can use the popitem() method to delete an arbitrary key-value pair from a dictionary. popitem() returns the item it deletes.

To remove and return a random key-value pair:

◆ Type *d*.popitem()

Python places the removed item in a two-item tuple in which the first item is the key and the second is the value.

d is a dictionary expression (**Figure 6.16**).

✔ Tips

■ To remove all of the key-value pairs from a dictionary, see "Clearing or Deleting a Dictionary" later in this chapter.

■ Python raises a KeyError exception if the dictionary is empty.

■ For technical types: popitem() can be used for (exhaustive) destructive iteration.

■ ◆NEW◆ Python 2.1 introduced popitem().

```
>>> {}.popitem()
Traceback (most recent call last):
  File "<stdin>", line 1, in ?
KeyError: popitem(): dictionary is empty
>>> a = killed.popitem()
>>> print a
('Qui-Gon Jinn', 'Darth Maul')
>>> killed.popitem()
('Darth Vader', 'Emperor Palpatine')
>>> killed.popitem()
('Yoda', 'Natural causes')
>>> print killed.keys()
['Obi-Wan Kenobi', 'Death Star crew', 'Porkins',
→ 'Boba Fett', 'Emperor Palpatine', 'Jabba
→ the Hutt', 'Darth Maul']
>>> b = mydicts[id(nums)].popitem()
>>> print b
('composite', [4, 6, 8, 9, 10])
>>> printdict(nums)
fibonacci : [1, 1, 2, 3, 5, 8]
prime : [2, 3, 5, 7]
square : [1, 4, 9]
triangular : [1, 3, 6, 10]
>>> while nums:
...    print nums.popitem()[0].
→ capitalize()
...
Fibonacci
Square
Triangular
Prime
>>> print nums
{}
```

Figure 6.16 popitem() can be used for random sampling without replacement.

```
>>> z = {}
>>> z.clear()
>>> print z
{}
>>> mydicts.clear()
>>> print mydicts
{}
>>> printdict(nums)
composite : [4, 6, 8, 9, 10]
fibonacci : [1, 1, 2, 3, 5, 8]
prime : [2, 3, 5, 7]
square : [1, 4, 9]
triangular : [1, 3, 6, 10]
>>> nums.clear()
>>> print nums
{}
>>> del killed
>>> print killed
Traceback (most recent call last):
  File "<stdin>", line 1, in ?
NameError: name 'killed' is not defined
```

Figure 6.17 Clearing (or deleting) mydicts doesn't affect its nested dictionaries; you must clear (or delete) them explicitly.

Clearing or Deleting a Dictionary

You can use the clear() method to delete all key-value pairs from a dictionary. Clearing a dictionary doesn't delete it but leaves an empty dictionary ({}). Use del to delete a dictionary altogether. See **Figure 6.17** for some examples.

To clear a dictionary:

◆ Type *d*.clear()
  d is a dictionary expression.

To delete a dictionary:

◆ Type del *d*
  d is a dictionary expression.

✔ Tips

■ clear() does its work as a side effect and returns None, so don't assign its result to a variable. Type this:

  d.clear()

  and not this:

  d = d.clear() # Wrong

  For information about side effects, see "Creating Expression Statements" in Chapter 2.

■ **LANG** Perl uses undef %hash to clear a hash. You also can use a foreach loop to clear a hash (inefficiently).

Combining Dictionaries

You can use the update() method to merge the key-value pairs of two dictionaries.

To combine two dictionaries:

◆ Type *d1*.update(*d2*) to update *d1* with all the key-value pairs of *d2*. If *d1* and *d2* contain matching keys, the *d2* items prevail.

d1 and *d2* are dictionary expressions (**Figure 6.18**).

✔ Tips

■ Keys are case-sensitive.

■ Updating doesn't change the second dictionary (*d2*).

■ update() does its work as a side effect and returns None, so don't assign its result to a variable. Type this:

d1.update(d2)

and not this:

d1 = d1.update(d2)   # Wrong

For information about side effects, see "Creating Expression Statements" in Chapter 2.

■ d1.update(d2) is equivalent to:

for key in d2.keys():
    d1[key] = d2[key]

■ **LANG** Perl uses ($hash1, $hash2) to merge hashes.

```
>>> odds = [1, 3, 5, 7, 9]
>>> evens = [2, 4, 6, 8, 10]
>>> new_nums = {
...   "odd": odds,
...   "even": evens
... }
>>> nums.update(new_nums)
>>> printdict(nums)
composite : [4, 6, 8, 9, 10]
even : [2, 4, 6, 8, 10]
fibonacci : [1, 1, 2, 3, 5, 8]
odd : [1, 3, 5, 7, 9]
prime : [2, 3, 5, 7]
square : [1, 4, 9]
triangular : [1, 3, 6, 10]
>>> updated_killers = {
...   "Boba Fett": "Digestion",
...   "Darth Maul": "Bisection",
...   "Darth Vader": "Patricide",
...   "Death Star crew":
→ "Atomization",
...   "Emperor Palpatine":
→ "Overconfidence",
...   "Jabba the Hutt": "Asphyxia",
...   "Obi-Wan Kenobi": "Just gave up",
...   "Porkins": "Incompetence",
...   "Qui-Gon Jinn": "Exhaustion",
...   "Yoda": "George Lucas"
... }
>>> killed.update(updated_killers)
>>> printdict(killed)
Boba Fett : Digestion
Darth Maul : Bisection
Darth Vader : Patricide
Death Star crew : Atomization
Emperor Palpatine : Overconfidence
Jabba the Hutt : Asphyxia
Obi-Wan Kenobi : Just gave up
Porkins : Incompetence
Qui-Gon Jinn : Exhaustion
Yoda : George Lucas
```

Figure 6.18 Here, I've used update() to add new items to nums and update all the items in killed.

COMBINING DICTIONARIES

```
>>> import copy
>>> shallow_nums = nums.copy()
>>> deep_nums = copy.deepcopy(nums)
>>> nums["square"][1] = "SEQUOIA"
>>> printdict(nums)
composite : [4, 6, 8, 9, 10]
fibonacci : [1, 1, 2, 3, 5, 8]
prime : [2, 3, 5, 7]
square : [1, 'SEQUOIA', 9]
triangular : [1, 3, 6, 10]
>>> print shallow_nums["square"]
[1, 'SEQUOIA', 9]
>>> print deep_nums["square"]
[1, 4, 9]
>>> shallow_killed = killed.copy()
>>> deep_killed =
↪ copy.deepcopy(killed)
>>> killed["Darth Vader"] =
↪ "Karoshi"
>>> print killed["Darth Vader"]
Karoshi
>>> print shallow_killed["Darth
↪ Vader"]
Emperor Palpatine
>>> print deep_killed["Darth Vader"]
Emperor Palpatine
```

Figure 6.19 The in-place change to the (mutable) list in nums appears in the shallow copy but not the deep one. The changed value in killed doesn't appear in either copy because immutable objects (such as strings) are always copied, not referenced.

Copying a Dictionary

"Copying a List or Tuple" in Chapter 5 explains the difference between shallow and deep copies. To summarize, a shallow copy may contain references to objects in the original, whereas a deep copy contains only copies of all the objects in the original. A shallow copy will change if a shared object is modified in the original (and vice versa). A deep copy won't change because the original and the copy are mutually independent. You may want to make a deep copy if any of your dictionary's values is a nested dictionary or list. If your dictionary contains only immutable values (numbers, strings, or tuples), a shallow copy will do.

You can use the copy() method to make a shallow copy of a dictionary. To make a deep copy, use the deepcopy() function in the copy module. **Figure 6.19** shows some examples.

To create a shallow copy of a dictionary:

◆ Type *d2* = *d1*.copy() to make a copy of the dictionary *d1* and assign it to the variable *d2*.

To create a deep copy of a dictionary:

◆ Type these statements:

import copy

d2 = copy.deepcopy(*d1*)

d1 is the dictionary you want to copy, and *d2* is the variable assigned the copy.

✔ Tip

■ The copy module also contains the copy() function to make a shallow copy of an object. This statement:

d2 = copy.copy(d1)

is equivalent to this one:

d2 = d1.copy()

Converting a Dictionary

Dictionary conversions are more limited than conversions of other data types. You can convert an entire dictionary to a string by using the str() and repr() functions; see "Converting Strings" in Chapter 4. You can't convert a string back to a dictionary.

To convert a dictionary to a string:

◆ Type str(*d*)

or

Type repr(*d*)

or

Type `` `d` ``

(Note the backquotes; a backquoted expression is equivalent to repr(*d*).)

d is a dictionary expression (**Figure 6.20**).

Normally, you won't want to convert an entire dictionary, but only its keys or values (either individually or as a group). As you saw earlier in this chapter, the keys(), values(), and items() methods convert all of a dictionary's keys, values, or key-value pairs to lists. You can convert these lists (or their individual items) to other data types by using the conversion functions described in "Converting..." sections of Chapters 3, 4, and 5.

✔ Tips

■ To convert a single dictionary value, use *d*[*key*] as a conversion-function argument.

■ The list() and tuple() functions can't convert entire dictionaries because they take only sequences (strings, lists, and tuples) as arguments.

```
>>> a = str(killed)
>>> print a
{'Qui-Gon Jinn': 'Darth Maul', 'Darth Vader':
→ 'Emperor Palpatine', 'Yoda': 'Natural causes',
→ 'Obi-Wan Kenobi': 'Darth Vader', 'Death
→ Star crew': 'Luke Skywalker', 'Porkins':
→ 'Death Star crew', 'Boba Fett': 'Sarlacc',
→ 'Emperor Palpatine': 'Darth Vader', 'Jabba
→ the Hutt': 'Leia Organa', 'Darth Maul':
→ 'Obi-Wan Kenobi'}
```

```
>>> repr(nums)
"{'composite': [4, 6, 8, 9, 10], 'fibonacci':
→ [1, 1, 2, 3, 5, 8], 'square': [1, 4, 9],
→ 'triangular': [1, 3, 6, 10], 'prime':
→ [2, 3, 5, 7]}"
```

```
>>> print `mydicts`
{10487580: {'composite': [4, 6, 8, 9, 10],
→ 'fibonacci': [1, 1, 2, 3, 5, 8], 'square':
→ [1, 4, 9], 'triangular': [1, 3, 6, 10],
→ 'prime': [2, 3, 5, 7]}, 10491348: {'Qui-Gon
→ Jinn': 'Darth Maul', 'Darth Vader': 'Emperor
→ Palpatine', 'Yoda': 'Natural causes',
→ 'Obi-Wan Kenobi': 'Darth Vader', 'Death
→ Star crew': 'Luke Skywalker', 'Porkins':
→ 'Death Star crew', 'Boba Fett': 'Sarlacc',
→ 'Emperor Palpatine': 'Darth Vader', 'Jabba
→ the Hutt': 'Leia Organa', 'Darth Maul':
→ 'Obi-Wan Kenobi'}}
```

Figure 6.20 String representations of dictionaries.

```
>>> import copy
>>> nums2 = copy.deepcopy(nums)
>>> nums == nums2
1
>>> nums.popitem()
('composite', [4, 6, 8, 9, 10])
>>> nums != nums2
1
>>> del nums2["composite"]
>>> nums == nums2
1
>>> nums["prime"][-1] = 97
>>> printdict(nums)
fibonacci : [1, 1, 2, 3, 5, 8]
prime : [2, 3, 5, 97]
square : [1, 4, 9]
triangular : [1, 3, 6, 10]
>>> nums > nums2
1
>>> nums.clear()
>>> nums2.clear()
>>> nums == nums2 == {}
1
```

Figure 6.21 Python compares dictionaries by their sorted key-value pairs.

Comparing Dictionaries

You can compare dictionaries by using the comparison operators introduced in "Using Comparison Operators" in Chapter 2. In practice, you'll want only to know whether two dictionaries are equivalent, that is, whether they have equivalent values stored under equivalent keys. The == operator determines equivalence. Comparisons return 1 (true) or 0 (false).

To compare dictionaries:

◆ Type *d1 op d2*

d1 and *d2* are two dictionary expressions, and *op* is the <, <=, >, >=, ==, or != operator (**Figure 6.21**).

Python compares dictionaries by comparing their sorted key-value pairs. To determine whether a dictionary is "less" than another, Python first sorts both dictionaries by key and compares their initial items. If the items are have different values, Python determines the truth of the comparison; otherwise, it compares the second items, and so on. If the compared items are the same object type, Python uses the comparison rules described in the "Comparing..." sections of Chapters 3, 4, and 5. Numbers are compared arithmetically, for example, and strings are compared lexicographically. Objects of different types always compare unequally.

continues on next page

COMPARING DICTIONARIES

✔ Tips

- Comparing dictionaries is computationally expensive because Python must sort the dictionaries first.

- Dictionary comparisons can be chained. The expression d1 < d2 != d3, for example, is legal; see "Chaining Comparisons" in Chapter 2.

- The == operator tests value equivalence, and the is operator tests object identity (**Figure 6.22**). For information about the is operator, see "Using Comparison Operators" in Chapter 2.

- The max() and min() functions don't work with dictionaries.

```
>>> gene1 = {
...    "OAT": "Gyrate atrophy",
...    "PAH": "Phenylketonuria"
...    }
>>> gene2 = {
...    "OAT": "Gyrate atrophy",
...    "PAH": "Phenylketonuria"
...    }
>>> gene1 == gene2
1
>>> gene1 is gene2
0
```

Figure 6.22 These two dictionaries have the same value but are separate objects.

```
>>> keys = killed.keys()

>>> print keys

['Qui-Gon Jinn', 'Darth Vader', 'Yoda',
→ 'Obi-Wan Kenobi', 'Death Star crew',
→ 'Porkins', 'Boba Fett', 'Emperor Palpatine',
→ 'Jabba the Hutt', 'Darth Maul']

>>> keys.sort()

>>> print keys

['Boba Fett', 'Darth Maul', 'Darth Vader',
→ 'Death Star crew', 'Emperor Palpatine',
→ 'Jabba the Hutt', 'Obi-Wan Kenobi', 'Porkins',
→ 'Qui-Gon Jinn', 'Yoda']

>>> nums_keys = nums.keys()

>>> nums_keys.sort()

>>> nums_keys.reverse()

>>> for key in nums_keys:

...    nums[key].reverse()

...    print key, ":", nums[key]

...

triangular : [10, 6, 3, 1]

square : [9, 4, 1]

prime : [7, 5, 3, 2]

fibonacci : [8, 5, 3, 2, 1, 1]

composite : [10, 9, 8, 6, 4]
```

Figure 6.23 Sorting a dictionary's keys in ascending and descending order.

Sorting a Dictionary

Dictionary items have no inherent order, and you can't control the order in which they're stored. Wanting to sort items by key is common, however. The printdict() function (refer to Script 6.1), for example, prints dictionary items sorted by key. You can retrieve a list of unsorted keys with the keys() method and then sort them with the sort() method.

To sort a dictionary's keys:

1. Type *keys* = *d*.keys() to store a list of a dictionary's keys in the variable *keys*. *d* is a dictionary expression.

2. Type *keys*.sort() to sort *keys* in ascending order.

3. Optionally, type *keys*.reverse() to sort *keys* in descending order (**Figure 6.23**).

✔ Tips

■ The sort() and reverse() methods are covered in "Sorting a List" and "Reversing a List" in Chapter 5. The comparison rules used for sorting objects are described in the "Comparing..." sections Chapters 3, 4, and 5.

■ You can also sort a dictionary's values or items by using values() or items() instead of keys() in step 1 of the preceding exercise. (An items() sort and a keys() sort yield the same sort order.)

■ To sort a list by using a custom sort order (a case-insensitive sort, for example), see "Defining a Custom List Sort Order" in Chapter 5.

■ **LANG** Perl uses sort(keys(%hash)) to sort a hash's keys.

Storing Computed Values in a Dictionary

This section uses some of the control statements covered in Chapter 7. A common Python technique is to use a dictionary to stockpile earlier results for fast retrieval. These memorized values are called *hints* or *memos*. This section shows you how to use dictionary in a function to avoid repeated calculations.

A prime number has no factors besides 1 and itself. The isprime() function (**Script 6.2**) returns 1 if n is prime, and 0 otherwise. If you run a few test cases, you'll notice that isprime() runs more slowly as n increases.

The isprime2() function (**Script 6.3**) performs the same calculations as isprime() but uses a dictionary to store previous results. The following steps refer to Script 6.3.

To store results in a dictionary:

1. `storage = {}`

   This statement creates an empty dictionary that will be used to store each result. This dictionary doesn't have to start out empty; you can add precomputed values.

2. `if storage.has_key(n):`
   `    return storage[n]`

   These statements determine whether you've already run isprime2() with the current value of n. If so, Python looks up the result, returns it, and quits.

3. `else:`

   The else clause takes over if the result for the current n wasn't in storage.

Script 6.2 The isprime() function determines whether its argument is prime.

```
def isprime(n):
  "Returns 1 if n is prime; 0 otherwise"
  count = n / 2
  while count > 1:
    if n % count == 0:
      return 0
    count -= 1
  return 1
```

Script 6.3 The isprime2() function returns the same result as isprime(), except that it stores previous results in a lookup dictionary for subsequent function calls.

```
storage = {}
def isprime2(n):
  "Returns 1 if n is prime; 0 otherwise"
  if storage.has_key(n):
    return storage[n]
  else:
    result = 1
    count = n / 2
    while count > 1:
      if n % count == 0:
        result = 0
      count -= 1
  storage[n] = result
  return result
```

```
>>> a = 2760727302517L
>>> isprime(a)  # 17.1 secs.
1
>>> isprime(a)  # 17.2 secs.
1
>>> isprime(a)  # 17.2 secs.
1
>>> isprime2(a)  # 17.2 secs.
1
>>> isprime2(a)  # <0.01 secs.
1
>>> isprime2(a)  # <0.01 secs.
1
```

Figure 6.24 Functions that use a dictionary to store earlier results run repeated calculations very fast.

4. ```
   result = 1
   count = n / 2
   while count > 1:
       if n % count == 0:
           result = 0
       count -= 1
   ```

   These statements replicate the time-consuming mathematical calculations in the original isprime() function.

5. `storage[n] = result`

   This statement adds the new result to the dictionary. This result will now be available for subsequent isprime2() function calls.

6. `return result`

   This statement returns the result of the calculations.

Figure 6.24 shows comparison runs and execution times for isprime() and isprime2(). All runs were for the same value of n. As expected, the three isprime() executions all took about the same time. The first isprime2() run took as long as isprime(), but subsequent runs were extremely fast thanks to dictionary lookup.

continues on next page

STORING COMPUTED VALUES IN A DICTIONARY
   ```

Figure 6.25 shows the dictionary after a few
isprime2() executions.

✔ Tips

■ This storage technique usually is used in
functions that are computationally intensive, recursive, or generally called with
limited combinations of arguments.

■ If a function has multiple arguments,
pass them as a tuple, as in this example:

```
if storage.has_key((x, y, z)):
        return storage[(x, y, z)]
```

```
>>> storage = {}
>>> print isprime2(1), isprime2(2)
1 1
>>> print isprime2(9), isprime2(10)
0 0
>>> import random
>>> for i in range(10):
...     temp = isprime2(int(random.
→ random() * 1000))
...
>>> isprime2(2760727302517L)
1
>>> printdict(storage)
1 : 1
2 : 1
9 : 0
10 : 0
90 : 0
99 : 0
274 : 0
287 : 0
330 : 0
373 : 1
566 : 0
662 : 0
819 : 0
916 : 0
2760727302517 : 1
```

Figure 6.25 The storage dictionary accumulates results
over multiple function executions.

CONTROL FLOW STATEMENTS

When the interpreter runs your program, it may execute statements in perfect sequence, skip statements, repeat others, or jump forward or back to still others. *Control flow* is the execution sequence of statements in your program, and you determine this flow with *control flow statements* (and with input data, but I'm not discussing that topic in this chapter.) The control flow statements if, while, and for use Boolean conditions or iteration to determine whether Python executes a series of statements.

The if statement is called a *conditional statement* because it executes a block of code based on whether a specified condition prevails.

The while and for statements are called *loops* or *iterative statements* because they repeat a block of code a specified number of times or until a particular condition becomes false.

This chapter also covers Python's line structure and loop control statements.

Note that try is a control flow statement too; I cover try in Chapter 11.

Splitting Statements Across Lines

A Python statement is terminated by a return (or newline), but long lines of code are difficult to read if you need to scroll horizontally to see the entire line. In "Creating a String" in Chapter 4, you saw that a triple-quoted string can be split over several lines. Python also allows you to split a single statement across two or more lines by using explicit or implicit line joining. *Explicit line joining* uses the backslash character (\), called the *line-continuation character,* to split lines. *Implicit line joining* allows you to split expressions enclosed in parentheses, brackets, or braces ((), [], or {}) without using a backslash. You can split a line wherever you normally would type white space, except inside a string.

To split a statement explicitly:

◆ Type \ at the end of a line, press Enter, and continue the statement on the next line (**Script 7.1**).

You may split a statement over many lines. When Python joins lines, it ignores the backslash and the return.

To split an expression implicitly:

◆ In an expression surrounded by (), [], or {}, press Enter, and continue the expression on the next line (**Script 7.2**).

You may split an expression over many lines. In Figure 6.1 in Chapter 6, I used implicit line joining to place each dictionary entry on its own line. You can use the same technique with lists and tuples (**Figure 7.1**).

Script 7.1 This script uses the line-continuation character (\) to split the second statement over four lines. I've indented the continuation lines below the first split to make the code easier to read. I like to add a space before the \.

```
year = 2001

leap_year = \
  year % 4 == 0 and \
  year % 100 != 0 or \
  year % 400 == 0
print leap_year
```

Script 7.2 Here's the same script as Script 7.1, except that I've added parentheses and dropped the backslashes. This script is a more elegant way to split a line. Implicit line joining also permits embedded comments.

```
year = 2000

leap_year = (
  year % 4 == 0 and  # Divisible by 4
  year % 100 != 0 or # but not by 100,
  year % 400 == 0)   # or divisible by 400
print leap_year
```

```
>>> days = ["Mon", "Tue",
...          "Wed", "Thu",
...          "Fri", "Sat",
...          "Sun"]
```

Figure 7.1 You can use implicit line joining to enter lists, tuples, dictionaries, and parenthesized expressions neatly.

```
>>> s = "mimetic" \
...      " " \
...      "polyalloy"
>>> s
'mimetic polyalloy'
```

Figure 7.2 Python concatenates string literals split by a backslash.

✔ Tips

■ In practice, implicit line joining mostly has supplanted explicit line joining because you can just add parentheses around the expression that you want to split.

■ A line ending in \ can't contain a trailing comment, but an implicit line join can carry a comment.

■ The indentation of continuation lines doesn't matter, but your code will be easier to read if you indent these lines one level below the initial line.

■ Blank continuation lines are permitted in script mode but not in interactive mode.

■ You can't put \ anywhere in a Python statement except in a string literal. (\ embedded in a string is considered to be part of the string and not a line-continuation character.)

■ You can use \ to join string literals (**Figure 7.2**).

■ You can't use \ to continue a comment.

■ **LANG** In Perl and C, a semicolon (;) terminates a line, so you don't need a line-continuation character.

SPLITTING STATEMENTS ACROSS LINES

Creating Compound Statements

A control flow statement is a *compound statement,* which consists of a header line followed by one or more indented statements:

```
Header:
    Statement1
    Statement2
    ...
    StatementN
```

The *header line* always begins on a new line and ends with a colon. In this chapter, I cover the if, while, and for headers. The header line in **Script 7.3** is while b:.

The group of indented statements is called a *block* or *body* (or sometimes *suite*). The interpreter treats the statements that comprise the block as a single unit. The block in Script 7.3 is the single statement a, b = b, a % b.

In script mode, the next-less-indented (or *dedented*) statement, print a, marks the end of a block but is not part of the block (refer to Script 7.3). In interactive mode, you must enter a blank line to signal the block's end (**Figure 7.3**).

✔ Tips

- Compound statements may contain compound statements (**Script 7.4**).

- In later chapters, you'll see that try statements (Chapter 11), function definitions (Chapter 8), and class definitions (Chapter 12) also are compound statements.

- **LANG** Perl, C, and Java use braces ({}) and Pascal uses keywords (begin/end) to delimit blocks.

Script 7.3 This while loop forms a compound statement with a single-statement block.

```
a, b = 35, 21
while b:
    a, b = b, a % b
print a
```

```
>>> a, b = 35, 21
>>> while b:
...     a, b = b, a % b
... print a
  File "<stdin>", line 3
    print a
        ^
SyntaxError: invalid syntax
>>>
>>> a, b = 35, 21
>>> while b:
...     a, b = b, a % b
...
>>> print a
7
```

Figure 7.3 In interactive mode, Python raises a SyntaxError exception if an unindented statement immediately follows a block. The correct syntax is to end a block with a blank line and then type the unindented statement. (A blank line is unnecessary in script mode.)

Script 7.4 A nested compound statement: The for loop is nested in the if conditional.

```
max = 10
s = range(max + 1)
if len(s):
    sumsq = 0
    for x in s:
        sumsq += x * x
    print sumsq
```

```
>>> x = 11
>>> if x % 2 == 0:
...    print x
... else:
...    pass  # Write this later
...
>>>
```

Figure 7.4 Python requires at least one statement in a block. The do-nothing pass statement can serve as a placeholder for code you haven't written yet.

Using *pass* to Create a Null Statement

Python's grammatical rules require that a block contain at least one statement. Sometimes, you need to create a block that does nothing, either because your logic requires it or (more commonly) because you plan to write the block of code later. You can use the pass statement to create a null statement.

To create a *pass* statement:

◆ Type:

pass

Nothing happens when Python executes a pass statement (**Figure 7.4**).

✔ Tips

■ In later chapters, you'll see that you also can use pass to hold a place in the bodies of functions and classes and to ignore exceptions.

■ **LANG** In Perl, C, and Java, an empty set of braces ({}) or an isolated semi-colon is like pass.

Indenting Blocks of Statements

Python detects the beginning and end of a block by the indentation of its statements: A block comprises statements indented the same distance to the right. You can indent statements with spaces, tabs, or a mix of the two. Your code may not line up correctly if you mix them, however, because:

- Different text editors expand tabs differently, so switching editors may cause alignment problems.

- The interpreter converts tabs internally to the number of spaces needed to indent a line to the next column that's a multiple of 8. A tab at column 12, for example, is converted to enough spaces to indent the line to column 16.

You can use a command-line option to warn you about a space-tab mix (see the tip in this section). The moral is be consistent: Pick either tabs or spaces and stick with them. In this book, I use two spaces for each indentation level to save space. In practice, it's common to use four spaces.

Following are the common indentation errors (with four-space indents to make the examples clearer):

- Indenting the first line of a program (**Figure 7.5**)

- Not indenting the line following a header line (**Figure 7.6**)

- Indenting a statement unexpectedly (**Figure 7.7**)

- Unindenting a statement inconsistently (**Figure 7.8**)

```
>>>     for i in range(10):
  File "<stdin>", line 1
    for i in range(10):

    ^
SyntaxError: invalid syntax
```

Figure 7.5 Start the first line of a program in column 1.

```
>>> x = 11
>>> if x % 2 == 0:
... print x
  File "<stdin>", line 2
    print x
          ^
IndentationError: expected an indented block
```

Figure 7.6 Always indent the line following a compound-statement header line.

```
>>> x = 11
>>>     if x % 2 == 0:
  File "<stdin>", line 1
    if x % 2 == 0:

    ^
SyntaxError: invalid syntax
```

Figure 7.7 Don't indent a line if it doesn't start a new block.

```
>>> x = 10
>>> while x > 0:
...     print x, "\t", x ** 0.5
...   x = x - 1
  File "<stdin>", line 3
    x = x - 1
        ^
IndentationError: unindent does not match
→ any outer indentation level
```

Figure 7.8 The indentation level of the statement x = x - 1 conflicts with the indentation levels of the preceding while and print statements, so the interpreter can't tell which block x = x - 1 belongs to.

Script 7.5 This script, sqroots.py, mixes space and tab indentation. The print statement is indented with a single tab, and the x = x - 1 statement is indented with eight spaces.

```
▓▓▓▓▓▓▓▓▓▓▓▓  script  ▓▓▓▓▓▓▓▓▓▓▓▓
x = 5
while x > 0:
  [tab] print x, "\t", x ** 0.5
........x = x - 1
```

```
E:\scripts>python -t sqroots.py
sqroots.py: inconsistent use of tabs and
→ spaces in indentation
5       2.2360679775
4       2.0
3       1.73205080757
2       1.41421356237
1       1.0


E:\scripts>python -tt sqroots.py
  File "sqroots.py", line 4
    x = x - 1
          ^
TabError: inconsistent use of tabs and spaces
→ in indentation
```

Figure 7.9 When you mix tabs and spaces in a script, the -t option prints a warning and runs the program. The -tt option raises a TabError exception and quits.

✔ Tip

■ You can use the -t and -tt command-line options to detect inconsistent use of tabs and spaces in your programs. The first line of the while block in **Script 7.5** is indented with a tab, and the second line is indented with spaces. **Figure 7.9** shows the result of running the interpreter with the -t option and the -tt option (see "Specifying Command-Line Options" in Chapter 1).

Putting Multiple Statements on a Line

It's good programming style to give each statement its own line, but Python lets you put more than one statement on a line if you separate statements with a semicolon (**Figure 7.10**). You also can move the body of a compound statement to the header line (**Figure 7.11**).

✔ Tips

- These techniques work best with short statements.

- You can't put nested statements on the same line.

- You can terminate a line containing a single statement with a semicolon.

```
>>> x = 5; y = x * x; print x, y
5 25
```

Figure 7.10 You can place multiple statements on a line if you separate the statements with a semicolon.

```
>>> x = 5
>>> while x: print x * x; x -= 1
...
25
16
9
4
1
>>> a = 11
>>> if a % 2: print "a is odd"
... else: print "a is even"
...
a is odd
```

Figure 7.11 A compound statement can occupy a single line.

```
>>> lst = [1, 2, 3]
>>> a = 1
>>> b = 0
>>> if b: print b
...
>>> if a and not b:
...    print a, "is true"
...    print not b, "is true"
...
1 is true
1 is true
>>> if a in lst:
...    print "a in lst"
...    if b in lst:
...       print "b in lst"
...
a in lst
>>> c = a * 3
>>> if c in lst:
...    if c % 2 != 0:
...       print c, "is odd"
...
3 is odd
>>> if (a > b) and (a in lst):
...    print (a > b), (a in lst)
...
1 1
>>> if lst:
...    x = len(lst)
...    if x in lst:
...       print x, "is in", lst
...
3 is in [1, 2, 3]
>>> if not ("" or 0 or [] or () or
→ {} or None):
...    print "All false"
...
All false
```

Figure 7.12 The if block executes if its condition is true.

Using *if* Conditionals

The if conditional executes a block of state-ments if a condition is true.

To create an *if* conditional:

◆ Type:

if *condition*:

   block

condition is evaluated. If it's true, *block* is executed (**Figure 7.12**).

block is an indented block of statements, and *condition* is a Boolean expression (see "Using Boolean Operators" in Chapter 2).

✔ Tips

■ I call conditions *Boolean expressions* to emphasize that they are evaluated as true or false. In fact, every expression (that is, every object) has a truth value (see Table 2.4 in Chapter 2).

■ You can nest if statements.

■ You can use if-else to execute code if the condition is false; see "Using *if-else* Conditionals" later in this chapter.

■ You can use if-elif-else to choose among several conditions; see "Using *if-elif-else* Conditionals" later in this chapter.

■ **LANG** Perl, C, and Java have an if con-ditional. Parentheses around the if condition are required in Perl, C, and Java but are optional in Python.

Using *if-else* Conditionals

You can add an else clause to an if statement to execute a block of statements if the condition is false.

To create an *if-else* conditional:

◆ Type:

```
if condition:
  block1
else:
  block2
```

condition is evaluated. If it's true, *block1* is executed; otherwise, *block2* is executed (**Figure 7.13**).

block1 and *block2* are indented blocks of statements, and *condition* is a Boolean expression (see "Using Boolean Operators" in Chapter 2).

✔ Tips

■ You can use if-elif-else to choose among several conditions (see "Using *if-elif-else* Conditionals" later in this chapter).

■ **LANG** Perl, C, and Java support an else clause. Python does not support the C and Java ternary operator ? :.

```
>>> a = 11
>>> if a % 2 == 0:
...     print a, "is even"
... else:
...     print a, "is odd"
...
11 is odd
>>>
>>> y = [2, 3, 7]
>>> if not y:
...     print y, "is empty"
... else:
...     t = y[-1]
...     if t % 2: print t, "is odd"
...     else: print t, "is even"
...
7 is odd
>>>
>>> from types import *
>>> s = "sequoia"
>>> x = 3
>>> if (type(s) == StringType and
...         type(x) == IntType):
...     if s:
...         if s[x] in "aeiou":
...             print s[x], "is a vowel"
...         else:
...             print s[x], "is a consonant"
...     else:
...         print s, "is an empty string"
... else:
...     print "Invalid arguments"
...
u is a vowel
```

Figure 7.13 Only one of the blocks in an if-else conditional is executed.

```
>>> test_score = 79
>>> if test_score >= 90:
...     grade = "A"
... elif test_score >= 80:
...     grade = "B"
... elif test_score >= 70:
...     grade = "C"
... elif test_score >= 60:
...     grade = "D"
... else:
...     grade = "F"
...
>>> print grade
C
>>>
>>> hex_digit = "e"
>>> if hex_digit in "0123456789":
...     print int(hex_digit)
... elif hex_digit in "ABCDEF":
...     print ord(hex_digit) -
→ ord("A") + 10
... elif hex_digit in "abcdef":
...     print ord(hex_digit) -
→ ord("a") + 10
... else:
...     print "Invalid hexadecimal digit"
...
14
```

Figure 7.14 The first if-elif-else conditional converts a numeric grade to a letter grade. The second conditional translates a hexadecimal digit to an integer. The hex digits are 0…9, A…F, and a…f, where A (or a) = 10, B (or b) = 11, and so on.

Using *if-elif-else* Conditionals

You can add an arbitrary number of elif (for *else if*) clauses to an if statement to test several independent conditions. A trailing else clause specifies code to execute if none of the preceding conditions is true.

To create an *if-elif-else* conditional:

◆ Type:

```
if condition1:
    block1
elif condition2:
    block2
...
elif conditionN:
    blockN
else:
    default_block
```

Each condition is evaluated in order. First, *condition1* is evaluated. If it's true, *block1* is executed; otherwise, *condition2* is evaluated. If *condition2* is true, *block2* is executed, and so on. If no conditions are true, *default_block* is executed. When a block is executed, the rest of the if structure is ignored (**Figure 7.14**).

block1, block2,... and *default_block* are indented blocks of statements, and *condition1, condition2,...* are Boolean expressions (see "Using Boolean Operators" in Chapter 2).

continues on next page

✔ Tips

- The else clause is optional.

- If the conditions are strings, numbers, or tuples (rather than, say, mutable objects or expressions that use Boolean or conditional operators), it may be clearer to use a dictionary rather than a long if-elif-else conditional (**Figure 7.15**).

- **LANG** Perl, C, and Java support an elif clause. In Perl, the clause is named elsif; in C and Java, it's named else if. Python has no switch (or case) statement, as do Perl, C, Java, and Pascal.

```
>>> gene = "OAT"
>>>
>>> # Using if-elif-else
... if gene == "IDDM2":
...   print "Diabetes"
... elif gene == "OAT":
...   print "Gyrate atrophy"
... elif gene == "PAH":
...   print "Phenylketonuria"
... elif gene == "VMD2":
...   print "Best disease"
... else:
...   print "Unknown gene"
...
Gyrate atrophy
>>>
>>> # Using a dictionary
... genes = {
...   "IDDM2": "Diabetes",
...   "OAT": "Gyrate atrophy",
...   "PAH": "Phenylketonuria",
...   "VMD2": "Best disease",
...   }
>>> if genes.has_key(gene):
...   print genes[gene]
... else:
...   print "Unknown gene"
...
Gyrate atrophy
```

Figure 7.15 Indexing a dictionary is an alternative to a creating a long series of elif tests. The dictionary method is more flexible because you can add or remove items while your program is running. The dictionary values also can be functions that perform complex actions.

```
>>> n = 5
>>> fact = 1
>>> while n > 0:
...   fact *= n
...   n -= 1
...
>>> print fact
120
```

Figure 7.16 This while loop calculates the factorial of 5. 5! = 5 * 4 * 3 * 2 * 1 = 120.

```
>>> n = 25
>>> a, b = 0, 1
>>> while b < n:
...   print b,
...   a, b = b, a + b
...
1 1 2 3 5 8 13 21
```

Figure 7.17 This while loop calculates each Fibonacci number as the sum of the two numbers that precede it.

Using *while* Loops

The while loop repeats a block of statements as long as a condition remains true.

To create a *while* loop:

◆ Type:

while *condition*:

  block

condition is evaluated. If it's true, *block* is executed. When block execution completes, *condition* is reevaluated, and if it's still true, *block* is executed again. This process repeats until *condition* becomes false; then the loop terminates.

block is an indented block of statements, and *condition* is a Boolean expression (see "Using Boolean Operators" in Chapter 2).

The while loop in **Figure 7.16** calculates the factorial of n. The factorial, denoted $n!$, is the result of multiplying the successive integers from 1 through n. $n! = n \times (n-1) \times (n-2) \times \cdots \times 1$.

The while loop in **Figure 7.17** prints the Fibonacci sequence up to n. The Fibonacci sequence is the sequence of numbers, 1, 1, 2, 3, 5, 8, 13,... in which each number is equal to the sum of the two preceding numbers.

continues on next page

✔ Tips

- Typically, a statement in the *block* modifies a value in the *condition,* although this logic is not required.

- A condition that remains true permanently causes an *infinite loop* (**Figure 7.18**). Infinite loops usually are the result of logic errors, but sometimes they are intentional and terminated by direct intervention, a side effect, a break statement, or a return statement. It's provably impossible to write a procedure that can determine whether a program has entered an infinite loop (in case you're considering doing so). This situation is called the *halting problem* in computer science.

- It's better to use a for loop than a while loop to traverse the items of a sequence (a string, list, or tuple). The while loop in **Figure 7.19** prints the squares of a sequence of integers. A clearer method would be to use a for loop and the range() function; see "Looping over a Range of Integers" later in this chapter.

- while loops often are used to read data from files (see Chapter 10).

- You can skip part of a loop iteration by using a continue statement or exit a loop by using a break statement; see "Skipping Part of a Loop Iteration" and "Exiting a Loop" later in this chapter.

- **LANG** Perl, C, and Java have a while loop. Python doesn't have do-while, do-unless, and until loops (but all these loops can be simulated with while). Parentheses around the loop condition are required in Perl, C, and Java but are optional in Python.

```
>>> n = 9
>>> while n != 0:
...     print n, "\t", n * n
...     n = n - 2
...
9       81
7       49
5       25
3       9
1       1
-1      1
-3      9
-5      25
-7      49
Traceback (most recent call last):
  File "<stdin>", line 2, in ?
KeyboardInterrupt
```

Figure 7.18 Here, I want to print the squares of the odd numbers from 0 through 9. But I created an infinite loop because the value of n jumps from 1 to –1 and never *equals* zero, as the condition n == 0 requires. To correct this problem, change the condition to n >= 0. I pressed Ctrl-C to break out of the infinite loop.

```
>>> i = 0
>>> while i < 5:
...     print i, i * i
...     i = i + 1
...
0 0
1 1
2 4
3 9
4 16
```

Figure 7.19 It's easier to traverse a sequence of integers with a for loop and the range() function. See the first example in Figure 7.31 later in this chapter.

```
>>> a = 0
>>> while a < 100:
...   if a / 2 == a / 3 + 1:
...     print a
...   a += 1
... else:
...   print "Done"
...
2
4
5
6
7
9
Done
```

Figure 7.20 Here, the else block will always execute, because the while block has no break condition.

Using *while-else* Loops

You can add an else clause to a while loop to execute a block of statements when the condition is false.

To create a *while-else* loop:

◆ Type:

while *condition*:

  block

else:

  post_block

As long as *condition* is true, *block* is executed. When *condition* becomes false (which may be the first time it's evaluated), *post_block* is executed; then the loop terminates (**Figure 7.20**).

block and *post_block* are indented blocks of statements, and *condition* is a Boolean expression (see "Using Boolean Operators" in Chapter 2).

✔ Tips

■ *post_block* won't execute if a break statement in *block* causes the loop to terminate; see "Exiting a Loop" later in this chapter.

■ The else clause isn't used much in practice. If *block* contains no break statement, the while-else loop is equivalent to this simpler structure:

while *condition*:

  block

post_block

Using *for* Loops

The for loop iterates over a sequence of values.

To create a *for* loop:

◆ Type:

for *target* in *sequence*:

   block

sequence is evaluated once (it should be a string, list, or tuple). *target* is assigned the first item in *sequence*, and *block* is executed; then *target* is assigned the second item in *sequence*, and *block* is executed again; and so on for each item in *sequence*. *block* executes len(*sequence*) times.

target is a variable, *sequence* is an expression that yields a sequence, and *block* is an indented block of statements.

The first example in **Figure 7.21** prints the items in a tuple, the second example sums the items in a list, and the third example prints the vowels in a string.

Figure 7.22 creates a list that contains the distinct items in a sequence.

```
>>> tup = ("mimetic", (2, 4), 4.5)
>>> for x in tup:
...     print x
...
mimetic
(2, 4)
4.5
>>>
>>> sum = 0
>>> for x in [1, 2, 3, 4]:
...     sum += x
...
>>> print sum
10
>>>
>>> s = "sequoia"
>>> for x in s:
...     if x in "aeiouAEIOU":
...         print x,
...
e u o i a
```

Figure 7.21 In these examples, x refers to the current item in the sequence.

```
>>> s = [1, 2, 2.0, "a", "A", "a",
⇢ (3, 4), (6/2, 8/2)]
>>> unique = []
>>> for x in s:
...     if x not in unique:
...         unique.append(x)
...
>>> print unique
[1, 2, 'a', 'A', (3, 4)]
```

Figure 7.22 The unique list contains the items in s with duplicates removed.

```
>>> s2 = "sequoia"
>>> s1 = "mimetic polyalloy"
>>> intersection = []
>>> for x in s1:
...   if x in s2:
...     if x not in intersection:
...       intersection.append(x)
...
>>> print intersection
['i', 'e', 'o', 'a']
```

Figure 7.23 The intersection list contains the items common to s1 and s2.

```
>>> s1 = [2, 3, 4]
>>> s2 = [1, 2, 3, 9]
>>> union = s1[:]  # Make a copy
>>> for x in s2:
...   if not x in s1:
...     union.append(x)
...
>>> print union
[2, 3, 4, 1, 9]
```

Figure 7.24 The union list contains the items that appear in both s1 and s2, without duplicates.

```
>>> s1 = (1, 5)
>>> s2 = (2, 6, 7)
>>> combined = []
>>> for x in s1:
...   for y in s2:
...     combined.append((x, y))
...
>>> print combined
[(1, 2), (1, 6), (1, 7), (5, 2), (5, 6), (5, 7)]
```

Figure 7.25 The combined list contains each item in s1 paired with each item in s2, as two-item tuples.

Figure 7.23 creates a list that is the intersection of two sequences, containing items shared by both sequences.

Figure 7.24 creates a list that is the union of two sequences, which is the smallest list that contains all the items of both sequences.

Figure 7.25 creates a list that is the item-wise combination of two sequences, which contains all possible pairs of the items in both sequences.

Figure 7.26 determines whether one sequence contains all the items of another sequence.

✔ Tips

- If the items in *sequence* are tuples of identical size, *target* can be a tuple of variables. If *sequence* contains only three-item tuples, for example, the following statement uses sequence unpacking (see "Creating a List or Tuple" in Chapter 5) to assign the items of each tuple to the corresponding *x, y,* and *z* variables in each iteration:

  for (*x, y, z*) in *sequence*:

  The parentheses surrounding the target variables are optional, but your code will be easier to read if you include them.

- Tuple unpacking often is used to process dictionaries. The items() method returns all of a dictionary's key-value pairs as a list of two-item tuples (see "Getting All of a Dictionary's Key-Value Pairs" in Chapter 6). The for loop in **Figure 7.27** formats and prints the keys and values (see "Printing Formatted Strings" in Chapter 4).

```
>>> s1 = "aeiou"
>>> s2 = "sequoia"
>>> all_in = 1
>>> for x in s1:
...     if x not in s2:
...         all_in = 0
...
>>> print all_in
1
```

Figure 7.26 This code prints 1 (true) if all the items in s1 appear in s2, or 0 (false) otherwise.

```
>>> nums = {
...     "composite": [4, 6, 8, 9, 10],
...     "fibonacci": [1, 1, 2, 3, 5, 8],
...     "prime": [2, 3, 5, 7],
...     "square": [1, 4, 9],
...     "triangular": [1, 3, 6, 10]
...     }
>>>
>>> for (key, value) in nums.items():
...     print "The %s numbers are %s"
→ % (key, value)
...
The composite numbers are [4, 6, 8, 9, 10]
The fibonacci numbers are [1, 1, 2, 3, 5, 8]
The square numbers are [1, 4, 9]
The triangular numbers are [1, 3, 6, 10]
The prime numbers are [2, 3, 5, 7]
```

Figure 7.27 This for loop uses tuple unpacking to print all the keys and values of the nums dictionary, introduced in Figure 6.1 in Chapter 6.

```
>>> s = [2, 4, 6, 1, 3, 5, 9, 8]
>>> for x in s:
...   if x % 2 != 0: s.remove(x)
...
>>> print s
[2, 4, 6, 3, 9, 8]
>>>
>>> s = [2, 4, 6, 1, 3, 5, 9, 8]
>>> for x in s[:]:
...   if x % 2 != 0: s.remove(x)
...
>>> print s
[2, 4, 6, 8]
```

Figure 7.28 Here, I want to remove the odd numbers from the list s. My first attempt fails because it's not safe to modify s in the body of the loop. My second attempt succeeds because I iterated over a temporary copy of s—that is, s[:].

■ If the sequence is a list, don't modify it in place in the body of the loop; if you do, Python may skip or repeat sequence items. Iterate over a copy of the sequence instead (**Figure 7.28**). This problem happens only for mutable sequences (that is, lists). To make a copy of a list, see "Copying a List or Tuple" in Chapter 5. To read more about how Python keeps track of sequence items in a for loop, see Section 7.3, "The for statement," in the *Python Reference Manual*.

■ Target variables are not deleted when the for loop terminates. If the sequence is empty, however, the block never executes, and the target variables are never assigned values.

■ If the block modifies a target variable, the value assigned to that variable in the next iteration isn't affected.

■ You can skip part of a loop iteration by using a continue statement or exit a loop by using a break statement; see "Skipping Part of a Loop Iteration" and "Exiting a Loop" later in this chapter.

■ A for loop often can be replaced by a list comprehension (see "Using List Comprehensions to Create Lists" in Chapter 8) or the join() method (see "Splitting and Joining Strings" in Chapter 4).

■ **LANG** Perl's foreach loop iterates over array elements. To emulate the behavior of C, Java, or Pascal counter-style loops, see "Looping over a Range of Integers" later in this chapter.

USING FOR LOOPS

Using *for-else* Loops

You can add an else clause to a for loop to execute a block of statements after for is done iterating over all the items in a sequence.

To create a *for-else* loop:

◆ Type:

for *target* in *sequence*:

  block

else:

  post_block

for loops over all the items in *sequence*, executing *block* at each iteration. When the items are exhausted (which is immediately if *sequence* is empty), *post_block* is executed; then the loop terminates (**Figure 7.29**).

block and *post_block* are indented blocks of statements, *target* is a variable, and *sequence* is an expression that yields a sequence.

✔ Tips

■ *post_block* won't execute if a break statement in *block* causes the loop to terminate; see "Exiting a Loop" later in this chapter.

■ The else clause isn't used much in practice. If *block* contains no break statement, the for-else loop is equivalent to this simpler structure:

for *target* in *sequence*:

  block

post_block

```
>>> for a in range(100):
...   if a / 2 == a / 3 + 1:
...     print a
... else:
...   print "Done"
...
2
4
5
6
7
9
Done
```

Figure 7.29 Here, the else block will always execute, because the for block has no break condition.

USING *FOR-ELSE* LOOPS

```
>>> range(0)
[]
>>> range(7)
[0, 1, 2, 3, 4, 5, 6]
>>> range(1, 7)
[1, 2, 3, 4, 5, 6]
>>> range(1, 7, 2)
[1, 3, 5]
>>> range(0, 7, 2)
[0, 2, 4, 6]
>>> range(0, 7, 3)
[0, 3, 6]
>>> range(0, 7, -1)
[]
>>> range(0, -7, -1)
[0, -1, -2, -3, -4, -5, -6]
>>> range(7, 0, -1)
[7, 6, 5, 4, 3, 2, 1]
>>> range(7, 0, -3)
[7, 4, 1]
>>> range(0, -7, -3)
[0, -3, -6]
>>> range(-7, 7, 3)
[-7, -4, -1, 2, 5]
```

Figure 7.30 The range() function returns a list of sequential integers.

Looping over a Range of Integers

At times, you will want to loop over a list of integers, often to index a sequence manually or to calculate mathematical formulas. You can use the range() function to create a list containing an arithmetic progression of integers to use in a for loop.

To create a list of integers:

◆ Type range([*start*,] *stop* [,*step*]) to return a list of integers from *start* to, but not including, *stop*.

step specifies the interval between integers. If *step* is negative, range() counts down from *start* to *stop*, and *start* should exceed *stop*; otherwise, an empty list is returned. If *start* is omitted, it defaults to 0; if *step* is omitted, it defaults to 1 (**Figure 7.30**).

start, stop, and *step* are integer expressions. If any argument is not an integer, its fractional part is truncated. If *step* is specified, *start* also must be specified, but not vice versa. If *step* is 0, Python raises a ValueError exception.

To create a *for* loop with the *range* function:

◆ Type:

for *target* in *range(...)*:

    block

range(...) is evaluated once. *target* is assigned the first integer in *range(...)*, and *block* is executed; then *target* is assigned the second integer in *range(...)*, and *block* is executed again; and so on for each integer in *range(...)*.

target is a variable, *range(...)* is a list of integers created with the range() function (see "To create a list of integers" earlier in this section), and *block* is an indented block of statements (**Figure 7.31**).

```
>>> for i in range(5):
...    print i, i * i
...
0 0
1 1
2 4
3 9
4 16
>>> for i in range(1, 4):
...    for j in range(1,4):
...      x = 1.0 / (i + j - 1)
...      print "%5.3f" % x,
...    print
...
1.000 0.500 0.333
0.500 0.333 0.250
0.333 0.250 0.200
>>> lst = [1, 3, -5, 0, -39]
>>> for i in range(len(lst)):
...    print i, ":", lst[i]
...
0 : 1
1 : 3
2 : -5
3 : 0
4 : -39
>>> s = "sequoia"
>>> for i in range(len(s)):
...    if s[i] in "aeiouAEIOU":
...      print s[i],
...
e u o i a
```

Figure 7.31 Using for and range() to iterate over a progression of integers.

```
>>> (MON, TUE, WED, THU, FRI, SAT,
→ SUN) = range(7)
>>> print MON, TUE, SUN
0 1 6
```

Figure 7.32 This assignment uses sequence unpacking (see "Creating a List or Tuple" in Chapter 5) and the range() function to enumerate variables representing the days of the week.

✔ Tips

■ Although the range() function usually is used in for loops, it is independent of for and can be used elsewhere in your programs. One common use of range() is to assign consecutive values to a group of variables to create an enumeration (**Figure 7.32**). This usage emulates C's enum specifier.

■ If the *stop* value is very large (say, 100,000 or greater), use the xrange() function instead of range() to increase execution speed. xrange() takes the same arguments as range() and returns the same list, but it doesn't build the list all at the same time. xrange() calculates each list item when it's needed instead storing all the values in memory simultaneously. xrange() also is useful when you don't need to calculate all the values in a range() list because you plan to exit the loop early with a break statement; see "Exiting a Loop" later in this chapter.

■ range() and xrange() don't work with long integers that exceed sys.maxint.

■ Use the tolist() method on an xrange() object to see its contents in list form.

■ **LANG** The for-range() loop emulates the behavior of a Perl, C, Java, and Pascal counter-style for loops.

Skipping Part of a Loop Iteration

By default, all statements in a loop block are executed during each iteration. You can use a continue statement in the body of a while or for loop to skip part of an iteration if a given condition prevails.

To skip part of a loop iteration:

◆ In the block of a while or for loop, type:

if *test_condition*:

    statements

    continue

The if conditional is not a requirement for using continue, but using continue without one is pointless. You may include optional *statements* to execute before the continue. When the interpreter encounters continue, it skips the rest of the statements in the loop, jumps back to the top of a loop, and goes back to either testing the loop condition (in a while loop) or continuing with the next sequence item (in a for loop) (**Figure 7.33**).

statements represents zero or more statements, and *test_condition* is a Boolean expression (see "Using Boolean Operators" in Chapter 2).

```
>>> import math
>>> a = [2, -3, 4, 5, -6, -7, 8, -9]
>>> for x in a:
...   if x < 0:
...     continue
...   print x, math.sqrt(x)
...
2 1.41421356237
4 2.0
5 2.2360679775
8 2.82842712475
```

Figure 7.33 This for loop uses continue to print the square roots of the positive numbers in a list.

```
>>> nums = {
...    "composite": [4, 6, 8, 9, 10],
...    "fibonacci": [1, 1, 2, 3, 5, 8],
...    "prime": [2, 3, 5, 7],
...    "square": [1, 4, 9],
...    "triangular": [1, 3, 6, 10]
...    }
>>>
>>> for key in nums.keys():
...    print key +":"
...    for x in nums[key]:
...       if x % 2 != 0:
...          continue
...       print x,
...    print "\n"
...
composite:
4 6 8 10

fibonacci:
2 8

square:
4

triangular:
6 10

prime:
2
```

Figure 7.34 This code prints the even numbers in each list in the nums dictionary. The outer loop (for key...) iterates over the dictionary keys, and the inner loop (for x...) iterates over the items of each key's associated list. Note that continue jumps to the top of the inner loop (the closest enclosing loop) and doesn't affect the flow of the outer loop.

✔ Tips

■ If a loop containing continue is nested in another loop, continue jumps to the top of the inner loop, not the outer one (**Figure 7.34**).

■ In practice, continue is used less often than break; see "Exiting a Loop" later in this chapter.

■ **NEW** Python 2.1 and later versions permit continue statements inside try blocks; see "Handling an Exception" in Chapter 11.

■ **LANG** Python's continue statement is equivalent to continue in C and Java and to next in Perl. Python doesn't support goto or labeled continue statements.

Exiting a Loop

By default, all statements in a loop block are executed during each iteration. You can use a break statement in the body of a while or for loop to jump out of a loop if a given condition prevails.

To exit a loop:

◆ In the block of a while or for loop, type:

if *test_condition*:

   statements

   break

The if conditional is not a requirement for using break, but using break without one is pointless. You may include optional *statements* to execute before the break. When the interpreter encounters break, it terminates the loop (**Figure 7.35**).

statements represents zero or more statements, and *test_condition* is a Boolean expression (see "Using Boolean Operators" in Chapter 2).

```
>>> a = [2, -3, 4, 5, -6, -7, 8, -9]
>>> for x in a:
...   if x < 0:
...     print x
...     break
...
-3
```

Figure 7.35 This for loop prints the first negative number in a list. It uses a break to exit the loop as soon as a negative number is found.

```
>>> m = [[1,   2,  3,  4],
...      [5,   6,  7,  8],
...      [9,  10, 11, 12],
...      [13, 14, 15, 16]]
>>> for i in range(len(m)):
...   for j in range(len(m[i])):
...     if i >= j:
...       print m[i][j],
...     else:
...       break
...   print
...
1
5 6
9 10 11
13 14 15 16
```

Figure 7.36 This code prints the bottom triangle of a matrix (a list of lists). The outer loop (for i...) iterates over the rows, and the inner loop (for j...) iterates over the columns. Note that break exits only the inner loop (the closest enclosing loop) and doesn't affect the flow of the outer loop.

```
>>> m = [[1,    2,   3,   4],
...      [5,    6,   7,   8],
...      [9,   10,  11,  12],
...      [13,  14,  15,  16]]
>>> target = 8
>>> found = 0
>>> for i in range(len(m)):
...     if found:
...         break
...     for j in range(len(m[i])):
...         if m[i][j] == target:
...             s = "Found " + `target`
...             s += " at m[" + `i`
...             s += "][" + `j` +"]"
...             print s
...             found = 1
...             break
... else:
...     print target, "not found"
...
Found 8 at m[1][3]
```

Figure 7.37 This code searches for a target value in m, and its structure is similar to the code in Figure 7.36. If target is found, its location is printed, the found flag is set to 1 (true), and break terminates the inner loop. The outer loop checks found at the start of each iteration and also terminates if target was located. The else clause executes and prints a "not found" message only if the target wasn't located.

✔ Tips

■ If a loop containing break is nested in another loop, break terminates the inner loop but not the outer one (**Figures 7.36** and **7.37**).

■ A break statement terminates a loop without executing the loop's else clause (if present); see "Using *while-else* Loops" and "Using *for-else* Loops" earlier in this chapter (refer to Figure 7.37).

■ **LANG** Python's break statement is equivalent to break in C and Java and to last in Perl. Python doesn't support goto or labeled break statements.

EXITING A LOOP

FUNCTIONS

Python lets you create your own functions. You've already seen a few of Python's built-in functions: id(), str(), len(), and range(), for example. And you've seen some functions in the standard modules: random.random() and copy.deepcopy(). Functions make programs modular and manageable; they encapsulate computations and separate the high-level logic from the details. Functions are reusable and allow you to perform a well-defined task multiple times in multiple places with various initial values.

In this chapter, I explain how to create and call your own functions. I also cover Python's functional programming tools, which allow you to apply functions to sequence items.

Defining a Function

A *function* is a named block of statements that performs an operation. The def statement is a compound statement (see "Creating Compound Statements" in Chapter 7) that creates a new function and defines its name, parameters, and the block of statements that it executes when it is called.

To define a function:

◆ Type:

```
def func(param_list):
    block
```

When executed, this compound statement creates a new function object and assigns it to the name *func* (**Figure 8.1**).

func is a valid Python name (see "Naming Variables" in Chapter 2), *param_list* represents zero or more comma-separated parameters (described later in this chapter, starting with "Specifying Positional Arguments"), and *block* is an indented block of statements.

✔ Tips

■ Defining a function does not execute it; a function is executed only when it's called; see "Calling a Function" later in this chapter.

■ As with all Python objects, you don't declare the object type of return values, parameters, or function variables. This flexibility means that you can define a single function for use with different object types, just as len(), for example, works with strings, lists, tuples, and dictionaries.

■ def is a compound statement, so you may write short functions on one line:

```
def square(x): return x * x
```

■ Functions may be defined within functions; see "Nesting Functions" in Chapter 9.

```
>>> def do_nothing():
...     pass
...
>>> def print_msg():
...     print "Mimetic polyalloy"
...
>>> def iseven(num):
...     print num % 2 == 0
...
>>>
```

Figure 8.1 These statements define three simple functions. The aptly named do_nothing function is the simplest possible Python function. print_msg prints a string. iseven has a parameter list; it prints 1 if its argument is an even number, or 0 otherwise.

- Functions are objects and can be assigned to variables; see "Assigning a Function to a Variable" later in this chapter.

- You also can create small, anonymous functions that are not bound to a function name; see "Using *lambda* Expressions to Create Functions" later in this chapter.

- You can assign arbitrary attributes to functions; see "Accessing Attributes" in Chapter 9.

- **LANG** A Python function is equivalent to a subroutine in Perl or a function in C. Perl uses sub to create subroutines. Note that unlike function definitions in Perl and C, def is an executable statement (that creates an object). C and Java require you to specify the data type of the function return value and each parameter; Python does not.

Parameters Aren't Arguments

In computer literature, sometimes you see the terms *parameter* and *argument* used interchangeably, but there's a difference. A *parameter* is a name in the parameter list of a function definition's header (the def statement). It receives a value from the caller of the function. An *argument* is the actual value or reference passed to a function by the caller.

In this function definition, for example:

```
def sum(x, y):

 return x + y
```

x and y are parameters, and in this function call:

```
z = sum(2, 3 * 5)
```

2 and 3 * 5 are arguments. For information about calling a function, see "Calling a Function" later in this chapter.

DEFINING A FUNCTION

Documenting a Function

So far, I've been using comments that start with # to describe my code (see "Documenting Programs" in Chapter 2). Python allows you to add an optional string literal as the first line of a function block. This string, called a *documentation string* or *docstring*, should show how to call the function and briefly describe what the function does.

A docstring is special because it's assigned to the function's __doc__ attribute and can be accessed with the dot operator at run time, unlike # comments.

To access a function's docstring:

◆ Type *func*.__doc__

func is a function name, which may be qualified with a module name. Don't include parentheses after *func* (**Figure 8.2**).

```
>>> def do_nothing():
...     "Does nothing."
...     pass
...
>>> def print_msg():
...     """Prints a string."""
...     print "Mimetic polyalloy"
...
>>> def iseven(num):
...     """iseven(integer) -> Boolean
...
... Prints 1 if num is an even
→ number; 0 otherwise."""
...     print num % 2 == 0
...
>>> do_nothing.__doc__
'Does nothing.'
>>> s = print_msg.__doc__
>>> print s
Prints a string.
>>> print iseven.__doc__
iseven(integer) -> Boolean

Prints 1 if num is an even number; 0 otherwise.
>>>
```

Figure 8.2 Here, I've added docstrings to the functions defined in Figure 8.1. Triple-quoted docstrings can span multiple lines and retain their formatting when printed.

```
>>> print str.__doc__
str(object) -> string


Return a nice string representation of the
→ object.

If the argument is a string, the return value
→ is the same object.
>>> print "".join.__doc__
S.join(sequence) -> string


Return a string which is the concatenation of
→ the strings in the sequence.  The separator
→ between elements is S.
>>> [].append.__doc__
'L.append(object) - append object to end'
>>> import math
>>> print math.sqrt.__doc__
sqrt(x)


Return the square root of x.
```

Figure 8.3 Printing the docstring of a built-in function is a quick way to get help.

✔ Tips

- The docstring must be the first line after the def statement.

- If you don't specify a docstring, the value of the function's __doc__ attribute defaults to None.

- Although I often omit docstrings in this book to save space, it's a good practice to add them to all your functions. Your users will appreciate them, and some tools use docstrings to create help documentation.

- You also can access the docstrings of built-in functions and methods (**Figure 8.3**).

- You can add a docstring to a module (see "Documenting a Module" in Chapter 9) or class definition (see "Documenting a Class" in Chapter 12).

Calling a Function

Functions don't run when they're defined; you must invoke them explicitly. A *function call* is an expression that executes a function. The part of a program from which a function is called is termed the *caller.* You've already seen calls to Python's built-in functions throughout this book (len(s), for example). User-defined functions are called in the same way: by using the name of the function followed by a parenthesized list of arguments.

To call a function:

◆ Type:

func(arg_list)

When executed, the caller stops until *func* finishes running, and control returns to the caller (**Figure 8.4**).

func is a function name, and *arg_list* represents zero or more comma-separated arguments that are passed to the function (discussed later in this chapter, starting with "Specifying Positional Arguments").

```
>>> do_nothing()
>>> print_msg()
Mimetic polyalloy
>>> num = 9
>>> iseven(num)
0
```

Figure 8.4 Calling the three functions defined in Figure 8.1.

```
>>> def f1():
...     print "f1"
...     f2()
...
>>> def f2():
...     print "f2"
...
>>> f1()
f1
f2
```

Figure 8.5 It's legal to refer to functions before they're defined, but not to call them. f2 can appear in f1's definition before f2 itself has been defined. But only after defining f2 can you call f1.

✔ Tips

■ Even if you're not passing a function any arguments, you still must include empty parentheses in the function call.

■ You must define a function before you call it. You can, however, refer to a function before it's defined (**Figure 8.5**).

■ To call a function that returns a value, see "Returning a Value from a Function" later in this chapter.

■ You can determine whether an object is callable by using the built-in function `callable(object)`. This function returns 1 (true) if the *object* argument is callable and 0 (false) otherwise. Callable objects include user-defined functions, built-in functions, methods of built-in objects, class objects, and methods of class instances.

CALLING A FUNCTION

Returning a Value from a Function

A *return value* is the result of a function that is sent back to the caller of the function. You can specify a return value by using a `return` statement.

To return a value from a function:

◆ In the body of the function, type:

return *expr*

This statement ends the current function call. It evaluates *expr* and sends it back to the caller as the return value.

expr is an expression. If *expr* is omitted, None is substituted.

```
>>> def iseven(num):
...     return num % 2 == 0
...
>>> def isprime(n):
...     count = n / 2
...     while count > 1:
...       if n % count == 0:
...         return 0
...       count -= 1
...     return 1
...
>>> def primes(m):
...     lst = []
...     for i in range(1, m):
...       if isprime(i):
...         lst.append(i)
...     return lst
...
>>> def vowels(s):
...     v = ""
...     for c in s:
...       if c in "aeiouAEIOU":
...         v += c
...     return v
...
>>> def ascii(s):
...     asc = {}
...     for c in s:
...       if not asc.has_key(c):
...         asc[c] = ord(c)
...     return asc
...
```

(figure continues on next page)

Figure 8.6 *continued*

```
>>> a = iseven(40)
>>> b = isprime(27)
>>> c = primes(20)
>>> d = vowels("sequoia")
>>> e = ascii("ick")
>>> print a
1
>>> print b
0
>>> print c
[1, 2, 3, 5, 7, 11, 13, 17, 19]
>>> print d
euoia
>>> print e
{'c': 99, 'k': 107, 'i': 105}
```

Figure 8.6 These functions return various types of values. iseven determines whether its argument is an even number and returns 1 (true) or 0 (false). isprime determines whether its argument is a prime number and returns 1 or 0. Note that isprime has two return statements; control returns to the caller when either statement is encountered. primes returns a list containing the prime numbers that are less than its argument. vowels returns a string containing the vowels of its argument. ascii returns a dictionary containing the ASCII codes (values) of the characters (keys) of its argument.

To call a function that returns a value:

◆ Type:

```
target = func(arg_list)
```

When executed, the caller stops until *func* finishes running, and control returns to the caller. *target* is assigned the function's return value (**Figure 8.6**).

target is a variable, *func* is a function name, and *arg_list* represents the arguments passed to the function.

In Figures 7.22 through 7.26 in Chapter 7, I wrote some examples that illustrated how the for loop worked. In **Scripts 8.1** through **8.5**, I've reworked those examples into practical and reusable functions. **Figure 8.7** shows some example function calls.

Script 8.1 The unique function takes a sequence and returns a list that contains the items of its argument with duplicates removed.

```
def unique(seq):
  result = []
  for x in seq:
    if x not in result:
      result.append(x)
  return result
```

Script 8.2 The intersection function takes two sequences and returns a list that contains the items common to both its arguments.

```
def intersection(seq1, seq2):
  result = []
  for x in seq1:
    if x in seq2:
      if x not in result:
        result.append(x)
  return result
```

Script 8.3 The union function takes two sequences and returns a list that contains the items that appear in both its arguments, without duplicates.

```
def union(seq1, seq2):
  result = seq1[:]  # Make a copy
  for x in seq2:
    if not x in seq1:
      result.append(x)
  return result
```

Script 8.4 The combine function takes two sequences and returns a list that contains each item in the first argument paired with each item in the second argument as two-item tuples.

```
def combine(seq1, seq2):
  result = []
  for x in seq1:
    for y in seq2:
      result.append((x, y))
  return result
```

Script 8.5 The all_in function takes two sequences and returns 1 (true) if all the items in the first argument appear in the second argument, or 0 (false) otherwise.

```
def all_in(seq1, seq2):
  result = 1
  for x in seq1:
    if x not in seq2:
      result = 0
      break
  return result
```

```
>>> s = [1, 2, 2.0, "a", "A", "a",
→ (3, 4), (6/2, 8/2)]
>>> print unique(s)
[1, 2, 'a', 'A', (3, 4)]
>>>
>>> s1 = "mimetic polyalloy"
>>> s2 = "sequoia"
>>> print intersection(s1, s2)
['i', 'e', 'o', 'a']
>>>
>>> s1 = [2, 3, 4]
>>> s2 = [1, 2, 3, 9]
>>> print union(s1, s2)
[2, 3, 4, 1, 9]
>>>
>>> s1 = (1, 5)
>>> s2 = (2, 6, 7)
>>> print combine(s1, s2)
[(1, 2), (1, 6), (1, 7), (5, 2), (5, 6), (5, 7)]
>>>
>>> s1 = "aeiou"
>>> s2 = "sequoia"
>>> all_in(s1, s2)
1
```

Figure 8.7 Example calls for the functions in Scripts 8.1 through 8.5.

```
>>> a = do_nothing()
>>> b = print_msg()
Mimetic polyalloy
>>> c = iseven(2)
1
>>> print a, b, c
None None None
```

Figure 8.8 All the functions defined in Figure 8.1 return None, which is the default return value for a function with no return statement (or a function in which a return exists but isn't executed).

✔ Tips

■ If control flows off the end of a function without encountering a return statement, None is returned (**Figure 8.8**).

■ A return statement may occur only within a function definition.

■ To return multiple values from a function, see "Returning Multiple Values from a Function" later in this chapter.

■ **LANG** Perl and C also use return to return values. When used as a return value, Python's None is similar to C's void. Perl's default return value is the value of the last expression evaluated in the block, whereas Python's default return value is None.

RETURNING A VALUE FROM A FUNCTION

Returning Multiple Values from a Function

If you have a small number of return values, you should return them in a tuple. With a tuple, you easily can assign each return value to its own variable by using tuple packing and unpacking in an assignment statement; see "Creating Variables" in Chapter 2. If you specify multiple expressions in a `return` statement, they are returned in a tuple.

To return multiple values from a function:

◆ In the body of a function, type:

`return expr1, expr2,...`

This statement ends the current function call. It evaluates *expr1, expr2,...* and sends them back to the caller as a tuple of return values.

expr1, expr2,... are two or more comma-separated expressions.

To call a function that returns multiple values:

◆ Type:

`target1, target2,... = func(arg_list)`

When executed, the caller stops until *func* finishes running, and control returns to the caller. *target1* is assigned the first item in the returned tuple, *target2* is assigned the second item, and so on (**Figure 8.9**).

func is a function name, *arg_list* represents the arguments passed to the function, and *target1, target2,...* are two or more comma-separated variables. You must have the same number of targets as there are items in the returned tuple.

✔ Tips

■ The items in the returned tuple may be different types of objects.

■ If the number of targets and the number of items in the returned tuple don't match, Python raises a `ValueError` exception.

```
>>> def fracint(x):
...   i = int(x)
...   f = x - i
...   return float(f), float(i)
...
>>> frac, int = fracint(-5.5)
>>> print frac
-0.5
>>> print int
-5.0
>>>
>>> def letters(s):
...     from string import letters,
→ whitespace
...     v = c = w = o = ""
...     s = str(s)
...     for ch in s:
...       if ch in "aeiouAEIOU":
...         v += ch
...       elif ch in letters:
...         c += ch
...       elif ch in whitespace:
...         w += ch
...       else:
...         o += ch
...     return v, c, w, o
...
>>> s ="mimetic polyalloy"
>>> v, c, w, o = letters(s)
>>> v, c, w, o
('ieioao', 'mmtcplylly', ' ', '')
```

Figure 8.9 `fracint` returns the fractional and integer parts of a number in a two-item tuple. (This emulates the `math.modf` function.) `letters` returns the vowels, consonants, white space, and other characters of its argument in a tuple of strings.

```
>>> def get_color(red, green, blue):
...    colors = {
...    (0,    0,    0)  : "black",
...    (0,    0,    255): "blue",
...    (0,    255,  0)  : "green",
...    (0,    255,  255): "cyan",
...    (255,  0,    0)  : "red",
...    (255,  0,    255): "magenta",
...    (255,  255,  0)  : "yellow",
...    (255,  255,  255): "white"
...    }
...    rgb = (red, green, blue)
...    if colors.has_key(rgb):
...        return colors[rgb]
...    else:
...        return rgb
...
>>> print get_color(255, 0, 255)
magenta
>>> print get_color(0, 0, 0)
black
>>> print get_color(0, 25, 18)
(0, 25, 18)
>>> print get_color(0, 255)
Traceback (most recent call last):
  File "<stdin>", line 1, in ?
TypeError: get_color() takes exactly 3
 → arguments (2 given)
```

Figure 8.10 The get_color function takes three positional arguments that represent a color's red, green, and blue color components and returns the name of the color, if known; otherwise, the function returns a tuple containing the argument values.

Specifying Positional Arguments

Positional arguments must be passed to a function in the exact order in which the parameters are given in the function definition. This method is the normal way to pass arguments; you've already seen it in calls to Python's built-in functions. In the absence of default parameter values (see the following section), the number of arguments passed must match the number of parameters in the function's parameter list. **Figure 8.10** shows some examples.

To define positional parameters in a function header:

◆ Type:

def *func(param1, param2,...):*
func is a function name, and *param1, param2,...* are one or more comma-separated positional parameter names.

To call a function by using positional arguments:

◆ Type:

func(arg1, arg2,...)
func is a function name, and *arg1, arg2,...* are one or more comma-separated arguments (expressions) that correspond to the function's positional parameters.

✔ Tip

■ If the number of positional arguments and the number of positional parameters don't match, Python raises a TypeError exception.

Specifying Default Parameter Values

A *default value* is assigned to a parameter automatically when no value is passed in the function call. You've already seen default values in Python's built-in functions. In round(*x* [, *n*]), for example, you need only supply a value for *x*; the default value of *n* is 0.

You specify default values in the parameter list of a function header (see "To define positional parameters in a function header" in the preceding section). Type *param* = *default_value* in place of *param* for each parameter that you want to assign a default value. *default_value* is an expression.

Parameters with default values must come after parameters without default values. This function header is illegal, for example:

def f(x = 1, y): # Illegal

In a function call, you may specify an optional argument to override the default parameter value. **Figure 8.11** shows some examples.

```
>>> def get_color(red = 0, green = 0,
→ blue = 0):
...    colors = {
...       (0,   0,   0)  : "black",
...       (0,   0,   255): "blue",
...       (0,   255, 0)  : "green",
...       (0,   255, 255): "cyan",
...       (255, 0,   0)  : "red",
...       (255, 0,   255): "magenta",
...       (255, 255, 0)  : "yellow",
...       (255, 255, 255): "white"
...       }
...    rgb = (red, green, blue)
...    if colors.has_key(rgb):
...       return colors[rgb]
...    else:
...       return rgb
...
>>> print get_color()
black
>>> print get_color(255)
red
>>> print get_color(0, 255)
green
>>> print get_color(0, 0, 255)
blue
>>> print get_color(25)
(25, 0, 0)
>>>
>>> def repeat(x, times = 1):
...    return str(x) * times
...
>>> print repeat("*")
*
>>> print repeat("-", 25)
-------------------------
>>> print repeat()
Traceback (most recent call last):
  File "<stdin>", line 1, in ?
TypeError: repeat() takes at least 1 argument
→ (0 given)
```

Figure 8.11 Here, I've changed the header of get_color in Figure 8.10. All of its parameters now default to zero. The first argument of the repeat function is required, and the second argument is optional.

```
>>> def affix(x, lst = []):
...   lst.append(x)
...   return lst
...
>>> print affix(1)
[1]
>>> print affix(2)
[1, 2]
>>> print affix(3)
[1, 2, 3]
>>>
>>> def affix2(x, lst = None):
...   if lst is None: lst = []
...   lst.append(x)
...   return lst
...
>>> print affix2(1)
[1]
>>> print affix2(2)
[2]
>>> print affix2(3)
[3]
```

Figure 8.12 The *affix* function appends x to the list lst (it modifies lst in place). Python evaluates the default value of lst only once, when *affix* is defined, so lst retains its value between repeated calls to *affix*. The *affix2* function moves the default value to the function body, so lst is evaluated anew each call (rather than shared between calls).

✔ Tips

■ It makes no sense to say that a parameter is optional; assigning its value is optional.

■ If you specify a default argument, you must specify every default argument to its left. You can't skip a default argument by leaving an empty slot in a function call. Given this function definition header, for example:

```
def f(a = 1, b = 2, c = 3):
```

you can't make a function call that omits b and specifies c; if you do, Python raises SyntaxError exception:

```
f(5,,10)   # Syntax error
```

You can circumvent this restriction by using keyword arguments (see the following section).

■ A default value is evaluated and saved only once when the function is defined and not when the function is called. This convention means that if the default value is a mutable object (list or dictionary), it will accumulate in-place changes over repeated function calls. This behavior may or may not be what you intend (usually not). **Figure 8.12** shows examples of how to share a default value between function calls and how *not* to share it by using None as a default value. If a default value is an immutable object (number, string, or tuple), no sharing occurs between function calls, because any change will create a new object, not modify the existing one. For information about passing arguments, see "Passing Mutable and Immutable Arguments to Functions" later in this chapter.

SPECIFYING DEFAULT PARAMETER VALUES

Specifying Keyword Arguments

You can pass a *keyword argument* to a function by using its corresponding parameter name, rather than its position: Simply type *keyword = arg* in the function call. A function definition requires no special syntax to enable keyword calls.

Passing keyword arguments is most useful for functions with a large number of parameters, most of which have a common default value. Suppose that you want to call the following (fictitious) function that searches for text in a file:

```
def search(text, file,
 match_case = 0,
 match_whole_word = 0,
 match_wilcards = 0,
 reverse = 0):
```

The reverse parameter reverses the search direction. If you want to search backward instead of forward and accept the other default values, the function call using positional arguments is:

```
search("sequoia", "trees.txt", 0, 0, 0, 1):
```

Here's the equivalent call using keyword arguments:

```
search("sequoia", "trees.txt", reverse = 1):
```

Note the benefits of the keyword call: It's more readable, you can omit optional arguments, and you can place keyword arguments in any order.

```
>>> def get_color(red = 0, green = 0,
→ blue = 0):
...   colors = {
...     (0,   0,   0)  : "black",
...     (0,   0,   255): "blue",
...     (0,   255, 0)  : "green",
...     (0,   255, 255): "cyan",
...     (255, 0,   0)  : "red",
...     (255, 0,   255): "magenta",
...     (255, 255, 0)  : "yellow",
...     (255, 255, 255): "white"
...     }
...   rgb = (red, green, blue)
...   if colors.has_key(rgb):
...     return colors[rgb]
...   else:
...     return rgb
...
>>> print get_color(red = 255)
red
>>> print get_color(green = 255,
→ blue = 255, red = 255)
white
>>> print get_color(255, 255,
→ blue = 255)
white
>>> print get_color(18, blue = 255)
(18, 0, 255)
>>> print get_color(red = 255, 0, 255)
SyntaxError: non-keyword arg after keyword arg
>>> print get_color(255, red = 255)
Traceback (most recent call last):
  File "<stdin>", line 1, in ?
TypeError: get_color() got multiple values
→ for keyword argument 'red'
>>> print get_color(puce = 255)
Traceback (most recent call last):
  File "<stdin>", line 1, in ?
TypeError: get_color() got an unexpected
→ keyword argument 'puce'
```

Figure 8.13 Examples of function calls using keyword call arguments and a few examples of common errors.

To call a function by using keyword arguments:

♦ Type:

func(pos_args, keyword1 = arg1, keyword2 = arg2,...)

func is a function name, *pos_args* are positional arguments (if any), and *arg1, arg2,...* are arguments (expressions) that are passed to the parameters named *keyword1, keyword2,...* in the function definition (**Figure 8.13**).

Here are some rules for using keyword arguments:

♦ Unlike positional arguments, keyword arguments needn't be in the same order as the parameters listed in the function definition.

♦ A positional argument can't follow a keyword argument (refer to Figure 8.13).

♦ You can't duplicate an argument by specifying it as both a positional argument and a keyword argument (refer to Figure 8.13).

✔ Tip

■ You can't use keyword arguments in built-in and standard module function calls; Python raises a TypeError exception if you try.

SPECIFYING KEYWORD ARGUMENTS

Specifying an Arbitrary Number of Positional Arguments

A function can take a variable (not fixed) number of positional arguments. You've already seen built-in functions such as max() and min(), which take variable-length argument lists. When you call the function, Python matches the normal positional arguments from left to right and then places any excess positional arguments in a tuple that you can use in the function.

To define a function that takes an arbitrary number of positional arguments:

◆ Type:

```
def func(pos_params, *args):
```

func is a function name, *pos_params* are positional parameters (if any), and *args* is a tuple that receives any excess positional arguments (the * is not part of the parameter name).

To call a function by using an arbitrary number of positional arguments:

◆ Type:

```
func(pos_args, arg1, arg2,...)
```

func is a function name, *pos_args* are normal positional arguments (if any), and *arg1, arg2,...* are zero or more excess arguments (expressions) that are placed in a tuple.

Figure 8.14 shows a function that calculates the mean (average) of an arbitrary number of arguments. Scripts 8.2 and 8.3 earlier in this chapter show functions that return the intersection and union of two sequences, respectively.

```
>>> def mean(*nums):
...   if len(nums) == 0:
...     return 0.0
...   else:
...     sum = 0.0
...     for x in nums: sum += x
...     return sum/len(nums)
...
>>> print mean()
0.0
>>> print mean(4)
4.0
>>> print mean(-1, 0, 2)
0.333333333333
```

Figure 8.14 The mean function takes an arbitrary number of arguments and returns their arithmetic average.

Script 8.6 The intersection function takes an arbitrary number of sequences and returns a list that contains the items common to all its arguments.

```
script
def intersection(*seqs):
  result = []
  for x in seqs[0]:
    for y in seqs[1:]:
      if x not in y:
        break
    else:
      result.append(x)
  return result
```

Script 8.7 The union function takes an arbitrary number of sequences and returns a list that contains the items that appear in all its arguments, without duplicates.

```
script
def union(*seqs):
  result = []
  for seq in seqs:
    for x in seq:
      if not x in result:
        result.append(x)
  return result
```

```
>>> s1 = "sequoia"
>>> s2 = "polyalloy"
>>> s3 = "formaldehyde"
>>> print intersection(s1, s2, s3)
['o', 'a']
>>> print union(s1, s2, s3)
['s', 'e', 'q', 'u', 'o', 'i', 'a', 'p', 'l',
→ 'y', 'f', 'r', 'm', 'd', 'h']
```

Figure 8.15 Example calls for the functions in Scripts 8.6 and 8.7.

Scripts 8.6 and **8.7** show the intersection and union functions rewritten to take an arbitrary number of sequences. **Figure 8.15** shows some example function calls of Scripts 8.6 and 8.7.

✔ Tips

■ If no excess arguments are passed, *args* defaults to an empty tuple.

■ To specify an arbitrary number of keyword arguments, see the next section.

■ NEW Python 2.0 introduced *args.

■ LANG Perl collects subroutine arguments in an array named @_. C uses ... and va_list to store variable-length argument lists.

Specifying an Arbitrary Number of Keyword Arguments

A function can take a variable (not fixed) number of keyword arguments if its final parameter name begins with **. When you call the function, Python matches the normal positional arguments from left to right, followed by any excess positional arguments (see the preceding section), and then places any excess keyword arguments in a dictionary that you can use in the function. See **Figure 8.16** for an example.

To define a function that takes an arbitrary number of keyword arguments:

◆ Type the function definition header:

def *func*(*pos_params*, **args*, ***kwargs*):

func is a function name, *pos_params* are normal positional parameters (if any), *args* is a tuple that receives excess positional arguments (if any), and *kwargs* is a dictionary that receives any excess keyword arguments (the ** is not part of the parameter name).

To call a function by using an arbitrary number of keyword arguments:

◆ Type:

func(*pos_args*, keyword1 = arg1, keyword2 = arg2,...)

func is a function name, *pos_args* are positional and excess positional arguments (if any), and *arg1, arg2,...* are zero or more excess keyword arguments (expressions) that are placed in a dictionary with corresponding keys *keyword1, keyword2,...*.

```
>>> def book(title, author, **other):
...     print "title :", title
...     print "author :", author
...     for (k, v) in other.items():
...         print k, ":", v
...
>>>
>>> book("Therapy",
...      "Lodge, David",
...      pub = "Penguin",
...      format = "paperback",
...      pages = 336,
...      year = 1996)
title : Therapy
author : Lodge, David
format : paperback
pub : Penguin
pages : 336
year : 1996
```

Figure 8.16 The book function collects excess keyword arguments in the other dictionary and prints its key-value pairs.

✔ Tips

■ If no excess keyword arguments are passed, *kwargs* defaults to an empty dictionary.

■ Nonkeyword arguments must appear before keyword arguments.

■ **NEW** Python 2.0 introduced **kwargs.

```
>>> def arg_demo(a, b = -99, *args,
→ **kwargs):
...     print "Normal args:"
...     print "\ta =", a, ", b =", b
...     print "Excess positional args:"
...     print "\t", args
...     print "Excess keyword args:"
...     print "\t", kwargs
...
>>> arg_demo(1)
Normal args:
        a = 1 , b = -99
Excess positional args:
        ()
Excess keyword args:
        {}
>>> arg_demo(b = 1, a = 2)
Normal args:
        a = 2 , b = 1
Excess positional args:
        ()
Excess keyword args:
        {}
>>> arg_demo(1, 2, 3, 4)
Normal args:
        a = 1 , b = 2
Excess positional args:
        (3, 4)
Excess keyword args:
        {}
>>> arg_demo(1, 2, 3, 4, x = 5, y = 6)
Normal args:
        a = 1 , b = 2
Excess positional args:
        (3, 4)
Excess keyword args:
        {'x': 5, 'y': 6}
```

(figure continues in next column)

Combining Argument-Passing Techniques

You can mix all the argument-passing techniques of the preceding five sections in a single function call. Deciphering how positional and excess arguments are assigned may become confusing, however, as a function call becomes more complex. The arg_demo function in **Figure 8.17** takes normal arguments, excess positional arguments, and excess keyword arguments. When you call arg_demo (or any other function), Python assigns arguments in this order:

1. Nonkeyword arguments by position

2. Keyword arguments by name

3. Excess nonkeyword arguments to the args tuple

4. Excess keyword arguments to the kwargs dictionary

After these assignments, any remaining unassigned arguments are given their default values.

✔ Tip

■ Function definitions and calls are explained in fierce detail in Section 7.5, "Function definitions," and Section 5.3.4, "Calls," in the *Python Reference Manual*.

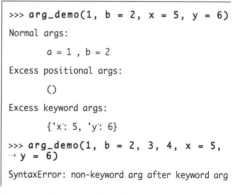

```
>>> arg_demo(1, b = 2, x = 5, y = 6)
Normal args:
        a = 1 , b = 2
Excess positional args:
        ()
Excess keyword args:
        {'x': 5, 'y': 6}
>>> arg_demo(1, b = 2, 3, 4, x = 5,
→ y = 6)
SyntaxError: non-keyword arg after keyword arg
```

Figure 8.17 These function calls show how Python assigns various combinations of positional, keyword, and excess arguments.

COMBINING ARGUMENT-PASSING TECHNIQUES

Creating Recursive Functions

Recursion is the capability of a function to call itself. In practice, recursion often is used to traverse treelike data structures such as directory hierarchies or to process arbitrarily nested data structures, such as lists of lists of.... When the `copy.deepcopy()` function creates a copy of a list, for example, it recursively copies deeply nested objects in the original list; see "Copying a List or Tuple" in Chapter 5.

Recursion also is used to compute recursively defined mathematical quantities. In Figures 7.16 and 7.17 in Chapter 7, I used `while` loops to calculate the factorial of a number and the numbers in the Fibonacci series. You can use recursion to make the same calculations.

The factorial of a number *n*, written *n*!, is the product of all the whole numbers up to *n*, so $n! = n \times (n-1) \times (n-2) \times \cdots \times 1$. The definition also specifies that $0! = 1$. In mathematical notation, the recursive definition is:

$0! = 1$

$n! = n \times (n-1)!$

Script 8.8 shows how to calculate a factorial by using recursion.

The Fibonacci sequence is the sequence of numbers—1, 1, 2, 3, 5, 8, 13,...—in which each successive number is equal to the sum of the two preceding numbers. In mathematical notation, the recursive definition is:

$fibonacci(0) = 1$

$fibonacci(1) = 1$

$fibonacci(n) = fibonacci(n-1) + fibonacci(n-2)$

Script 8.9 shows how to calculate a Fibonacci number by using recursion.

Script 8.8 The `factorial` function recursively calculates the factorial of n.

```
def factorial(n):
  if n == 0:
    return 1
  else:
    return n * factorial(n - 1)
```

Script 8.9 The `fibonacci` function recursively calculates the n-th number in the Fibonacci series.

```
def fibonacci(n):
  if n < 2:
    return 1
  else:
    return fibonacci(n - 1) + fibonacci(n - 2)
```

```
>>> for i in range(6):
...     print str(i) + "! =",
→ factorial(i)
...
0! = 1
1! = 1
2! = 2
3! = 6
4! = 24
5! = 120
>>>
>>> for i in range(11):
...     print fibonacci(i),
...
1 1 2 3 5 8 13 21 34 55 89
```

Figure 8.18 Example calls for the functions in Scripts 8.8 and 8.9.

Figure 8.18 shows example runs of Scripts 8.8 and 8.9.

✔ Tips

■ A recursive function that always calls itself will never terminate, so a terminating condition under which the function can return a value without calling itself is required. In Script 8.8, the terminating condition is n == 0; in Script 8.9, it's n < 2.

■ Although recursion enables you to write certain routines with small, simple functions, it doesn't guarantee speed or efficiency. Often, it's clearer and easier to write equivalent iterative routines by using while or for loops.

■ The erroneous use of recursion can cause your program to run out of memory and crash Python. You can retrieve or set the maximum recursion depth with the sys.getrecursionlimit() and sys.setrecursionlimit() functions. The default limit is 1000. Python raises a RuntimeError exception when recursion depth is exceeded. See Section 3.1 "sys—System-specific parameters and functions" in the *Python Library Reference*.

■ Perl, C, and Java support recursion.

Passing Mutable and Immutable Arguments to Functions

When you call a function, Python passes the object references of the arguments from the caller to the function. Recall from "Creating Variables" in Chapter 2 that object references are pointers to objects residing in memory.

For immutable objects (numbers, strings, and tuples), this behavior effectively creates a local, temporary copy of the argument inside the called function; the function cannot change the original object.

The story is different for mutable objects (lists and dictionaries). Passing a reference creates an alias of the original object inside the called function. Recall from "Creating References to the Same Object" in Chapter 2 that aliases are variables that share references to the same object. The original object (in the caller) will change if you modify the passed-in object in place (in the function). On the other hand, if you reassign the aliased parameter a value, the reference to the original object is lost, and changes in the function won't be reflected in the caller.

Figure 8.19 illustrates this argument-passing behavior.

```
>>> def change_args(x, seq1, seq2):
...     x = ""
...     seq1[0] = -99
...     seq2 = []
...
>>> s = "mimetic"
>>> lst1 = [1, 2, 3]
>>> lst2 = [4, 5, 6]
>>> change_args(s, lst1, lst2)
>>> print s
mimetic
>>> print lst1
[-99, 2, 3]
>>> print lst2
[4, 5, 6]
```

Figure 8.19 Reassigning x inside change_args has no effect on s outside, because s is immutable, so x effectively is a copy of s. The in-place alteration of seq1 is reflected in lst1 because lst1 is mutable, so lst1 and seq1 are aliases. lst2 and seq2 are aliases initially, but assigning seq2 a new object destroys its reference to the shared object, so changes within the function aren't visible to lst2.

✔ Tips

■ To avoid modifying a shared mutable object in a function, pass in a copy of the object. lst1, for example, won't be modified if you change the function call in Figure 8.19 from:

`change_args(s, lst1, lst2)`

to:

`change_args(s, lst1[:], lst2)`

For information about copying lists or dictionaries, see "Copying a List or Tuple" in Chapter 5 or "Copying a Dictionary" in Chapter 6.

■ In-place changes of mutable objects within functions cause side effects. Although side effects sometimes are useful, you should favor using return to return function results. See also "Using Functional Programming Tools" later in this chapter.

■ It's good practice to make local copies of mutable arguments in a function to ensure absolutely that there are no side effects. It should be the responsibility of the function, and not its caller, to prevent side effects.

■ For information about using mutable objects as default parameter values, see "Specifying Default Parameter Values" earlier in this chapter.

■ **LANG** Passing an immutable object is like call-by-value in C. Passing a mutable object is like passing a C pointer.

PASSING MUTABLE AND IMMUTABLE ARGUMENTS

Declaring Global Variables

When you create a variable inside a function, only code within that function can read or change the variable's value because its scope is *local* to that function. All variables in the function's parameter list are also local variables (**Figure 8.20**).

A variable's *scope* defines the extent to which it can be referenced within a block. Scope can be local or global. A *global* variable created outside a function can be accessed and changed by any function that declares it global by using the global statement.

To declare variables as global:

◆ In the body of the function, type:

global *var1, var2,...*

var1, var2,... are one or more comma-separated variable names.

In **Figure 8.21**, Python assumes that x is a local variable and complains when I try to access x before setting it. **Figure 8.22** fixes the problem by declaring x to be a global variable.

```
>>> def printsum(a, b):
...     x = a + b
...     print x
...
>>> printsum(3,9)
12
>>> x
Traceback (most recent call last):
  File "<stdin>", line 1, in ?
NameError: name 'x' is not defined
```

Figure 8.20 The variable x is local to the printsum function. When printsum terminates, x is destroyed. Python raises a NameError exception if you try to use x outside printsum. a and b also are destroyed when printsum terminates.

```
>>> x = 39
>>> def add1():
...     x = x + 1
...
>>> add1()
Traceback (most recent call last):
  File "<stdin>", line 1, in ?
  File "<stdin>", line 2, in add1
UnboundLocalError: local variable 'x'
→ referenced before assignment
```

Figure 8.21 add1 isn't aware of the x variable declared outside it.

```
>>> x = 39
>>> def add1():
...     global x
...     x = x + 1
...
>>> add1()
>>> x
40
```

Figure 8.22 When x is declared as a global variable, add1 looks for it outside its local scope.

```
>>> def accessor():
...     print a
...
>>> def assigner():
...     a = -99
...
>>> a = 10
>>> accessor()
10
>>> assigner()
>>> print a
10
```

Figure 8.23 Python lets you access (but not change) a variable outside a function without declaring it to be global. a exists outside the accessor and assigner functions. Although accessor is able to print a, assigner is unable to change its value, because the assignment renders a a local variable inside assigner.

✔ Tips

- I've glossed over Python's elaborate set of scoping rules in this section; for a complete explanation, see "Understanding Scoping Rules" in Chapter 9.

- The global statement can appear anywhere in a function, but its variables must be used only after the statement.

- Don't use a global variable as the target control variable in a for loop or as a parameter in a function definition, class definition, or import statement.

- If you want simply to access, rather than change, a variable that exists outside the function, Python lets you do so without a global declaration (**Figure 8.23**). This technique is only an example of what Python allows owing to its scoping rules; I don't recommend it, because the resulting code is unclear. You should declare the variable to be global or (preferably) design the function to accept the variable as an argument.

- Although broadly scoped variables are useful in some situations, overuse of globals frequently leads to messy dependencies and protracted debugging sessions. Often, programmers who use globals excessively are severely punished. You should communicate with functions via arguments and return values.

DECLARING GLOBAL VARIABLES

Assigning a Function to a Variable

A function, like everything else in Python, is an object and as such may be assigned to a variable. The assignment creates an alias that refers to the same function object as the original name; see "Creating References to the Same Object" in Chapter 2.

To assign a function to a variable:

◆ Type *target* = *func*

target is a variable name, and *func* is a function name. Type only the function name, without parentheses or parameters.

In addition to being called, a function object can be assigned, stored, passed, and so on, just like lists, strings, and other objects (**Figure 8.24**).

```
>>> def square(x): return x*x
...
>>> def cube(x): return x*x*x
...
>>> pow2 = square
>>> pow3 = cube
>>> type(pow2)
<type 'function'>
>>> print pow2
<function square at 007A7FAC>
>>> print pow2(3)
9
>>> print pow3(pow2(2))
64
>>> dict = {
...     "pow2": pow2,
...     "pow3": pow3
...     }
>>> print dict["pow2"](4)
16
>>> print dict["pow3"](3)
27
>>> n = 3
>>> lst = [(pow2, n), (pow3, n)]
>>> for (func, arg) in lst:
...     print func(arg)
...
9
27
>>> def callfunc(func, arg):
...     return func(arg)
...
>>> x = callfunc(pow3, 3)
>>> print x
27
```

Figure 8.24 The square and cube function objects are assigned to the aliases pow2 and pow3, respectively. You can call pow2 and pow3 as you would square and cube. You can store function objects in data structures such as lists (lst) and dictionaries (dict) and then access them the normal way. You also can pass a function object as an argument, as done in callfunc.

```
>>> truncate = int
>>> print truncate(1.5)
1
>>> type(truncate)
<type 'builtin_function_or_method'>
>>> print truncate
<built-in function int>
```

Figure 8.25 You also can alias Python's built-in functions, as done here with `int`.

✔ Tips

- You also can assign built-in functions to variables (**Figure 8.25**).

- Invoking a function through an alias is called an *indirect function call*.

- Reassigning an alias maintains the link to the original function. In these statements, for example:

  ```
  def func(): pass
  a = func
  b = a
  ```

  func, a, and b all have the same `id()` value and so refer to the same object; see "Determining an Object's Identity" and "Creating References to the Same Object" in Chapter 2.

- Python's functional programming tools use function objects extensively; see "Using Functional Programming Tools" later in this chapter.

- **LANG** Function assignments are similar to function pointers in C.

ASSIGNING A FUNCTION TO A VARIABLE

Using Functional Programming Tools

In "Creating Expression Statements" in Chapter 2, you saw that some built-in functions and methods cause side effects. The sort() method, for example, sorts a list in place as a side effect. In "Passing Mutable and Immutable Arguments to Functions" earlier in this chapter, you saw that passing and modifying mutable arguments causes side effects.

In some quarters, side effects are frowned upon by those who believe programming should emphasize expression evaluation rather than command execution. *Functional programming languages* prohibit side effects. This means that functions and expressions cannot change any values in other functions, so the languages have no assignment statements, no global variables, no call-by-reference, no pointers, and so on.

Depending on who you ask, Python is considered to be a *procedural language* (owing to its reliance on functions) or an *object-oriented language* (because it supports the use of objects). But Python also offers some built-in functional programming tools that apply functions to sequence items. These tools are described in remainder of this chapter (**Table 8.1**).

Table 8.1

Functional Programming Tools	
Tool	**Description**
lambda	Creates small, anonymous functions
apply()	Indirectly calls a function and passes it positional and keyword arguments
map()	Applies a function to sequence items and returns a list containing the results
zip()	Takes a variable number of sequences and returns a list of tuples, where the *n*-th tuple contains the *n*-th item of each sequence
filter()	Returns a list containing the items of a sequence that satisfy a given condition
reduce()	Applies a function to sequence items, starting with the first two items and successively using the result of a function call together with the next item, ultimately reducing the sequence to a single value
List comprehension	A concise syntactic structure that constructs a list by emulating the behavior of nested for loops and if conditionals

✔ Tips

■ Python provides these tools as convenience functions; their use is optional. You can always use a def statement instead of a lambda expression or replicate the logic of the other tools by using if, while, and for statements. These tools are used frequently in Python programs, however, and you should become familiar with them (or perhaps even fond of them).

■ These tools work with all callable objects: user-defined or built-in functions or methods, or class objects. To determine whether an object is callable, type callable(*object*) to return 1 (true) if *object* is callable, or 0 (false) otherwise.

■ For more information about functional programming in Python, refer to the following references.

"Charming Python: Functional programming in Python" by David Mertz at www.106.ibm.com/developerworks/library/l-prog.html.

"Python for Lisp Programmers" by Peter Norvig at www.norvig.com/python-lisp.html.

For general information, see "Frequently Asked Questions for comp.lang.functional" at www.cs.nott.ac.uk/~gmh//faq.html.

■ **LANG** Lisp, Scheme, and Haskell are examples of functional programming languages, but they're not considered to be "pure." Lisp, for example, permits global variables.

Using *lambda* Expressions to Create Functions

As with def, you can create a function object with a lambda expression. lambda functions are small, one-line functions. They are not named when they are created, so sometimes they are called *anonymous functions*.

To use a *lambda* expression to create a function:

◆ Type lambda *param_list*: *expr*

  param_list is a list of zero or more comma-separated parameters, and *expr* is an expression that uses those parameters. Like def functions, lambda functions may have default parameter values and can take positional, keyword, and excess arguments.

The function object returned by a lambda expression behaves almost identically like an equivalent def function (**Figure 8.26**). The function definition:

def *name*(*param_list*):

  return expr

is equivalent to:

name = lambda *param_list*: *expr*

def and lambda differ in these ways:

◆ lambda is an expression, whereas def is a statement. You can use a lambda expression anywhere you'd use a normal expression: as an argument, as a list item, as a dictionary value, and so on.

◆ The def block permits multiple statements, whereas the lambda body must be a single expression.

```
>>> def product(x,y): return x*y
...
>>> product(3,4)
12
>>> times = lambda x,y: x*y
>>> times(3,4)
12
>>> type(product)
<type 'function'>
>>> type(times)
<type 'function'>
>>> print (lambda x,y: x*y)(3,4)
12
```

Figure 8.26 The lambda function times accomplishes the same thing as the def function above it. lambda and def both return function objects. The lambda expression in the print statement is an inline function; you can't do that with a def statement.

```
>>> dict = {
...     "pow2": (lambda x: x*x),
...     "pow3": (lambda x: x*x*x)
...     }
>>> print dict["pow2"](4)
16
>>> print dict["pow3"](3)
27
>>> n = 3
>>> lst = [lambda x: x*x, lambda x:
→ x*x*x]
>>> for func in lst: print func(n),
...
9 27
>>> print lst[-1](n)
27
>>> draw_line = lambda x="-", n=10: x*n
>>> draw_line()
'----------'
>>> draw_line("*", n = 20)
'********************'
```

Figure 8.27 You can use lambda expressions anywhere you would use a normal expression, such as in lists or as dictionary values, as done here. I've called the lambda functions by referring to them in the normal way: by list index or by dictionary key. The draw_line function shows that lambda functions, like def functions, can define default parameter values and accept positional or keyword arguments.

```
>>> a = "Travis trips trapshooting
→ Trappist traders".split()
>>> print a
['Travis', 'trips', 'trapshooting',
'Trappist', 'traders']
>>>
>>> a.sort(lambda x,y:
→ cmp(x.lower(), y.lower()))
>>> print a
['traders', 'Trappist', 'trapshooting',
→ 'Travis', 'trips']
```

Figure 8.28 My original case-insensitive sort used a def statement to define a custom sort-order function (refer to Figure 5.45 in Chapter 5). Here, I've deleted the def function and inserted the sorting logic directly into the sort method as a lambda expression.

◆ Nonexpression statements such as if, while, for, and print are forbidden in the body of a lambda expression, which restricts the number of operations you can cram into a lambda function.

◆ You can use a lambda expression without assigning it a name.

Figure 8.27 shows some examples. In **Figure 8.28**, I've used a lambda expression to rewrite the case-insensitive sort in Figure 5.45 (see "Defining a Custom List Sort Order" in Chapter 5).

✔ Tips

■ lambda expressions are a convenient, shorthand alternative to def functions, but their use is optional and a matter of style. lambda functions are helpful if you don't want to clutter your programs with a lot of small, nonreusable functions.

■ lambda expressions follow the same scoping rules as functions (see "Declaring Global Variables" earlier in this chapter, and "Understanding Scoping Rules" in Chapter 9).

■ **LANG** lambda gets its name from a similar Lisp feature.

Using *apply* to Call a Function

The apply() function takes a function, a tuple, and a dictionary as arguments. It calls the function by using the tuple items as positional arguments and the dictionary items as keyword arguments, and returns the result of the function call.

To use *apply* to call a function:

◆ Type apply(*func* [, *args*[, *kwargs*]])

func is a function or other callable object, *args* is a tuple containing positional arguments that are passed to *func,* and *kwargs* is a dictionary containing keyword arguments that are passed to *func*. The *kwargs* keys must be strings. If *args* or *kwargs* is omitted, their values are not supplied to *func* (**Figure 8.29**).

```
>>> apply(lambda x,y: x*y, (2,3))
6
>>> def get_color(red = 0, green = 0,
→ blue = 0):
...   colors = {
...     (0,   0,   0)  : "black",
...     (0,   0,   255): "blue",
...     (0,   255, 0)  : "green",
...     (0,   255, 255): "cyan",
...     (255, 0,   0)  : "red",
...     (255, 0,   255): "magenta",
...     (255, 255, 0)  : "yellow",
...     (255, 255, 255): "white"
...     }
...   rgb = (red, green, blue)
...   if colors.has_key(rgb):
...     return colors[rgb]
...   else:
...     return rgb
...
>>> apply(get_color)
'black'
>>> apply(get_color, (255, 0 , 0))
'red'
>>> apply(get_color, (255, 0),
→ {"blue": 255})
'magenta'
>>> apply(get_color, (), {"blue": 255,
→ "green": 255,"red": 255,})
'white'
>>>
```

(figure continues on next page)

Using *APPLY* TO CALL A FUNCTION

Figure 8.36 *continued*

```
>>> def circle(radius):
...     return 3.14159 * radius *
→ radius
...
>>> def square(side):
...     return side * side
...
>>> def rectangle(base, height):
...     return base * height
...
>>> shape = "circle"
>>> radius = 2
>>> if shape == "circle":
...     func, args = circle, (radius,)
... elif shape == "square":
...     func, args = square, (side,)
... elif shape == "rectangle":
...     func, args = rectangle, (base,
→ height)
...
>>> print shape, "area is",
→ apply(func, args)
circle area is 12.56636
```

Figure 8.29 `apply()` matches passed-in arguments to a passed-in function's parameters, calls the function, and returns the result of the call.

✔ Tips

- This function call:

  apply(*func*, *args*, *kwargs*)

  is equivalent to this one:

  func(**args*, ***kwargs*)

  For information about positional and keyword arguments, see "Specifying an Arbitrary Number of Positional Arguments" and "Specifying an Arbitrary Number of Keyword Arguments" earlier in this chapter.

- The function calls apply(*func*, *args*) and *func*(*args*) aren't equivalent. In the former, the number of items in the *args* tuple is the number of arguments passed to *func*. In the latter, *func* is passed one argument: the *args* tuple.

- The *args* argument can be any sequence (string, list, or tuple). If *args* is not a tuple, it's converted to one.

- **NEW** In antediluvian versions of Python, using apply() was the only way to pass excess positional and keyword arguments to a function.

Using *map* to Apply a Function to Sequence Items

The map() function takes a function and one or more sequences as arguments. It repeatedly calls the function, using the sequence items in turn as arguments, and returns a list containing the values returned by each function call.

To use *map* to apply a function to sequence items:

◆ Type map(*func*, *seq1* [,*seq2*,...])

func is a function or other callable object, and *seq1, seq2*,... are one or more comma-separated sequences (strings, lists, or tuples) whose items are passed to *func*. *func* must take as many arguments as there are sequences. map() always returns a list no matter what sequence types you pass it.

If you provide only one sequence argument, the *i*-th item in the returned list is *func*(*seq1*[*i*]) (**Figure 8.30**).

If you provide more than one sequence argument, the *i*-th item in the returned list is *func*(*seq1*[*i*], *seq2*[*i*],...). If the sequences have unequal lengths, map() extends shorter sequences with None items to match the length of the longest sequence. The returned list has the same length as the longest sequence (**Figure 8.31**).

```
>>> map(lambda x: x*x, range(5))
[0, 1, 4, 9, 16]
>>> map(ord, "mimetic")
[109, 105, 109, 101, 116, 105, 99]
>>> def frac(x): return x - int(x)
...
>>> map(frac, [2.0, 0.5, -2.5])
[0.0, 0.5, -0.5]
>>> map(int, map(lambda x:2*x,
→ [2.9, 3.1, 4.0]))
[5, 6, 8]
>>> dict = {1: "one", 2: "two",
→ 3: "three"}
>>> map(lambda s: s.upper(),
→ dict.values())
['THREE', 'TWO', 'ONE']
```

Figure 8.30 map() calls a function repeatedly, each time using a successive sequence item as an argument, and returns a list containing the results of all the function calls.

```
>>> map(max, [1, 5, 9], [0, 6, 4],
→ [8, 3, 5])
[8, 6, 9]
>>> map(min, [1, 5, 9], [0, 6, 4],
→ [8, 3, 5, 99])
[0, 3, 4, None]
>>> map(lambda x,y: x*y, [1, 2, 3],
→ [4, 5, 6])
[4, 10, 18]
>>> def sumprod(x, y):
...     return (x+y, x*y)
...
>>> map(sumprod, [1, 2, 3], [4, 5, 6])
[(5, 4), (7, 10), (9, 18)]
>>> m = [[1, 2, 3],
...      [4, 5, 6]]
>>> map(*[lambda *args: list(args)] + m)
[[1, 4], [2, 5], [3, 6]]
```

Figure 8.31 In the max example, the largest of the *i*-th items of all the sequences is placed in the *i*-th slot of the returned list. In the min example, Python pads shorter sequences with None items to make them equal in length to the longest sequence. The sumprod function returns a tuple, so the returned list contains tuples. The final example transposes the matrix m (a list of lists).

```
>>> map(None, [1, 2, 3])
[1, 2, 3]
>>> map(None, "abc")
['a', 'b', 'c']
>>> map(None, [1, 2, 3], "abc")
[(1, 'a'), (2, 'b'), (3, 'c')]
>>> map(None, [1, 2, 3], [4, 5, 6])
[(1, 4), (2, 5), (3, 6)]
>>> map(None, [1, 2], [3, 4], [5, 6])
[(1, 3, 5), (2, 4, 6)]
>>> map(None, [1, 2, 3], [])
[(1, None), (2, None), (3, None)]
>>> map(None, [1, 2, 3], [4, 5])
[(1, 4), (2, 5), (3, None)]
>>> seq = range(1, 6)
>>> map(None, seq, map(lambda x:
  ↪ x*x, seq))
[(1, 1), (2, 4), (3, 9), (4, 16), (5, 25)]
```

Figure 8.32 If None is mapped to a single sequence, map() returns the original sequence (as a list). If None is mapped to multiple sequences, map() returns a list of tuples in which each tuple contains an item from each sequence.

If *func* is None, map() substitutes the identity function lambda *x:x. If one sequence argument is provided, map() simply returns the sequence, converted to a list if necessary—that is, it returns list(*seq1*). If multiple sequence arguments are provided, map() returns a list of tuples in which the *i*-th tuple contains the *i*-th item of each sequence. If the sequences have unequal lengths, map() pads shorter sequences with None items, as described in the preceding paragraph (**Figure 8.32**).

✔ Tips

■ This expression:

map(*func*, *seq*)

is similar to this code:

```
if func is None:
   return list(seq)
result = []
for i in seq:
   result.append(func(i))
return result
```

■ If you're mapping None to a sequence, consider using zip() instead of map(); see the following section.

■ Consider using a list comprehension instead of map(). This expression:

map(*func*, *seq*)

is equivalent to this list comprehension:

[*func*(x) for x in *seq*]

See "Using List Comprehensions to Create Lists" later in this chapter.

USING MAP WITH SEQUENCE ITEMS

Using *zip* to Group Sequence Items

The zip() function takes one or more sequences as arguments. It returns a list of tuples in which the i-th tuple contains the i-th item of each sequence. The returned list is truncated to the length of the shortest sequence.

To use *zip* to group sequence items:

◆ Type zip(*seq1* [, *seq2*, ...])

seq1, seq2,... are one or more comma-separated sequences (strings, lists, or tuples). zip() always returns a list of tuples no matter what sequence types you pass it (**Figure 8.33**).

✔ Tips

■ If you provide one argument, zip() returns a list of one-item tuples.

■ If you provide two or more equal-length arguments, zip(*seq1*, *seq2*, ...) is equivalent to map(None, *seq1*, *seq2*, ...).

■ ◆NEW Python 2.0 introduced zip().

```
>>> zip([1, 2, 3])
[(1,), (2,), (3,)]
>>> zip("abc")
[('a',), ('b',), ('c',)]
>>> zip([1, 2, 3], "abc")
[(1, 'a'), (2, 'b'), (3, 'c')]
>>> zip([1, 2, 3], [4, 5, 6])
[(1, 4), (2, 5), (3, 6)]
>>> zip([1, 2], [3, 4], [5, 6])
[(1, 3, 5), (2, 4, 6)]
>>> zip([1, 2, 3], [])
[]
>>> zip([1, 2, 3], [4, 5])
[(1, 4), (2, 5)]
```

Figure 8.33 zip() returns a list of tuples in which the i-th tuple is (seq1[i], seq2[i],...). The returned list is truncated to the length of the shortest sequence.

```
>>> def isvowel(c):
...    return c in "aeiouAEIUO"
...
>>> filter(isvowel, "sequoia")
'euoia'
>>>
>>> filter((lambda x: x % 2), range(10))
[1, 3, 5, 7, 9]
>>>
>>> a = [1, 2, 3, 1, 5]
>>> b = [5, 6, 4, 4, 2]
>>> zip(a,b)
[(1, 5), (2, 6), (3, 4), (1, 4), (5, 2)]
>>> filter(lambda (x,y): x+y > 6,
→ zip(a,b))
[(2, 6), (3, 4), (5, 2)]
>>>
>>> d1 = {"a": 1, "b": 2, "c": 3}
>>> d2 = {"b": 20, "c": 30, "d": 40}
>>> intersect = filter(d2.has_key,
→ d1.keys())
>>> print intersect
['b', 'c']
>>>
>>> def primes(n):
...    nums = range(2, n)
...    i = 0
...    while i < len(nums):
...      nums = filter(
...        lambda x, y=nums[i]:
...        x%y or x<=y, nums)
...      i += 1
...    return nums
...
>>> primes(20)
[2, 3, 5, 7, 11, 13, 17, 19]
```

Figure 8.34 The first example returns the vowels of a string, and the second example removes even numbers from a `range()` list. The following example returns a list of tuples whose items sum to more than 6. The following example returns a list of keys common to two dictionaries. The final example returns a lists of primes up to n.

Using *filter* to Remove Sequence Items Conditionally

The filter() function takes a function and a sequence as arguments. It evaluates each item in a sequence, using the function and returns a sequence that contains the items for which the function returned true. filter() doesn't modify the original sequence.

To use *filter* to remove sequence items conditionally:

◆ Type filter(*func*, *seq*)

func is a function or other callable object that returns true or false, and *seq* is a sequence (string, list, or tuple) whose items are evaluated by *func*. filter() returns the same type of sequence you pass it. If *func* is None, filter() returns a sequence that contains all items of *seq* that evaluate to true (**Figure 8.34**).

✔ Tips

■ This expression:

filter(*func*, *seq*)

is similar to this code:

result = []

for i in *seq*:

  if (*func*(i) or

    (i and (*func* is None))):

    result.append(i)

return result

■ For information about truth values, see "Using Boolean Operators" in Chapter 2.

■ Consider using a list comprehension instead of filter(). This expression:

filter(*func*, *seq*)

is equivalent to this list comprehension:

[x for x in *seq* if *func*(x)]

See "Using List Comprehensions to Create Lists" later in this chapter.

Using *reduce* to Reduce a Sequence

The reduce() function takes a function and a sequence as arguments. It calls the function, using the first two sequence items as arguments; then it calls the function again, using the result of the preceding call and the third sequence item as arguments, and so on until the sequence is exhausted. reduce() returns the result of the final function call. The expression reduce(func, [a, b, c]), for example, is equivalent to func(func(a, b), c).

To use *reduce* to reduce a sequence:

◆ Type reduce(*func*, *seq* [,*init*])

func is a function or other callable object, and *seq* is a sequence (string, list, or tuple) whose items are passed successively to *func*. *func* must accept two arguments and return a single value. *init* is an optional starting value (expression) that is used in the first computation or as the default return value if *seq* is empty. Python raises a TypeError exception if *seq* is empty and *init* is omitted (**Figure 8.35**).

✔ Tip

■ This expression:

reduce(*func*, *seq*, *init*)

is similar to this code (assuming that the default value of *init* is None):

```
if list(seq) == []:
  return init
if init != None:
  seq.insert(0, init)
result = seq[0]
for next in seq[1:]:
  result = func(result, next)
return result
```

```
>>> nums = range(1,6)
>>> print nums
[1, 2, 3, 4, 5]
>>> sum = reduce(lambda x,y: x+y,
→ nums)
>>> mean = reduce(lambda x,y: x+y,
→ nums)/float(len(nums))
>>> sumsq = reduce(lambda x,y: x+y,
→ map(lambda x: x*x, nums))
>>> print sum, mean, sumsq
15 3.0 55
>>>
>>> n = 5
>>> factorial = reduce((lambda a,
→ b: a*b), range(1, n+1))
>>> print factorial
120
>>>
>>> lst = [1, 2, 0, 4]
>>> first_false = reduce(lambda x,
→ y: x and y, lst)
>>> print first_false
0
>>>
>>> m = [[1, 2, 3],
...      [4, 5, 6],
...      [7, 8, 9]]
>>> n = 1
>>> def col_sum(m, n):
...    return reduce(lambda x,y: x+y,
→ map(lambda x,n=n: x[n], m))
...
>>> for i in range(len(m)):
...    print col_sum(m, i)
...
12
15
18
```

Figure 8.35 sum, mean, and sumsq calculate the sum, average, and sum of squares of a list of numbers. factorial calculates the factorial of n (see Figure 7.16 in Chapter 7). first_false returns the first false value in a list (change *and* to *or* to return the first true value). The col_sum function returns the sum of the items in the n-th column of the matrix m (a lists of lists).

Using List Comprehensions to Create Lists

A *list comprehension* is a concise and often clearer alternative to creating lists by using lambda, map(), and filter(). **Figure 8.36** shows some examples.

In its simplest form, a list comprehension maps one list into another by applying an expression to each item in a sequence.

To use a simple list comprehension:

◆ Type [*expr* for *var* in *seq*]

expr is an expression, *var* is a variable, and *seq* is a sequence (string, list, or tuple). Python loops through *seq* and assigns each item to *var,* one by one, evaluating *expr* for each. The returned list contains successive values of *expr.*

You can add an if condition to the end of a list comprehension to exclude items from the returned list.

To use a simple list comprehension with an *if* condition:

◆ Type [*expr* for *var* in *seq* if *cond*]

This list comprehension behaves like the one described in the preceding exercise, except that *expr* is evaluated only if *cond* is true.

In its extended form, a list comprehension may have an arbitrary number of nested for loops, and each loop may have its own if condition. In practice, list comprehensions typically have three or fewer for loops.

A list comprehension is a single expression; I've indented the example in the following exercise and split it across lines for clarity.

To use an extended list comprehension:

◆ Type:

```
[expr for var1 in seq1 if cond1
    for var2 in seq2 if cond2
    ...
    for varN in seqN if condN]
```

Another common form includes a single if condition:

```
[expr for var1 in seq1
    for var2 in seq2
    ...
    for varN in seqN
    if cond]
```

This is roughly equivalent to:

```
result = []
for var1 in seq1:
  for var2 in seq2:
    ...
      for varN in seqN:
        if cond:
          result.append(expr)
```

```
>>> s = range(8)
>>> print s
[0, 1, 2, 3, 4, 5, 6, 7]
>>> [2*x for x in s]
[0, 2, 4, 6, 8, 10, 12, 14]
>>> [x*x for x in s]
[0, 1, 4, 9, 16, 25, 36, 49]
>>> [x*x for x in s if x % 2]
[1, 9, 25, 49]
>>> [(x, x*x) for x in s if x % 2]
[(1, 1), (3, 9), (5, 25), (7, 49)]
>>>
>>> s1 = [1, 2, 3]
>>> s2 = [4, 5, 6]
>>> s3 = [7, 8, 9]
>>> [x+y+z for (x,y,z) in
→ zip(s1,s2,s3)]
[12, 15, 18]
>>>
>>> s1 = "aeiou"
>>> s2 = "sequoia"
>>> ords = [(c, ord(c)) for c in s1]
>>> print ords
[('a', 97), ('e', 101), ('i', 105), ('o', 111),
→ ('u', 117)]
>>> all_in = 0 not in [c in s2 for c
→ in s1]
>>> any_in = 1 in [c in s2 for c in s1]
>>> print all_in, any_in
1 1
>>>
>>> d1 = {"a": 1, "b": 2, "c": 3}
>>> values = [d1[key] for key in
→ d1.keys()]
>>> print values
[2, 3, 1]
>>> ["%s=%s" % (k, v) for (k, v) in
→ d1.items()]
['b=2', 'c=3', 'a=1']
>>> d2 = {"b": 20, "c": 30, "d": 40}
```

(figure continues on next page)

Figure 8.36 *continued*

```
>>> intersection = [key for key in
→ d1.keys() if d2.has_key(key)]
>>> print intersection
['b', 'c']
>>>
>>> s = [[1, 2], [], [3, 4, 5], [6]]
>>> flatten = [x for nested in s for
→ x in nested]
>>> print flatten
[1, 2, 3, 4, 5, 6]
>>>
>>> s1 = [1, 2, 3]
>>> s2 = [5, 4, 3]
>>> pairs = [(x,y) for x in s1 for y
→ in s2]
>>> bigpairs = [(x,y) for x in s1
...                   for y in s2
...                   if x*y > 6]
>>> print pairs
[(1, 5), (1, 4), (1, 3), (2, 5), (2, 4), (2, 3),
→ (3, 5), (3, 4), (3, 3)]
>>> print bigpairs
[(2, 5), (2, 4), (3, 5), (3, 4), (3, 3)]
>>> lst1 = [0, 1, 2, 3, 4]
>>> lst2 = [5, 6, 7, 8, 9]
>>> [(x,y) for x in lst1 if x > 2
→ for y in lst2 if y < 7]
[(3, 5), (3, 6), (4, 5), (4, 6)]
```

Figure 8.36 The first few examples show common numeric list comprehensions. The following example uses zip() to sum positional items in sequences. ords is a list of tuples in which each tuple contains a character and its ASCII code. all_in determines whether *all* of the characters in s1 are in s2; any_in determines whether *any* of the characters in s1 are in s2. values contains the values of the dictionary d1. intersection is a list of keys that d1 and d2 have in common. flatten is a common operation that "unnests" nested lists. pairs contains all the two-item combinations of two lists, and bigpairs contains the two-item combinations in which the product of the items exceeds 6.

✔ Tips

- The variables defined in a list comprehension (*var1, var2,...*) overwrite same-named variables in the current scope and remain defined after the list is created. In [x for x in seq], for example, x is set to the last item of seq after the list comprehension has executed.

- Sequences may be unequal lengths, as each sequence is part of its own nested for loop.

- If a list comprehension creates a list of tuples, you must enclose the expression in parentheses. [(x, x*x) for x in seq], for example, is valid, whereas [x, x*x for x in seq] is not.

- **NEW** Python 2.0 introduced list comprehensions.

MODULES

A *module* is a single text file that contains a related collection of variables, functions, and other objects. Python includes a large number of modules; you've already seen the math module, for example, which contains mathematical functions and constants. You'll want to organize a large program as a set of modules to make it more manageable. You'll be able to reuse those modules in other programs.

Modules also are used to prevent name conflicts. You can write your own len() function, for example, and qualify it with the module name to prevent it from clashing with Python's built-in len() function or a len() function in another module. The names associated with an object are called its *attributes*.

Modules can contain Python code, or they can be compiled C (or C++) objects. Both types are used in the same way, and many of the standard modules are C extensions. I cover only Python-coded modules in this book. For information about C extensions, refer to the standard Python manuals *Extending and Embedding the Python Interpreter* and *Python/C API Reference Manual.*

Structuring a Module

You should lay out your modules in a consistent and logical manner. In this book, I use the structure shown in **Script 9.1**. Each module section is optional; the sections are:

1. You can add a Unix shebang line if you're going to run the module as a program rather than import it into other modules. The shebang line is unnecessary (and ignored) in Windows and Mac OS. If present, the shebang line must be the first line in the file. See "Running Programs in Script Mode" in Chapter 1.

2. This string literal is the documentation string. It describes the module's purpose and functionality. See "Documenting a Module" later in this chapter.

3. These statements load other modules whose functions or objects are required to run the code in the current module. See "Loading a Module with import" later in this chapter.

4. These statements are the module's global variables and initialization code. The names defined here are called *top-level* or *module-level names* because they're not nested in the module's functions and class definitions. These names can be used by functions and classes within this module and by programs that import this module.

5. These statements are this module's class definitions; see Chapter 12.

6. These statements are this module's function definitions; see Chapter 8.

7. When the module code runs, this if statement checks whether this module is running as a program or has been imported as a module. See "Determining Whether a Module Is Running As a Program" later in this chapter.

Script 9.1 A common structure for Python modules.

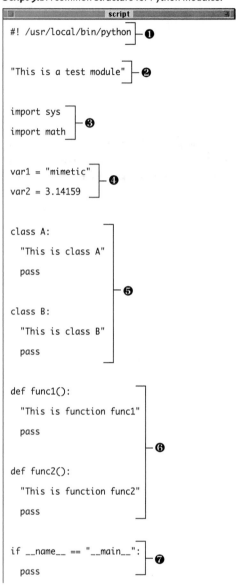

Script 9.2 The *area* module defines functions that calculate the areas of geometric shapes.

```
"Provides functions that calculate areas of
geometric shapes"


pi = 3.14159


def circle(radius):

    "Returns the area of a circle, given its
    → radius"

    return pi * radius * radius


def rectangle(base, height):

    "Returns the area of a rectangle, given its
    → base and height"

    return float(base * height)


def square(side):

    "Returns the area of a square, given one side"

    return float(side * side)


def triangle(base, height):

    "Returns the area of a triangle, given its
    → base and height"

    return 0.5 * base * height
```

Creating a Module

A *module* is a text file of Python statements that you can create with your favorite text editor (Notepad, vi, or BBEdit, for example) or with IDLE (see "Using IDLE" in Chapter 1). Module file names carry the *.py* extension.

To create a module:

1. Start a text editor.

2. Type Python definitions and statements, structuring your module as described in the preceding section.

3. Save the file as *module*.py.

   module is a valid Python name, so it may not contain blanks or special characters even if your operating system permits them; see "Naming Variables" in Chapter 2. Use a concise, descriptive name, as the module name is its file name without the *.py* suffix.

The *area* module in **Script 9.2** defines functions that calculate the areas of various two-dimensional geometric shapes. Note that it also defines a global variable pi, which is used in the circle() function.

The stats module in **Script 9.3** defines functions that calculate simple statistics for a list of numbers. Note that it imports the math module so that it may use the math.sqrt() function in the stdev() function.

I'll use these modules in subsequent examples in this chapter.

✔ Tips

- A module is just a listing of Python source code, so you can run it as a program or import it as a module. Although no special syntax distinguishes a program from a module, there's a way to check whether a module is running as a program or has been imported as a module; see "Determining Whether a Module Is Running As a Program" later in this chapter.

- You must load a module to use its functions and other objects; see "Loading a Module with *import*" later in this chapter.

- If a module file name doesn't end in *.py,* you'll still be able run the file as a program, but you won't be able to import it as a module object.

- If you're an Emacs user, try Python mode at www.python.org/emacs/python-mode/.

- **LANG** Python modules are similar to Perl modules (*.lib* or *.pm* files), C libraries, and Java packages.

Script 9.3 The stats module defines functions that calculate statistics for lists of numbers.

```
"Provides statistical functions that operate
→ on a list of numbers"


import math


def mean(nums):

  "Returns the arithmetic mean of a list of
  → numbers"

  return sum(nums)/float(len(nums))


def median(nums):

  "Returns the median of a list of numbers"

  numscopy = nums[:]  # Don't sort original

  numscopy.sort()

  n = len(numscopy)

  mid = n/2

  if (n % 2) == 0:

    return (numscopy[mid] + numscopy[mid-1])
    → /2.0

  else:

    return float(numscopy[mid])


def stdev(nums):

  "Returns the sample standard deviation of a
  → list of numbers"

  devs = map(lambda x, avg=mean(nums): x-avg,
  → nums)

  return math.sqrt(sumsq(devs)/(len(nums)-1))


def sum(nums):

  "Returns the sum of a list of numbers"

  return float(reduce(lambda x,y: x+y, nums))


def sumsq(nums):

  "Returns the sum of squares of a list of
  → numbers"

  return sum(map(lambda x: x*x, nums))
```

CREATING A MODULE

```
>>> import area
>>> import stats
>>> print area.__doc__
Provides functions that calculate areas of
→ geometric shapes
>>> print stats.__doc__
Provides statistical functions that operate
→ on a list of numbers
```

Figure 9.1 These are the module docstrings specified in the modules in Scripts 9.2 and 9.3 earlier in this chapter.

```
>>> import copy
>>> print copy.__doc__
Generic (shallow and deep) copying operations.


Interface summary:

        import copy


        x = copy.copy(y)        # make a
→ shallow copy of y

        x = copy.deepcopy(y)    # make a deep
→ copy of y


For module specific errors, copy.error is
→ raised.


The difference between shallow and deep
→ copying is only relevant for compound
→ objects (objects that contain other
→ objects, like lists or class instances).


- A shallow copy constructs a new compound
→ object and then (to the extent possible)
→ inserts *the same objects* into in that
→ the original contains.


- A deep copy constructs a new compound
→ object and then, recursively, inserts
→ *copies* into it of the objects found in
→ the original.

...<snip>...
```

Figure 9.2 Module docstrings often provide comprehensive information about the module's assumptions, variables, functions, and classes. In practice, your module's docstring should resemble that of copy here (abridged to save space) rather than the terse docstrings I created for the area and stats modules.

Documenting a Module

As with functions (see "Documenting a Function" in Chapter 8), Python allows you to add an optional documentation string as the first line of a module file (or the first line after the shebang line, if present). A module's docstring should comprehensively describe the module's purpose and functionality and should be more elaborate than a function docstring.

Docstrings are assigned to the module's __doc__ attribute and, unlike # comments, can be accessed with the dot operator at run time.

To access a module's docstring:

1. If necessary, import the module (see the following section) by typing this line:

import *module*

module is a module name.

2. Type *module*.__doc__ (**Figure 9.1**).

✔ Tips

- If you don't specify a docstring, the default value of the __doc__ attribute is None.

- Although I often omit docstrings in this book to save space, it's a good practice to add them to all your modules. Your users will appreciate them, and some tools use docstrings to create help documentation.

- You can access the docstrings of built-in modules; many of which are comprehensive in scope (**Figure 9.2**).

- You also can add a docstring to a class definition; see "Documenting a Class" in Chapter 12.

Loading a Module with *import*

To use the objects defined in a module, you must load the module with an `import` statement. The name of a module is its file name without the *.py* extension (remember that Python names are case-sensitive). Here are some salient points about `import`:

◆ The first time you load a module, Python executes all the code in the module.

◆ Module code is executed *only once* during the first import, regardless of how many times the module appears in subsequent `import` statements anywhere in your program. This behavior is desirable: If different modules in your program all import the sys module, for example, it would be time-consuming and redundant to execute the sys code each time.

◆ `import` can appear anywhere in a program, including inside functions and in the bodies of control flow statements.

◆ `import` turns a text file into a module object and assigns that object to a name.

◆ Python searches for modules in `sys.path`; see "Specifying the Module Search Path" later in this chapter.

To load a module:

◆ To load a module, type:

`import module`

module is a module name.

or

To load multiple modules, type:

`import module1, module2, . . .`

module1, module2,... are one or more comma-separated module names (**Figure 9.3**).

```
>>> import area
>>> import stats
>>> type(area)
<type 'module'>
>>> type(stats)
<type 'module'>
>>>
>>> import math, copy, sys
>>>
```

Figure 9.3 When you import a module, Python converts it to a module object.

Bytecode Files

When the interpreter first imports (or reloads) a module, it executes all the module's code. If the code contains an error, Python raises an exception; otherwise, it quietly creates a compiled bytecode file. *Bytecodes* are portable, low-level (not human-readable) instructions that can run on any machine with a Python interpreter. A bytecode file has the same name as its corresponding *.py* module file, except that its extension is *.pyc*. These *.pyc* files will appear in your module directories after you run a program. Technically speaking, Python actually loads these *.pyc* files, and not the *.py* files, when you import a module. Python will compile a module into a new *.pyc* file only if it can't find an existing *.pyc* file (because you've deleted it or you've never loaded the module before) or if the existing *.pyc* file's time stamp is older than its corresponding *.py* file's time stamp (because you've modified the *.py* source code since the last import). This scheme prevents needless recompilation when you run your program.

```
>>> import area
>>> print area.pi
3.14159
>>> area.pi = 3
>>> import area
>>> print area.pi
3
```

Figure 9.4 The pi attribute is defined the first time *area* is loaded. The second import doesn't rerun *area*'s code, so pi isn't reinitialized; instead, it retains its modified value.

✔ Tips

■ When modules import other modules, it's customary to place all the import statements at the start of the importing module.

■ Because Python doesn't rerun module code after the first import, a variable created in a module won't revert to its initial value on subsequent imports (**Figure 9.4**). To rerun module code, see "Reloading a Module with *reload*" later in this chapter.

■ To load specific module objects, see "Loading Specific Module Names with *from*" later in this chapter.

■ To import a module under a different name, see "Loading a Module Under a Different Name with *as*" later in this chapter.

■ The import statement invokes the built-in __import__ function. When you become proficient in Python, you can use __import__ to override the default import behavior for loading your own modules. For information about __import__, see Section 2.3, "Built-in Functions," of the *Python Library Reference*.

■ **LANG** Python's import statement is similar to Perl's require, C's #include, and Java's import statements. Unlike C's #include, Python's import is an executable statement, not a preprocessor (compile-time) declaration.

Accessing Attributes

When Python executes module code during an import, statements that assign names (=, def, class, and so on) create attributes. Attributes include names of variables, functions, classes, and other objects. To access an object's attribute, *qualify* the attribute with the object name by using the dot operator. After you import a module, Python raises a NameError exception if you to try to access one of its attributes without qualification (**Figure 9.5**).

To access an attribute:

◆ Type *object.attr*

object is an object (expression), and *attr* is an attribute name (**Figure 9.6**).

```
>>> import stats
>>> nums = [1, 2, 4, 5]
>>> mean(nums)
Traceback (most recent call last):
  File "<stdin>", line 1, in ?
NameError: name 'mean' is not defined
```

Figure 9.5 Here, Python complains because the mean() function isn't qualified by the stats module.

```
>>> import area, stats
>>> print area.pi
3.14159
>>> print stats.mean
<function mean at 007EE594>
>>> area.circle(2)
12.56636
>>> nums = [1, 2, 4, 5]
>>> stats.mean(nums)
3.0
>>> print map(area.square, nums)
[1.0, 4.0, 16.0, 25.0]
```

Figure 9.6 After importing a module, you can access its objects by qualifying them with the module's name. You can use these objects in the same way that you would use Python's built-in objects.

```
>>> import math, area
>>> print math.pi
3.14159265359
>>> print area.pi
3.14159
```

Figure 9.7 My *area* module and the built-in *math* module both define the variable *pi*. You can differentiate the two *pi* objects by using qualification. Note that *area.pi* has fewer significant digits than *math.pi*.

✔ Tips

- Qualification works on all objects with attributes: modules, lists, strings, functions, classes, and so on.

- Qualification is necessary to distinguish like-named attributes in different modules (**Figure 9.7**).

- If you don't qualify a name, Python searches for it by using scoping rules; see "Understanding Scoping Rules" later in this chapter.

- Names imported with a from statement don't require qualification; see "Loading Specific Module Names with *from*" later in this chapter.

- You can attach arbitrary information to functions and methods by assigning them custom attributes. These statements, for example, create the cube() function and assign it an attribute named category with the value "math":

  ```
  >>> def cube(x):
  ...   return x * x * x
  ...
  >>> cube.category = "math"
  ```

  Note that the attribute is defined outside the function body. Function attributes are an alternative to docstrings for storing function information that's available at run time; they are stored in a dictionary that's available as the __dict__ attribute of the function or method.

- **NEW** Python 2.1 introduced function attributes.

- **LANG** Python's . operator is similar to Perl's :: and Java's . operators.

Listing an Object's Attributes

The dir() function is a useful tool for inter-active experimenting and learning about built-in and user-defined objects. dir() returns a sorted list of the names of an object's important attributes, including its variables, functions, and methods.

To list an object's attributes:

◆ Type dir(*object*)

object is an object (expression) (**Figure 9.8**).

✔ Tips

■ Without an argument, dir() returns a list of names in the current local namespace; see "Accessing Namespaces" later in this chapter.

■ Technically speaking, dir() retrieves attributes from an object's __dict__, __methods__, and __members__ attributes.

```
>>> dir(39)
□
>>> dir("")
['capitalize', 'center', 'count'
...<snip>...
'title', 'translate', 'upper']
>>> dir(())
□
>>> dir([])
['append', 'count', 'extend', 'index',
→ 'insert', 'pop', 'remove', 'reverse',
→ 'sort']
>>> dir({})
['clear', 'copy', 'get', 'has_key', 'items',
→ 'keys', 'popitem', 'setdefault', 'update',
→ 'values']
>>> import math, area
>>> dir(math)
['__doc__', '__name__', 'acos', 'asin',
→ 'atan', 'atan2', 'ceil',
...<snip>...
'sinh', 'sqrt', 'tan', 'tanh']
>>> dir(math.sqrt)
['__doc__', '__name__', '__self__']
>>> dir(area)
['__builtins__', '__doc__', '__file__',
→ '__name__', 'circle', 'pi', 'rectangle',
→ 'square', 'triangle']
>>> dir(area.pi)
□
>>> dir(area.circle)
['__dict__', '__doc__', '__name__',
→ 'func_closure', 'func_code',
→ 'func_defaults', 'func_dict', 'func_doc',
→ 'func_globals', 'func_name']
```

Figure 9.8 The dir() function returns a list of an object's important attributes. Note that numbers and tuples have no methods.

```
>>> import math
>>> obj = math
>>> attr = "sqrt"
>>> if hasattr(obj, attr):
...   a = getattr(obj, attr)
...   print "Attribute", attr,
→ "is a", type(a)
... else:
...   print "Attribute",
→ attr,"doesn't exist"
...
Attribute sqrt is a <type
→ 'builtin_function_or_method'>
>>>
>>> import area
>>> print area.pi
3.14159
>>> delattr(area, "pi")
>>> print area.pi
Traceback (most recent call last):
  File "<stdin>", line 1, in ?
AttributeError: 'area' module has no
→ attribute 'pi'
>>>
>>> import stats
>>> average = getattr(stats, "mean")
>>> average([1,2,4,5])
3.0
>>>
>>> print getattr(getattr(stats,
→ "median"), "__doc__")
Returns the median of a list of numbers
```

Figure 9.9 Python's built-in functions for manipulating attributes.

■ The expression delattr(*object*, *attr*) is equivalent to del *object.attr*.

Manipulating Attributes

Python has several built-in functions that manipulate attributes. **Figure 9.9** shows some examples.

To determine whether a particular attribute exists:

◆ Type hasattr(*object*, *attr*) to return 1 (true) if *object* has an attribute named *attr*, or 0 (false) otherwise.

object is an object (expression), and *attr* is a string.

To retrieve an attribute:

◆ Type getattr(*object*, *attr* [,*default*]) to return attribute *attr* of *object* or *default* if *attr* doesn't exist.

If *attr* doesn't exist and *default* is omitted, Python raises an AttributeError exception.

object is an object (expression), *attr* is a string, and *default* is an expression.

To set an attribute value:

◆ Type setattr(*object*, *attr* ,*value*) to assign *value* to attribute *attr* of *object* or create a new attribute if *attr* doesn't exist.

object is an object (expression), *attr* is a string, and *value* is an expression.

To delete an attribute:

◆ Type delattr(*object*, *attr*) to delete the attribute *attr* of *object*.

If *attr* doesn't exist, Python raises an AttributeError exception.

object is an object (expression), and *attr* is a string.

✔ Tips

■ The expression getattr(*object*, *attr*) is equivalent to *object.attr*.

■ The expression setattr(*object*, *attr*, *value*) is equivalent to *object.attr* = *value*.

Loading Specific Module Names with *from*

Whereas import loads a module as a whole, the from statement loads only the objects (names) you specify. Objects imported with from are copied to the current namespace, so you can refer directly to them without quali-fication (see "Accessing Attributes" earlier in this chapter). from has two forms: One form loads the specified names, and the other loads *all* of a module's names.

To load specific module names:

◆ Type:

from *module* import *name1, name2,...*

module is a module name, and *name1, name2,...* are one or more comma-separated attribute names (**Figure 9.10**).

To load all module names:

◆ Type:

from *module* import *

module is a module name, and * repre-sents all the attribute names in *module* (**Figure 9.11**).

```
>>> from area import pi, circle
>>> print pi
3.14159
>>> circle(2)
12.56636
>>> triangle(3, 4)
Traceback (most recent call last):
  File "<stdin>", line 1, in ?
NameError: name 'triangle' is not defined
```

Figure 9.10 This from statement imports only the names pi and circle from the *area* module, so these names can be used without qualification. If you try to use one of *area*'s other names, such as triangle, Python raises a NameError exception.

```
>>> from stats import *
>>> nums = [1, 2, 3, 6]
>>> mean(nums)
3.0
>>> median(nums)
2.5
>>> stdev(nums)
2.1602468994692869
>>> sum(nums)
12.0
>>> sumsq(nums)
50.0
```

Figure 9.11 This form of the from statement imports all of a module's names.

```
>>> from math import pi
>>> from area import pi
>>> print pi
3.14159
>>>
>>> import math
>>> print math.pi
3.14159265359
>>> import area
>>> print area.pi
3.14159
```

Figure 9.12 A naming conflict: I've used from to import pi from both the built-in math module and my area module. Python used the most recently imported name (from area) and overwrote math.pi. (area.pi has fewer significant digits than math.pi.) You can avoid this problem by using import instead of from, and qualifying the names.

```
>>> from area import pi
>>> print pi
3.14159
>>> print area.pi
Traceback (most recent call last):
  File "<stdin>", line 1, in ?
NameError: name 'area' is not defined
```

Figure 9.13 Python doesn't recognize the area module here, because from only copies names; it doesn't create a module object.

✔ Tips

- from is handy for importing frequently used names; using unqualified names saves typing and leaves code less cluttered. But you should use from judiciously. It invites name conflicts, and it can be difficult for other programmers to determine where unqualified names originate (**Figure 9.12**).

- from doesn't create a module object; it only copies objects (names) from the module file to the importer. If you try to refer to the module or qualify one of its names, Python won't recognize the module and will raise a NameError exception (**Figure 9.13**).

continues on next page

LOADING SPECIFIC MODULE NAMES WITH *FROM*

- In-place changes to mutable objects imported with from are visible to aliases. Reassignments to mutable and immutable objects aren't visible (**Script 9.4** and **Figure 9.14**). This behavior is consistent with that discussed in "Passing Mutable and Immutable Arguments to Functions" in Chapter 8. For information about aliases, see "Creating References to the Same Object" in Chapter 2.

- As with import, module code is executed only once during the first from; see "Loading a Module with *import*" earlier in this chapter.

- from *module* import * can occur only at the top level of a module, not inside function and class definitions.

- from *module* import * doesn't import names that begin with an underscore, which are termed *private names*. You must use the other form of from or an import statement to import private names.

- from, like import, searches for modules in sys.path; see "Specifying the Module Search Path" later in this chapter.

- To import a module under a different name, see "Loading a Module Under a Different Name with *as*" later in this chapter.

- **LANG** Python's from statement is similar to Perl's use statement.

Script 9.4 This module file, *somevars.py*, creates a few top-level variables.

```script
s = "mimetic"
lst1 = [1, 2, 3]
lst2 = [4, 5, 6]
```

```
>>> from somevars import s, lst1, lst2
>>> s = ""
>>> lst1[0] = -99
>>> lst2 = []
>>>
>>> import somevars
>>> print somevars.s
mimetic
>>> print somevars.lst1
[-99, 2, 3]
>>> print somevars.lst2
[4, 5, 6]
```

Figure 9.14 Assigning a new value to the name s that I got from the from assignment changes only a local copy and has no effect on somevars.s. The in-place alteration of the name lst1 (from the from assignment) is reflected in its alias, somevars.lst1. The name lst2 (from the from assignment) and somevars.lst2 are aliases initially, but assigning lst2 a new object destroys its reference to the shared object, so changes aren't visible to somevars.lst2.

```
>>> import area as geometry
>>> geometry.circle(2)
12.56636
>>> geometry.square(3)
9.0
>>>
>>> from stats import mean as
→ average, stdev as sample_sd
>>> nums = [1, 2, 3, 4]
>>> average(nums)
2.5
>>> sample_sd(nums)
1.2909944487358056
>>> mean(nums)
Traceback (most recent call last):
  File "<stdin>", line 1, in ?
NameError: name 'mean' is not defined
```

Figure 9.15 Here, I use the *as* extension to import the *area* module, the stats.mean function, and the stats.stdev functions under different names. Note that Python recognizes only the "as" names of these objects, not their "real" names.

✔ Tips

■ This statement:

`import *module* as *name*`

is equivalent to this code:

`import *module*`
`*name* = *module*`
`del *module*`

■ When importing multiple modules or attribute names, you may omit the *as* extension for any particular name. The statement `import mod1 as my_mod1, mod2, mod3 as my_mod3`, for example, is legal.

■ *as* is not a Python keyword and is recognized only in the import and from contexts, so you may use *as* as a variable name or function name.

■ **NEW** Python 2.0 introduced *as*.

Loading a Module Under a Different Name with *as*

Python allows you to import an entire module or a specific module name under a different name by using the *as* extension of the import and from statements. This capability is useful to prevent name conflicts, for example. See **Figure 9.15** for some examples.

To load a module under a different name:

◆ To load a module under a different name, type:

`import *module* as *imp_name*`

module is a module name, and *imp_name* is the name *module* is imported as.

To load multiple modules under different names:

◆ Type:

`import *module1* as *imp_name1*, *module2* as *imp_name2*,...`

module1, module2,... are module names, and *imp_name1, imp_name2,...* are the corresponding names they are imported as.

To load specific module names under different names:

◆ Type:

`from *module* import *name1* as *imp_name1*, *name2* as *imp_name2*,...`

module is a module name; *name1, name2,...* are attribute names; and *imp_name1, imp_name2,...* are the corresponding names they are imported as.

Enabling Language Features

Each new version of Python introduces new features (bug fixes aside). Most new features are benign in the sense that they don't cause the results of programs written for earlier versions of Python to change. Occasionally, a new feature introduces *backward-incompatible behavior* that "breaks" existing programs because they depend on old behavior. If a new feature redefines how an operator works, for example, an expression that uses that operator will return different values for old and new Python versions.

The Python team takes a conservative approach to this predicament. Rather than irrevocably discarding an old feature in favor of a new one, they grant a transition period between the release of the transitional version and the release of the backward-incompatible version. During this period, new backward-incompatible features are available in the transitional version but must be enabled explicitly by a special form of the from statement.

To enable a language feature:

◆ Type:

```
from __future__ import feature
```

feature is the name of the optional feature, given in the Python release notes.

The from __future__ statement has some special restrictions:

◆ It can appear only at the top of a module (after the docstring).

◆ It must precede any Python code or normal import statements.

✔ Tips

■ When a feature eventually becomes a standard part of the language, its from __future__ directive is no longer required.

■ As with the normal from statement, you can import multiple features by separating the feature names with commas: *feature1, feature2,...*.

■ Python 2.1 introduced nested scopes (see "Nesting Functions" later in this chapter), which must be enabled in Python 2.1 with:

```
from __future__ import nested_scopes
```

In Python 2.2, nested scopes became a standard part of the language, so their use no longer needs to be enabled (in versions 2.2 and later) with a from __future__ directive.

■ Python 2.2 introduced true division and generators, which must be enabled with:

```
from __future__ import true_division
```

and

```
from __future__ import generators
```

More information about these new features is available at www.amk.ca/python/2.2/.

■ Python 2.1 introduced from __future__.

```
>>> import area
>>> print area.pi
3.14159
>>> area.pi = 3
>>> print area.pi
3
>>> reload(area)
<module 'area' from 'area.pyc'>
>>> print area.pi
3.14159
```

Figure 9.16 Reloading *area* reruns the code in *area.py*, thus reinitializing the value of pi. Compare this behavior with that of import in Figure 9.4 earlier in this chapter.

```
>>> import area
>>> print area.pi
3.14159
>>> # Edits to source code in
>>> # area.py happen here
...
>>> reload(area)
<module 'area' from 'area.py'>
>>> print area.pi
3
```

Figure 9.17 Between importing and reloading *area*, I changed the value of pi in the source code; see Figure 9.18.

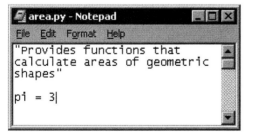

Figure 9.18 Here, after the import but before the reload() in Figure 9.17, I changed the value of pi from 3.14159 to 3 in the *area.py* file.

Reloading a Module with *reload*

Recall from "Loading a Module with *import*" earlier in this chapter that Python executes module code only once, during the first import. You can force Python to reload and rerun a module's code by using the built-in reload() function. This function is useful when you want to see module changes without stopping Python.

reload() is suitable only in the contexts of program development and debugging. reload() takes a module object, not the name of a *.py* file, so you must import a module successfully with import before you can reload it.

To reload a module:

◆ Type reload(*module*)

   module is a module object created by import (**Figure 9.16**).

During program development, reloading typically is used for on-the-fly recompilation of edited module files (**Figures 9.17** and **9.18**).

continues on next page

✔ Tips

- Note that reload() is a function, whereas import is a statement.

- Operations that follow a reload() will use the newly reloaded objects, but Python won't update old objects retroactively, so it's possible to have a mix of old and new versions of objects while your program is running. A class instance that existed before a reload will continue to use old methods, for example.

- Other modules that import a reloaded module with import will use the newly reloaded objects; but modules that import a reloaded module with from will continue to use the old objects (unless you reissue a from statement after reloading).

- Reloading a module won't also reload any modules that the reloaded module happens to import. If mod1 contains the statement import mod2, for example, reload(mod1) won't also reload mod2.

- Reloading changes a module in place, so objects in the old module that aren't over-written by the new module are retained in the new module.

- C/C++ extensions can't be reloaded by reload().

```
>>> import sys

>>> print sys.path

['', 'e:\\python21', 'e:\\python21\\dlls',
→ 'e:\\python21\\lib',
→ 'e:\\python21\\lib\\plat-win',
→ 'e:\\python21\\lib\\lib-tk']
```

Figure 9.19 This is the module search path for my Windows PC. The list's first item is an empty string, which represents the current directory. Search paths vary by system.

```
>>> sys.path.append('e:\\scripts')

>>> print sys.path

['', 'e:\\python21', 'e:\\python21\\dlls',
→ 'e:\\python21\\lib',
→ 'e:\\python21\\lib\\plat-win',
→ 'e:\\python21\\lib\\lib-tk',
→ 'e:\\scripts']
```

Figure 9.20 Here, I've added the directory e:\scripts to my search path. In Windows, use the \\ escape sequence to represent a backslash (see "Inserting Special Characters into a String" in Chapter 4).

✔ Tips

■ Python raises an ImportError exception if it can't find a module.

■ If you're just experimenting with Python, the simplest approach is to keep all your files in the current directory. If you're creating production programs, create specific directories in which to store your modules and either add those directories to PYTHONPATH or append them to sys.path. You should *not* store modules in one of the default search directories, because your modules may be deleted if someone installs a new version of Python.

■ You can explore the search path graphically if you're using IDLE; choose File > Path Browser. (See "Using IDLE" in Chapter 1.)

■ **LANG** Python's PYTHONPATH is similar to Java's CLASSPATH.

Specifying the Module Search Path

When Python loads a module, it searches for it in the list of directories in the path attribute of the built-in sys module. Python initializes sys.path with the directories in the environment variable PYTHONPATH (if it exists; see "Using Python Environment Variables" in Chapter 1) and then adds some installation-dependent directories.

Python searches the directories in the listed order. The first item in the list is always the current directory, represented by the actual directory name or by an empty string. Python inserts the current directory before the PYTHONPATH directories, so it's always the first place searched.

To get the module search path:

◆ Type:

```
import sys
sys.path
```

sys.path contains a list of directories, as strings (**Figure 9.19**).

sys.path is a list, so you can use the append() method to add a new directory to the path while your program is running. You can, in fact, use any list operation or method to modify the search path; see "Modifying a List" in Chapter 5.

To add a directory to the module search path:

◆ Type:

```
import sys
sys.path.append(dir)
```

dir is a string containing a directory name (**Figure 9.20**).

Determining Whether a Module Is Running As a Program

A module is just a collection of Python statements, so you can load it in one of two ways: import it for use in other modules or run it as a stand-alone program. You can determine how a module has been loaded by inspecting its built-in __name__ attribute. __name__ contains a string whose value depends on how the module is used. If you import a module, __name__ contains the name of the module file without the *.py* extension. If you run the module as a program, __name__ contains the string "__main__".

Script 9.5 contains a statement that prints the value of its *__name__* attribute. **Figure 9.21** shows the result of an import, and **Figure 9.22** shows the script running as a program.

Script 9.5 This script, *printname.py,* simply echoes the value of its *__name__* attribute.

```
print "__name__ = ", __name__
```

```
>>> import printname
__name__ = printname
```

Figure 9.21 If you import a module, its *__name__* attribute contains the module file name without the *.py* extension.

```
E:\scripts>python printname.py
__name__ = __main__
```

Figure 9.22 If you run a module as a program, its *__name__* attribute contains the string "__main__".

Script 9.6 I've appended this self-test routine to the end of the stats module (refer to Script 9.3).

```
if __name__ == "__main__":

  #Benchmarks

  bm_mean = 3.0

  bm_median = 2.5

  bm_stdev = 2.160247

  bm_sum = 12.0

  bm_sumsq = 50.0

  # Run tests

  nums = [1, 2 ,3, 6]

  print "1 means OK; 0 means NOT OK"

  print "mean():", bm_mean == mean(nums)

  print "median():", bm_median == median(nums)

  print "stdev():", bm_stdev ==
→ round(stdev(nums),6)

  print "sum():", bm_sum == sum(nums)

  print "suqsq():", bm_sumsq == sumsq(nums)
```

```
E:\scripts>python stats.py

1 means OK; 0 means NOT OK

mean(): 1

median(): 1

stdev(): 1

sum(): 1

suqsq(): 1
```

Figure 9.23 The self-test code executes only when you run stats as a program, not when you import it.

To determine whether a module is running as a program:

◆ Type:
```
if __name__ == "__main__":
    block
```
block is an indented block of statements that executes if the module is running as a program. By convention, this statement is placed at the end of a module.

Python programmers often use this if conditional to run self-test routines. A self-test routine compares program results against independently derived benchmark values and reports any variations. This technique is used to verify the correctness of code and flag the reintroduction of bugs in code that already worked. **Script 9.6** shows an (inadequate) self-test routine for the stats module, and **Figure 9.23** shows the results of running stats as a program.

✔ Tips

■ Self-test routines go by a variety of names: regression tests, test suites, test beds, and test harnesses, for example.

■ **OS** For the __name__ == "__main__" method to work in the Mac OS IDE, click the black triangle in the top-right corner of the module window and choose the Run As __main__ option.

Determining Which Modules Are Loaded

The sys.modules dictionary contains all the modules that have been loaded in the current Python session. The dictionary's keys are the module names, and the values are the corresponding module objects. Python automatically loads some modules at startup, so the dictionary will contain more than just the modules your program loaded.

To determine which modules are loaded:

◆ Type:

```
import sys
sys.modules.keys()
```

The keys() method retrieves module names from the dictionary; you can retrieve the module objects by using the values() method or retrieve the key-value pairs by using the items() method (**Figure 9.24**).

✔ Tip

■ You shouldn't modify the sys.modules dictionary unless you know what you're doing.

```
E:\scripts>python
>>> import sys, math, area
>>> print "\n".join(sys.modules.keys())
os.path
os
exceptions
__main__
ntpath
nt
sys
__builtin__
site
math
signal
UserDict
area
stat
```

Figure 9.24 The sys.modules dictionary contains all loaded modules: the ones your program loads and the ones Python preloads at startup. I've used the join() method to print one name per line. (Note that the built-in stat module is different from my stats module.)

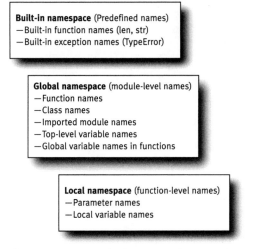

Figure 9.25 These are the three types of namespaces that Python uses to keep track of variables at run time. Namespaces are dictionaries that contain names (as keys) and their corresponding objects (as values).

Understanding Namespaces

Recall from "Creating Variables" in Chapter 2 that a variable is just a name bound to an object. The statements s = "mimetic" and def sum(x,y):, for example, bind the name s to the string object "mimetic", and the name sum to the function object sum. A *namespace* is a dictionary that stores names as keys and their corresponding objects as values. The namespace for the preceding statements is {'s': 'mimetic', 'sum': <function sum at 007A8014>}.

Python uses its own namespaces to keep track of variables; it automatically and invisibly creates, updates, and deletes these namespaces while your program runs.

There are three types of namespaces (**Figure 9.25**):

◆ **Local namespaces.** Python creates a new local namespace whenever a function is called. The local namespace contains a key-value pair for each function parameter and each local variable defined in the function's body. Variables in functions that are declared global are *not* in this namespace (they're in a global namespace). Each function has its own local namespace, which Python deletes when the function returns a value or raises an exception.

◆ **Global namespaces.** Python creates a new global namespace when a module is first loaded via import. The global namespace contains a key-value pair for each top-level (global) variable, function, class and imported module. Each module has its own global namespace, which Python deletes when the interpreter halts.

continues on next page

◆ **Built-in namespace.** Python creates the built-in namespace when the interpreter starts. The built-in namespace contains a key-value pair for each of Python's built-in functions (len, str, and so on) and exception (TypeError, SyntaxError, and so on) names. There's only one built-in namespace, which Python deletes when the interpreter halts.

✔ Tips

■ If namespaces seem to be less than riveting, bear with me; this discussion is leading to "Understanding Scoping Rules" later in this chapter.

■ The key-value pairs in a namespace are called *bindings*.

■ In recursive functions, Python creates a separate local namespace for each recursive call; see "Creating Recursive Functions" in Chapter 8.

■ Retrieving an attribute is actually a namespace lookup. Callable objects (modules, functions, methods, classes, and instances) have a built-in __dict__ attribute that holds their attribute names and values in a dictionary. object.attr, for example, is equivalent to object.__dict__["attr"], and object.attr = x, is equivalent to object.__dict__["attr"] = x. For information about the __dict__ attribute, see Section 3.2, "The standard type hierarchy," in the *Python Reference Manual*.

```
E:\scripts>python

>>> locals()

{'__doc__': None, '__name__': '__main__',
↪ '__builtins__': <module '__builtin__'
↪ (built-in)>}

>>> globals()

{'__doc__': None, '__name__': '__main__',
↪ '__builtins__': <module '__builtin__'
↪ (built-in)>}
```

Figure 9.26 The local and global namespaces of a new interactive session are the same. They contain these predefined names: __doc__ (the documentation string), __name__ (the name of the module, which is always named __main__ in an interactive session and in a program run from a file), and __builtins__ (which refers to the __builtin__ module, which contains the functions and exceptions that are always available to the interpreter).

```
E:\scripts>python

>>> s, x = "mimetic", 39

>>> import math

>>> from area import circle

>>> def product(x,y): x*y

...

>>> ",".join(locals().keys())

'math,__doc__,product,circle,x,__builtins__,
↪ __name__,s'

>>> ",".join(globals().keys())

'math,__doc__,product,circle,x,__builtins__,
↪ __name__,s'
```

Figure 9.27 In this new interactive session, I've defined and imported a few names, which Python adds to the global namespace and its mirror image (at the module level), the local namespace.

Accessing Namespaces

Although Python creates and maintains many namespaces at run time (one for each module and each function, for example), only three are visible and accessible at any particular point in a program: one local, one global, and one built-in. The rules for determining which namespaces are visible are:

◆ **Within a function**, the visible namespaces are the local namespace for the current function, the global namespace of the module in which the current function is defined, and the built-in namespace.

◆ **Outside a function**—that is, at the top level of a module or at a prompt in interactive mode, the visible namespaces are the global namespace for the current module, and the built-in namespace. In this context, Python equates the local namespace with the global namespace. (When in interactive mode, you're actually in a module named __main__; to check this, type __name__ at the >>> prompt.)

The built-in locals() and globals() functions provide access to local and global namespaces. Keep in mind that these functions are context-sensitive: Their return values depend on the place at which they're called.

To get the local namespace:

◆ Type locals() to return a dictionary corresponding to the current local namespace.

To get the global namespace:

◆ Type globals() to return a dictionary corresponding to the current global namespace.

Figures 9.26 shows the local and global namespaces for a new interactive session. **Figure 9.27** shows an interactive session after a few names are created and imported;

continues on next page

for clarity, I've printed only the names (that is, the namespace keys). **Figure 9.28** shows local and global namespaces inside a function call.

Recall from "Listing an Object's Attributes" earlier in this chapter that the built-in `dir()` function returns a list of a given object's attributes. You can use `dir()` without an argument to get the current local namespace names (the same names in `locals().keys()`).

To get a list of names in the local namespace:

◆ Type `dir()` to return a sorted list of names in the current local namespace (**Figure 9.29**).

The built-in `vars()` function returns the local namespace of a specific object. Technically speaking, `vars()` returns the values in an object's `__dict__` attribute.

```
>>> def vowels(s):
...     print "globals (in vowels):",
→ ",".join(globals().keys())
...     print "locals (entering vowels):",
→ ",".join(locals().keys())
...     v = ""
...     for c in s:
...         if c in "aeiouAEIOU":
...             v += c
...     print "locals (exiting vowels):",
→ ",".join(locals().keys())
...     return v
...
>>> x = "sequoia"
>>> ",".join(globals().keys())
'__doc__,vowels,x,__name__,__builtins__'
>>> vowels(x)
globals (in vowels):
→ __doc__,vowels,x,__name__,__builtins__
locals (entering vowels): s
locals (exiting vowels): v,c,s
'euoia'
```

Figure 9.28 Here, I've modified the vowels() function (see Figure 8.6 in Chapter 8) to print its global namespace names and its local namespace names at its entry and exit points. At the function's entry point, Python adds the parameter s to the function's local namespace. At its exit point, Python also has added the variables v and c, which were defined inside vowels(). The module-level variable x (and the rest of the module's global names) also are in the function's global namespace.

```
>>> dir()
['__builtins__', '__doc__', '__name__']
>>> def product(x,y):
...     print dir()
...     return x * y
...
>>> a = b = 5
>>> product(a,b)
['x', 'y']
25
```

Figure 9.29 dir() returns a sorted list of the names that are in the local namespace.

ACCESSING NAMESPACES

```
>>> import area
>>> vars(area).keys()
['rectangle', '__doc__', 'pi', 'circle',
→ '__name__', '__builtins__', '__file__',
→ 'triangle', 'square']
>>> print vars(area)['pi']
3.14159
>>> def product(x,y):
...    print vars()
...    return x * y
...
>>> a = b = 5
>>> product(a,b)
{'x': 5, 'y': 5}
25
```

Figure 9.30 vars() returns a dictionary corresponding to the local namespace of a specified object.

```
>>> dir(__builtins__)
['ArithmeticError', 'AssertionError',
→ 'AttributeError', 'DeprecationWarning',

...<snip>...

'slice', 'str', 'tuple', 'type', 'unichr',
→ 'unicode', 'vars', 'xrange', 'zip']
>>> vars(__builtins__)
{'WindowsError': <class
→ exceptions.WindowsError at 0080AE34>,
→ 'OverflowError': <class exceptions.
→ OverflowError at 0080CB34>,

...<snip>...

'SyntaxError': <class exceptions.SyntaxError
→ at 0080B99C>, 'pow': <built-in function pow>,
→ 'vars': <built-in function vars>}
```

Figure 9.31 Here, dir() returns just the keys of the built-in namespace, and vars() returns the entire dictionary.

To get the local namespace of a specific object:

◆ Type vars(*object*) to return a dictionary corresponding to the local namespace of *object*.

object is an object (expression). If *object* is omitted, vars() returns the current local namespace (equivalent to locals()) (**Figure 9.30**).

You can pass the __builtin__ module of the dir() or vars() function to get the built-in namespace.

To get the built-in namespace:

◆ Type dir(__builtin__) to return a sorted list of names in the built-in namespace.

or

Type vars(__builtin__) to return a dictionary corresponding to the built-in namespace (**Figure 9.31**).

Understanding Scoping Rules

If you've been playing with the interpreter, you've probably seen more than one `NameError` exception, which Python raises when you try to use a variable that you haven't defined. This error typically occurs because you've mistyped a variable name. In the background, Python actually conducts a mildly elaborate search for a variable before it finally raises a `NameError` exception.

Recall from "Creating Global Variables" in Chapter 8 that a variable's scope determines its visibility within a program; it's the region of code within which the variable represents a certain value. Python uses *scoping rules* to resolve a variable's value. When Python encounters a variable—say, x—in a program, it searches for x in the visible namespaces in this order (**Figure 9.32**):

1. **Local namespace.** If the current function or method has a parameter x or defines a local variable x, Python uses it and stops searching; otherwise, it looks for x in the global namespace.

2. **Global namespace.** If the current module defines or imports a variable, function, class, or module named x, Python uses it and stops searching; otherwise, it looks for x in the built-in namespace.

3. **Built-in namespace.** If the built-in namespace, which is available to all modules, defines a function or exception named x, Python uses it and stops searching; otherwise, it raises a `NameError` exception.

```
>>> a = "mimetic"
>>>
>>> def concat(b):
...   c = a + b
...   return c
...
>>> concat(" polyalloy")
'mimetic polyalloy'
```

Figure 9.32 *a* and concat are global names because they're defined at the top level of a module. *b* and *c* are local names because they are defined inside a function. *b* and *c* are required only while concat is running and are destroyed automatically when concat terminates.

```
>>> list("syzygy")
['s', 'y', 'z', 'y', 'g', 'y']
>>> list = [1, 2, 3]
>>> list("syzygy")
Traceback (most recent call last):
  File "<stdin>", line 1, in ?
TypeError: object is not callable: [1, 2, 3]
>>> del list
>>> list("syzygy")
['s', 'y', 'z', 'y', 'g', 'y']
```

Figure 9.33 Here, the list variable shadows the list() function. list() becomes accessible again when I delete list.

✔ Tip

- It's a common mistake to override a built-in function with one of your own variable names. If you create a list named `list` or a string named `str`, for example, you won't be able to use the built-in `list()` or `str()` functions, because Python will find your variables in the local or global namespace and stop searching, never reaching the built-in namespace in which the `list()` and `str()` functions live. In the vernacular, your variable has *shadowed* or *occluded* the built-in function. To fix this problem, change the variable name. If you're in interactive mode, delete the variable with `del` to restore the built-in function; see "Deleting Variables" in Chapter 2 (**Figure 9.33**).

```
>>> def primes(m):
...
...    def isprime(n):
...      count = n / 2
...      while count > 1:
...        if n % count == 0:
...          return 0
...        count -= 1
...      return 1
...
...    lst = []
...    for i in range(1, m):
...      if isprime(i):
...        lst.append(i)
...    return lst
...
>>> primes(20)
[1, 2, 3, 5, 7, 11, 13, 17, 19]
>>> x = isprime(19)
Traceback (most recent call last):
  File "<stdin>", line 1, in ?
NameError: name 'isprime' is not defined
```

Figure 9.34 The isprime() function is nested within its parent function, primes(), and thus may be called only from within primes(). Python raises a NameError exception when I try to invoke isprime() outside its parent.

Nesting Functions

You can define one function within another. The nested function can be called only from within the function in which it's defined, called its *parent function* (**Figure 9.34**).

There's a surprise here: According to Python's scoping rules, if function A is function B's parent, B's variables aren't visible in A. Recall from the preceding section that at any given time, Python uses exactly three namespaces to look up variable names: local (function-level), global (module-level), and built-in. When you refer to a variable within a nested function, Python searches for that variable in the current function's namespace and then in the module's namespace; it never looks in the parent function's namespace. These lookup rules may cause results that don't match your expectations (**Figure 9.35**).

continues on next page

To solve this problem, Python 2.1 introduced *nested scopes*. Python 2.1 and later will search for the variable in the current function's namespace, *then in the parent function's namespace,* and finally in the module's namespace (**Figure 9.36**).

Nested scopes is an optional feature in Python 2.1, and you must enable it by including this statement in your program:

```
from __future__ import nested_scopes
```

In Python 2.2, nested scopes is a standard feature, and the `from __future__` statement isn't required. For information about enabling optional features, see "Enabling Language Features" earlier in this chapter.

✔ Tips

- If nested scopes are enabled and functions are multiply nested, Python searches all ancestors, not just the immediate parent. If function C is defined within function B and B is defined within function A, for example, C's variables are visible in both A and B.

- A `lambda` function defined within a function behaves just like a nested function; see "Using *lambda* Expressions to Create Functions" in Chapter 8.

```
>>> def squares():
...
...     def printit():
...         print x, x*x
...
...     x = 5
...     while x > 0:
...         printit()
...         x -= 1
...
<stdin>:1: SyntaxWarning: local name 'x' in
→ 'squares' shadows use of 'x' as global in
→ nested scope 'printit'
>>> squares()
Traceback (most recent call last):
  File "<stdin>", line 1, in ?
  File "<stdin>", line 8, in squares
  File "<stdin>", line 4, in printit
NameError: global name 'x' is not defined
```

Figure 9.35 This function fails with a `NameError` because, when the nested function `printit()` runs, Python searches for x first within `printit()` itself and then in the module; it never looks for x in the parent function, `squares()`.

```
>>> from __future__ import nested_scopes
>>> def squares():
...
...     def printit():
...         print x, x*x
...
...     x = 5
...     while x > 0:
...         printit()
...         x -= 1
...
>>> squares()
5 25
4 16
3 9
2 4
1 1
```

Figure 9.36 Enabling nested scopes fixes the problem. After searching for x in `printit()`, Python searches for—and finds—x in `squares()`.

Grouping Modules into Packages

Python allows you to group related modules into a *package*. Packages are an advanced tool and are beyond the scope of this book; for more information, see the *Python Tutorial* and www.python.org/doc/essays/packages.html. I'll mention a few salient points:

◆ The structure of modules in a package is analogous to that of a directory tree: packages can have subpackages, which can have sub-subpackages, and so on.

◆ The top-level package directory has the same name as the package.

◆ Python executes the __init__.py script in the top-level package directory when the package is imported. This script defines the package's structure and runs initialization code.

◆ You can use packages to reduce the likelihood of name clashes between modules.

◆ Package modules are accessed and imported by using dot notation. The expression A.B.c.func(), for example, calls the function func() in the module c in the subpackage B in the package A.

Terminating a Program Explicitly

In script mode, the Python interpreter normally runs until there are no more statements to execute in the program. In interactive mode, you can type an end-of-file character to exit the interpreter: Ctrl-Z (Windows) or Ctrl-D (Unix). You also can exit a program by calling the sys.exit() function (**Figure 9.37**).

To terminate a program explicitly:

◆ Type:

```
import sys
sys.exit()
```

✔ Tips

■ exit() takes an optional argument that indicates the exit code (defaulting to zero). Most systems consider zero to be a normal termination and any nonzero value to be an unsuccessful termination. If you specify a string exit status—sys.exit ("informative error message"), for example—it's printed to sys.stderr, and an exit code of 1 is used. For information about sys.stderr, see "Accessing Standard Input and Output Files" in Chapter 10.

■ See also "Running Programs in Interactive Mode" and "Running Programs in Script Mode" in Chapter 1.

■ sys.exit() is equivalent to raise SystemExit; see "Understanding the Exception Hierarchy" in Chapter 11.

```
E:\scripts>python
>>> def quit(code):
...     if code == 0:
...         import sys
...         sys.exit()
...
>>> quit(1)
>>> quit(0)

E:\scripts>
```

Figure 9.37 A program can exit the Python interpreter by calling the sys.exit() function.

```
>>> eval_code = compile("1 + 2",
→ "<string>", 'eval')
>>> eval(eval_code)

3

>>>

>>> single_code = compile("print
→ 'mimetic polyalloy'", "<string>",
→ 'single')
>>> eval(single_code)

mimetic polyalloy

>>>

>>> exec_code = compile("""

... for x in range(6):

...    print x, x*x

... """, "<string>", 'exec')
>>> exec exec_code

0 0

1 1

2 4

3 9

4 16

5 25

>>>

>>> eval("int(3.14159)")

3

>>> eval("int(x)", {'x': 3.14159})

3

>>>

>>> exec "print 'mimetic',; print
→ 'polyalloy'"

mimetic polyalloy
```

(figure continues on next page)

Running Code Programmatically

This section covers an advanced topic that you may skip without loss of continuity. Python provides several built-in tools that let you precompile and execute frequently used pieces of code inside a Python program. See **Figure 9.38** for some examples.

To compile a string into a code object:

◆ Type compile(string, filename, kind)

string is a string that represents the Python code to compile.

filename is a string that specifies the code's origin. If the code originates in a file, specify the file's name (for use in tracebacks). compile(), however, normally is used to create a code object from a dynamically generated string of Python code; in this case, *filename* is set to "" or "<string>" by convention.

kind specifies the type of code object type to return, which can be used with exec or eval(). Set *kind* to 'eval' if *string* is an expression (to be used with eval()), 'exec' if it's a sequence of statements (to be used with exec), or 'single' if it's a single interactive statement (to be used with exec). If *kind* is 'single', Python prints expression statements that evaluate to something other than None.

compile() returns a code object.

To evaluate a string or code object:

◆ Type eval(*expr* [,*globals* [,*locals*]])

expr is a string that represents a Python expression or a code object created with compile().

globals and *locals* are optional dictionaries that eval() uses as the local and global namespaces when evaluating *expr*. If *locals* is omitted, it defaults to *globals;* if both dictionaries are omitted, the expression is evaluated in the namespace of the caller.

eval() returns the result of the evaluated expression.

To execute a string, file object, or code object:

◆ Type:

exec [in *globals* [,*locals*]]

code is a string that represents Python statements, a file object containing Python statements, or a code object created with compile().

globals and *locals* are optional dictionaries that exec uses as the local and global namespaces when executing *code*. If *locals* is omitted, it defaults to *globals;* if both dictionaries are omitted, the code is executed in the namespace of the caller.

To execute a source-code file:

◆ Type:

execfile(*filename* [,*globals* [,*locals*]])

filename is a file containing Python statements.

globals and *locals* are optional dictionaries that execfile uses as the local and global namespaces when executing *filename*. If *locals* is omitted, it defaults to *globals;* if both dictionaries are omitted, the code is executed in the namespace of the caller.

execfile() returns None.

Figure 9.38 continued

```
>>> exec "print a, b" in {'a':
→ 'mimetic', 'b': 'polyalloy'}
mimetic polyalloy
>>> exec "print a, b" in {'a':
→ 'mimetic', 'b': 'polyalloy'},
→ {'a': 1, 'b': 2}
1 2
>>>
>>> f = open("squares.py", "r")
>>> exec f
1 1
2 4
3 9
4 16
5 25
>>> f.close
<built-in method close of file object at
→ 007F3BB0>
>>>
>>> execfile("squares.py")
1 1
2 4
3 9
4 16
5 25
```

Figure 9.38 These are examples of how to compile and run Python code programmatically. The code in script *squares.py* that is used in some of the examples is listed in Script 1.1 in Chapter 1. File objects are covered in Chapter 10.

FILES

So far, I've been typing input data directly in the interpreter and printing output in the window where I started my Python program. In practice, often it's necessary to access files from within a program to read, write, and manipulate stored data. The operating system manages your files, and Python's file tools allow you to access them from inside programs. In this chapter, I'll show you how to perform common tasks with files and directories. I'll also describe Python's other input/output tools for redirecting output to a file, retrieving input directly from the keyboard, accessing your file system through the os module, and saving objects as files.

Opening a File

Python file operations are done by using file objects rather than file names. Before you can read from or write to a file, you must open it as a file object. The built-in open() function opens a file and returns a file object.

To open a file:

◆ Type open(*filename* [,*mode*])

filename is a file name (string) that may include a relative or absolute path; if no path is given, Python looks in the current directory. *mode* is a string that indicates how the file is to be opened—for reading, writing, or both. *mode* can be one of the values listed in **Table 10.1**. If omitted, *mode* defaults to 'r'.

Figures 10.1 and **10.2** show a few files that I'll use in this chapter's examples. I'll also use the file *flips.py,* which contains Script i.1 in the Introduction. **Figure 10.3** shows some examples of open().

✔ Tips

■ When a file operation fails for an input/output-related reason, Python raises an IOError exception. Some common reasons for I/O errors are trying to open a nonexistent file, trying to write to a file opened for reading, trying to open a read-only file for writing, and lacking permission to access a file.

■ For information about paths, see the sidebar in "Using the File System" later in this chapter.

■ The open() function takes an optional third argument, *bufsize,* that indicates the type of buffered file access. A *buffer* is an area of memory that holds file data that is waiting to be transferred to and from your disk. Buffering is used to accumulate data before doing a time-consuming disk access;

Table 10.1

MODE	DESCRIPTION
File Modes	
'r'	Only read from the file. *filename* must already exist.
'w'	Only write to the file. If *filename* doesn't already exist, it's created; otherwise, *filename*'s existing contents are overwritten.
'a'	Only append to the file. If *filename* doesn't already exist, it's created; new data is appended to the end of *filename*.
'r+'	Read from and write to the file. *filename* must already exist.
'w+'	Read from and write to the file. If *filename* doesn't already exist, it's created; otherwise, *filename*'s existing contents are deleted before writing.
'a+'	Read from and write to the file. If *filename* doesn't already exist, it's created; new data is appended to the end of *filename*.

```
Line 1.
Line 2.
Line 3.
```

Figure 10.1 A simple test file, test.txt.

```
Phlebas the Phoenician, a fortnight dead,
Forgot the cry of gulls, and the deep sea swell
And the profit and loss.

A current under sea
Picked his bones in whispers. As he rose and
→ fell
He passed the stages of his age and youth
Entering the whirlpool.

Gentile or Jew
O you who turn the wheel and look to windward,
Consider Phlebas, who was once handsome and
→ tall as you.
```

Figure 10.2 The file water.txt contains *Death by Water* from *The Waste Land* (1922) by T.S. Eliot.

```
>>> water = open("water.txt")

>>> test = open("test.txt", "r+")

>>> flips = open("E:\\scripts\\
→ flips.py", "a")

>>> type(water)

<type 'file'>

>>> water

<open file 'water.txt', mode 'r' at 007C4E58>

>>> xxx = open("xxx.txt", "r")
→ # File doesn't exist

Traceback (most recent call last):

  File "<stdin>", line 1, in ?

IOError: [Errno 2] No such file or directory:
→ 'xxx.txt'

>>> xxx = open("xxx.txt", "w")
→ # Creates xxx.txt

>>>
```

Figure 10.3 Here are some examples of opening files. Note that the file xxx.txt doesn't exist. When I tried to open it for reading, Python raised an IOError exception; when I opened it for writing, Python created a new empty file.

■ **LANG** Perl's open and C's fopen functions open files. Python's file-access modes mirror C's file-access modes. Perl uses binmode to access binary files. Many of Python's file methods have analogues in the stdio.h C standard library.

it also is used to allow file reading and writing to operate at different speeds or on different-size blocks of data. Normally, you needn't be concerned with buffering; but if you are, you can pass open() an integer argument for *bufsize*. If *bufsize* is omitted or negative, the system default is used; the value 0 yields unbuffered reading and writing; the value 1 buffers one line at a time; and values greater than 1 use a buffer of approximately that size.

■ The fdopen(), popen(), tmpfile(), popen2(), popen3(), and popen4() functions in the os module also create file objects. For information about these functions, see Section 6.1, "os—Miscellaneous OS interfaces," of the *Python Library Reference*.

■ You can get information about a file object, including its mode and name, by using the attributes and methods described in "Getting File Object Information" later in this chapter.

■ **OS** In Windows paths, use the \\ escape sequence to represent a backslash; see "Inserting Special Characters into a String" in Chapter 4.

■ **OS** If you're opening a binary file in Windows or Mac OS, you must append "b" to *mode,* so that open() allows modes such as "rb", "wb", and "r+b". A *binary file* is a non-human-readable file that contains "invisible" control characters, as opposed to a text file containing only printable ASCII characters. An *.exe* executable file is a binary file, for example. Unix doesn't distinguish text and binary files and ignores the "b". The expression open("disk.sys", "rb"), for example, opens the binary file *disk.sys* for reading.

OPENING A FILE

Reading from a File

The open() function creates a file object but doesn't read from it. For that, you'll need to use the file object's read(), readline(), or readlines() methods. These methods allow you to read a file's contents character by character (that is, byte by byte), line by line, or all at once.

Python tracks your current position internally when you read from a file, so each read operation starts where the preceding one left off. Python stops reading when it encounters the end of the file (*EOF*). A read operation that starts at EOF returns an empty string (or an empty list, in the case of readlines()). Note that a blank line in a file is not an empty string, but a string that contains only a newline ("\n").

To read characters from a file:

◆ Type f.read([*size*]) to read *size* characters from the file *f* and return them in a string.

f is a file object, and *size* is an integer expression. If *size* is omitted or negative, all (remaining) file characters are read (**Figure 10.4**).

```
>>> test = open("test.txt", "r")
>>> test.read(1)
'L'
>>> test.read(3)
'ine'
>>> s = test.read()
>>> s
' 1.\nLine 2.\nLine 3.\n'
>>> print s
 1.
Line 2.
Line 3.

>>> test.read()   #EOF
''
>>> water = open("water.txt")
>>> s = water.read()
>>> print s
Phlebas the Phoenician, a fortnight dead,
...<snip>...
Consider Phlebas, who was once handsome and
→ tall as you.
```

Figure 10.4 The read() function reads a specified number of characters into a string, including newline characters. If you don't specify the number of characters, Python places all the file data in a single string. Note that read() returns an empty string if you're already at the end of the file.

```
>>> water = open("water.txt", "r")
>>> water.readline(22)
'Phlebas the Phoenician'
>>> water.readline()
', a fortnight dead,\n'
>>> water.readline()
'Forgot the cry of gulls, and the deep sea
→ swell\n'
>>> test = open("test.txt", "r")
>>> test.readline()
'Line 1.\n'
>>> test.readline(99999)
'Line 2.\n'
>>> test.readline()
'Line 3.\n'
>>> test.readline()
''
```

Figure 10.5 The readline() function reads a line into a string, including the terminating newline character. To read part of a line, specify the number of characters to read. readline() returns an empty string if you're already at the end of the file or "\n" for a blank line.

```
>>> test = open("test.txt", "r")
>>> test.readlines()
['Line 1.\n', 'Line 2.\n', 'Line 3.\n']
>>> water = open("water.txt", "r")
>>> lines = water.readlines()
>>> len(lines)
12
>>> lines[0]
'Phlebas the Phoenician, a fortnight dead,\n'
>>> lines[3]
'\n'
>>> lines[4]
'A current under sea\n'
>>> lines[-1]
'Consider Phlebas, who was once handsome and
→ tall as you.'
```

Figure 10.6 The readlines() function reads all lines into a list of strings.

To read a line from a file:

◆ Type f.readline([*size*]) to read *size* characters from the current line in the file *f* and return them in a string, which includes a terminating newline.

If the line is longer than *size*, the entire line is returned.

f is a file object, and *size* is an integer expression. If *size* is omitted or negative, the entire line is read (**Figure 10.5**).

To read all the lines from a file:

◆ Type f.readlines() to read all the lines in the file *f* and return them in a list of strings.

Each string includes a terminating newline.

f is a file object (**Figure 10.6**).

✔ Tips

■ You can use a list comprehension and the rstrip() method to remove terminating newlines (and other trailing white space) from all the strings in the readlines() list (**Figure 10.7**).

continues on next page

```
>>> test = open("test.txt", "r")
>>> lines = test.readlines()
>>> lines
['Line 1.\n', 'Line 2.\n', 'Line 3.\n']
>>> [s.rstrip() for s in lines]
['Line 1.', 'Line 2.', 'Line 3.']
```

Figure 10.7 Stripping terminating newlines by using a list comprehension.

```
>>> water = open("water.txt",
→ "r").readlines()
>>> test = open("test.txt",
→ "r").readlines()
>>>
>>> # Count number of lines
... len(water)
12
>>>
>>> n = 2
>>> # Print the first n lines.
... print "\n".join([s.rstrip() for s
→ in water[:n]])
Phlebas the Phoenician, a fortnight dead,
Forgot the cry of gulls, and the deep sea swell
>>>
>>> # Print the last n lines.
... print "\n".join([s.rstrip() for s
→ in water[-n:]])
O you who turn the wheel and look to windward,
Consider Phlebas, who was once handsome and
→ tall as you.
>>>
>>> # Print every n-th line.
... for i in range(n-1, len(water), n):
...    print water[i],
...
Forgot the cry of gulls, and the deep sea swell

Picked his bones in whispers. As he rose and fell
Entering the whirlpool.
Gentile or Jew
Consider Phlebas, who was once handsome and
→ tall as you.
>>>
>>> # Print the n-th word of every line.
... for line in water:
...    try:
...       print line.split()[n-1],
...    except:
...       pass
...
```

(figure continues in next column)

Figure 10.8 *continued*

```
the the the current his passed the or you
→ Phlebas,
>>>
>>> # Print lines that start with s.
... s = "A"
>>> for line in water:
...    if line[:len(s)] == s:
...       print line,
...
And the profit and loss.
A current under sea
>>>
>>> # Count occurrences of s.
... s = "Phlebas"
>>> print "".join(water).count(s)
2
>>>
>>> # Replace occurrences of old with new.
... old = "Phoenician"
>>> new = "Alsatian"
>>> print "".join(water).
→ replace(old, new)
Phlebas the Alsatian, a fortnight dead,
...<snip>...
>>>
>>> # Make every letter lowercase
... [s.lower() for s in test]
['line 1.\n', 'line 2.\n', 'line 3.\n']
>>>
>>> # Randomize file lines
... import random
>>> random.shuffle(test)
>>> test
['Line 3.\n', 'Line 1.\n', 'Line 2.\n']
```

Figure 10.8 Some common file tasks.

```
>>> water = open("water.txt")
>>> for line in water.xreadlines():
...     if line.count("who"):
...         print line.rstrip()
...
O you who turn the wheel and look to windward,
Consider Phlebas, who was once handsome and
→ tall as you.
```

Figure 10.9 Each iteration through the xreadlines() list returns a new line.

- You can combine list and string operations on the readlines() list to perform common file tasks (**Figure 10.8**).

- If your file is huge, use the xreadlines() method instead of readlines() to save memory. xreadlines() returns the same list as readlines(), but it doesn't build the list all at the same time. xreadlines() retrieves each list item when it's needed instead of storing all list items in memory simultaneously (**Figure 10.9**).

- **NEW** Python 2.1 introduced xreadlines().

- **OS** Python automatically accommodates the different Windows, Mac OS, and Unix end-of-line (EOL) characters by converting \r\n (Windows) and \r (Mac OS) characters to \n during read operations. No conversion is needed for Unix. You can determine the EOL character for your operating system with os.linesep; see "Using the File System" later in this chapter.

- **LANG** Perl's read, getc, while(*<filehandle>*), and @array = *<filehandle>* expressions, and C's fread, fgetc, and fgets functions read from files.

Writing to a File

The write() method writes a string to an open file, and the writelines() method writes a list of strings to an open file. Neither method appends a newline (\n) to the strings.

As it does with the read methods, Python tracks your current position internally when you write to a file, so each write operation starts where the preceding one left off. To insert a blank line into a file, write a newline, not an empty string.

Remember to open() a file in write mode to overwrite its contents or in append mode to add data to the end; see "Opening a File" earlier in this chapter.

To write a string to a file:

◆ Type f.write(s) to write s to the file f.

f is a file object, and s is a string expression. This method returns None.

To write strings to a file:

◆ Type f.writelines(list) to write the strings in list to the file f.

f is a file object, and list is a list containing string expressions. This method returns None.

```
>>> test = open("test.txt", "a")
→   # Append
>>> test.write("Li")
>>> test.write("ne 4.\n")
>>> lst = ["Line 5.\n", "Line 6.\n"]
>>> test.writelines(lst)
>>> test.flush()
>>>
>>> water = open("water.txt", "w")
→ # Overwrite
>>> lst = ["Where Alph, the sacred
→ river, ran\n", "Through caverns
→ measureless to man\n"]
>>> water.writelines(lst)
>>> water.flush()
>>>
>>> quote = open("quote.txt", "w")
→ # New file
>>> quote.write("Feather-footed
→ through the plashy fen passes the
→ questing vole.\n")
>>> quote.flush()
```

Figure 10.10 Here, I append lines to the file test.txt and overwrite the contents of water.txt. I called the flush() method to commit the changes in the files to my disk.

```
Line 1.

Line 2.

Line 3.

Line 4.

Line 5.

Line 6.
```

Figure 10.11 The code in Figure 10.10 appended lines to test.txt.

```
Where Alph, the sacred river, ran

Through caverns measureless to man
```

Figure 10.12 The code in Figure 10.10 overwrote the contents of water.txt.

```
Feather-footed through the plashy fen passes
→ the questing vole.
```

Figure 10.13 The code in Figure 10.10 created the file quote.txt.

Figure 10.10 shows examples that use write() and writelines() to append to, overwrite, and create a file. **Figures 10.11**, **10.12**, and **10.13** show the files after the write operations.

✔ Tips

■ Because of buffering (see the tips in "Opening a File" earlier in this chapter), data that you write may not actually appear in the file until you call the f.flush() or f.close() method. f.flush() causes any buffered but unwritten data to be written to the file object f. f.close() is covered in "Closing a File" later in this chapter.

■ Written strings can have binary data (including null characters), not just text; see the tips in "Opening a File" earlier in this chapter.

■ Remember that writelines() doesn't add newlines to the end of each string in *list*. If you don't add them yourself, writelines() effectively concatenates *list*'s items as it writes them to a file. You easily can append newlines to every item in *list* with this list comprehension:

```
[s + "\n" for s in list]
```

■ **OS** When you write to Windows or Mac OS files, Python converts \n end-of-line characters to \r\n (Windows) or \r (Mac OS). For Unix, Python retains the \n.

■ **LANG** Perl's print and C's fwrite, fputc, and fputs functions write to files. C's fflush function flushes a buffer.

Closing a File

When you're finished writing to or reading from files, you should close them to free memory. Closing files is not strictly required because Python closes them automatically when your script finishes, but having many open files occupies resources that Python could otherwise reclaim.

To close to a file:

◆ Type f.close()

   f is a file object. This method returns None (**Figure 10.14**).

✔ Tips

■ You can't read from or write to a closed file, Python raises a ValueError exception if you try.

■ You can determine whether a file object is closed by inspecting its closed attribute; see "Getting File Object Information" later in this chapter.

■ You can close() the same file more than once.

■ It's good programming style to close a file before reopening it elsewhere in the program in another context.

■ Because of buffering (see the tips in "Opening a File" earlier in this chapter), data that you write may not actually appear in the file until you call close().

■ **LANG** Perl's close and C's fclose functions close files.

```
>>> test = open("test.txt", "a")
>>> test.write("Line 4.\n")
>>> test.close()
>>> test
<closed file 'test.txt', mode 'a' at 007C4EB8>
>>> test.write("Line 5.\n")
Traceback (most recent call last):
  File "<stdin>", line 1, in ?
ValueError: I/O operation on closed file
```

Figure 10.14 You don't have to close files in simple scripts, but in larger or long-running programs, you should close files to prevent memory problems.

```
>>> test = open("test.txt", "r")
>>> print test.tell()
0
>>> test.read(5)
'Line '
>>> print test.tell()
5
>>> test.read(10)
'1.\nLine 2.'
>>> print test.tell()
16
>>> test.read()
'\nLine 3.\n'
>>> print test.tell()
27
```

Figure 10.15 tell() tells you the position where the next read or write operation will take place. The first character in the file is at position 0.

Changing Position in a File

Recall that Python tracks the file position internally during read and write operations. You can determine the current file position with the tell() method and set it with the seek() method. tell() is useful if you want to know where the next read or write operation will begin, and seek() is useful if you want to perform a read or write operation in the middle of a line.

To get the current file position:

◆ Type f.tell() to return the current file position as the number of characters (bytes) from the start of the file f.

The first character is at position 0.

f is a file object (**Figure 10.15**).

To set the current file position:

◆ Type f.seek(*offset* [,*where*]) to change the current file position by *offset* characters (bytes) relative to *where* in the file *f*. To move backward, specify a negative *offset*.

f is a file object, *offset* is an integer expression, and *where* is one of the integer values in **Table 10.2**. If omitted, *where* defaults to 0 (absolute positioning). This method returns None (**Figure 10.16**).

✔ Tips

■ seek(0) rewinds to the beginning of a file.

■ If you try to move to before a file's first character, Python raises an IOError exception.

■ An invisible character, such as a newline or tab, is counted as one character.

■ seek() often is used to process database records whose fields have fixed start and end columns.

■ **LANG** Perl's tell and seek functions and C's ftell and fseek functions get and set a file position.

Table 10.2

Relative Offset Positions	
VALUE	DESCRIPTION
0	Absolute file position: seek() determines the new position by counting characters from the start of the file. *offset* can't be negative for this value of *where*. seek(5, 0), for example, moves the file position to the sixth character in the file (position 5).
1	Seek relative to the current file position: seek() determines the new position by counting characters from the current file position. seek(-5, 1), for example, moves the file position to the first character in the file if the current position is at the sixth character.
2	Seek relative to the end of the file: seek() determines the new position by counting characters from the end of the file. seek(-5, 2), for example, moves the file position to the fifth character from the end of the file.

```
>>> # Open file for reading and writing
... test = open("test.txt", "r+")
>>> test.tell()
0
>>> test.seek(5, 0)
>>> test.write("4")  # Replace "1"
>>> test.seek(8, 1)
>>> test.write("5")  # Replace "2"
>>> test.seek(-4, 2)
>>> test.write("6")  # Replace "3"
>>> test.seek(0, 2)  # End of the file
>>> lines = ["Line 7.\n", "Line 8.\n"]
>>> test.writelines(lines)
>>> test.seek(0)  # Back to the start
>>> print test.read()
Line 4.
Line 5.
Line 6.
Line 7.
Line 8.
```

Figure 10.16 seek() allows you to perform read or write operations at various places in a file.

```
>>> # Open file for reading and writing
... water = open("water.txt", "r+")
>>> water.seek(22)
>>> water.truncate()
>>> water.seek(0)
>>> print water.read()
Phlebas the Phoenician
>>> water.seek(0)
>>> water.truncate(7)
>>> print water.read()
Phlebas
```

Figure 10.17 truncate() deletes characters from the end of a file. You can specify the number of characters to leave in the file.

Truncating a File

You can delete the contents of a file starting from the current position to the end of the file.

To truncate a file:

◆ Type f.truncate([size]) to truncate the file f to at most size characters (bytes).

f is a file object, and size is an integer expression. If size is omitted, truncate() deletes characters starting at the current position. This method returns None (**Figure 10.17**).

✔ Tips

■ truncate(0) clears a file.

■ **OS** truncate() isn't available in some flavors of Unix.

Getting File Object Information

Table 10.3 summarizes the built-in methods and attributes that return characteristic information about a file object *f* (**Figure 10.18**).

✔ Tips

■ The file descriptor returned by `fileno()` is used in low-level file operations; see, for example, Section 6.1.3, "File Descriptor Operations," of the *Python Library Reference*.

■ The `softspace` attribute is used infrequently in routine programming tasks; see Section 2.1.7.9, "File Objects," of the *Python Library Reference*.

Table 10.3

File Object Information	
ATTRIBUTE/METHOD	**DESCRIPTION**
`f.closed`	Indicates the file state: 1 if *f* is closed; 0 if *f* is open. Read-only.
`f.mode`	The I/O mode (string) of *f*; this is the value of the *mode* parameter if *f* was created with open(). Read-only.
`f.name`	The name (string) of *f* if *f* was created with open(). Read-only.
`f.softspace`	A Boolean (0 or 1) attribute that indicates whether Python should print a space before the next value is printed with a print statement. Read/write.
`f.isatty()`	Returns 1 if *f* is connected to an interactive terminal; returns 0 otherwise.
`f.fileno()`	Returns the integer file-descriptor used by functions in the os and other modules.

```
>>> water = open("water.txt", "r+")
>>> water.closed
0
>>> water.mode
'r+'
>>> water.name
'water.txt'
>>> water.softspace
0
>>> water.isatty()
0
>>> water.fileno()
3
```

Figure 10.18 A file object has various attributes and functions that give characteristic information.

```
>>> squares = open("squares.txt", "w")
>>> print >> squares, "n", "n**2"
>>> print >> squares, "-", "----"
>>> for i in range(6):
...   print >> squares, i, i*i
...
>>> squares.close()
```

Figure 10.19 These extended print statements write to the file squares.txt.

```
n n**2
- ----
0 0
1 1
2 4
3 9
4 16
5 25
```

Figure 10.20 The statements in Figure 10.19 created the file squares.txt.

Printing to a File

The print statement has an extended form that lets you redirect output to a file object instead of to the screen. print otherwise behaves as described in "Printing Objects" in Chapter 2.

To print to a file:

◆ Type:

print >> f, expr1, expr2,...

f is a file object, and *expr1, expr2,...* are zero or more comma-separated expressions that are evaluated and written to *f* (**Figures 10.19** and **10.20**).

✔ Tips

■ You can add a trailing comma to print to suppress the trailing newline.

■ You also can print to a file by redirecting sys.stdout; see "Accessing Standard Input and Output Files" later in this chapter.

■ **NEW** Python 2.0 introduced print >>.

Accessing Standard Input and Output Files

When you start the interpreter, Python provides three file objects named *standard input*, *standard output*, and *standard error*. You can use these files to manage input and output (I/O) tasks in your programs. The files are accessible in the sys module.

To access standard input and output files:

◆ Type:

```
import sys
sys.iofile
```

iofile is stdin for standard input, stdout for standard output, or stderr for standard error.

By default, sys.stdin gets user input from the keyboard, and sys.stdout prints text to the user's screen. The print statement, for example, actually writes to sys.stdout; see "Printing Objects" in Chapter 2 (**Figure 10.21**). sys.stderr, which is used to write error messages, also prints to the user's screen by default. When Python raises an exception, for example, it writes to sys.stderr.

As with normal files, the read(), readline(), and readlines() methods are used with sys.stdin to capture input typed by the user; see "Reading from a File" earlier in this chapter. The write() and writelines() methods are used with sys.stdout and sys.stderr to print text; see "Writing to a File" earlier in this chapter.

Figure 10.22 shows a simple standard I/O example within the interpreter.

```
>>> print "sequoia"
sequoia
>>>
>>> import sys
>>> sys.stdout.write("sequoia\n")
sequoia
```

Figure 10.21 The print statement is equivalent to sys.stdout.write().

```
>>> import sys
>>> s = sys.stdin.readline()
Down to a sunless sea.
>>> sys.stdout.write(s)
Down to a sunless sea.
>>>
```

Figure 10.22 By default, sys.stdin reads the keyboard, and sys.stdout writes to the screen.

Script 10.1 This script, count.py, reads text from standard input and writes the number of lines, words, and characters in the text to standard output.

```
                        script
import sys
charcount = wordcount = linecount = 0
for line in sys.stdin.readlines():
    linecount += 1
    charcount += len(line)
    line = line.strip()
    for word in line.split():
        wordcount += 1
sys.stdout.write("Lines: " + str(linecount)
→ + "\n")
sys.stdout.write("Words: " + str(wordcount)
→ + "\n")
sys.stdout.write("Characters:
→ " + str(charcount))
```

```
E:\scripts>python count.py < water.txt
Lines: 12
Words: 70
Characters: 372
E:\scripts>python count.py <
→ water.txt > count.txt

E:\scripts>type count.txt
Lines: 12
Words: 70
Characters: 372
E:\scripts>type water.txt | python
→ count.py
Lines: 12
Words: 70
Characters: 372
```

Figure 10.23 You can use the redirection operators to read from (<) and write to (>) files, or the pipe operator (|) to take input from another command. Here, I'm using Windows, but these commands work in Unix too. In Unix, substitute cat for type to print a file.

Script 10.2 This script, replace.py, finds and replaces text. It reads text from standard input or a file and writes to standard output or a file.

```
                    script
import sys
if len(sys.argv) <= 2:

  print "usage: replace.py old_text new_text
  → [in_file [out_file]]"
else:

  old_text = sys.argv[1]

  new_text = sys.argv[2]

  in_file = sys.stdin

  out_file = sys.stdout

  if len(sys.argv) > 3:

    in_file = open(sys.argv[3])

  if len(sys.argv) > 4:

    out_file = open(sys.argv[4], 'w')

  for line in in_file.xreadlines():

    out_file.write(line.replace(old_text,
    → new_text))
```

You can use the Windows and Unix redirection operators to read from and write to files. **Script 10.1**, named count.py, counts the number of lines, words, and characters in text. **Figure 10.23** shows how to run count.py from the command-prompt window. The < redirection operator takes input from the file water.txt rather than from the keyboard. The > redirection operator sends output to the file count.txt rather than to the screen. The | pipe operator takes input from another command rather than from the keyboard. See your operating system's documentation for information about redirection and pipelines.

Script 10.2, named replace.py, finds and replaces text. (Scripts like this appear all over the Web.) The script takes up to four command-line arguments; see "Passing Arguments to a Script" in Chapter 1. Its syntax is:

replace.py *old_text new_text* [*in_file* [*out_file*]]

old_text is the text to search for, and *new_text* is the replacement text. If *in_file* is omitted, replace.py takes text from standard input (the keyboard); otherwise, text is read from the file *in_file*. If *out_file* is omitted, replace.py prints the results to standard output (the screen); otherwise, it prints to the file *out_file*. **Figure 10.24** shows an example run.

continues on next page

ACCESSING STANDARD INPUT AND OUTPUT FILES

You can use the isatty() method (see "Getting File Object Information" earlier in this chapter) to detect whether a script is used interactively (from the keyboard) or whether it's used with redirected or piped I/O (**Script 10.3** and **Figure 10.25**).

✔ Tips

- Python lets you programmatically redirect standard input to read from a file and standard output (and standard error) to write to a file. You can restore standard input and output files to their original values by subsequently reassigning them the values in sys.__stdin__, sys.__stdout__, and sys.__stderr__, which contain the values that sys.stdin, sys.stdout, and sys.stderr had at interpreter startup.

  Polite programmers restore original values when they're done with standard I/O redirection, because such redirection affects print and raw_input(), for example (**Figures 10.26** and **10.27**).

- When a user presses Ctrl-C in the middle of your program, Python raises a KeyboardInterrupt exception, which you can catch and handle; see Chapter 11.

- If a file is too big to read all at once, use xreadlines() instead of readlines(). Alternatively, you may read character by character with read(1) or line by line with readline(); see "Reading from a File" earlier in this chapter.

```
E:\scripts>type test.txt
Line 1.
Line 2.
Line 3.

E:\scripts>python replace.py "Line "
→ "Line #" test.txt
Line #1.
Line #2.
Line #3.
```

Figure 10.24 Here, replace.py reads input from a file and writes results to the screen.

Script 10.3 This script, mode.py, indicates whether it's being used interactively or whether it's being used with redirected or piped I/O.

```
script
import sys
if sys.stdin.isatty():
    print "Interactive"
else:
    print "Redirected/piped"
```

```
E:\scripts>python mode.py
Interactive

E:\scripts>python mode.py < test.txt
Redirected/piped

E:\scripts>type test.txt | python mode.py
Redirected/piped
```

Figure 10.25 Here, mode.py displays the mode in which it's running.

```
>>> import sys
>>> out = open("out.txt", "w")
>>> sys.stdout = out
>>> print "This string goes to out.txt"
>>> sys.stdout.write("So does this\n")
>>> "And so does this"
>>> # Restore standard output
... sys.stdout = sys.__stdout__
>>> out.close()
>>> print "Back to normal"
Back to normal
>>>
```

Figure 10.26 Here, I temporarily redirect standard output from the screen to the file out.txt and print a few lines. Then I restore the original startup value of standard output by using sys.__stdout__.

```
E:\scripts>type out.txt
This string goes to out.txt
So does this
'And so does this'
```

Figure 10.27 Here are the contents of the file out.txt after running the statements in Figure 10.26.

■ Standard error is useful when you want to direct error messages to a place other than that of your program's normal output. If your program creates an output file, for example, it's wise to write diagnostic error messages to an error log or to print them on the screen, where they'll be noticed, rather than write them in the file along with the normal results, where they could interfere with other programs that use the program's output file.

■ Some IDEs, such as IDLE (see "Using IDLE" in Chapter 1), alter the definitions of the standard I/O files. If you're using an IDE and getting unexpected results, try your program in a command-prompt window instead.

■ **LANG** Perl's standard I/O files are STDIN, STDOUT, and STDERR. C's are stdin, stdout, and stderr.

Prompting for User Input

Python provides two built-in functions, raw_input() and input(), to retrieve a line of text from standard input. Both functions take an optional *prompt* string to display while awaiting user input. input() is equivalent to eval(raw_input()). For information about eval(), see "Running Code Programmatically" in Chapter 9.

You should prefer raw_input() to input() because input() expects a valid Python expression and so is sensitive to user errors: Python raises a SyntaxError if it can't evaluate the input expression. If you use raw_input() instead, you can inspect the input expression safely before evaluating it.

To prompt for user input:

◆ Type raw_input([*prompt*]) to read a line from standard input (sys.stdin), convert it to a string (stripping the trailing newline), and return it.

  prompt is an optional string that's first printed to the screen (standard output). Python raises an EOFError exception if it encounters the end of a file without getting any user input (**Figure 10.28**).

```
>>> age = raw_input("Enter your age:")
Enter your age:39
>>> print "You used to be",
→ str(int(age) - 1)
You used to be 38
```

Figure 10.28 The raw_input() function displays an optional prompt and retrieves a string from standard input.

Table 10.4

Cross-Platform OS **Attributes**

ATTRIBUTE	DESCRIPTION
os.altsep	An alternative character used by the OS to separate pathname components, or None if only one separator character exists. '/' for Windows, where os.sep is a backslash.
os.curdir	The string that refers to the current directory. '.' for Windows and Unix, and ':' for Mac OS.
os.linesep	The string used to terminate lines on the current platform. '\n' for Unix, '\r\n' for Windows, and '\r' for Mac OS.
os.name	The name of the OS-dependent module: 'posix', 'nt', 'dos', 'mac', 'os2', 'ce', or 'java'.
os.pardir	The string that refers to the parent directory of the current directory. '..' for Windows and Unix, and '::' for Mac OS.
os.pathsep	The character that separates search-path components, as in the PATH environment variable. ':' for Unix and ';' for Windows.
os.sep	The character that separates pathname components. '/' for Unix, '\\' for Windows, and ':' for Mac OS. (Note that '\\' is the escape sequence for a single \.)

Using the File System

So far, I've been performing basic file input and output: reading from and writing to files. Python's os module and its os.path submodule let you access your file system to manipulate files and directories (folders).

All popular operating systems use a hierarchical tree structure to organize files and directories. The precise syntax, however, differs across OSes. The character that separates pathname components, for example, is a slash (/) in Unix, a backslash (\) in Windows, and a colon (:) in Mac OS. The os module has attributes that allow you to account for these differences when you write cross-platform programs (**Table 10.4**). **Figure 10.29** shows some examples.

```
>>> import os
>>> os.altsep   # None
>>> os.curdir
'.'
>>> os.linesep
'\r\n'
>>> os.name
'nt'
>>> os.pardir
'..'
>>> os.pathsep
';'
>>> os.sep
'\\'
```

Figure 10.29 OS attributes for Windows 2000.

✔ Tips

- The examples in the subsequent sections assume that you have the proper permissions to create, modify, access, and delete files and directories.

- The os module is documented in Section 6.1, "os—Miscellaneous OS interfaces," of the *Python Library Reference*.

- The os.path submodule is loaded automatically when you import the os module. os.path is documented in Section 6.2, "os.path—Common pathname manipulations," of the *Python Library Reference*.

- **OS** When you import the os module, Python actually loads an OS-dependent module, whose name is given by os.name. You should not try to import an OS-dependent module directly; just import os and let Python load the appropriate module invisibly.

Paths

A *path*, or *pathname*, specifies the location of a directory or file in a hierarchical file system. An *absolute path* specifies a location completely by listing its entire path starting at the topmost node of the directory tree, called the *root*. A *relative path* specifies a location relative to the current working directory. In Windows, an absolute path starts with a backslash or with a drive letter followed by a colon and a backslash. In Unix, an absolute path starts with a slash.

C:\Program Files\WebWasher (Windows) and /usr/local/bin/python (Unix) are absolute paths. books\petty\chap01.doc (Windows) and doc/readme.txt (Unix) are relative paths.

See also "Getting Path Information" later in this chapter.

```
>>> import os

>>> print os.environ.keys()

['USERPROFILE', 'OS', 'OS2LIBPATH', 'HOMEPATH',
→ 'PROCESSOR_LEVEL', 'ALLUSERSPROFILE',
→ 'NUMBER_OF_PROCESSORS',
→ 'PROCESSOR_ARCHITECTURE', 'SYSTEMDRIVE',
→ 'PATHEXT', 'APPDATA', 'SYSTEMROOT',
→ 'WINDIR', 'TMP', 'PATH', 'TK_LIBRARY',
→ 'PROCESSOR_REVISION', 'PROGRAMFILES',
→ 'PROCESSOR_IDENTIFIER', 'COMMONPROGRAMFILES',
→ 'HOMEDRIVE', 'TCL_LIBRARY', 'TEMP',
→ 'USERDOMAIN', 'COMSPEC', 'LOGONSERVER',
→ 'COMPUTERNAME', 'USERNAME']

>>> os.environ["USERNAME"]

'chris'

>>> os.environ["TEMP"]

'E:\\temp'

>>> os.environ["PATH"]

'E:\\WINNT\\system32;E:\\WINNT;E:\\bin;
→ e:\\Python21\\'

>>> os.environ["PATH"] += os.pathsep
→ + "E:\\scripts"

>>> os.environ["PATH"]

'E:\\WINNT\\system32;E:\\WINNT;E:\\bin;
→ e:\\Python21\\;E:\\scripts'

>>> os.environ["TESTDATA"] = "test.txt"

>>> os.environ["TESTDATA"]

'test.txt'
```

Figure 10.30 The os.environ dictionary contains copies of environment variables that existed when you loaded os. Changes in os.environ aren't visible outside Python.

✔ Tips

■ Changes in os.environ are visible only in the context of the current Python session.

■ For information about environment variables, see "Setting Your Path" in Chapter 1.

■ **LANG** Perl's ENV accesses environment variables.

Accessing Environment Variables

When you load the os module, it populates the os.environ dictionary with copies of the names and values of the current environment variables. You can retrieve and modify these variables by using the normal dictionary operations described in Chapter 6. **Figure 10.30** shows some examples.

To get the values of all the environment variables:

◆ Type:

import os

os.environ

This expression returns a dictionary in which the keys are environment-variable names (strings) and the values are the corresponding values (strings).

To get the value of an environment variable:

◆ Type:

import os

os.environ[*varname*]

varname is the name (string expression) of an environment variable.

To add or replace an environment variable:

◆ Type:

import os

os.environ[*varname*] = *value*

This statement adds a new key-value pair if *varname* doesn't appear in os.environ or replaces an existing pair if it does.

varname is the name (string expression) of an environment variable, and *value* is a string expression representing the new value.

Changing the Working Directory

The *current working directory* is the directory in which you started the Python interpreter. This directory may be different from the directory in which your script resides. If you want to work with files in another directory, you can specify a path for each file or change the working directory and just use the file name. The latter option often is preferable. **Figure 10.31** shows some examples.

To get the current working directory:

◆ Type:

    import os

    os.getcwd()

This function returns a string representing the absolute path of the current working directory.

To change the current working directory:

◆ Type:

    import os

    os.chdir(path)

path is an absolute or relative pathname (string expression) that identifies the new working directory.

✔ Tip

■ 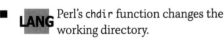 Perl's chdir function changes the working directory.

```
>>> import os
>>> os.getcwd()
'E:\\scripts'
>>> os.chdir("test")   # Relative path
>>> os.getcwd()
'E:\\scripts\\test'
>>> os.chdir("..")   # Parent directory
>>> os.getcwd()
'E:\\scripts'
>>> os.chdir("E:\\projects")
↪ # Absolute path
>>> os.getcwd()
'E:\\projects'
```

Figure 10.31 You can use an absolute or relative path to indicate the new working directory.

```
>>> import os
>>> os.listdir(os.getcwd())
['count.py', 'flips.py', 'mode.py', 'replace.py',
→ 'test', 'test.txt', 'water.txt']
>>> os.listdir("E:\\temp")
[]
>>> import glob
>>> glob.glob("*.py")
['count.py', 'flips.py', 'mode.py', 'replace.py']
>>> glob.glob("?o*.py")
['count.py', 'mode.py']
>>> glob.glob("[rf]*.py")
['flips.py', 'replace.py']
>>> glob.glob("[!rf]*.py")
['count.py', 'mode.py']
```

Figure 10.32 The os.listdir() function lists the files and directories that a given directory contains. The glob.glob() function lets you specify wildcard characters for listing files and directories.

Listing Directory Contents

You can see the files and subdirectories contained in a specified directory. **Figure 10.32** shows some examples.

To list a directory's contents:

◆ Type:

```
import os
os.listdir(path)
```

This function returns a list containing the names (strings) of the files and subdirectories in *path*.

path is an absolute or relative pathname (string expression) that identifies a directory.

To list a directory's contents by using wildcard characters:

◆ Type:

```
import glob
glob.glob(path)
```

This function returns a list containing the names (strings) of the files and subdirectories in *path*.

path is an absolute or relative pathname (string expression) that can contain wildcard characters: * matches everything, ? matches any single character, [*seq*] matches any character in *seq*, and [!*seq*] matches any character not in *seq*.

✔ Tips

■ The list returned by os.listdir() is in arbitrary order and doesn't contain the special entries '.' and '..' for the current and parent directories.

■ glob.glob() wildcard characters are Unix shell-style wildcards, which aren't the same as regular expressions.

■ **LANG** Perl's readdir function reads directory contents.

Creating a Directory

Python allows you to create new, empty directories programmatically. **Figure 10.33** shows some examples.

To create a directory:

♦ Type:

```
import os
```

```
os.mkdir(path)
```

This function creates the directory *path*. The directory is created within the working directory if *path* is a relative pathname.

path is an absolute or relative pathname (string expression) of a directory.

To create a directory and its intermediate-level directories:

♦ Type:

```
import os
```

```
os.makedirs(path)
```

This function creates a directory the way that os.mkdir() does, but it also creates all the intermediate-level (parent) directories needed to contain the directory. The directories are created within the working directory if *path* is a relative pathname.

path is an absolute or relative pathname (string expression) of a directory.

✔ Tips

■ Python raises an OSError exception if it can't create the directory or if you try to create a directory that already exists.

■ **OS** In Unix, the script that creates the directory is the directory's owner.

■ **LANG** Perl's mkdir function creates a directory.

```
>>> import os
>>> os.mkdir("E:\\projects")
>>> os.makedirs
→ ("E:\\projects\\python\\weather")
>>> cwd = os.getcwd()
>>> os.listdir(cwd)
['count.py', 'flips.py', 'mode.py',
→ 'replace.py', 'test', 'test.txt',
→ 'water.txt']
>>> os.mkdir("temp")
>>> os.makedirs("chap01\\sect01")
>>> os.makedirs("chap01\\sect02")
>>> os.listdir(cwd)
['chap01', 'count.py', 'flips.py', 'mode.py',
→ 'replace.py', 'temp', 'test', 'test.txt',
→ 'water.txt']
>>> os.listdir(cwd + os.sep + "chap01")
['sect01', 'sect02']
```

Figure 10.33 The os.mkdir() function creates a new directory. os.makedirs() creates a new directory and any intermediate-level directories needed along the way.

■ **OS** The mkdir() and makedirs() functions each take an optional second argument, *mode,* that specifies the Unix file permission. *mode* is a numeric octal representation of the permission and defaults to 0777 (universal permission). For information on permissions, see your Unix system documentation or type man umask or man chmod at the Unix prompt. On non-Unix systems, *mode* may be ignored or may have no effect.

You can use the os.access(), os.chmod(), and os.umask() functions to verify, change, and set permissions, and the os.chown() to change the owner and group IDs; see Section 6.1.4, "Files and Directories," in the *Python Library Reference*.

```
>>> import os

>>> os.removedirs
→ ("E:\\projects\\python\\weather")

>>> cwd = os.getcwd()

>>> os.listdir(cwd)

['chap01', 'count.py', 'flips.py', 'mode.py',
→ 'replace.py', 'temp', 'test', 'test.txt',
→ 'water.txt']

>>> os.rmdir("temp")

>>> os.rmdir("chap01\\sect01")

>>> os.removedirs("chap01\\sect02")

>>> os.listdir(cwd)

['count.py', 'flips.py', 'mode.py', 'replace.py',
→ 'test', 'test.txt', 'water.txt']
```

Figure 10.34 These statements remove the directories I created in Figure 10.33 in the preceding section.

Removing a Directory

Python allows you to delete empty directories programmatically. **Figure 10.34** shows some examples.

To remove a directory:

◆ Type:

```
import os
```

```
os.rmdir(path)
```

This function removes the directory *path*. Python looks in the working directory if *path* is a relative pathname.

path is the absolute or relative pathname (string expression) of an existing empty directory.

To remove a directory and its intermediate-level directories:

◆ Type:

```
import os
```

```
os.removedirs(path)
```

This function attempts to remove all the directories in *path*. Python first removes the rightmost directory in *path* then it removes its parent directory and so on until it removes all the parent directories in *path* or encounters a non-empty parent directory (in which case it raises an OSError exception). Python looks in the working directory if *path* is a relative pathname.

path is the absolute or relative pathname (string expression) of an existing empty directory.

✔ Tips

- Python raises an OSError exception if it can't remove a directory, if you try to remove a nonexistent directory, or if you try to remove a directory that is not empty.

- To delete files from a directory, see "Removing a File" later in this chapter.

- **LANG** Perl's rmdir function removes a directory.

- To delete directories that contain files, use shutil.rmtree(); see Section 6.23, "shutil—High-level file operations," in the *Python Library Reference*. Be cautious with this function; if you tell it to do so, it'll erase your entire hard drive.

Renaming a File or Directory

Python allows you to rename a file or directory programmatically. **Figure 10.35** shows some examples.

To rename a file or directory:

◆ Type:

```
import os

os.rename(old, new)
```

This function renames a file or directory named *old* to *new*. Python looks in the working directory if a relative path is given.

old and *new* are the absolute or relative paths (string expressions) of the file or directory.

To rename an entire path:

◆ Type:

```
import os

os.renames(old, new)
```

This function renames an entire path from *old* to *new,* creating new directories in *new* as needed and removing empty directories in *old*. Python looks in the working directory if a relative path is given.

old and *new* are the absolute or relative paths (string expressions) of the file or directory.

✔ Tips

■ Python raises an OSError exception if it can't rename a file or directory or if you try to rename a nonexistent file or directory.

■ os.renames() often is used to move a file to a different directory.

■ **LANG** Perl's *rename* function renames a file.

```
>>> import os
>>> os.rename("E:\\projects",
→ "E:\\myprojects")
>>> cwd = os.getcwd()
>>> os.listdir(cwd)
['count.py', 'flips.py', 'mode.py', 'replace.py',
→ 'test', 'test.txt', 'water.txt']
>>> os.rename("water.txt",
→ "phlebas.txt")
>>> os.renames("flips.py",
→ "E:\\backup\\chap01\\
→ flips_0903.bak")
>>> os.listdir(cwd)
['count.py', 'mode.py', 'phlebas.txt',
→ 'replace.py', 'test', 'test.txt']
>>> os.listdir("E:\\backup\\chap01")
['flips_0903.bak']
```

Figure 10.35 The os.rename() function renames a file or directory. In this example, os.renames() renamed the file flips.py to flips_0903.bak and moved it to the directory E:\backup\chap01\, which it created in the process. Python couldn't delete the directory containing the original flips.py because it wasn't empty after the move.

```
>>> import os
>>> os.remove("E:\\temp\\log.tmp")
>>> os.remove("flips.py")
```

Figure 10.36 The os.remove() function deletes a file.

Removing a File

Python allows you to delete a file program-matically. **Figure 10.36** shows some examples.

To remove a file:

◆ Type:

os.remove(*path*)

This function removes the file *path*.
Python looks in the working directory if
path is a relative pathname.

path is the absolute or relative pathname
(string expression) of an existing file.

✔ Tips

■ Python raises an OSError exception if it
can't remove a file or if you try to remove
a nonexistent file.

■ To remove a directory, see "Removing a
Directory" earlier in this chapter.

■ The os.unlink(*path*) function is identical to os.remove(*path*); *unlink* is a traditional Unix name.

■ **LANG** Perl's unlink function removes
a file.

Getting Path Information

You can get information about paths by using functions in the os.path module. **Figure 10.37** shows some examples.

To determine whether a path exists:

◆ Type:

import os

os.path.exists(*path*)

This function returns 1 (true) if *path* refers to an existing path or 0 (false) otherwise.

path is the absolute or relative pathname (string expression).

To determine whether a path is a directory:

◆ Type:

import os

os.path.isdir(*path*)

This function returns 1 (true) if *path* is an existing directory or 0 (false) otherwise.

path is the absolute or relative pathname (string expression).

To determine whether a path is a file:

◆ Type:

import os

os.path.isfile(*path*)

This function returns 1 (true) if *path* is an existing file or 0 (false) otherwise.

path is the absolute or relative pathname (string expression).

To determine whether a path is an absolute path:

◆ Type:

import os

os.path.isabs(*path*)

This function returns 1 (true) if *path* is an absolute pathname or 0 (false) otherwise.

path is the absolute or relative pathname (string expression).

```
>>> import os
>>> paths = [os.getcwd(), "C:\\",
→ "flips.py", "\\temp\\temp.log"]
>>> for path in paths:
...     print
...     print path
...     print "    exists:",
→ os.path.exists(path)
...     print "    isdir:",
→ os.path.isdir(path)
...     print "    isfile",
→ os.path.isfile(path)
...     print "    isabs",
→ os.path.isabs(path)
...     print "    ismount:",
→ os.path.ismount(path)
...

E:\scripts
    exists: 1
    isdir: 1
    isfile 0
    isabs 1
    ismount: 0

C:\
    exists: 1
    isdir: 1
    isfile 0
    isabs 1
    ismount: 1

flips.py
    exists: 1
    isdir: 0
    isfile 1
    isabs 0
    ismount: 0

\temp\temp.log
    exists: 1
    isdir: 0
    isfile 1
    isabs 1
    ismount: 0
```

Figure 10.37 These os.path functions return path information.

To determine whether a path is a mount point:

◆ Type:

```
import os
os.path.ismount(path)
```

This function returns 1 (true) if *path* is a mount point, or 0 (false) otherwise. A *mount point* is a directory in a file system that corresponds to the root directory of some other file system. In Windows, a mount point takes the form C:\ or \\plato\, for example. In Unix, ismount() checks whether *path* and its parent are on different devices; see Section 6.2, "os.path— Common pathname manipulations," of the *Python Library Reference*.

path is the absolute or relative pathname (string expression).

✔ Tips

■ **OS** In Unix, isdir() and isfile() follow symbolic links and return true if the path is a link to a directory or file. You can use os.path.islink(*path*) to determine whether *path* is a symbolic link and os.readlink(*path*) to return the actual path to which the symbolic link points.

■ **LANG** Perl's file-test operators (-e, -d, and so on) check a file's status.

Getting File Information

You can get information about files by using os.path functions. **Figure 10.38** shows some examples.

To get a file's size:

◆ Type:

```
import os
os.path.getsize(filename)
```

This function returns the size of *filename* in bytes, as an integer.

filename is the absolute or relative pathname of a file (string expression).

To get the time when a file was last accessed:

◆ Type:

```
import os
os.path.getatime(filename)
```

This function returns the time when *filename* was last accessed as the integer number of seconds since the epoch (see the tips in this section).

filename is the absolute or relative pathname of a file (string expression).

To get the time when a file was last modified:

◆ Type:

```
import os
os.path.getmtime(filename)
```

This function returns the time when *filename* was last modified as the integer number of seconds since the epoch (see the tips in this section).

filename is the absolute or relative pathname of a file (string expression).

```
>>> import os, time
>>> filename = "flips.py"
>>> os.path.getsize(filename)
774
>>> atime = os.path.getatime
→ (filename)
>>> print atime
999546180
>>> print time.ctime(atime)
Mon Sep 03 12:43:00 2001
>>> mtime = os.path.getmtime(filename)
>>> print mtime
987356901
>>> print time.ctime(mtime)
Sun Apr 15 10:48:21 2001
```

Figure 10.38 These os.path functions return file information.

✔ Tips

- The results of `getatime()` and `getmtime()` are expressed in seconds since the epoch. The *epoch* is the point at which time starts for an operating system—that is, the time and date corresponding to 0 in an operating system's clock and time-stamp values. In Windows and most Unix versions, the epoch is 00:00:00 January 1, 1970 (GMT); in Mac OS, it's 00:00:00 January 1, 1904 (GMT). The built-in `time` module provides various time-related functions. In the examples in this section, I use `time.ctime(seconds)` to convert a time expressed in seconds since the epoch to a string representing local time; see Section 6.9, "`time`—Time access and conversions," of the *Python Library Reference*.

- The `os.stat(filename)` function lets you get several pieces of file information at the same time. The function returns a tuple that contains a file's size, access time, modification time, and other properties; see Section 6.1.4, "Files and Directories," of the *Python Library Reference*.

- **LANG** Perl's `stat` function returns file statistics.

Splitting Paths

Python provides several functions that split pathnames into components. These functions account for cross-platform differences in pathname syntax; see "Using the File System" earlier in this chapter. **Figure 10.39** shows some examples.

To get the base name of a path:

◆ Type:

    import os

    os.path.basename(*path*)

This function returns the base name of *path* as a string. The *base name* is the last component of a path, after the final separator.

path is the absolute or relative pathname (string expression).

To get the directory name of a path:

◆ Type:

    import os

    os.path.dirname(*path*)

This function returns the directory name of *path*, as a string. The directory name is the entire path except for the last component.

path is the absolute or relative pathname (string expression).

To split a path into a directory name and a base name:

◆ Type:

    import os

    os.path.split(*path*)

This function returns a tuple that contains two strings. The first item contains *path*'s directory name, and the second item contains its base name.

path is the absolute or relative pathname (string expression).

```
>>> import os
>>> paths = [os.getcwd(), "C:\\",
→ "flips.py", "\\temp\\temp.log"]
>>> for path in paths:
...     print
...     print path
...     print "    basename:",
→ os.path.basename(path)
...     print "    dirname:",
→ os.path.dirname(path)
...     print "    split:",
→ os.path.split(path)
...     print "    splitdrive:",
→ os.path.splitdrive(path)
...     print "    splitext:",
→ os.path.splitext(path)
...     print "    abspath:",
→ os.path.abspath(path)
...

E:\scripts
    basename: scripts
    dirname: E:\
    split: ('E:\\', 'scripts')
    splitdrive: ('E:', '\\scripts')
    splitext: ('E:\\scripts', '')
    abspath: E:\scripts

C:\
    basename:
    dirname: C:\
    split: ('C:\\', '')
    splitdrive: ('C:', '\\')
    splitext: ('C:\\', '')
    abspath: C:\
```

(figure continues on next page)

Figure 10.39 *continued*

```
flips.py
    basename: flips.py
    dirname:
    split: ('', 'flips.py')
    splitdrive: ('', 'flips.py')
    splitext: ('flips', '.py')
    abspath: E:\scripts\flips.py

\temp\temp.log
    basename: temp.log
    dirname: \temp
    split: ('\\temp', 'temp.log')
    splitdrive: ('', '\\temp\\temp.log')
    splitext: ('\\temp\\temp', '.log')
    abspath: \temp\temp.log
```

Figure 10.39 These os.path functions split paths into components. I ran these examples in Windows.

To split the drive from a path:

◆ Type:

import os

os.path.splitdrive(*path*)

This function returns a tuple that contains two strings. The first item contains *path*'s drive, and the second item contains the rest of *path*. If no drive is specified or if your operating system doesn't use drive specifications (Unix, for example), the first item will be an empty string.

path is the absolute or relative pathname (string expression).

To split the file extension from a path:

◆ Type:

import os

os.path.splitext(*path*)

This function returns a tuple that contains two strings. The first item contains *path* up to but not including the file extension; the second item contains the file extension, including the dot. If no file extension is specified, the second item will be an empty string.

path is the absolute or relative pathname (string expression).

To get the absolute version of a path:

◆ Type:

import os

os.path.abspath(*path*)

This function returns the absolute version of *path* as a string, taking the current working directory into account. *path* need not exist.

path is the absolute or relative pathname (string expression).

Joining Paths

Python provides a function that intelligently joins one or more pathname components into a single path. This function accounts for cross-platform differences in pathname syntax; see "Using the File System" earlier in this chapter. **Figure 10.40** shows some examples.

To join pathname components into a single path:

◆ Type:

    import os

    os.path.join(*path1* [,*path2* [,...]])

This function returns a path that is valid for the current operating system, constructed from the specified components. If any component is an absolute path, all the previous components are discarded, and joining continues.

path1, path2,... are one or more pathname components (string expressions).

✔ Tips

■ os.path.join() doesn't check the validity of its result on the current operating system, so it's possible to construct an illegal path.

■ **os** For Windows paths, include a backslash in a drive component. Specify "C:\\", for example, not "C:".

```
>>> import os
>>> os.path.join("winnt", "system32")
'winnt\\system32'
>>> os.path.join("C:\\", "winnt",
→ "system32")
'C:\\winnt\\system32'
>>> os.path.join("projects\\books",
→ "petty\\chap01.txt")
'projects\\books\\petty\\chap01.txt'
>>> os.path.join(os.getcwd(), "test")
'E:\\scripts\\test'
>>> os.path.join(os.pardir, os.pardir,
→ "temp")
'..\\..\\temp'
>>> os.path.join("\games", "\go",
→ "current")
'\\go\\current'
>>> os.path.join("\\")
'\\'
>>> os.path.join("")
''
>>>
>>> dirs=['usr','local','bin','python']
>>> print reduce(os.path.join, dirs)
usr\local\bin\python
```

Figure 10.40 The os.path.join() function intelligently joins one or more pathname components into a single path that is suitable for the current operating system. I ran these examples in Windows.

Saving Objects As Files

Python allows you to convert an object to a stream of bytes in such a way that the byte stream can be reconverted to a copy of the object. This conversion process is called *pickling* in Python and *serializing* or *marshalling* in other languages. Pickled objects often are called *persistent objects* because they continue to exist (in some form) after your program stops. A pickled object can be, for example:

◆ Saved in a file

◆ Stored in a string

◆ Stored in a database

◆ Transferred across a network

You can pickle these objects:

◆ `None`

◆ Numbers (any type)

◆ Strings and Unicode strings

◆ Lists, tuples, and dictionaries containing only objects that can be pickled

◆ Functions defined at the top level of a module

◆ Built-in functions

◆ Classes defined at the top level in a module

◆ Instances of classes defined at the top level in a module

Pickling objects

Python's `pickle` and `cPickle` modules provide identical pickling and unpickling functionality, but `pickle` is written in Python, whereas `cPickle` is written in C and is orders of magnitude faster (see the tips in this section for another difference). Objects pickled by `pickle` and `cPickle` are interchangeable. I use `cPickle` in the examples in this section, but you may substitute `pickle` if you prefer; the syntax otherwise is identical.

To pickle an object:

1. Type `import cPickle` to load the cPickle module.

2. Type `file = open(`*`filename`*`, "w")` to open a file object *file* for writing.

   filename is the name of the file in which the pickled object will be stored. *filename* will be created (or overwritten) on disk. See "Opening a File" earlier in this chapter.

3. Type `cPickle.dump(`*`object`*`, `*`file`* `[,`*`binary`*`])` to write a pickled representation of *object* to the file object *file* and create the file *filename*.

   If the optional *binary* argument is present and nonzero, the binary pickle format is used; if the argument is zero or omitted, the (less efficient but more human-readable) text pickle format is used.

4. Type `file.close()` to close *file*.

   See "Closing a File" earlier in this chapter.

To unpickle an object:

1. Type `import cPickle` to load the cPickle module.

2. Type `file = open(`*`filename`*`, "r")` to open a file object *file* for reading.

   filename is the disk file in which a pickled object resides; see "To pickle an object" earlier in this section.

3. Type `target = cPickle.load(`*`file`*`)` to read the pickled representation of an object from *file*, unpickle it, and store it in the variable *target*.

4. Type `file.close()` to close *file*.

Figures 10.41 and **10.42** show examples of pickling and unpickling an object.

```
>>> import cPickle
>>> file = open("sequoia.obj", "w")
>>> s = "sequoia"
>>> cPickle.dump(s, file)
>>> file.close()
```

Figure 10.41 Here, I'm pickling the string `"sequoia"` and storing it in the file `sequoia.obj`, which is created in the current working directory.

```
>>> import cPickle
>>> file = open("sequoia.obj", "r")
>>> s = cPickle.load(file)
>>> file.close()
>>> s
'sequoia'
```

Figure 10.42 Here, I'm unpickling the object I pickled in Figure 10.41.

```
>>> import cPickle
>>> lst = [1, 2, 3]
>>> pickled = cPickle.dumps(lst)
>>> pickled
'(lp1\nI1\naI2\naI3\na.'
>>> unpickled = cPickle.loads(pickled)
>>> unpickled
[1, 2, 3]
```

Figure 10.43 You can use the dumps() and loads() functions to pickle and unpickle objects as strings instead of files.

```
>>> import shelve
>>> db = shelve.open("numbers", "c")
>>> db["composite"] = [4, 6, 8, 9, 10]
>>> db["fibonacci"] = [1, 1, 2, 3, 5, 8]
>>> db["prime"] = [2, 3, 5, 7]
>>> db["square"] = [1, 4, 9]
>>> db["triangular"] = [1, 3, 6, 10]
>>> db.close()
>>>
>>> db = shelve.open("numbers")
>>> db["square"] = [1, 4, 9, 16, 25]
>>> db["square"]
[1, 4, 9, 16, 25]
>>> del db["triangular"]
>>> db.has_key("square")
1
>>> db.keys()
['fibonacci', 'composite', 'prime',
↪ 'square']
>>> db.sync()   # Write data to disk
>>> db.close()
```

Figure 10.44 The shelve module allows you to store pickled objects in a database that behaves like a dictionary.

You also can write pickled objects to strings instead of files. cPickle.dumps(*object* [,*binary*]) returns the pickled representation of *object* as a string, and *binary* is described in step 3 of "To pickle an object" earlier in this section. cPickle.loads(string) reads a pickled object from a string; characters in the string past the pickled object's representation are ignored (**Figure 10.43**).

Shelving objects

Python's shelve module allows you to store pickled objects in a persistent, database-like object called a *shelf*. Shelves are useful for storing large amounts of data, because Python performs shelf lookups as needed rather than loading the entire shelf file into memory.

To open or create a shelf:

◆ Type:

import shelve

shelve.open(*filename* [,*flag*])

filename is the name of the database (shelf) file without an extension. *flag* is 'r' to open the existing database for reading only; 'w' to open the existing database for reading and writing; 'c' to open the database for reading and writing, creating it if it doesn't exist; or 'n' to create a new, empty database that is open for reading and writing. If omitted, *flag* defaults to 'c'.

Within a Python program, a shelf acts like a dictionary (see Chapter 6), except that its keys can be only strings (not numbers or tuples), and its values can be only objects that can be pickled. A shelf supports these dictionary operations: d[*key*], d[*key*] = *value*, del d[*key*], d.has_key(*key*), and d.keys(). Additionally, you can call d.close() to write unsaved changes to disk and close the shelf, or d.sync() to write unsaved changes to disk without closing the shelf (**Figure 10.44**).

✔ Tips

- If Python is unable to pickle or unpickle an object, it raises a PicklingError or an UnpicklingError exception.

- See the *Python Library Reference* for more information about the pickle, cPickle, and shelve modules: Section 3.14, "pickle—Python object serialization"; Section 3.15, "cPickle—Alternate implementation of pickle"; and Section 3.17, "shelve—Python object persistence."

- In practice, a programmer would pickle the storage dictionary created in "Storing Computed Values in a Dictionary" in Chapter 6. This is an example of a useful real-world application of pickling.

- If you pickle a container (list, tuple, or dictionary) that contains aliases that refer to the same object, the items in the unpickled object will still be aliases (**Figure 10.45**). For information about aliases, see "Creating References to the Same Object" in Chapter 2.

- When you pickle a class instance, its class definition and methods aren't saved, so you'll still be able to read the unpickled instance even if you change the class definition later; see Chapter 12.

- pickle defines Pickler() and Unpickler() classes that can be subclassed. In cPickle, Pickler() and Unpickler() are functions and not classes, so they can't be subclassed. This restriction shouldn't be an issue in most cases. (Classes are covered in Chapter 12.)

- **LANG** Java's Serializable interface permits objects to be serialized.

```
>>> import cPickle
>>> lst1 = [1, 2]
>>> lst2 = [lst1, lst1]
>>> lst2[0] is lst2[1]   # Same object
1
>>> pickled = cPickle.dumps(lst2)
>>> unpickled = cPickle.loads(pickled)
>>> unpickled[0] is unpickled[1]
→ # Still the same
1
```

Figure 10.45 Aliases remain aliases through pickling and unpickling.

EXCEPTIONS

Three main types of errors can occur in your programs: logic errors, syntax errors, and run-time errors. A *logic error,* such as a faulty algorithm, causes your program to produce incorrect results but does not prevent it from running. These errors can be difficult to find. A *syntax error* violates one of Python's grammatical rules and prevents your program from running. These errors are easy to fix. A *run-time error* is an execution error that occurs while your program runs. Some common causes of run-time errors are nonsensical input data, arithmetic errors, illegal object types, out-of-range sequence indexes, non-existent dictionary keys, misspelled attribute names, uninitialized variables, and operating-system-related problems.

Although it can't help you with logic errors, Python raises an exception when it detects a syntax error (**Figure 11.1**) or a run-time error (**Figure 11.2**). So far, I've passively accepted Python's default exception behavior: The interpreter stops the program and prints a diagnostic error message, called a *traceback*, that indicates the exception type and shows (approximately) where the error occurred.

This chapter describes how to intercept, or *catch*, exceptions when they occur and how to handle them gracefully, before Python terminates your program. I also show you how to raise and create exceptions yourself.

```
>>> x === 5
  File "<stdin>", line 1
    x === 5
        ^
SyntaxError: invalid syntax
```

Figure 11.1 You must fix syntax errors before Python can compile and run your code. Syntax errors also can occur when you import a faulty module.

```
>>> 5 * (1/0)
Traceback (most recent call last):
  File "<stdin>", line 1, in ?
ZeroDivisionError: integer division or
→ modulo by zero
>>> 5 + "five"
Traceback (most recent call last):
  File "<stdin>", line 1, in ?
TypeError: unsupported operand types for +
>>> x + 5
Traceback (most recent call last):
  File "<stdin>", line 1, in ?
NameError: name 'x' is not defined
>>> f = open("xxx.txt", "r")
Traceback (most recent call last):
  File "<stdin>", line 1, in ?
IOError: [Errno 2] No such file or directory:
→ 'xxx.txt'
>>> (1, 2, 3)[8]
Traceback (most recent call last):
  File "<stdin>", line 1, in ?
IndexError: tuple index out of range
```

Figure 11.2 Some common run-time errors.

```
>>> type(IndexError)
<type 'class'>
>>> dir(IndexError)
['__doc__', '__module__']
>>> IndexError.__doc__
'Sequence index out of range.'
```

Figure 11.3 Exceptions, like all objects, have a type, identity, and value. You can read an exception's docstring (__doc__ attribute) to get its summary information.

```
>>> filter(lambda x: type(eval(x))
→ is type(IndexError),
→ dir(__builtins__))
['ArithmeticError', 'AssertionError',
→ 'AttributeError', 'DeprecationWarning',
→ 'EOFError', 'EnvironmentError', 'Exception',
→ 'FloatingPointError', 'IOError',
→ 'ImportError', 'IndentationError',
→ 'IndexError', 'KeyError',
→ 'KeyboardInterrupt', 'LookupError',
→ 'MemoryError', 'NameError',
→ 'NotImplementedError', 'OSError',
→ 'OverflowError', 'RuntimeError',
→ 'RuntimeWarning', 'StandardError',
→ 'SyntaxError', 'SyntaxWarning',
→ 'SystemError', 'SystemExit', 'TabError',
→ 'TypeError', 'UnboundLocalError',
→ 'UnicodeError', 'UserWarning',
→ 'ValueError', 'Warning', 'WindowsError',
→ 'ZeroDivisionError']
```

Figure 11.4 You can query the __builtins__ module to get a list of built-in exceptions.

Understanding the Exception Hierarchy

Exceptions, like almost everything in Python, are objects (**Figure 11.3**). You can access built-in exceptions in the always-available __builtins__ module (**Figure 11.4**).

Python organizes exceptions in a hierarchical tree. **Table 11.1** lists and describes all the built-in exceptions; the indentation indicates how the exceptions are structured hierarchically. Each exception type is a Python class; I don't cover classes until Chapter 12, but the class-related concepts that I use in this chapter will be plain from their context.

At the top of the exception tree is Exception, from which all other built-in exceptions are derived. Exception is the parent, or base, of two children: SystemExit and StandardError. The sys.exit() function generates the SystemExit exception, which you can catch when you kill a program explicitly; see "Terminating a Program Explicitly" in Chapter 9. (SystemExit is an exception but not an error.) StandardError is the base of all other exceptions. In this chapter, I cover mostly StandardError and its descendants.

You can take advantage of the hierarchy to detect and handle exceptions as a group rather than individually. If you have a block of statements that performs mathematical calculations, for example, you can catch just ArithmeticError rather than catch all its children—FloatingPointError, OverflowError, and ZeroDivisionError—individually (assuming that you want to handle all arithmetic exceptions in the same way).

Built-In Exceptions

EXCEPTION	DESCRIPTION
Exception	The root of all exceptions.
SystemExit	Raised by the sys.exit() function. If you don't handle this exception, the Python inter- preter terminates your program without printing a traceback. If you call sys.exit(), Python translates the call into an exception and runs its exception handlers (the finally clauses of try statements).
StandardError	Base for all built-in exceptions except SystemExit.
ArithmeticError	Parent for exceptions that Python raises for various arithmetic errors.
FloatingPointError	Raised when a floating-point operation fails.
OverflowError	Raised when the result of an arithmetic operation is too large to be represented. This exception can't occur for long integers; Python raises a MemoryError instead.
ZeroDivisionError	Raised when the second argument of a normal or modular division is zero.
AssertionError	Raised when an assert statement fails; see "Making an Assertion" later in this chapter.
AttributeError	Raised when an attribute reference or assignment fails. If an object doesn't support attribute references or attribute assignments, Python raises a TypeError exception instead.
EnvironmentError	Parent for exceptions that occur outside Python.
IOError	Raised when an input/output operation (such as a print statement, an open() func- tion call, or a file-object method) fails for an I/O-related reason: "file not found" or "disk full," for example.
OSError	Raised when an operating-system-related error occurs (outside Python). A numeric error code usually accompanies this exception. This exception is used primarily as the os module's os.error exception; see Section 6.1, "os—Miscellaneous OS interfaces," of the *Python Library Reference*.
WindowsError	Raised when a Windows-specific error occurs.
EOFError	Raised when input() or raw_input() encounters an end-of-file condition (EOF) with- out reading any data. (Note that the file-object read() and readline() methods return an empty string when they encounter EOF.)
ImportError	Raised when import fails to find a module or when from-import fails to find a name.
KeyboardInterrupt	Raised when the user presses the interrupt key (normally, Ctrl-C or Del). Python regu- larly checks for interrupts during program execution. Python also raises this exception if the user types an interrupt while input() or raw_input() is waiting for input.
LookupError	Parent for exceptions that Python raises when a dictionary key or sequence (string, list, or tuple) index is invalid.
IndexError	Raised when a sequence index is out of range. Recall that Python silently constrains slice indexes to fall in the allowed range; see "Slicing a List or Tuple (Extracting a Segment)" in Chapter 5. If an index is not a plain integer, Python raises a TypeError exception.
KeyError	Raised when Python can't find a dictionary key.
MemoryError	Raised when an operation runs out of memory but the program may still be rescued by deleting some objects. The interpreter may not always be able to recover completely from this situation but raises this exception so that it can print a traceback indicating the source of the problem.

table continues on next page

UNDERSTANDING THE EXCEPTION HIERARCHY

Table 11.1 *continued*

Built-In Exceptions	
EXCEPTION	DESCRIPTION
NameError	Raised when Python can't find a local or global name. This exception applies only to unqualified names; see "Accessing Attributes" in Chapter 9. The exception argument is a string that indicates the missing name.
UnboundLocalError	Raised when you reference a local variable in a function or method, but no value has been assigned to that variable.
RuntimeError	Raised when Python detects a generic error that doesn't fall in any of the other categories. The exception argument is a string that indicates what went wrong. Python rarely raises this catch-all exception.
NotImplementedError	Raised when you invoke a method that hasn't been implemented. An abstract method in a user-defined base class should raise this exception if it requires a derived class to override the method (see Chapter 12).
SyntaxError	Raised when the Python interpreter detects a syntax error in interactive or script mode. This exception may occur in an import statement, in an exec statement, in an eval() or input() call, when reading a script initially, or when reading standard input.
TabError	Raised when you use the -tt command-line option with a program that uses tabs and spaces inconsistently; see "Indenting Blocks of Statements" in Chapter 7.
IndentationError	Raised when program breaks Python's indentation rules; see "Indenting Blocks of Statements" in Chapter 7.
SystemError	Raised when the Python interpreter encounters an internal error that isn't serious enough to cause the interpreter to quit. The exception argument is a string indicating what went wrong (in low-level terms).
TypeError	Raised when you apply a built-in operation or function to an object of inappropriate type. The exception argument is a string that gives details about the type mismatch.
ValueError	Raised when you pass a built-in operation or function an argument that has the right type but an inappropriate value, and the situation isn't described by a more precise exception, such as IndexError.
UnicodeError	Raised when a Unicode-related encoding or decoding error occurs; see "Creating a Unicode String" in Chapter 4.

UNDERSTANDING THE EXCEPTION HIERARCHY

✔ Tips

■ For a complete description of exceptions, see Section 2.2, "Built-in Exceptions," of the *Python Library Reference*.

■ Technically, the exceptions module defines exceptions. It's unnecessary to import this module explicitly, as the built-in namespace provides exceptions.

■ The warnings module includes warnings, which also are organized as a hierarchy (**Table 11.2**). You can use warnings to print messages that alert the user to a potential problem without raising an exception or stopping program execution. I don't cover warnings in this book; for information about them, see Section 3.20, "warnings—Warning control," of the *Python Library Reference*.

■ **NEW** Python 2.1 introduced warnings. Python 2.0 introduced the WindowsError, UnicodeError, and UnboundLocalError exceptions. Python 1.5 implemented all the built-in exceptions as classes rather than strings. String exceptions are still permitted but are used infrequently; I don't cover them in this book.

■ **LANG** Java, C++, and several other languages support exceptions.

Table 11.2

Warnings	
WARNING	DESCRIPTION
Warning	The root of all warnings
DeprecationWarning	Warns about deprecated (obsolete) features
SyntaxWarning	Warns about dubious syntax
RuntimeWarning	Warns about dubious run-time behavior
UserWarning	User-defined warnings

Handling an Exception

When Python raises an exception, you must catch and handle the exception; otherwise, Python terminates your program. Exception handling forces you to consider what can go wrong in your program and what you should do about it. It's impractical (and nearly impossible) to try to account for and handle *everything* that can go wrong. Instead, you should check for conditions that (generally speaking) you can reasonably recover from at run time by using a corrective block of code, called an *exception handler*. Your exception handler can take remedial action itself without user interaction, can ask the user to provide additional or acceptable data to fix the problem, or in some circumstances can terminate the program with sys.exit(). (The point of exceptions, however, is to prevent such abrupt and fatal situations.)

Python's try statement detects and handles exceptions. try is a compound statement like if or while and follows the indentation rules given in "Creating Compound Statements" in Chapter 7. try also changes the normal control flow in a program. (Recall that *control flow* is the execution sequence of statements in your program.)

To handle an exception:

◆ Type:

```
try:
    try_block
except ex:
    except_block
```

Python runs the code in *try_block* until it finishes successfully or an exception occurs. If it finishes successfully, Python skips the *except_block*, and execution continues at the statement following *except_block*. If an exception occurs, Python skips the rest of the *try_block*

continues on next page

statements and examines the value *ex* in the except clause to see whether the type of exception raised matches the type declared by *ex*.

If the exception matches *ex*, Python runs *except_block*, and control flows to the statement following *except_block*. If the exception doesn't match *ex*, the exception percolates out of the try statement into any enclosing try statements that might have an except clause to handle it. If no surrounding except clauses handle the exception, Python terminates the program and prints an error message (**Figures 11.5** and **11.6**).

try_block and *except_block* are indented blocks of statements, and *ex* is an exception type.

```
>>> try:
...     5 + "five"
... except TypeError:
...     print "Can't add number and
→ nonnumber."
...
Can't add number and nonnumber.
>>>
>>> try:
...     x + 5
... except NameError:
...     print "Can't find a local or
→ global variable."
...
Can't find a local or global variable.
>>>
>>> filename = "xxx.txt"
>>> try:
...     f = open(filename, "r")
... except IOError:
...     print "Unable to open file",
→ filename
...
Unable to open file xxx.txt
>>>
>>> for x in range(-2, 3):
...     print x, "\t",
...     try:
...         print 1.0 / x
...     except ZeroDivisionError:
...         print 'uninvertable'
...
-2      -0.5
-1      -1.0
0       uninvertable
1       1.0
2       0.5
>>>
>>> def safe_index(sequence, index):
...     try:
...         return sequence[index]
```

(figure continues on next page)

Figure 11.5 *continued*

```
...    except IndexError:
...      if len(sequence):
...        if int(index) < 0:
...          return sequence[0]
...        else:
...          return sequence[-1]
...
>>> safe_index([1,2,3], -25)
1
>>> safe_index([1,2,3], 1)
2
>>> safe_index([1,2,3], 50)
3
>>> safe_index([], 2)
>>>
```

Figure 11.5 These examples use try-except statements to catch and handle exceptions. Note that the exception handler in the safe_index() function doesn't simply print an error message; instead, it fixes the problem by constraining the sequence index to a valid value.

```
>>> def divide(x,y):
...    try:
...      return(x/y)
...    except ZeroDivisionError:
...      print "Can't divide by zero."
...
>>> x = 5
>>> y = "c"
>>> try:
...    divide(x,y)
... except TypeError:
...    print "Can't divide nonnumbers."
...
Can't divide nonnumbers.
```

Figure 11.6 The divide() function divides its arguments; its except clause handles the ZeroDivisionError exception (and no others). When I try to divide 5 by the letter "c" illegally, Python raises a TypeError exception inside divide(). Because divide() doesn't catch the TypeError exception, the exception propagates up to the try statement in the caller, which handles it.

✔ Tips

■ Python kills an exception when it catches one in an except clause, so the exception won't percolate to other try statements (unless you raise it again with raise; see "Raising an Exception Explicitly" later in this chapter).

■ You can nest try statements to an arbitrary depth. If an except clause in an inner try statement doesn't handle an exception, Python looks at except clauses in the outer try statement(s).

■ You can embed a try statement in an except clause if there's a chance that your exception handler itself may raise an exception.

■ Because a try statement's blocks may call functions located elsewhere in your program, the source of an exception may reside outside the try.

continues on next page

- Exceptions aren't always used for when things go wrong; you can use them to catch valid conditions, too (**Figure 11.7**).

- Before Python 2.1 introduced nested scopes (see "Nesting Functions" in Chapter 9), you could determine whether a variable, such as x, was defined (that is, assigned a value) by using the expressions locals().has_key("x") and globals().has_key("x"). With nested scopes, however, a defined variable may not necessarily be in the local scope or global scope. In Python 2.1 or later, you can determine whether a variable is defined by attempting to access the variable and catch the possible NameError exception (**Figure 11.8**).

```
>>> def isnum(x):
...    try:
...        float(x)
...        return 1
...    except ValueError:
...        return 0
...
>>> isnum("Remedios Varo")
0
>>> isnum("1.5")
1
>>> isnum("39")
1
```

Figure 11.7 Exceptions are useful outside the context of errors. Here, the isnum() function uses an exception to determine whether a string represents a number.

```
>>> try:
...    x
... except NameError:
...    "Not defined."
...
'Not defined.'
```

Figure 11.8 You can determine whether a variable is defined by using a try-except statement. This statement works with nested scopes, too.

```
>>> import sys
>>> filename = "xxx.txt"
>>> try:
...   f = open(filename, "r")
... except IOError:
...   type, value =
→ sys.exc_info()[:2]
...   print "type:", type
...   print "value:", value
...
type: exceptions.IOError
value: [Errno 2] No such file or directory:
→ 'xxx.txt'
>>>
>>> # Now outside the except clause
... sys.exc_info()
(None, None, None)
```

Figure 11.9 The sys.exc_info() function returns the type and value of the current exception.

■ You can use the sys.exc_info() function to retrieve detailed information about the current exception. sys.exc_info() returns a three-item tuple (*type, value, traceback*). *type* is the exception type of the exception that is being handled (a class object). *value* is the exception's argument (an instance object) or the second argument of the raise statement (see "Getting an Exception's Argument" and "Raising an Exception Explicitly" later in this chapter). *traceback* is a traceback object that has special attributes, including the line number where the error occurred. You should *not* assign *traceback* to a local variable in the function handling the exception, as this assignment will cause a circular reference. You may assign *type* and *value* to variables, however. Outside an error handler, sys.exc_info() returns (None, None, None). For information about traceback objects, see Section 3.2, "The standard type hierarchy," of the *Python Reference Manual*. For information about sys.exc_info(), see Section 3.1, "sys—System-specific parameters and functions," of the *Python Reference Manual* (**Figure 11.9**).

■ **NEW** Python 2.1 and later versions permit continue statements inside try blocks; see "Skipping Part of a Loop Iteration" in Chapter 7.

■ **LANG** Java's try-catch statement handles exceptions.

Ignoring an Exception

To ignore an exception, use a solitary pass statement as an except clause block; see "Using pass to Create a Null Statement" in Chapter 7.

To ignore an exception:

◆ Type:

```
try:
    try_block
except ex:
    pass
```

This statement behaves as described in "Handling an Exception" earlier in this chapter, except that if an exception occurs, Python ignores it and control flows to the statement following pass (**Figure 11.10**).

try_block is an indented block of statements, and *ex* is an exception type.

✔ Tip

■ **LANG** In Java, empty braces ({ }) in a catch clause ignore an exception.

```
>>> import os
>>> try:
...     os.remove("E:\\temp\\log.tmp")
... except OSError:
...     pass
...
>>>
```

Figure 11.10 When I delete this temporary file, I don't care whether it actually exists.

```
>>> try:
...     5 * (1/0)
... except ZeroDivisionError, e:
...     print e
...     print "dir(e):", dir(e)
...     print "e.args:", e.args
...
integer division or modulo by zero
dir(e): ['args']
e.args: ('integer division or modulo by
→ zero',)
>>>
>>> try:
...     5 + "five"
... except TypeError, e:
...     print e
...
unsupported operand types for +
>>>
>>> try:
...     x + 5
... except NameError, e:
...     print e
...
```

(figure continues on next page)

Figure 11.11 *continued*

```
name 'x' is not defined
>>>
>>> try:
...    print (1, 2, 3)[8]
... except IndexError, e:
...    print e
...

tuple index out of range
>>>
>>> try:
...    f = open("xxx.txt", "r")
... except IOError, e:
...    print e
...    print "dir(e):", dir(e)
...    print "e.args:", e.args
...    print "e.errno:", e.errno
...    print "e.filename:",
→ e.filename
...    print "e.strerror:",
→ e.strerror
...

[Errno 2] No such file or directory:
→ 'xxx.txt'
dir(e): ['args', 'errno', 'filename',
→ 'strerror']
e.args: (2, 'No such file or directory')
e.errno: 2
e.filename: xxx.txt
e.strerror: No such file or directory
```

Figure 11.11 Specify a variable after the exception name to receive the exception argument's value. OS-related exception arguments have extra attributes that contain information returned by the operating system.

Getting an Exception's Argument

When an exception occurs, it may have an associated value, also known as its *argument*. The argument's value and type depend on the exception type. For most exceptions, the argument is a one-item tuple that contains a string indicating the error's cause. For operating-system errors such as IOError, the argument contains extra attributes that give OS information, such as an error number or file name. You can use the dir() function to list an argument's attributes; see "Listing an Object's Attributes" in Chapter 9.

To retrieve an argument's value, specify a variable after the exception name in the except clause.

To get an exception's argument:

◆ Type:

```
try:
    try_block
except ex, target:
    except_block
```

This statement behaves as described in "Handling an Exception" earlier in this chapter, except that if an exception occurs, Python assigns the exception argument to *target* (**Figure 11.11**).

try_block and *except_block* are indented blocks of statements, *ex* is an exception type, and *target* is a variable name.

✔ Tips

- If an exception doesn't have an argument, the value of *target* defaults to None.

- Type print *target* or str(*target*) to present *target* as a nicely formatted string.

- *target* remains available after *except_block* finishes.

- An exception argument is an instance of a class (see Chapter 12), so you can access its __class__ attribute to retrieve more information about it (**Figure 11.12**).

- **LANG** Java's exceptions inherit informational methods from Throwable.

```
>>> try:
...   5 + "five"
... except TypeError, e:
...   print e
...
unsupported operand types for +
>>> e
<exceptions.TypeError instance at 007F3324>
>>> type(e)
<type 'instance'>
>>> e.__class__
<class exceptions.TypeError at 007AA204>
>>> e.__class__.__name__
'TypeError'
>>> e.__class__.__doc__
'Inappropriate argument type.'
```

Figure 11.12 An argument object's __class__ attribute provides more information about the object.

```
>>> def divide(x,y):
...   try:
...     return(x/y)
...   except:
...     print "Can't divide", x,
→ "by", y
...
>>> divide(5,0)
Can't divide 5 by 0
>>> divide(5,"a")
Can't divide 5 by a
>>> divide(5,1)
5
>>>
>>> try:
...   f = open("nums.txt", "r")
...   s = f.readline()
...   i = int(s)
... except:
...   import sys
...   type, value = sys.exc_info()[:2]
...   print type
...   print value
...
exceptions.ValueError
invalid literal for int(): 39.75
```

Figure 11.13 An except clause with no exception name or argument name catches all exceptions. In general, you shouldn't use this catch-all except clause, because it can hide real programming errors.

Handling All Exceptions

To catch all exceptions, specify an except clause with no exception name or argument name. A catch-all except clause generally is a poor choice for an error handler because it catches *any* exception, not just the ones that interest you; furthermore, it can conceal genuine bugs in your program.

To handle all exceptions:

◆ Type:

    try:

        try_block

    except:

        except_block

This statement behaves as described in "Handling an Exception" earlier in this chapter, except that the *except_block* handles all exceptions (**Figure 11.13**).

try_block and *except_block* are indented blocks of statements.

✔ Tips

■ You can use the following statement to catch all built-in exceptions:

    try:

        try_block

    except StandardError:

        except_block

■ **LANG** Java's catch-all catch clause catches exceptions of type Exception.

Running Code in the Absence of an Exception

You can add an else clause to a try statement to run a block of statements only if the try clause doesn't cause an exception. The else clause must follow the last except clause.

To run code in the absence of an exception:

◆ Type:

try:

   try_block

except [...]:

   except_block

else:

   else_block

This statement behaves as described in "Handling an Exception" earlier in this chapter, except that Python runs *else_block* only if *try_block* doesn't cause an exception (**Figure 11.14**).

try_block, except_block, and *else_block* are indented blocks of statements.

```
>>> try:
...     f = open("nums.txt", "r")
... except IOError, e:
...     print "Can't open file:",
→ e.filename
... else:
...     s = f.readline()
...     print s,
...     f.close()
...
39.75
```

Figure 11.14 The else block runs only if Python can open the file nums.txt, which it can in this case.

```
>>> def divide(x,y):
...   try:
...     return(x/y)
...   except (TypeError,
→ ZeroDivisionError):
...       print "Can't divide", x,
→ "by", y
...
>>> divide(5,0)
Can't divide 5 by 0
>>> divide(5,"a")
Can't divide 5 by a
>>>
>>> try:
...   f = open("nums.txt", "r")
...   s = f.readline()
...   i = int(s)
... except (IOError, ValueError), e:
...   print e
...
invalid literal for int(): 39.75
```

Figure 11.15 You can catch multiple exceptions in a single except clause to use the same handler for more than one exception.

Handling Multiple Exceptions

You can use a single except clause to catch multiple exception types or use multiple except clauses to define multiple exception-handling blocks.

To handle multiple exceptions with a single handler:

◆ Type:

```
try:
    try_block
except (ex1, ex2,...)[,target]:
    except_block
```

This statement behaves as described in "Handling an Exception" earlier in this chapter, except that the except clause catches any of the listed exceptions (*ex1, ex2,...*) and runs the same *except_block* for all of them. *target* is an optional variable that takes the exception's argument; see "Getting an Exception's Argument" earlier in this chapter (**Figure 11.15**).

try_block and *except_block* are indented blocks of statements, *ex1, ex2,...* are two or more comma-separated exception types, and *target* is a variable name.

To handle multiple exceptions with multiple handlers:

◆ Type:

try:

   try_block

except *ex1* [, *target1*]:

   except_block1

except *ex2* [, *target2*]:

   except_block2

...

except *exN* [, *targetN*]:

   except_blockN

This statement behaves as described in "Handling an Exception" earlier in this chapter, except that Python examines each except clause in turn, from first to last, to determine whether the type of exception raised matches the type declared by *ex1, ex2,..., exN.*

target1, target2,..., targetN are optional variables that take the corresponding exception's argument; see "Getting an Exception's Argument" earlier in this chapter (**Figure 11.16**).

try_block and *except_block1, except_block2,..., except_blockN* are indented blocks of statements, *ex1, ex2,..., exN* are exception types, and *target1, target2,..., targetN* are variable names.

```
>>> def divide(x,y):
...   try:
...     return(x/y)
...   except ZeroDivisionError:
...     print "Can't divide", x,
→ "by zero"
...   except TypeError, e:
...     print e
...
>>> divide(5,0)
Can't divide 5 by zero
>>> divide(5,"a")
unsupported operand type(s) for /
>>>
>>> try:
...   f = open("nums.txt", "r")
...   s = f.readline()
...   i = int(s)
... except IOError, e:
...   print "Can't open file:",
→ e.filename
... except ValueError:
...   print "Can't convert",
→ s.strip(), "to integer"
...
Can't convert 39.75 to integer
```

Figure 11.16 You can use multiple except clauses to handle different types of exceptions.

Combining the try, except, and else clauses from this section and the preceding sections yields the try statement's most general form, which follows. Note that the catch-all except clause follows the named except clauses and that the else clause follows the last except clause.

```
try:
    try_block
except (ex, ex,...)[,target]:
    except_block
except ex [,target]:
    except_block
...
except (ex, ex,...):
    except_block
except:
    except_block
else:
    else_block
```

✔ Tips

- To catch all the exceptions in a particular group of the exception hierarchy, specify the group's name in an except clause. This, for example:

```
try:
    try_block
except LookupError:
    except_block
```

  is equivalent to this:

```
try:
    try_block
except (IndexError, KeyError):
    except_block
```

- **LANG** Java's try statement supports multiple catch clauses.

HANDLING MULTIPLE EXCEPTIONS

Running Mandatory Cleanup Code

You can use the try-finally statement to run code regardless of whether Python raises an exception. Unlike an except clause, a finally clause doesn't catch exceptions; it defines cleanup actions that must be performed under all circumstances, regardless of whether an error occurs.

A finally clause and an except clause can't appear together within a single try statement. Programmers typically nest a try-finally statement in a try-except statement to handle exceptions raised in the try-finally statement. Furthermore, you can't add an else clause to a try-finally statement.

To run cleanup code:

◆ Type:

```
try:
    try_block
finally:
    finally_block
```

Python runs the code in *finally_block* after it runs the code in *try_block*. Python runs *finally_block* no matter how *try_block* completes—whether normally, through an exception, or via a control-flow statement such as break or return. If an exception occurs in *try_block*, however, Python skips the rest of *try_block*, runs *finally_block*, and then raises the exception again to be caught by a higher-level try-except statement (**Figure 11.17**).

try_block and *finally_block* are indented blocks of statements.

```
>>> try:
...     f = open("nums.txt", "r")
...     try:
...         s = f.readline()
...         i = int(s)
...     finally:
...         f.close()
...         print "file closed"
... except IOError, e:
...     print "Can't open file:",
→ e.filename
... except ValueError:
...     print "Can't convert",
→ s.strip(), "to integer"
...
file closed
Can't convert 39.75 to integer
```

Figure 11.17 If open() fails, the except IOError clause handles it, and Python never runs the nested try-finally statement. If open() succeeds (as it does here), Python attempts to read from the file and convert its contents to an integer. Here, the conversion fails and raises a ValueError exception, so Python first runs the finally code and then catches the exception in the outer try statement's except ValueError clause.

```
>>> def isnum(x):
...     try:
...         float(x)
...         return 1
...     except ValueError:
...         return 0
...
>>> def check_rectangle(height,
→ width):
...     if not isnum(height) or not
→ isnum(width):
...         raise TypeError
...     if height <= 0 or width <= 0:
...         arg = ("Nonpositive
→ dimensions:", height, width)
```

(figure continues on next page)

Figure 11.18 *continued*

```
...     raise ValueError, arg
...   else:
...     return(height, width)
...
>>> def make_rectangle(height, width):
...   try:
...     return check_rectangle
→(height, width)
...   except TypeError:
...     print "Dimensions must be
→numeric"
...   except ValueError, arg:
...     print arg[0], "height:",
→arg[1], "width:", arg[2]
...
>>>
>>> make_rectangle(1, 5)
(1, 5)
>>>
>>> make_rectangle(1, -5)
Nonpositive dimensions: height: 1 width: -5
>>>
>>> make_rectangle("Seneca", 5)
Dimensions must be numeric
```

Figure 11.18 The check_rectangle() function raises an exception explicitly if the dimensions of a rectangle are invalid (that is, they are nonnumeric or nonpositive). The make_rectangle() function catches and handles the exceptions that check_rectangle() raises.

- You can create and raise user-defined exceptions; see "Creating User-Defined Exceptions" later in this chapter.

- Type raise SystemExit to quit the interpreter.

- **LANG** Java's throw statement raises, or *throws,* exceptions. C's setjmp and longjmp functions are somewhat similar to Python's try and raise clauses.

Raising an Exception Explicitly

You can use the raise statement to force a specified exception to occur.

To raise an exception explicitly:

- Type:

  raise *ex*

  or

  raise *ex*, *arg*

  or

  raise *ex*, (*arg1*, *arg2*,...)

  Python raises the exception *ex* with optional arguments that give specific details about the exception; see "Getting an Exception's Argument" earlier in this chapter. The exception argument can be a single value, *arg,* or a tuple of values (*arg1, arg2,...*). If omitted, the exception argument defaults to None (**Figure 11.18**).

  ex is an exception type, and *arg, arg1, arg2,...* are expressions.

✔ Tips

- Type raise with no arguments to raise the current exception again (in the current scope). If there's no current exception to raise, Python raises a TypeError exception.

- For alternative forms of raise, see "Creating User-Defined Exceptions" later in this chapter.

- The raise statement takes an optional third argument, *traceback,* which is a traceback object. Python substitutes *traceback* instead of creating a new traceback object for the current exception. *traceback* is not used much in practice, but it's handy if you want to raise an exception again in an except clause; see Section 3.2, "The standard type hierarchy," of the *Python Reference Manual.*

Creating User-Defined Exceptions

This section requires that you understand class definitions; see Chapter 12.

Exceptions can be strings, classes, or instances. String exceptions are obsolete, so I don't discuss them in this book (although Python still supports them for backward compatibility). I cover class-based exceptions in this section.

You can create user-defined exceptions by using the class statement (see "Defining a Class" in Chapter 12). I recommend that you base your exceptions on Python's root exception, Exception (see "Understanding the Exception Hierarchy" earlier in this chapter). You can handle user-defined exceptions the same way that you would built-in exceptions. **Figures 11.19** and **11.20** show some examples.

To create a user-defined exception:

◆ Type:

```
class ex(Exception):
    def __init__(self, arg = None):
        self.arg = arg
    def __str__(self):
        return str(self.arg)
```

This definition creates a new exception class, *ex*, which inherits from Exception. The __init__() method creates the exception's argument, *arg* (see "Getting an Exception's Argument" earlier in this chapter). The __str__() method creates the nicely formatted string form of *arg* that's printed in tracebacks.

ex is an exception type, and *arg* is a variable name.

```
>>> class MyError(Exception):
...    def __init__(self, arg = None):
...       self.arg = arg
...    def __str__(self):
...       return str(self.arg)
...
>>> raise MyError
Traceback (most recent call last):
  File "<stdin>", line 1, in ?
__main__.MyError: None
>>>
>>> raise MyError()
Traceback (most recent call last):
  File "<stdin>", line 1, in ?
__main__.MyError: None
>>>
>>> raise MyError, "testing"
Traceback (most recent call last):
  File "<stdin>", line 1, in ?
__main__.MyError: testing
>>>
>>> raise MyError("testing")
Traceback (most recent call last):
  File"<stdin>", line 1, in ?
__main__.MyError: testing
>>>
>>> try:
...    raise MyError, "testing"
... except MyError, e:
...    print e
...
testing
```

Figure 11.19 You can raise, catch, and handle user-defined exceptions as you would built-in exceptions.

```
>>> class DimensionError
→ (Exception):
...   def __init__(self, msg, height,
→ width):
...     self.arg = (msg, height, width)
...     self.msg = msg
...     self.height = height
...     self.width = width
...   def __str__(self):
...     return str(self.arg)
...
>>> def check_rectangle(height, width):
...   if height <= 0 or width <= 0:
...     raise DimensionError
→ ("Nonpositive dimensions",
→ height, width)
...   else:
...     return(height, width)
...
>>> def make_rectangle(height, width):
...   try:
...     return check_rectangle
→ (height, width)
...   except DimensionError, e:
...     print e.msg +":", "height:",
→ e.height, "width:", e.width
...
>>> make_rectangle(1, 5)
(1, 5)
>>>
>>> make_rectangle(1, -5)
Nonpositive dimensions: height: 1 width: -5
```

Figure 11.20 You can create a class constructor
(__init__) that takes multiple exception arguments.

To raise an exception without an exception argument:

◆ Type:

raise ex

or

raise ex()

ex is an exception type.

To raise an exception with a single exception argument:

◆ Type:

raise ex, arg

or

raise ex(arg)

ex is an exception type, and *arg* is an
expression.

To raise an exception with multiple exception arguments:

◆ Type:

raise ex, (arg1, arg2,...)

or

raise ex(arg1, arg2,...)

ex is an exception type, and *arg1, arg2,...* are
one or more comma-separated expressions.

CREATING USER-DEFINED EXCEPTIONS

✔ Tips

- You can use class exceptions to create a hierarchy of exceptions; see "Understanding the Exception Hierarchy" earlier in this chapter (**Figure 11.21**).

- Python converts exception arguments to instances automatically, but you can raise an exception that uses an explicit class instance.

  raise *instance*

  is equivalent to:

  raise *instance*.__class__, *instance*

- **LANG** User-defined exceptions in Java extend the class Throwable or one of its subclasses, such as Exception.

```
>>> # Inherits from DimensionError
... class NonnumericDimError
→ (DimensionError):
...     pass
...
>>> # Inherits from DimensionError
... class NonpositiveDimError
→ (DimensionError):
...     pass
...
>>> try:
...     raise NonnumericDimError
→ ("NonnumericDimError", "a", -5)
... except DimensionError:
...     import sys
...     type, value = sys.exc_info()[:2]
...     print type
...     print value
...
__main__.NonnumericDimError
('NonnumericDimError', 'a', -5)
```

Figure 11.21 Here, I used the DimensionError exception defined in Figure 11.20 as the base class for the more-specific NonnumericDimError and NonpositiveDimError exceptions. The except DimensionError clause catches any exception derived from DimensionError. The sys.exc_info() function returns a tuple that contains the specific type of error raised and its argument; see the tips in "Handling an Exception" earlier in this chapter.

```
>>> x = 5.5
>>> if x % 3 == 0:
...   pass
... elif x % 3 == 1:
...   pass
... else:  # Assume x%3 == 2
...   assert x % 3 == 2, "x%3==2"
...   pass
...
Traceback (most recent call last):
  File "<stdin>", line 6, in ?
AssertionError: x%3==2
>>>
>>> suit = "mimetic"
>>> try:
...   if suit == "clubs":
...     pass
...   elif suit == "diamonds":
...     pass
...   elif suit == "hearts":
...     pass
...   elif suit == "spades":
...     pass
...   else:
...     # Should never reach here
...     assert 0, "AssertionError:
→ Bad suit: " + `suit`
... except AssertionError, e:
...   print e
...
AssertionError: Bad suit: 'mimeti'
```

Figure 11.22 The assertion in the first example flags a faulty assumption. The assert statement in the default else clause fails because % can compute remainders that are not whole numbers (see "Getting the Remainder of a Division" in Chapter 3). The assertion in the second example tests the assumption that one of the four if/elif statements is always executed; the assert always asserts false because the default else clause should be unreachable.

Making an Assertion

This section covers an advanced topic that you may skip without loss of continuity.

An *assertion* is a debugging tool that you can use to print diagnostic information while your program runs. Python's assert statement contains a Boolean expression that, if false, indicates an error. The expression is always one that you believe to be true at the time that it's evaluated. If the expression evaluates to false, Python raises an AssertionError exception, which you can catch and handle like any other exception. By verifying that the expression is true, Python corroborates your knowledge of your program, thus reducing the possibility of bugs.

To make an assertion:

◆ Type:

    assert expr [,arg]

expr is a test expression that evaluates to true or false. If *expr* is false, Python raises an AssertionError exception with the optional argument *arg*. If *expr* is true, assert takes no action (**Figure 11.22**).

expr is a Boolean expression (see "Using Boolean Operators" in Chapter 2), and *arg* is an expression. If omitted, *arg* defaults to None.

Python translates the assert statement internally to this code:

    if __debug__:
      if not expr:
        raise AssertionError, arg

__debug__ is a built-in, read-only variable that is 1 (true) by default. To change __debug__ to 0 (false), specify the -O or the -OO (uppercase letter ohs) command-line option to start Python in optimized mode and ignore assertions; see "Specifying Command-Line Options" in Chapter 1.

To disable assertions:

◆ Type python -0 *script.py*

script.py is the name of a script file containing assert statements.

✔ Tips

■ Use assertions for debugging purposes only, not for tasks such as checking the validity of user input.

■ Don't use assertion expressions for code that's required to make your program run correctly. Because assertions may be disabled, your program shouldn't assume that the assertion's expression will be evaluated; in particular, these expressions shouldn't cause side effects.

■ If *expr* is true, assert acts like a pass statement.

■ It's common practice to print assertion results to sys.stderr; see "Accessing Standard Input and Output Files" in Chapter 10.

■ You can use __debug__ to include any kind of debugging code in your programs, not just assertions.

■ As an alternative to specifying -0 or -00, you can set the Python environment variable PYTHONOPTIMIZE to 0 or 1 to disable or enable assertions; see "Using Python Environment Variables" in Chapter 1.

■ **LANG** Java's assert statement raises an AssertionError. C's assert function makes assertions.

MAKING AN ASSERTION

CLASSES

So far, I've written programs that use only the built-in object types in Python's standard type hierarchy: numbers, sequences, dictionaries, callable types, and internal types (see "Built-In Types" in the Introduction). Python, like all object-oriented programming languages, provides tools that you can use to create new types of objects. The notions of classes and objects are the bases for these tools.

A *class* is a template or blueprint for an *object.* Conceptually, classes are comparable to categories that you use to organize real-world information, such as *animal, vegetable,* and *mineral.* (*Mosquito, lettuce,* and *schist,* for example, are instances of objects.) In programs, you use a class to define a generalized category that describes a group of more specific items (objects) that can exist within it. These objects have associated variables and methods that characterize the object as a member of a class.

Object-oriented programming (*OOP*) is the use of programming techniques based on the concepts of classes and objects: You organize your program as a collection of discrete, self-contained objects that hold data and define methods that interact with other objects. In Python, OOP is optional; you can get by with just the tools and techniques that I've covered so far. But Python's OOP tools are a powerful and often-used part of the language, as you'll see in this chapter.

Understanding OOP Terminology

I lack the room to give a full exposition of object-oriented programming, and many other books do that, so I'll discuss only the OOP features available in Python. OOP takes practice, and it's important that you design a flexible and extensible class hierarchy in the early stages of your project. OO programmers typically spend considerable time planning their programs before they write a line of code.

OOP comes with its own vocabulary. Many of these terms might sound like jargon, but they're useful and accepted parlance. **Table 12.1** defines some important terms; I discuss each term in more detail when it arises.

Table 12.1

OOP Terms	
TERM	**DEFINITION**
Class	A user-defined prototype for an object that defines a set of attributes that characterize any object of the class. The attributes are data members (class variables and instance variables) and methods, accessed via dot notation.
Class variable	A variable that is shared by all instances of a class. Class variables are defined within a class but outside any of the class's methods. Class variables aren't used as frequently as instance variables are.
Initialization method	A special method, named `__init__`, that's invoked automatically when an object of that class is instantiated. Instance variables typically are defined in this method.
Data member	A class variable or instance variable that holds data associated with a class and its objects.
Function overloading	The assignment of more than one behavior to a particular function. The operation performed varies by the types of objects (arguments) involved.
Instance variable	A variable that is defined inside a method and belongs only to the current instance of a class.
Inheritance	The transfer of the characteristics of a class to other classes that are derived from it. If Shape is a class, for example, the classes `Circle` and `Square` can be derived from it, and each will inherit Shape's data and methods: area, perimeter, and so on. Each class holds a position in a class hierarchy: Data and methods in one class can be inherited from a parent (or *superclass*) or passed down the hierarchy to a child (or *subclass*). A child class may override any of its parent's attributes, as well as add attributes of its own.
Instance	An individual object of a certain class. An object c that belongs to a class `Circle`, for example, is an instance of the class `Circle`.
Instantiation	The creation of an instance of a class.
Method	A special kind of function that is defined in a class definition. An instance uses its methods to perform actions that operate on its own data, such as printing itself. Contrast methods with functions, which handle different types of objects.
Object	A unique instance of a data structure that's defined by its class. An object comprises both data members (class variables and instance variables) and methods.
Operator overloading	The assignment of more than one function to a particular operator. The operation performed varies by the types of objects (operands) involved.

```
>>> class Point:
...     pass
...
>>> class Shape:
...     pass
...
>>> type(Point)
<type 'class'>
>>> str(Point)
'__main__.Point'
>>> repr(Point)
'<class __main__.Point at 007C5654>'
```

Figure 12.1 These minimal class definitions have (as yet) no data members or methods; I'll expand these definitions in the examples later in this chapter.

Defining a Class

Classes are Python's means of creating user-defined data types. The class statement is a compound statement (see "Creating Compound Statements" in Chapter 7) that creates a new class and that defines the class's name, data attributes (class and instance variables), and methods.

To define a class:

◆ Type:

class *class*:

   block

This compound statement defines a new class object and assigns it to the name *class*. The statements inside *block* define the class's attributes—that is, its data members and methods (**Figure 12.1**).

class is a valid Python name (see "Naming Variables" in Chapter 2), and *block* is an indented block of statements.

✔ Tips

■ By convention, class names are capitalized.

■ A class definition doesn't create an instance of a class, but defines the attributes that all instances of the class share. To create an instance, see "Creating an Instance" later in this chapter.

■ You can use the pass statement to define a null class, as I do in Figure 12.1; see "Using *pass* to Create a Null Statement" in Chapter 7.

■ Class definitions usually are placed near the top of a module, after the import statements and global-variable definitions; see "Structuring a Module" in Chapter 9.

■ You also can create a new class by deriving it from one or more existing classes; see "Deriving New Classes from Existing Classes" later in this chapter.

■ **LANG** Java's class statement defines a class.

■ Python executes the statements in *block* when a class is first defined or loaded.

Documenting a Class

As it does with functions and modules, Python allows you to add an optional documentation string as the first line of a class definition. A class docstring should summarize the class's purpose.

Docstrings are assigned to the class's __doc__ attribute and, unlike # comments, can be accessed with the dot operator at run time.

To access a class's docstring:

◆ Type *class*.__doc__

class is a class name (**Figure 12.2**).

✔ Tips

■ If you don't specify a docstring, the default value of the __doc__ attribute is None.

■ Although I often omit docstrings in this book to save space, it's good practice to add them to all your classes. Your users will appreciate them, and some tools use docstrings to create help documentation.

■ You can access the docstrings of built-in classes (**Figure 12.3**).

■ You also can add docstrings to class methods in the same way that you can add them to functions; see "Documenting a Function" in Chapter 8.

```
>>> class Point:
...     """
...     A location on a
...     2-dimensional plane
...     """
...     pass
...
>>> class Shape:
...     'A geometric shape'
...     pass
...
>>> print Point.__doc__

    A location on a
    2-dimensional plane

>>> Shape.__doc__
'A geometric shape'
```

Figure 12.2 Here, I've added docstrings to the classes defined in Figure 12.1. Triple-quoted docstrings can span multiple lines and retain their formatting when printed.

```
>>> Exception.__doc__
'Common base class for all exceptions.'
>>> IndexError.__doc__
'Sequence index out of range.'
>>> NameError.__doc__
'Name not found globally.'
>>> ValueError.__doc__
'Inappropriate argument value (of correct type).'
>>> ZeroDivisionError.__doc__
'Second argument to a division or modulo
→ operation was zero.'
```

Figure 12.3 Printing the docstring of a built-in class is a quick way to get help.

Table 12.2

Built-In Class Attributes	
ATTRIBUTE	**DESCRIPTION**
__dict__	Dictionary containing the class's namespace. For information about namespaces, see "Understanding Namespaces" in Chapter 9.
__doc__	Class documentation string, or None if undefined.
__name__	Class name.
__module__	Module name in which the class is defined; this attribute is "__main__" in interactive mode.
__bases__	A possibly empty tuple containing the base classes, in the order of their occurrence in the base class list; see "Deriving New Classes from Existing Classes" later in this chapter.

```
>>> Point.__dict__

{'__module__': '__main__', '__doc__':
→ 'A location on a 2-dimensional plane'}

>>> Point.__doc__

'A location on a 2-dimensional plane'

>>> Point.__name__

'Point'

>>> Point.__module__

'__main__'

>>> Point.__bases__

()
```

Figure 12.4 These are built-in class attributes.

Accessing Built-In Class Attributes

Python provides several predefined class attributes, listed in **Table 12.2**. You can access these attributes by using dot notation to qualify the attribute with the class name; see "Accessing Attributes" in Chapter 9.

To access a class attribute:

◆ Type $class.attr$

$class$ is a class name, and $attr$ is an attribute name (**Figure 12.4**).

✔ Tips

■ You also can access built-in instance attributes; see "Accessing Built-In Instance Attributes" later in this chapter.

■ Retrieving a class attribute actually is a namespace lookup. The class's __dict__ attribute holds the class's attribute names and values in a dictionary. $class.attr$, for example, is equivalent to $class.$__dict__$["attr"]$, and $class.attr = x$ is equivalent to $class.$__dict__$["attr"] = x$. For information about namespaces, see "Understanding Namespaces" in Chapter 9.

■ A class attribute assignment such as $class.attr = x$ always updates the __dict__ attribute of $class$, not the namespaces of any base classes.

■ If Python can't find a class attribute in the class's __dict__ namespace, it searches the base classes depth first, left to right in the order in which base classes are specified in the class definition. For information about base classes, see "Deriving New Classes from Existing Classes" later in this chapter.

■ You also can manipulate class attributes by using the built-in hasattr(), getattr(), setattr(), and delattr() functions, described in "Manipulating Attributes" in Chapter 9. You shouldn't change or delete built-in attributes.

Creating an Instance

After you've defined a class, you can create an instance of that class by calling the class object as a function. The process of creating an object from a class definition is known as *instantiation;* thus, objects often are called *instance objects* or just *instances.* All instances are accessed via object references. Any variable that appears to hold an object actually contains a reference to that object; see "Creating Variables" in Chapter 2.

To create an instance:

◆ Type *inst = class()* to create a new instance of the class *class* and assign it to the variable *inst* (**Figure 12.5**).

   inst is a variable name, and *class* is a class name; see "Defining a Class" earlier in this chapter.

✔ Tips

■ Calling a class object implies a call to the class's __init__() method (if it exists); see "Creating Instance Variables with an Initialization Method" later in this chapter.

■ **LANG** Java objects are created with expressions that use the new operator.

```
>>> class Point:
...    pass
...
>>> point = Point()
>>> type(point)
<type 'instance'>
>>> repr(point)
'<__main__.Point instance at 007F8A4C>'
```

Figure 12.5 When you call a class object, Python creates and returns a new class instance.

Table 12.3

Built-In Instance Attributes	
ATTRIBUTE	DESCRIPTION
__dict__	Dictionary containing the instance's namespace. For information about namespaces, see "Understanding Namespaces" in Chapter 9.
__class__	Name of the instance's class.

```
>>> class Point:
...   pass
...
>>> point = Point()
>>> point.__dict__
{}
>>> point.__class__
<class __main__.Point at 007A7E64>
>>> point.__class__.__name__
'Point'
```

Figure 12.6 These are built-in instance attributes. The __dict__ dictionary is empty because the class defines no data members or methods. You can use an instance's __class__ attribute to access the attributes of its class.

- An instance attribute assignment such as *inst.attr* = *x* always updates the __dict__ attribute of *inst,* not the namespaces of *inst's* class or base classes.

- You also can manipulate instance attributes by using the built-in hasattr(), getattr(), setattr(), and delattr() functions, described in "Manipulating Attributes" in Chapter 9. You shouldn't change or delete built-in attributes.

Accessing Built-In Instance Attributes

Python provides several predefined instance attributes, listed in **Table 12.3**. You can access these attributes by using dot notation to qualify the attribute with the instance name; see "Accessing Attributes" in Chapter 9.

To access an instance attribute:

- ◆ Type *inst.attr*

    inst is an instance name, and *attr* is an attribute name (**Figure 12.6**).

✔ Tips

- You also can access built-in class attributes; see "Accessing Built-In Class Attributes" earlier in this chapter.

- Retrieving an instance attribute actually is a namespace lookup. The instance's __dict__ attribute holds the instance's attribute names and values in a dictionary. *inst.attr*, for example, is equivalent to *inst.*__dict__["*attr*"], and *inst.attr* = *x* is equivalent to *inst.*__dict__["*attr*"] = *x*. For information about namespaces, see "Understanding Namespaces" in Chapter 9.

- If Python can't find an instance attribute in the instance's (local) __dict__ namespace, it searches in the class defined by the instance's __class__ attribute. If Python finds no match there, it searches the base classes depth first, left to right in the order in which base classes are specified in the class definition. If Python still finds no match, it performs the lookup by using the instance's __getattr__() method, if it exists. For information about base classes, see "Deriving New Classes from Existing Classes" later in this chapter. For information about the __getattr__() method, see "Accessing Instance Attributes" later in this chapter.

Creating Class Variables

Python lets you create *class variables*, which are values shared among all instances of a particular class. In other words, class variables are specific to the class, as opposed to instances of the class. You can access a class variable by using dot notation and qualifying the variable with a class object or an instance object.

To create a class variable:

◆ Type an assignment statement within a class definition but outside any of the class's method definitions.

For information about assignment statements, see "Creating Variables" in Chapter 2 (**Figure 12.7**).

To access a class variable:

◆ Type *class.attr* or *inst.attr*

See the tips in this section for information about changing a class variable's value.

class is a class name, *inst* is an instance of *class*, and *attr* is a class variable name (**Figure 12.8**).

✔ Tips

■ A class variable exists independently of class instances. The variable is available no matter how many class instances are created, even if none is created.

■ If you change a class variable's value at run time by qualifying it with the class object (*class.attr = value*), Python dynamically changes the value of *attr* to *value* in all existing (and future) *class* instances (**Figure 12.9**).

```
>>> class Point:
...     origin = (0,0)
```

Figure 12.7 This assignment creates the Point class variable origin.

```
>>> class Point:
...     origin = (0,0)
...
>>> Point.origin
(0, 0)
>>> pt1 = Point()
>>> pt2 = Point()
>>> print pt1.origin
(0, 0)
>>> print pt2.origin
(0, 0)
>>> pt1.__class__.origin
(0, 0)
```

Figure 12.8 The class variable origin is accessible by all instances of Point. Note that I can access origin before I create an instance of Point.

```
>>> class Point:
...     origin = (0,0)
...
>>> pt1 = Point()
>>> print pt1.origin
(0, 0)
>>> Point.origin = (3,9)
>>> print pt1.origin
(3, 9)
>>> pt2 = Point()
>>> print pt2.origin
(3, 9)
```

Figure 12.9 Here, I change the value of Point's class variable origin by qualifying origin with Point class itself. The change is visible to the existing Point instance pt1 and the new Point instance pt2.

```
>>> class Point:
...   origin = (0,0)
...
>>> pt1 = Point()
>>> pt1.__dict__   # Original pt1 namespace
{}
>>> pt2 = Point()
>>> print pt1.origin, pt2.origin,
→ Point.origin
(0, 0) (0, 0) (0, 0)
>>> pt1.origin = (3,9)
>>> print pt1.origin, pt2.origin,
→ Point.origin
(3, 9) (0, 0) (0, 0)
>>> pt1.__dict__   # pt1 namespace changes
{'origin': (3, 9)}
>>> Point.__dict__
{'__doc__': None, '__module__': '__main__',
→ 'origin': (0, 0)}
```

Figure 12.10 Here, I change the value of Point's class variable origin by qualifying origin with the Point instance p1. The change affects only p1; the Point class and the Point instance p2 retain their original origin values. In terms of namespaces, Python adds the new local variable origin to p1's namespace (__dict__) but leaves Point's namespace unchanged.

```
>>> class Point:
...   num_points = 0
...   def __init__(self):
...     Point.num_points += 1
...
>>> print Point.num_points
0
>>> pt1 = Point()
>>> print pt1.num_points
1
>>> pt2 = Point()
>>> print pt1.num_points,
→ pt2.num_points
2 2
```

Figure 12.11 The class variable num_points counts the Point instances you've created. For information about __init__(), see "Creating Instance Variables with an Initialization Method" later in this chapter.

- If you change a class variable's value at run time by qualifying it with an instance (*inst.attr = value*), Python creates a new (local) instance variable named *attr* with the value *value* in *inst*. This change affects only the current instance *inst*; it has no effect on the class variable *attr* of *inst*'s class or on other existing (or future) class instances (**Figure 12.10**).

- Class variables appear in the class's __dict__ (namespace) attribute; see the tips in "Accessing Built-In Class Attributes" earlier in this chapter.

- When you access a class variable, Python searches for its name by using the rules described in the tips in "Accessing Built-In Class Attributes" earlier in this chapter. An instance variable shadows a class variable with the same name.

- You also can manipulate class variables by using the built-in hasattr(), getattr(), setattr(), and delattr() functions, described in "Manipulating Attributes" in Chapter 9.

- Class variables, although not needed as often as instance variables, have their uses. A class variable can count the number of class instances created, for example (**Figure 12.11**).

- You can use class variables with immutable values as defaults for instance variables.

- **LANG** Class variables in Java are called *static fields* or *class fields*.

CREATING CLASS VARIABLES

Using Special Methods to Overload Standard Behavior

A *method* is a function that is associated with a particular class. You define the operations of a particular class via its methods, which operate on an instance's data to obtain results. Python provides several special methods that you can implement to overload the standard behavior of Python's built-in functions and operators so that they can handle instances of new classes that you define, in addition to built-in types.

Function overloading is the capability of having functions with the same name behave differently depending on the type or class of arguments involved; Python selects the correct behavior automatically, based on the parameters. Python invokes the special method __str__(), for example, when you call str(x), and x is an instance of a class that implements __str__().

Operator overloading is the assignment of more than one function to a particular operator (+, -, *, **, !=, and so on); the operation performed depends on the type or class of the operands involved. You've already seen operator overloading: The + operator performs addition when its operands are numbers or concatenation when its operands are strings. The special method __add__(), for example, lets you define how Python evaluates x + y when x and y are class instances.

The names of the special methods always begin and end with double underscores (__init__, for example). Python triggers these methods automatically at run time when the interpreter encounters the built-in function or operator that corresponds to the special method. Python has special methods for:

◆ Creating and destroying instances

◆ Creating string representations of instances

◆ Defining the truth value of an instance

◆ Comparing instances

◆ Accessing instance attributes

◆ Treating instances like sequences and dictionaries

◆ Performing mathematical operations on instances

✔ Tips

■ The behavior of a class depends on the special methods and user-defined methods it implements.

■ You can't use special methods to change the behavior of built-in types.

■ I don't discuss the details of every special method in this book. For descriptions of all the special methods, see Section 3.3, "Special method names," of the *Python Reference Manual.*

Creating Instance Variables with an Initialization Method

An *instance variable* is a variable that may have a different value for each instance of a given class. You can define an instance variable in a class method; each instance of the class will have its own copy of that variable. Programmers use instance variables much more often than they use class variables.

Python provides several ways to create instance variables. After you create an instance, you can type *instance.variable = value*, for example, to create an on-the-fly instance variable (**Figure 12.12**). You should define instance variables in class methods, however, because they're easier to find and manage that way, and that's where other programmers expect them to be.

You typically (but not always) define instance variables in a class's initialization method, which is a special method that Python invokes automatically to initialize a newly created instance. The initialization special method is named __init__ and is defined, as are all class methods, with a def statement; see "Defining a Function" in Chapter 8.

You define a method as you would define a normal function, except that the method's first parameter always is *self. self* is a special reference that you can use to refer to the current instance on which the method is invoked. Python passes *self* to the method implicitly; *don't* include *self* in the argument list when you invoke a method.

To define an initialization method:

◆ Type:

```
class class:
  def __init__(self, param_list)
    block
```

```
>>> class Point:
...     pass
...
>>> pt = Point()
>>> pt.x = 3
>>> pt.y = 9
```

Figure 12.12 These assignments create on-the-fly instance variables pt.x and pt.y. This technique is useful if you want to emulate a C struct or Pascal record, but in most circumstances, you should create instance variables in the class's __init__() method.

```
>>> class Point:
...    def __init__(self):
...       self.x = 0
...       self.y = 0
...
>>> pt = Point()
>>> print pt.x, pt.y
0 0
>>> pt.x = 5
>>> print pt.x, pt.y
5 0
```

Figure 12.13 This __init__() method takes no arguments and assigns the default value o to the instance variables self.x and self.y. You can change the values of pt.x and pt.y after you create an instance.

```
>>> class Point:
...    def __init__(self, x=0, y=0):
...       self.x = x
...       self.y = y
...
>>> pt1 = Point()
>>> pt2 = Point(3)
>>> pt3 = Point(3,9)
>>> print pt1.x, pt1.y
0 0
>>> print pt2.x, pt2.y
3 0
>>> print pt3.x, pt3.y
3 9
```

Figure 12.14 This improved version of __init__() assigns two arguments to the instance variables self.x and self.y. There's no conflict between the instance variable self.x and the parameter x, because the dot operator specifies which variable I'm referring to. Each instance—pt1, pt2, and pt3—contains its own independent copies of x and y. Note that method parameters can take default values, just as normal function parameters can.

Python invokes this method immediately after the interpreter creates a new instance of *class*. *self* refers to the newly created instance. The statements in *block* may refer to the parameters (instance variables) in *param_list* as *self.param1, self.param2,* and so on. You can pass arguments to __init__() when you create an instance of *class*.

param_list represents zero or more comma-separated parameters, and *block* is an indented block of statements.

To pass arguments to an initialization method:

◆ Type *inst = class(arg_list)* to create a new instance *inst* of the class *class,* and pass the arguments in *arg_list* to *class*'s __init__() method.

  arg_list must omit an argument for the method's *self* parameter.

  inst is a variable name, *class* is a class name, and *arg_list* represents zero or more expressions.

To access an instance variable:

◆ Type *inst.attr*

  You must specify the instance variable's instance explicitly. If you refer to *attr* by itself (without qualification), Python considers *attr* to be a local variable in the current method. To refer to the current instance on which the method is invoked, set *inst* equal to *self*.

  inst is a class instance, and *attr* is an instance variable name.

The Point class has two instance variables, x and y, that represent the *x* and *y* coordinates of a point on a two-dimensional grid. **Figures 12.13** and **12.14** show various ways to initialize a Point instance by using an initialization method.

✔ Tips

- By convention, __init__() is the first method defined in a class.

- In __init__(), *self* refers to the newly created instance; in other methods, *self* refers to the instance whose method is called.

- You don't have to name a method's first parameter self, but doing so is a strong Python convention.

- __init__() should return None.

- This statement:

  pt = Point(3, 9)

  is equivalent to this one internally:

  Point.__init__(pt, 3, 9)

- Instance variables appear in the instance's __dict__ (namespace) attribute; see the tips in "Accessing Built-In Instance Attributes" earlier in this chapter.

- When you access an instance variable, Python searches for its name by using the rules described in the tips in "Accessing Built-In Instance Attributes" earlier in this chapter. An instance variable shadows a class variable with the same name.

- You also can manipulate instance variables by using the built-in hasattr(), getattr(), setattr(), and delattr() functions, described in "Manipulating Attributes" in Chapter 9.

- You can use class variables with immutable values as defaults for instance variables.

- **LANG** Java supports instance variables, called *fields*. Python's __init__() method is similar to a Java constructor. Python's self reference is similar to Java's this reference. In Java, you can refer to fields without an explicit instance reference, whereas Python requires an instance reference.

```
>>> a = 39    # Create object <39>
>>> b = a     # Increase ref. count of <39>
>>> c = [b]   # Increase ref. count of <39>
>>>
>>> del a     # Decrease ref. count of <39>
>>> b = -99   # Decrease ref. count of <39>
>>> c[0] = 1  # Decrease ref. count of <39>
```

Figure 12.15 An object's reference count increases when it's assigned a new name or placed in a container (list, tuple, or dictionary). The object's reference count decreases when it's deleted with del, its reference is reassigned, or its reference goes out of scope. When an object's reference count reaches zero, Python collects it.

Destroying an Instance

This section covers an advanced topic that you may skip without loss of continuity.

As I've mentioned a few times in preceding chapters, Python deletes unneeded objects (built-in types or class instances) automatically to free memory space. The process by which Python periodically reclaims blocks of memory that no longer are in use is termed *garbage collection*. Python's garbage collector runs during program execution and is triggered when an object's reference count reaches zero. An object's *reference count* changes as the number of aliases that point to it changes; see "Creating References to the Same Object" in Chapter 2 (**Figure 12.15**).

You normally won't notice when the garbage collector destroys an orphaned instance and reclaims its space. But a class can implement the special method __del__(), called a *destructor,* that is invoked when the instance is about to be destroyed. This method might be used to clean up any nonmemory resources used by an instance.

__del__() rarely is used in practice, because there's no guarantee that __del__() will be called in any specific time period; it may never be called at all. So it's unwise to rely on a destructor for resource-releasing operations, such as closing a file. A better approach is to define some sort of close() method that you can call explicitly to clean up.

Script 12.1 shows an implementation of
__del__(), and **Figure 12.16** shows an
example invocation.

To define a destructor:

♦ In a class definition, type:

def __del__(*self*)

  block

Python invokes this method when an
instance is about to be destroyed; it's
invoked at most once per instance. *self*
refers to the instance on which __del__()
is invoked.

block is an indented block of statements.

✔ Tips

■ The del statement doesn't call __del__()
directly. The former decrements an
instance's reference count by one, and the
latter is called only when an instance's
reference count reaches zero.

■ You can control the garbage collector
by using the gc module; see Section 3.2,
"gc—Garbage Collector interface," of the
Python Library Reference.

■ Reference counting fails in the face of circular data structures, or *cycles,* which are
objects that refer to each other. If *x* and *y*
reference each other, neither object's
counter will become zero, so neither will
be collected (nor will any object to which
x or *y* refer). To cope with this situation,
Python periodically runs a cycle-detection
routine that deletes cycles. Python's garbage
collector won't collect cyclic instances for
which __del__() is defined (another reason
not to define __del__()).

■ **NEW** Python 2.0 introduced the gc module
and garbage collection of circular
data structures.

■ **LANG** Java supports garbage collection.
Python's __del__() method is
similar to Java's finalize method.

Script 12.1 This __del__() destructor prints the class
name of an instance that is about to be destroyed.

```
class Point:

  def __init__(self, x=0, y=0):

    self.x = x

    self.y = y


  def __del__(self):

    class_name = self.__class__.__name__

    print class_name, "destroyed"
```

```
>>> from point import Point
>>> pt1 = Point()
>>> pt2 = pt1
>>> pt3 = pt1
>>> print id(pt1), id(pt2), id(pt3)
8192764 8192764 8192764
>>> del pt1
>>> del pt2
>>> del pt3
Point destroyed
```

Figure 12.16 The three aliases pt1, pt2, and pt3 all refer
to the same object. Python invokes the destructor when
the final alias is removed and the instance's reference
count is zero.

Script 12.2 The __str__() and __repr__() methods return informal and formal string representations of an instance.

```
class Point:

  def __init__(self, x=0, y=0):

    self.x = x

    self.y = y


  def __str__(self):

    return "(%g,%g)" % (self.x, self.y)


  def __repr__(self):

    return "Point(%s,%s)" % (self.x, self.y)
```

```
>>> from point import Point
>>> pt = Point(3,9)
>>> str(pt)
'(3,9)'
>>> print pt
(3,9)
>>> repr(pt)
'Point(3,9)'
>>> `pt`
'Point(3,9)'
```

Figure 12.17 An instance's informal string representation is returned by str() and print; its formal string representation is returned by repr() and ``. The formal string representation can be used to create a copy of the instance.

Creating a String Representation of an Instance

You can use the special methods __str__() and __repr__() to create a string representation of an instance. Recall from "Converting a String" in Chapter 4 that str() creates a string that's intended for neatly formatted output, whereas repr() returns a valid Python expression that can evaluated to re-create an object with the same value.

Script 12.2 shows an implementation of __str__() and __repr__(), and **Figure 12.17** shows some example invocations.

To create an informal string representation of an instance:

◆ In a class definition, type:

  def __str__(self)

    block

  Python invokes this method when an instance is used as an argument to str() or print. self refers to the instance on which __str__() is invoked. The return value must be a string object.

  block is an indented block of statements.

REPRESENTING AN INSTANCE AS A STRING

To create a formal string representation of an instance:

◆ In a class definition, type:

```
def __repr__(self)
    block
```

Python invokes this method when an instance is used as an argument to `repr()` or is surrounded by backquotes. *self* refers to the instance on which `__repr__()` is invoked. The return value must be a string object.

block is an indented block of statements.

✔ Tips

■ The formal string representation typically is used for debugging purposes, so it's important that `__repr__()` return a string that is especially informative and unambiguous.

■ If it's not possible for `__repr__()` to return a valid Python expression, it should return a string of the form `"<...description...>"`, where *description* provides detailed information about the instance.

■ **LANG** Java's `toString` method returns a string representation of an object.

Script 12.3 This __nonzero__() method returns 0 (false) if a Point instance's x and y coordinates both are equal to zero, or 1 (true) otherwise.

```
script
class Point:
  def __init__(self, x=0, y=0):
    self.x = x
    self.y = y

  def __str__(self):
    return "(%g,%g)" % (self.x, self.y)

  def __nonzero__(self):
    if self.x == 0 and self.y == 0:
      return 0
    else:
      return 1
```

```
>>> from point import Point
>>> pt1 = Point(0,1)
>>> pt2 = Point(0,0)
>>> pt3 = Point(1,5)
>>> for pt in [pt1, pt2, pt3]:
...   if pt:
...     print pt, "is true"
...   else:
...     print pt, "is false"
...
(0,1) is true
(0,0) is false
(1,5) is true
>>> print pt1 and pt2
(0,0)
>>> print pt2 or pt3
(1,5)
>>> not pt2
1
```

Figure 12.18 pt1 and pt3 are true, and pt2 is false. You can use instances in Boolean expressions as you would use standard objects.

Setting the Truth Value of an Instance

Recall from "Using Boolean Operators" in Chapter 2 that all objects have a truth value, which is true or false. By default, an instance's truth value is true, but you can use the special method __nonzero__() to return 0 (false) or 1 (true) for truth-value testing.

Script 12.3 shows an implementation of __nonzero__(), and **Figure 12.18** shows some example invocations.

To set the truth value of an instance:

◆ In a class definition, type:

```
def __nonzero__(self)
  block
```

Python invokes this method when an instance is used in a Boolean expression. *self* refers to the instance on which __nonzero__() is invoked. The return value must be 1 (true) or 0 (false).

block is an indented block of statements.

✔ Tips

■ If you don't define __nonzero__(), Python invokes __len__(); see "Treating an Instance Like a List or Dictionary" later in this chapter. If a class defines neither __nonzero__() nor __len__(), all of its instances are considered to be true.

■ **LANG** Java's Boolean class can be used to determine an instance's truth value.

Comparing Instances

You can use the special methods listed in **Table 12.4** to compare instances by using Python's built-in comparison operators (<, <=, >, >=, ==, and !=); see "Using Comparison Operators" in Chapter 2. These methods are called *rich comparison* methods.

Script 12.4 shows an implementation of the rich comparison methods, and **Figure 12.19** shows some example invocations.

To define a comparison method:

◆ In a class definition, type:

def __comp__(self, other)

  block

__comp__() is one of the comparison methods listed in Table 12.4. Python invokes these methods when an instance is used in a comparison expression. *self* refers to the instance on which __comp__() is invoked, and *other* is the instance to which *self* is compared. A comparison method can return any value, but if the comparison operator is used in a Boolean context, the return value should be interpretable as a Boolean value (1 for true, or 0 for false); otherwise, Python raises a TypeError exception.

other is an instance, and *block* is an indented block of statements.

Table 12.4

Comparison Methods	
METHOD	**RESULT**
__lt__(self, other)	self < other
__le__(self, other)	self <= other
__gt__(self, other)	self > other
__ge__(self, other)	self >= other
__eq__(self, other)	self == other
__ne__(self, other)	self != other

Script 12.4 These comparison methods compare Point instances by Euclidean distance from the origin (0,0). The math.hypot(x,y) function calculates Euclidean distance, which equals math.sqrt(x*x + y*y).

```
script

from math import hypot

class Point:

    def __init__(self, x=0, y=0):

        self.x = x

        self.y = y

    def __lt__(self, other):

        return hypot(self.x, self.y) <
        ↪ hypot(other.x, other.y)

    def __le__(self, other):

        return hypot(self.x, self.y) <=
        ↪ hypot(other.x, other.y)

    def __gt__(self, other):

        return hypot(self.x, self.y) >
        ↪ hypot(other.x, other.y)

    def __ge__(self, other):

        return hypot(self.x, self.y) >=
        ↪ hypot(other.x, other.y)

    def __eq__(self, other):

        return hypot(self.x, self.y) ==
        ↪ hypot(other.x, other.y)

    def __ne__(self, other):

        return hypot(self.x, self.y) !=
        ↪ hypot(other.x, other.y)
```

COMPARING INSTANCES

```
>>> from point import Point
>>> pt1 = Point(0,0)    # Distance = 0
>>> pt2 = Point(2,2)    # Distance = 2.83
>>> pt3 = Point(3,4)    # Distance = 5
>>> pt4 = Point(-3,4)   # Distance = 5
>>> pt1 > pt2
0
>>> pt2 <= pt3 == pt4
1
```

Figure 12.19 You can chain instance comparisons just as you would chain normal comparisons.

Script 12.5 This __eq__() method performs an itemwise comparison of two lists and returns a list with the results.

```
                    script
class MyList:

  def __init__(self, lst):
    self.lst = lst


  def __eq__(self, other):
    result = []
    for i in range(len(self.lst)):
      if self.lst[i] == other.lst[i]:
        result.append(1)
      else:
        result.append(0)
    return result
```

```
>>> from mylist import MyList
>>> lst1 = MyList([1, 2, 3, 4, 5])
>>> lst2 = MyList([1, 9, 3, 4, 9])
>>> lst1 == lst2
[1, 0, 1, 1, 0]
```

Figure 12.20 The result of this comparison is a new list that contains ones where the items of two compared lists are equal or zeros where they're unequal.

✔ Tips

■ The rich comparison methods can return any type of object, not just the Boolean values 1 and 0. **Script 12.5** shows an implementation of a rich comparison method that returns a list, and **Figure 12.20** shows an example invocation.

■ Python doesn't force (coerce) explicit type conversions of comparison-method arguments. A rich comparison method may raise a NotImplementedError exception if it doesn't implement the operation for a given pair of arguments; see "Understanding the Exception Hierarchy" in Chapter 11.

■ **NEW** Python 2.1 introduced rich comparisons. If you're using an earlier version, or if you have not defined the rich-comparison methods, Python calls the __cmp__(*self*, *other*) method, which should return a negative integer if *self* < *other*, zero if *self* == *other*, or a positive integer if *self* > *other*. If __cmp__() is undefined, Python compares instances by object identity. If you define __cmp__(), you also should define the __hash__() method to calculate an integer hash key to use in dictionary operations. (The hash value also is returned by the built-in hash() function.) For information about hash(), see Section 2.3, "Built-in Functions," of the *Python Library Reference*. For information about __hash__(), see Section 3.3.1, "Basic customization," of the *Python Reference Manual*.

■ **LANG** Java's compareTo and equals methods are used to compare objects.

Accessing Instance Attributes

You can use the special methods listed in **Table 12.5** to read, modify, and delete the attributes of an instance by using the dot operator and the del statement; see "Accessing Attributes" and "Manipulating Instance Attributes" in Chapter 9.

In this section and subsequent sections, I won't show the steps for defining each special method, as they are similar syntactically to the method definitions I've shown in the preceding sections. **Script 12.6** shows an implementation of the attribute access methods, and **Figure 12.21** shows some example invocations.

Table 12.5

Attribute Access Methods	
METHOD	**DESCRIPTION**
__getattr__ → (self, name)	Returns the attribute self.name
__setattr__ → (self, name, value)	Sets the attribute self.name = value
__delattr__ → (self, name)	Deletes the attribute self.name

Script 12.6 In this alternative version of Point, named SimplePoint, I define the attribute access methods to restrict an instance's permitted attributes to just x and y. __delattr__() treats x and y as a pair: If one is deleted, so is the other.

```
class SimplePoint:

    def __getattr__(self,name):
        if name in ["x", "y"]:
            return self.name
        else:
            raise AttributeError, name

    def __setattr__(self,name,value):
        if name in ["x", "y"]:
            self.__dict__[name] = value
        else:
            raise AttributeError, name

    def __delattr__(self,name):
        if name in ["x", "y"]:
            del self.__dict__["x"]
            del self.__dict__["y"]
        else:
            raise AttributeError, name
```

```
>>> from simplepoint import
→ SimplePoint
>>> pt = SimplePoint()
>>> pt.__dict__
{}
>>> pt.x = 3
>>> pt.y = 9
>>> pt.z = 27
Traceback (most recent call last):
  File "<stdin>", line 1, in ?
  File "simplepoint.py", line 13, in __setattr__
    raise AttributeError, name
AttributeError: z
>>> pt.__dict__
{'x': 3, 'y': 9}
>>> pt.x, pt.y
(3, 9)
>>> del pt.x
>>> pt.__dict__
{}
```

Figure 12.21 The instance attribute dictionary shows pt's attributes. SimplePoint won't let me add the attribute z to pt, and when I delete x, y also is deleted.

✔ Tips

- ■ __getattr__() is invoked only if Python can't find the attribute in the normal places (that is, the instance's local dictionary or self's class tree). If Python finds the attribute through the normal mechanism, __getattr__() isn't called.

- ■ __getattr__() should return an attribute value or raise an AttributeError exception on failure.

- ■ __setattr__() is invoked when you attempt to assign an attribute. Unlike __getattr__(), __setattr__() is invoked *instead* of the normal mechanism (that is, storing the value in the instance's local dictionary).

- ■ If you want to assign an instance attribute in __setattr__(), use *self.*__dict__[*name*] = *value*. If you use *self.name* = *value*, you will cause a recursive call to __setattr__().

Treating an Instance Like a List or Dictionary

You can use the special methods listed in **Table 12.6** to emulate list (sequence) and dictionary operations such as slicing, indexing, and key lookup; see Chapters 5 and 6.

Script 12.7 shows implementations of some of the sequence and dictionary methods, and **Figure 12.22** shows some example invocations.

Table 12.6

Sequence and Dictionary Methods	
METHOD	DESCRIPTION
__len__(*self*)	Returns len(self)
__getitem__ → (*self*, *index*)	Returns *self*[*index*]
__setitem__(*self*, → *index*, *value*)	Returns *self*[*index*] = *value*
__delitem__ → (*self*, *index*)	Deletes *self*[*index*]
__getslice__ → (*self*, *i*, *j*)	Returns *self*[*i:j*]
__setslice__(*self*, → *i*, *j*, *sequence*)	Sets *self*[*i:j*] = *sequence*
__delslice__ → (*self*, *i*, *j*)	Deletes *self*[*i:j*]
__contains__ → (*self*, *item*)	Returns *item* in *self*, or *item* not in *self*

Script 12.7 These methods allow you to index the coordinates of a Point instance as you would index items in a list.

```
class Point:
  def __init__(self, x=0, y=0):
    self.x = x
    self.y = y

  def __len__(self):
    return 2

  def __contains__(self,item):
    try:
      return item in [self.x, self.y]
    except (TypeError, AttributeError), e:
      print e

  def __getitem__(self,index):
    if index == 0: return self.x
    elif index == 1: return self.y
    else: raise IndexError, index

  def __setitem__(self,index,value):
    if index == 0: self.x = value
    elif index == 1: self.y = value
    else: raise IndexError, index

  def __delitem__(self,index):
    if index == 0: del self.x
    elif index == 1: del self.y
    else: raise IndexError, index
```

```
>>> from point import Point
>>> pt = Point(3,9)
>>> len(pt)
2
>>> 3 in pt
1
>>> 9 not in pt
0
>>> for i in range(len(pt)):
...   print pt[i]
...
3
9
>>> print pt[4]
Traceback (most recent call last):
  File "<stdin>", line 1, in ?
  File "point.py", line 18, in __getitem__
    else: raise IndexError, index
IndexError: 4
>>> pt[0], pt[1] = 1, 5
>>> print pt[0], pt[1]
1 5
>>> del pt[1]
>>> print pt.__dict__
{'x': 1}
```

Figure 12.22 The x coordinate of pt is at index 0, and the y coordinate is at index 1.

✔ Tips

■ __len__() should return an integer greater than or equal to zero. If you don't define a __nonzero__() method, Python uses __len__() to determine the instance's truth value; see "Setting the Truth Value of an Instance" earlier in this chapter.

■ In __getitem__(), __setitem__(), and __delitem__(), *index* can be any object but typically is an integer for sequences.

■ Python invokes __delitem__() whenever the del operation is applied to a single item.

■ Immutable sequences (strings and tuples) should define only __getslice__(); mutable sequences (lists) should define __getslice__(), __setslice__(), and __delslice__(). *i* and *j* must be integers. Python replaces a missing *i* or *j* with zero or sys.maxint, respectively.

■ __getslice__() should return the same type of sequence that it is passed.

■ Use __contains__() to implement the in operator; see "Using Comparison Operators" in Chapter 2.

■ Sequences and dictionaries also should implement concatenation (addition) and repetition (multiplication) by defining the mathematical methods __add__(), __radd__(), __iadd__(), __mul__(), __rmul__(), and __imul__(); see "Performing Mathematical Operations on Instances" on the next page.

TREATING AN INSTANCE LIKE A LIST OR DICTIONARY

Performing Mathematical Operations on Instances

You can use the special methods listed in Tables 12.7 to 12.11 to perform mathematical operations on instances by using Python's built-in mathematical operators and functions.

Python invokes the methods listed in **Table 12.7** to implement binary arithmetic operators. These operators associate from left to right; Python tries to evaluate the expression x + y, for example, by invoking x.__add__(y).

The methods in **Table 12.8** support binary operations with reversed (swapped) operands, which Python invokes only if the left operand doesn't support the corresponding operation. To evaluate the expression x + y, for example, where x doesn't support the __add__() method, Python invokes y.__radd__(x). For information about binary arithmetic operators, see "Performing Basic Arithmetic" in Chapter 3.

Python invokes the methods listed in **Table 12.9** to implement augmented assignment operators (also called in-place operators). You should use these methods to perform in-place modifications of *self* and return the result (which could be, but does not have to be, *self*). If a specific augmented assignment isn't defined, Python falls back to the normal methods. To evaluate the expression x += y, for example, where x is an instance of a class that has an __iadd__() method, Python invokes x.__iadd__(y). If x is an instance of a class that doesn't define the __iadd()__ method, Python tries x.__add__(y) and y.__radd__(x), as with the evaluation of x + y. For information about augmented assignment operators, see "Making Augmented Assignments" in Chapter 3.

Table 12.7

Binary Operator Methods	
METHOD	**RESULT**
__add__(*self*,*other*)	*self* + *other*
__sub__(*self*,*other*)	*self* - *other*
__mul__(*self*,*other*)	*self* * *other*
__div__(*self*,*other*)	*self* / *other*
__mod__(*self*,*other*)	*self* % *other*
__divmod__(*self*,*other*)	divmod(*self*,*other*)
__pow__(*self*,*other*)	*self* ** *other*, pow(*self*,*other*)
__lshift__(*self*,*other*)	*self* << *other*
__rshift__(*self*,*other*)	*self* >> *other*
__and__(*self*,*other*)	*self* & *other*
__or__(*self*,*other*)	*self* | *other*
__xor__(*self*,*other*)	*self* ^ *other*

Table 12.8

Reversed Binary Operator Methods	
METHOD	**RESULT**
__radd__(*self*,*other*)	*other* + *self*
__rsub__(*self*,*other*)	*other* - *self*
__rmul__(*self*,*other*)	*other* * *self*
__rdiv__(*self*,*other*)	*other* / *self*
__rmod__(*self*,*other*)	*other* % *self*
__rdivmod__(*self*,*other*)	divmod(*other*,*self*)
__rpow__(*self*,*other*)	*other* ** *self*
__rlshift__(*self*,*other*)	*other* << *self*
__rrshift__(*self*,*other*)	*other* >> *self*
__rand__(*self*,*other*)	*other* & *self*
__ror__(*self*,*other*)	*other* | *self*
__rxor__(*self*,*other*)	*other* ^ *self*

Table 12.9

Augmented Assignment Methods	
METHOD	RESULT
__iadd__(self,other)	self += other
__isub__(self,other)	self -= other
__imul__(self,other)	self *= other
__idiv__(self,other)	self /= other
__imod__(self,other)	self %= other
__ipow__(self,other)	self **= other
__ilshift__(self,other)	self <<= other
__irshift__(self,other)	self >>= other
__iand__(self,other)	self &= other
__ior__(self,other)	self |= other
__ixor__(self,other)	self ^= other

Table 12.10

Unary Operator Methods	
METHOD	RESULT
__neg__(self)	-self
__pos__(self)	+self
__abs__(self)	abs(self)
__invert__(self)	~self

Table 12.11

Conversion Methods	
METHOD	RESULT
__int__(self)	int(self)
__long__(self)	long(self)
__float__(self)	float(self)
__complex__(self)	complex(self)
__oct__(self)	oct(self)
__hex__(self)	hex(self)
__coerce__(self)	coerce(self)

Python invokes the methods listed in **Table 12.10** to implement unary arithmetic operations; see "Performing Basic Arithmetic" and "Using Mathematical Functions" in Chapter 3.

Python invokes the methods listed in **Table 12.11** to implement arithmetic conversion operations; see "Converting Among Number Types" in Chapter 3.

Script 12.8 shows implementations of some of the mathematical methods, and **Figure 12.23** shows some example invocations.

✔ Tips

■ __int__(), __long__(), __float__(), and __complex__() should convert values to the appropriate built-in numeric type.

■ __oct__() and __hex__() should return octal and hexadecimal strings.

■ Python invokes __coerce__() in mixed-mode numeric arithmetic; see "Understanding Promotion" in Chapter 3. Your implementation of __coerce__() should follow the coercion rules given in Section 3.3.6, "Emulating numeric types," of the *Python Reference Manual*.

■ The mathematical methods support some mixed-type operations. If x is a string, x % y invokes string formatting, regardless of y's type; see "Printing Formatted Strings" in Chapter 4. If x is a sequence, x + y invokes sequence concatenation; see "Concatenating Lists or Tuples" in Chapter 5. If x or y is a sequence and the other operand is an integer, x * y invokes sequence repetition; see "Repeating a List or Tuple" in Chapter 5.

Script 12.8 These methods allow you to use mathematical operators and functions with Point instances.

```
                    script
class Point:
  def __init__(self, x=0, y=0):
    self.x = x
    self.y = y


  def __str__(self):
    return "(%g,%g)" % (self.x, self.y)


  def __add__(self, other):
    #Allow Point + Point, and Point + scalar
    if hasattr(other,"__class__") and
    ⟶ other.__class__ is Point:
      return Point(self.x + other.x, self.y +
      ⟶ other.y)
    else:
      return Point(self.x + other, self.y +
      ⟶ other)


  __radd__ = __add__   # Allow scalar + Point


  def __mul__(self, other):
    #Allow Point * Point, and Point * scalar
    if hasattr(other,"__class__") and
    ⟶ other.__class__ is Point:
      return Point(self.x * other.x, self.y *
      ⟶ other.y)
    else:
      return Point(self.x * other, self.y *
      ⟶ other)


  __rmul__ = __mul__   # Allow scalar * Point


  def __pow__(self, other):
    return Point(self.x ** other, self.y **
    ⟶ other)


  def __neg__(self):
    return Point(-self.x, -self.y)


  def __float__(self):
    return Point(float(self.x),
    ⟶ float(self.y))
```

```
>>> from point import Point
>>> pt1 = Point(3,9)
>>> pt2 = Point(1,4)
>>> pt = pt1 + pt2    # __add__()
>>> print pt
(4,13)
>>> print pt1 * pt2  # __mul__()
(3,36)
>>> print pt1 * 2    # __mul__()
(6,18)
>>> print 2 * pt1    # __rmul__()
(6,18)
>>> print pt2 ** 2   # __pow__()
(1,16)
>>> print -pt1       # __neg__()
(-3,-9)
>>> pt = float(pt1)  # __float__()
>>> pt.x, pt.y
(3.0, 9.0)
```

Figure 12.23 The __add__() method allows you to add a Point instance to a scalar (number) or to another Point instance. The __radd__() method permits the scalar to appear as the left operand. The __mult__() and __rmult__() methods perform the same operations for multiplication.

```
>>> class Printer:
...    def __call__(self, *args):
...       for i in range(len(args)):
...          print args[i]
...
>>> p = Printer()
>>> p()
>>> p("mimetic", 39)
mimetic
39
```

Figure 12.24 The __call__() method allows you to invoke an instance as a function. An instance of the class Printer simply prints its arguments when called.

Calling an Instance

To make an instance callable, use the special method __call__(*self* [,*args*]). If an instance x provides the __call__() method, this expression:

x(*arg1, arg2,...*)

invokes:

x.__call__(*self, arg1, arg2,...*)

Figure 12.24 shows an example.

Defining and Invoking a Custom Method

In addition to the special methods, Python lets you define your own methods. You define a method in a class definition the same way that you define a function (see "Defining a Function" in Chapter 8), except that the first parameter must be *self*. Use dot notation to invoke a method on an instance.

Script 12.9 shows implementations of some user-defined methods, and **Figure 12.25** shows some example invocations.

To define a custom method:

◆ In a class definition, type:

    def *method*(self, *param_list*)
      block

    method is a valid Python name (see "Naming Variables" in Chapter 2), *param_list* represents zero or more comma-separated parameters, *block* is an indented block of statements, and *self* refers to the instance on which *method* is invoked.

To invoke a custom method:

◆ Type:

    inst.method(*arg_list*)

    inst is an instance of the class in which *method* is defined, *method* is a method name, and *arg_list* represents zero or more comma-separated arguments that are passed to the method. *arg_list* must omit the argument for *method*'s *self* parameter.

✔ Tips

■ You can't define class methods that don't operate on instances (**Figure 12.26**).

■ Names in a class's namespace (__dict__ attribute) aren't visible in the class's methods, so you must fully qualify names that refer to class attributes outside a method (**Figure 12.27**).

Script 12.9 You can define custom methods within a class.

```
class Point:
  def __init__(self, x=0, y=0):
    self.x = x
    self.y = y

  def __str__(self):
    return "(%g,%g)" % (self.x, self.y)

  def clear(self):
    "Zeroes a point's coordinates"
    self.x = 0
    self.y = 0

  def distance(self, other):
    "Returns the distance between two points"
    xdiff = self.x - other.x
    ydiff = self.y - other.y
    return (xdiff * xdiff + ydiff * ydiff)
    → ** 0.5

  def dot(self, other):
    "Returns the dot product of two points"
    return self.x * other.x + self.y * other.y

  def move(self, delta_x, delta_y):
    "Moves a point"
    self.x += delta_x
    self.y += delta_y

  def norm(self):
    "Returns the length of a vector"
    return self.dot(self) ** 0.5
```

```
>>> from point import Point
>>> pt1 = Point(2,5)
>>> pt2 = Point(3,4)
>>> pt1.distance(pt2)
1.4142135623730951
>>> pt1.dot(pt2)
26
>>> pt2.norm()
5.0
>>> pt1.clear()
>>> print pt1
(0,0)
>>> pt2.move(-2,3)
>>> print pt2
(1,7)
```

Figure 12.25 These methods perform common operations on Point instances.

```
>>> class Adder:
...     def add(self,x,y):
...         return x + y
...
>>> a = Adder.add(2,3)
Traceback (most recent call last):
  File "<stdin>", line 1, in ?
TypeError: unbound method add() must be called
→ with instance as first argument
>>> b = Adder()
>>> b.add(2,3)
5
```

Figure 12.26 Python raises a TypeError exception because a class instance must be passed as a method's first argument (self).

- When assigning attributes, Python updates only the local dictionary of the instance. When accessing attributes, Python uses the namespace and search rules described in the tips in "Accessing Built-In Instance Attributes" earlier in this chapter.

- User-defined methods can define default parameter values, and take positional arguments, keyword arguments, and an arbitrary number of arguments just like normal functions; see Chapter 8.

- **LANG** Python's methods are similar to Java's object methods. Python has no analogue of Java's class methods.

```
>>> class Broken:
...     def print1(self):
...         print "print1"
...     def print2(self):
...         print1(self)
...
>>> x = Broken()
>>> x.print2()
Traceback (most recent call last):
  File "<stdin>", line 1, in ?
  File "<stdin>", line 5, in print2
NameError: global name 'print1' is not defined
>>>
>>> class Fixed:
...     def print1(self):
...         print "print1"
...     def print2(self):
...         Fixed.print1(self)
...
>>> y = Fixed()
>>> y.print2()
print1
```

Figure 12.27 In the class Broken, the statement print1(self) raises a NameError exception because the print1() method isn't visible in the print2() method. In the class Fixed, print1() is visible in print2() because I qualified print1() with the class name: Fixed.print1(self).

Deriving New Classes from Existing Classes

Python lets you derive a new class from an existing class. In this technique, called *inheritance,* the original class is called the *base class* or *superclass,* and the new class is a *derived class* or *subclass.* Inheritance has two major benefits:

◆ **Code reuse.** You can reuse the code in the superclass because the subclass acquires, or *inherits,* the attributes defined by its superclass. The subclass may, however, enhance, restrict, or modify its inherited attributes or may add new attributes of its own.

◆ **Specialization.** The subclass defines new behavior and so becomes a specialized version of its superclass.

Script 12.10 implements a class hierarchy: The subclasses Circle and Square both inherit attributes from their superclass, Shape. **Figure 12.28** shows some example invocations.

To define a subclass:

◆ Type:

```
class subclass(superclass)
```

This class definition defines a new class named *subclass* that inherits *superclass*'s attributes.

subclass and *superclass* are class names.

Script 12.10 Circle and Square inherit the x and y coordinates from Shape but define their own instance variables (radius and side) and methods (area()). You must qualify calls to inherited methods: Circle and Square must invoke Shape.__init__() and Shape.__str__(), not just __init__() and __str__(). Each subclass also inherits the superclass's class variables origin and shape_name.

```
class Shape:
  origin = (0,0)
  shape_name = None
  def __init__(self, x=0, y=0):
    self.x = x
    self.y = y

  def __str__(self):
    return "%s,x=%g,y=%g" % (self.shape_name,
    → self.x, self.y)

  def move(self, delta_x, delta_y):
    self.x += delta_x
    self.y += delta_y

class Circle(Shape):
  shape_name = "circle"
  def __init__(self, x=0, y=0, radius=1):
    Shape.__init__(self, x, y)
    self.radius = radius

  def __str__(self):
    return Shape.__str__(self) +
    → (",radius=%g" % (self.radius))

  def area(self):
    return self.radius * self.radius *
    → 3.14159

class Square(Shape):
  shape_name = "square"
  def __init__(self, x=0, y=0, side=1):
    Shape.__init__(self, x, y)
    self.side = side

  def __str__(self):
    return Shape.__str__(self) + (",side=%g"
    → % (self.side))

  def area(self):
    return self.side* self.side
```

```
>>> from shape import Shape, Circle,
→ Square
>>> circle =  Circle(0,0,2)
>>> square = Square(0,0,3)
>>> print circle
circle,x=0,y=0,radius=2
>>> print square
square,x=0,y=0,side=3
>>> print circle.origin, square.origin
(0, 0) (0, 0)
>>> circle.area()
12.56636
>>> square.area()
9
>>> circle.move(-1,-2)
>>> print circle
circle,x=-1,y=-2,radius=2
>>> square.move(2,3)
>>> print square
square,x=2,y=3,side=3
```

Figure 12.28 Inheritance kicks in when I try to invoke a method (move()) or access a variable (origin) that's not defined in the subclass. If Python can't find an attribute in a subclass, it searches the superclass.

```
>>> class A: pass
...
>>> class B: pass
...
>>> class C(A): pass
...
>>> class D(A): pass
...
>>> class E(C,D,B): pass
```

Figure 12.29 This is an example of multiple inheritance. If Python can't find a variable or method name in class E, it searches E's superclasses in the order C, A, D, B. If multiple superclasses define the same name, Python uses the first matching name it encounters.

Python also supports *multiple inheritance*, which allows a subclass to have two or more superclasses.

To define a subclass with multiple superclasses:

◆ Type:

    class *subclass(superclass1, superclass2, ...)*

    This class definition defines a new class named *subclass* that inherits attributes from *superclass1, superclass2,...* (**Figure 12.29**).

    subclass, superclass1, superclass2,... are class names.

Multiple inheritance is an advanced topic and is beyond the scope of this book. Many programmers find class hierarchies that involve multiple inheritance to be confusing and difficult to maintain, owing to the complicated rules needed to resolve name conflicts. Python resolves such conflicts by searching superclasses in a clearly defined (but sometimes difficult to follow) order. If Python can't find an attribute in an instance's local namespace, it performs a depth-first search of the superclasses in the same order in which the superclasses are specified in the class definition.

✔ Tips

- If a subclass defines an attribute with the same name as an attribute in its superclass, instances of the subclass use the subclass's attribute, unless the attribute is qualified explicitly with the name of the superclass (by using the dot operator).

- From within a subclass instance, Python first searches for an attribute name in this order:

  1. Instance namespace. This namespace, accessible via self, contains instance variables, private instance variables, and superclass instance variables.

  2. Class namespace. This namespace contains methods, class variables, private methods, and private class variables.

  3. Superclass namespace. This namespace contains superclass methods, superclass variables, private superclass methods, and private superclass class variables.

  For information about namespaces, see "Understanding Namespaces" in Chapter 9.

- If a class is in a different module from its superclass, you can qualify the superclass with the module name:

  ```
  class subclass(module.superclass)
  ```

- A class's superclasses are accessible via its __bases__ attribute; see "Accessing Built-In Class Attributes" earlier in this chapter.

- **LANG** Java uses the extends and implements operators to create class hierarchies.

```
>>> class Point:
...    __origin = (0,0)
...    def change_origin(self, x, y):
...        self.__origin = (x,y)
...        print "New origin:",
→ self.__origin
...
>>> pt = Point()
>>> pt.change_origin(-1,1)
New origin: (-1, 1)
>>> pt.__origin
Traceback (most recent call last):
  File "<stdin>", line 1, in ?
AttributeError: Point instance has no
→ attribute '__origin'
>>> pt._Point__origin
(-1, 1)
```

Figure 12.30 A private name is inaccessible outside the class in which it's defined—unless you use its mangled name.

Hiding Private Data

By default, an instance's attributes are accessible without restriction. All of a superclass's attributes, for example, are accessible within its subclasses. Python lets you define private variables and methods that allow you to protect attributes from outside code (and prevent namespace conflicts). Private attributes are invisible outside the class in which they're defined.

To hide an attribute:

◆ Type:
   __attrname
   Private names begin—but don't end—with a double underscore (**Figure 12.30**).
   attrname is a variable or method name.

✔ Tips

■ Python raises an AttributeError exception if you try to access a private name.

■ Python hides a private name by changing its name internally to _classname__attrname. The protection that this technique, called name mangling, affords actually is an illusion—you can access and change a private attribute by using its mangled name (refer to Figure 12.30).

■ **LANG** Java uses the public, protected, and private operators to define a member's visibility.

Determining Class Membership

You can use the built-in isinstance() function to test for membership in a class and the built-in issubclass() function to test whether a class is a subclass of another class. **Figure 12.31** shows some examples.

To determine whether an object is an instance of a given class:

◆ Type isinstance(*object*, *class*) to return 1 (true) if *object* is an instance of *class* or of a direct or indirect subclass thereof, or 0 (false) otherwise.

  If *class* is neither a class object nor a type object, Python raises a TypeError exception.

  object is an instance or an expression, and *class* is a class object or type object.

To determine whether a class is a subclass of a given class:

◆ Type issubclass(*class1*, *class2*) to return 1 (true) if *class1* is a direct or indirect subclass of *class2*.

  A class is considered to be a subclass of itself. If either argument is not a class object, Python raises a TypeError exception.

  class1 and *class2* are class objects.

✔ Tips

■ You can use isinstance() to perform type checking against Python's built-in types; see "Determining an Object's Type" in Chapter 2 (**Figure 12.32**).

■ You can't use the expression type(*a*) == type(*b*) to determine whether instances *a* and *b* were created from the same class; all instances are of the same type, types.InstanceType, even if they were created by different classes.

■ **LANG** Java uses the instanceof operator to test class membership.

```
>>> class A: pass
...
>>> class B(A): pass
...
>>> class C: pass
...
>>> a = A()
>>> b = B()
>>> c = C()
>>> isinstance(a, A)
1
>>> isinstance(b, A)
1
>>> isinstance(b, C)
0
>>> isinstance(c, C)
1
>>> issubclass(B,A)
1
>>> issubclass(B,B)
1
>>> issubclass(C,A)
0
```

Figure 12.31 Python provides built-in functions that test class membership.

```
>>> import types
>>> isinstance(2.0, types.IntType)
0
>>> isinstance(2.0, types.FloatType)
1
>>> isinstance("2.0", types.StringType)
1
>>> isinstance(lambda x: x*x,
→ types.LambdaType)
1
>>> isinstance([], types.ListType)
1
```

Figure 12.32 You can use isinstance() to type-check against built-in types.

APPENDIX

This appendix points you toward additional Python resources, including online tutorials; places to get your questions answered; newsgroups and mailing lists; development tools; and other people's freely available scripts, modules, and projects.

Printed material about the Web dates quickly. If you can't find any of the links listed herein, try locating the sites by using a search engine such as Google (www.google.com). You also can check the Python Language Web site (www.python.org) for new developments and updated links.

Learning Python

Besides this book and the *Python Tutorial* (see "Reading Python Documentation" in Chapter 1), you may want to look at some of these other Python tutorials and resources:

◆ The Python for Beginners guide at www.python.org/doc/Newbies.html (**Figure A.1**).

◆ If you're new to programming, consult the Python version of *How to Think Like a Computer Scientist*, by Allen Downey, Jeff Elkner, and Chris Meyers, at www.ibiblio.org/obp/thinkCSpy (**Figure A.2**).

◆ If you're an experienced programmer, consult *Dive into Python*, by Mark Pilgrim, at www.diveintopython.org (**Figure A.3**).

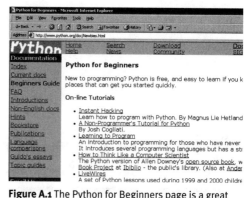

Figure A.1 The Python for Beginners page is a great starting point for learning to program in Python.

Figure A.2 *How to Think Like a Computer Scientist* is a free introductory computer-science book that uses Python to teach fundamental programming concepts.

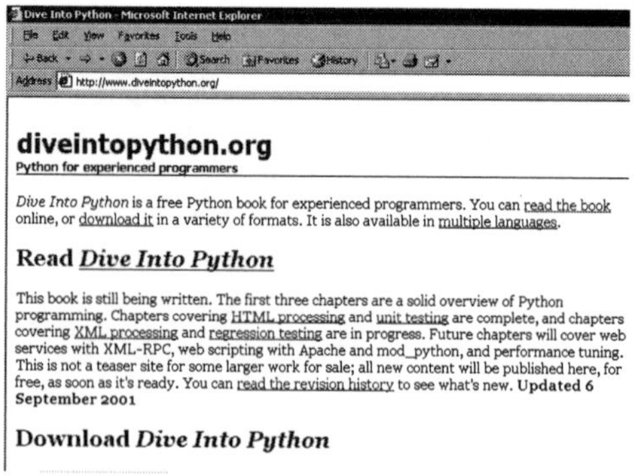

Figure A.3 *Dive into Python* is a free Python book for experienced programmers. You can read the book online or download it in a variety of formats.

LEARNING PYTHON

Figure A.4 Use the Search Python Resources page to perform basic and advanced keyword searches of Python-related sites.

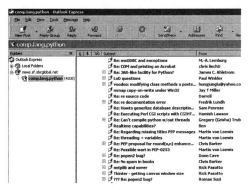

Figure A.5 Always consult the Python FAQ before submitting a question to a newsgroup; otherwise, you may be ignored (or teased) for asking a common question.

Figure A.6 comp.lang.python is a high-volume, open newsgroup for general discussions and questions about Python.

Getting Support

If you're having problems using Python, and online and printed documentation doesn't help, you can search for an answer on the Internet; read the Python FAQ (a document that answers Frequently Asked Questions about Python); or, if these avenues are unhelpful, ask for help from real people.

Search resources

◆ The Python help page, www.python.org/ Help.html, is organized by topic.

◆ You can use the Search Python Resources page, www.python.org/search, to perform keyword searches on Python-related sites (**Figure A.4**).

FAQs

◆ The official Python FAQ is at www. python.org/doc/FAQ.html (**Figure A.5**).

◆ The FAQTS Python Knowledge Base is at www.faqts.com/knowledge_base/index. phtml/fid/199.

◆ The Python CGI FAQ is at starship. python.net/crew/davem/cgifaq/faqw.cgi.

Real people

◆ The Python users' newsgroup, comp. lang.python, provides a friendly and helpful atmosphere for asking questions. It's also available as a mailing list; see the tips in this section for information about Python mailing lists (**Figure A.6**).

◆ You can send email to the Python help desk at help@python.org to ask a group of knowledgeable volunteers questions about all your Python problems.

◆ You also can send email to tutor@python. org; this low-volume mailing list is for folks who want to ask questions regarding how to learn computer programming with the Python language.

News

◆ The newsgroup `comp.lang.python.announce` is a low-volume moderated newsgroup for Python-related announcements (**Figure A.7**).

◆ The PythonWare Daily Python-URL! page, `www.pythonware.com/daily`, provides daily updates and Python news summaries.

◆ The Dr. Dobb's Python-URL! page, `www.ddj.com/topics/pythonurl`, provides weekly postings on the latest Python conferences, papers, releases, links, and more.

◆ The O'Reilly Python DevCenter page, `www.onlamp.com/python`, regularly publishes Python news and articles.

✔ Tips

■ For an overview of Python mailing lists and news resources, see `www.python.org/psa/MailingLists.html`.

■ Python HOWTO documents cover a single, specific topic fairly completely. HOWTO topics include regular expressions, sorting, XML, and socket programming; see `py-howto.sourceforge.net`.

■ Python topic guides provide overviews of Python resources associated with specific topics such as XML, databases, and Web (CGI) programming; see `www.python.org/topics/`.

■ Don't send technical questions to the Python Webmaster.

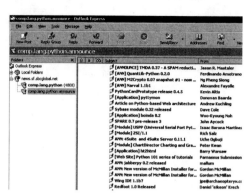

Figure A.7 `comp.lang.python.announce` is a moderated low-volume newsgroup reserved for announcing Python-related happenings.

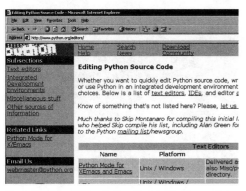

Figure A.8 The Editing Python Source Code page lists a wide range of text editors, IDEs, and editor add-ons that support Python.

Editing and Debugging Code

When you advance beyond the simple scripts presented in this book, you'll need a professional editor to edit Python source code or an Integrated Development Environment (IDE) to write or debug whole Python programs. You can find a list of Python programming tools at www.python.org/editors (**Figure A.8**).

✔ Tips

- Python IDEs also are listed on the Vaults of Parnassus Editor/IDE page at www.vex.net/parnassus/apyllo.py?i=979528604.

- There's a review of Python IDEs at www-106.ibm.com/developerworks/linux/library/l-pide.

Programming Resources

Good programmers are lazy; they never write code that somebody else has already written and is giving away (or selling at a reasonable price). You can find thousands of Python programs all over the Web, but here are a few good places to look:

◆ The Vaults of Parnassus, `www.vex.net/ parnassus`, is a treasure trove of Python source code. It lists hundreds of links to third-party modules (**Figure A.9**).

◆ Starship Python, `starship.python.net`, is a hosted, searchable Web site for the Python community.

◆ The Python Cookbook, `aspn.activestate. com/ASPN/Python/Cookbook`, is a collaborative Web site where programmers contribute code, comments, and ratings for Python "recipes."

◆ The SourceForge code snippet library, `sourceforge.net/snippet/browse.php? by=lang&lang=6`, contains useful utility programs.

There are several large-scale open-source Python projects. These projects are freely available for both commercial and non-commercial use and are distributed with source code.

◆ Python source code, documentation, and enhancement proposals are available at the Python project SourceForge repository; see `python.sourceforge.net` (**Figure A.10**).

◆ Jython is an implementation of Python seamlessly integrated with the Java platform. Jython is especially suited for embedded scripting, interactive experimentation, and rapid application development; see `www.jython.org`.

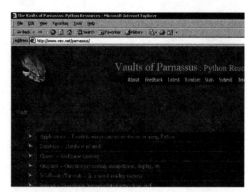

Figure A.9 The Vaults of Parnassus contains links to third-party modules. It's a great place to search for a particular module or for a module that does a particular thing.

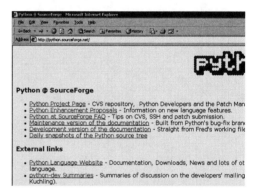

Figure A.10 You can get Python's source code at SourceForge.

- Zope is the leading open-source Web application server. Zope enables teams to collaborate in the creation and management of dynamic Web-based business applications such as intranets and portals; see www.zope.org.

- Numerical Python (NumPy) adds a fast, compact, multidimensional array type to Python. This facility gives Python the number-crunching power of numeric languages such as MATLAB while maintaining all the advantages of Python as a general-purpose programming language; see www.pfdubois.com/numpy.

- mod_python is an Apache module that embeds the Python interpreter within the server. With mod_python, you can write Web-based applications in Python that run many times faster than traditional CGI and have access to advanced features, such as the capability to retain database connections and other data between hits and access to Apache internals; see www.modpython.org.

- PyGame is a set of Python modules designed for writing games. This library is written on top of the SDL library and allows you to create portable games and multimedia programs in Python; see pygame.org.

PROGRAMMING RESOURCES

INDEX

INDEX

INDEX

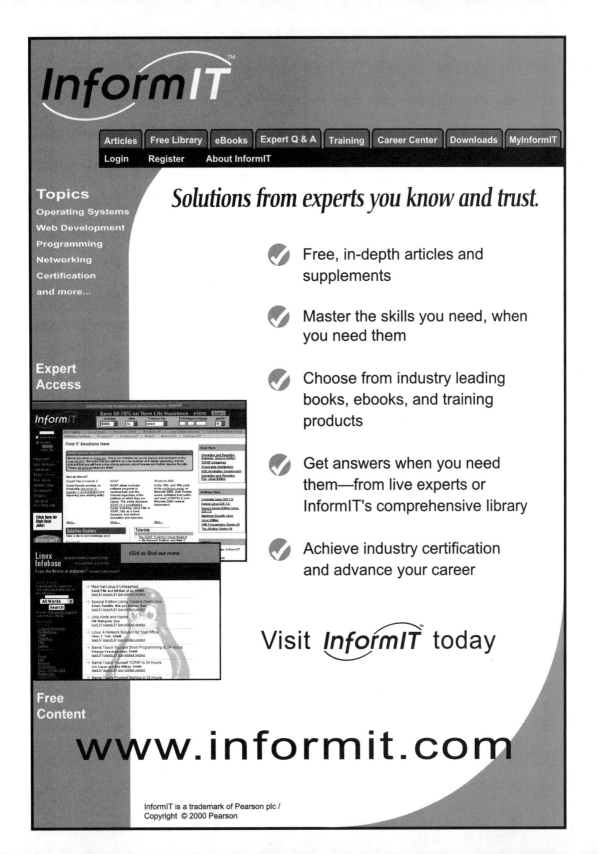